DOS 4.1

Disk Operating System

Second Edition

Walland Philip Vrbancic, Jr.

Second Edition

ISBN 978-0-578-85915-6

*I am ever so proud to dedicate this Book on the
DOS 4.1 Disk Operating System Second Edition
and all my previous achievements
to my Parents Wally and Melba
who continuously nourished my intellectual curiosity.*

I am ever so grateful to my partner
Carlton D. Wong
*who delightfully pretends to understand
what the Hell I am talking about!*

If I have seen further than others it is because I have stood on the shoulders of giants.
~~~ Isaac Newton ~~~

Disclaimer of All Liability

Do not use the *DOS 4.1 Disk Operating System* or this Book for any mission-critical applications or for any purpose in which a software error or a software failure could cause you financial or material loss. The *DOS 4.1 Disk Operating System* and this Book are designed to enhance your Apple][computing experience, but they may contain design flaws that could inhibit the proper operation of your computer or result in the loss of recorded data on any storage device connected to your computer. When using the *DOS 4.1 Disk Operating System* or this Book, you assume all risks associated with the operation of your computer and the potential loss of your data. If these terms are not acceptable to you, do not use the *DOS 4.1 Disk Operating System* or this Book.

Walland Philip Vrbancic, Jr., the administrator of applecored.net, makes no warranties either expressed or implied with respect to the *DOS 4.1 Disk Operating System* or with respect to this Book, its quality, performance, or fitness for any particular purpose. Any risk of incidental or consequential damages resulting from the use of the *DOS 4.1 Disk Operating System* or the use of information contained in this Book shall be assumed by you, the User. In no event will Walland Philip Vrbancic, Jr., or applecored.net be liable for any direct, indirect, incidental, or consequential damages resulting from any defect or deficiency in the *DOS 4.1 Disk Operating System* or in this Book.

While all possible attempts have been made to ensure that the information contained within this Book is complete and accurate, the author shall have no liability or responsibility for any errors or omissions, or for any damages or data loss resulting from the use of the information, circuit diagrams, and example software programs contained herein. The author reserves the right to make any changes and/or any improvements to the *DOS 4.1 Disk Operating System* or to the contents of this Book at any time and without any prior notice.

Preface to the Second Edition

When Brian Wiser and Bill Martens discovered my DOS 4.1 documentation and software at applecored.net, they immediately contacted me and wanted Apple Pugetsound Program Library Exchange (A.P.P.L.E.) to publish my *DOS 4.1 Manual*. Ha! If only this would have happened back in 1982. That's when my co-worker, Randy at Rockwell, and I were actively reading many publications on Apple software and hardware, and Call-A.P.P.L.E. was one of our favorite publications. Needless to say, to be published by any of those computer journals at that time would have been crazy exciting, and certainly a cherished memory for a lifetime. I actually was very close to finishing DOS 4.1 when I agreed to have Call-A.P.P.L.E. publish the *DOS 4.1 Manual*, Build 45, and provide demo diskette images for DOS 4.1L and DOS 4.1H.

I wanted both versions of DOS 4.1 to provide the user with virtually the same computing experience, albeit the `HELP` command is found only in DOS 4.1H. This desire proved to be somewhat troublesome in that I was limited in memory for DOS 4.1L and I had ample memory for DOS 4.1H. It was the unused memory in DOS 4.1H that was the impetus to introduce the `HELP` command in the first place. At the onset I warned both Mr. Wiser and Mr. Martens that I could not stop creating more functionality in DOS 4.1, but they were rather insistent on publishing the *DOS 4.1 Manual* for the Apple][community as it was. I finished DOS 4.1 with Build 46 after the *DOS 4.1 Manual* was published. Now, only the Build 46 software can be downloaded at applecored.net.

In my excitement to share with the Apple][community enthusiasts all of my DOS 4.1 innovations and the knowledge that I had gained while creating DOS 4.1, I did not even consider asking Mr. Wiser or Mr. Martens for a share in the revenues this publication may certainly generate. And, Mr. Wiser or Mr. Martens did not offer me a share in any of the revenues generated by this publication nor an insight into how many copies Call-A.P.P.L.E. sold to their readers. Yet, I realized and thought their investment in DOS 4.1 in using their experience and their time in preparing my manuscript for publication, securing the necessary legal identifiers, and creating the artwork for the front, back, and spine of the book was perhaps worth a share in the revenues. That is, I considered the entire publishing experience to be worth a share in the publication revenues for this book until I purchased and received a copy of *The DOS 4.1 Manual*. If I had seen a preliminary printing of *The DOS 4.1 Manual* I would have never agreed to its publication in that format. Seeing how the Apple][text screens appeared in *The DOS 4.1 Manual* simply appalled me. I would have gladly taken any amount of additional time to create a better looking display format. And, the additional time would have given me the opportunity to conclude my development of DOS 4.1 with Build 46. It is for these reasons that I am publishing the contents of the *DOS 4.1 Manual* again and calling it the *DOS 4.1 Disk Operating System Second Edition.*

The knowledge I gained in publishing the *DOS 4.3 File Management System* book without assistance was a phenomenal learning experience. That experience helped me mature as an author in order to document and explain what I have innovated by utilizing my deep understanding of software development, testing, and integration within the confines of a vintage and highly unique hardware environment. This current publication provides me a second opportunity to present the development and features of DOS 4.1 using far more elegant and visually appealing formats in the display of data, software algorithms, diagrams, and descriptive information.

Just because I am publishing the *DOS 4.1 Disk Operating System Second Edition* after I have published the *DOS 4.3 File Management System*, it is not my intention to change, update, or modify the DOS 4.1 software in any way. I am not releasing another DOS 4.1 software build with this publication. Build 46 continues to be the last and final version of DOS 4.1. And, I have identified all the Figures, Tables, and paragraphs that were not yet developed for the *DOS 4.1 Manual* and I have included them in the *DOS 4.1 Disk Operating System Second Edition.*

I know the user will discover the many fascinating developments found in the *DOS 4.1 Disk Operating System Second Edition* presented with the clarity of a far better format: he will be left wondering how he accomplished anything in a timely fashion without having had those developments in any other version of a previous Apple Disk Operating System. I would take that as my greatest compliment.

Enjoy the ride!

Table of Contents

List of Figures

List of Tables

I. Designing a New DOS

This book describes the process and products I created when I decided to design, write, and program a new Disk Operating System (DOS) for my Apple //e. Wherever I am able I have included schematic diagrams, code samples, equations, figures, tables, and representative screen shots to help explain what I have created and the reasons why I did so. Today, this has been an incredible journey for me in re-imagining that time when I mostly lived, breathed, and worked on Apple][computers, hardware, and software development continuously for a good period of my life many, many years ago.

1. Introduction

I have been an avid Apple][computer enthusiast, hobbyist, and professional programmer since 1983 when I became the proud owner of an Apple][+ computer. My complete system initially included an Apple][Language Card, a Disk][with an Apple][Disk Controller slot card, an Amdek color monitor, and an Epson MX100 printer with a Grappler+ Printer Interface slot card. During those early years I designed and built Apple][peripheral slot cards, made electrical and hardware modifications to my Apple][+ motherboard and keyboard, and wrote a substantial number of software programs using Applesoft BASIC (Applesoft hereafter) and 6502 assembly language. I soon acquired a Videx UltraTerm video display slot card and a Microsoft Z80 slot card, and I began writing Fortran programs that analyzed tomographic reconstructions of the human spinal column. A year or so later I added the Southern California Research Group quikLoader and PROmGRAMER slot cards, a Johnathon Freeman Designs (JFD) Parallel Printer Buffer, and an Axlon RAM Disk 320 and its interface slot card to my system.

Now that I am retired from the aerospace industry where I used C language for the software development of ultra-high-speed data collection systems for tactical radar and sensor development, I have always wanted to dig into, tear apart, and learn the intricacies of the last available Apple][DOS for the Apple][+, that is, DOS 3.3, published on August 25, 1980. Then I came across another version of DOS 3.3 published on January 1, 1983, which contains even more patches for the DOS APPEND command and an Apple //e initialization patch. What I learned from the 1980 publication flabbergasted me: the code is exciting in its originality and concept vis-à-vis it was released just after the publication of Integer BASIC, but I found it somewhat juvenile in structure and implementation. Apparently very little attention was paid to code design and review because it appeared to me Apple made a strong push to release "something or anything" to consumers and third-party vendors in order to market software products on diskettes.

And history does reveal that Apple Computer did outsource DOS and contracted for it to be delivered within 35 days for $13,000 in April 1978. Paul Laughton at Shepardson Microsystems wrote Apple's initial disk operating system using Hollerith cards, a card reader, and a minicomputer. Now I have the time and the continuing curiosity to delve into Apple][DOS, and I have the opportunity to create my own version of DOS that contains the power and the flexibility I always thought DOS ought to and could have. I call my version of Apple][DOS, DOS 4.1. And this is my 46th build of DOS 4.1. What a ride I have been on! Why? To see what I could do for this wonderful machine and its magnificent architecture!

I know there are a great many ProDOS users in the Apple][community, but I never became interested in ProDOS. The work I did at Hughes Aircraft in the mid 1980's consisted of using assembly language for programming an operating system executive and interface driver routines for Gould SEL 2780, 6780, and 9780 mainframe computers. These computers hosted a proprietary operating system that allowed our team to simulate a radar processor traveling above the earth's surface virtually in real time. In order to accomplish that goal and simulate real time navigation the computer's file system was flat: each user had their own directory, and these user directories contained no subdirectories. So I was very comfortable with the idea of a flat file system, very much like that of Apple's DOS 3.3. I was simply not comfortable with a slew of subdirectories exemplified by Apple's ProDOS. My thought was always "How does one remember the path to follow to find anything?" With the advent of the Macintosh computer and later when I became familiar with the UNIX file system, my subdirectory fears vanished and I cannot imagine a modern computer directory system without subdirectories. However, I still remain passionate about Apple][DOS and I leave ProDOS to those who are comfortable with that operating system architecture. Though what I have seen of ProDOS recently, I believe it could definitely use a facelift, seriously.

I am sure many are curious and want to know what is new and different in Build 46, and what makes this build so special. Looking back over my previous build manuals I realized that I should have included this vital build enhancement information with every build, if only for historical reasons. Like, which build did I solve the Track 0x00 utilization quest? Which build did I start labeling volumes? Which build did I solve the "Disk Full" logic error? Taken all together, I have done an incredible amount of research, writing, and software development to reach Build 46. And, to say the least, I have done an incredible amount of testing for every function under normal and abnormal (or error) conditions. However small the list of items unique to Build 46 may seem, I have spent countless hours developing and testing those items alone and in concert with the entire DOS package.

Build 45 did introduce another File Manager opcode to be used only by the DOS TS command. Build 46 adds the TSSAV 16-bit variable to the operation of this File Manager opcode so that the TS handler does not interfere with the DIRTS 16-bit variable as in previous builds. It must be emphasized that the File Manager FMTSCD opcode is not for external use. It is simply a means to utilize the error handling capabilities of the File Manager on behalf of the DOS TS command. In Build 46 both the Boot and Volume INIT functions now utilize the BOOTCFG table. This ensures total consistency between what the INIT function creates and how the created volume actually boots. Build 46 allows the creation of the volume Catalog with a minimum of one sector, or any number up to 15 sectors. Previously, the minimum number of volume Catalog sectors was set to seven. Build 46 sets the default volume Catalog to five sectors, or enough room to support 35 files. New to Build 46 are two new variables FIRSTCAT and LASTRACK found at the end of the CMDVALS data structure. These variables hold the default number of volume Catalog sectors and the default number of Tracks/Volume, respectively. Currently, these variables contain 0x05 for FIRSTCAT and 0x23 for LASTRACK. These variables are provided so that DOS 4.1 does not need to be reassembled in order to change these default values. Build 46 adds a new keyword, the B keyword, to the DOS SAVE, BSAVE, LSAVE, and TSAVE commands in order to implement the "File Delete/File Save" strategy. Many times when a highly edited file is saved, some of the T/S entries in the file's TSL are not utilized, and some disk space is wasted. When a file is deleted, then saved, those unused data sectors are retrieved and made available for other files to use. Using the B-keyword with these DOS commands will automatically delete the file, then save the file as intended. Finally, the DOS CATALOG command output can be terminated by pressing the ESC key.

2. General Software Design Strategy

My career in designing software, building software systems, and constructing data conversion and data manipulation algorithms required me to understand the hardware capabilities of the computers chosen for those tasks, down to the last detail. How else was I to construct a real time digital "time frame" on a computer having a given operating system and processor throughput, fixed addressable memory, and unique peripheral interfaces (e.g. the support of direct I/O) unless I understood the complete machine architecture. I believe this design approach is fully applicable to the Apple][computer: either code or data occupies fixed addressable memory where some defined memory locations are reserved for text, graphics, control, and peripheral slot cards, and code development is further restricted by the rather limited 6502 microprocessor Instruction Set. My obvious goal strategy is to design software in such a way as to create the most functionality with the least amount of code and data space. I believe this methodology will yield the highest degree of code effectiveness.

So I began my DOS design first with a "wish list" of some of the DOS capabilities and enhancements I wanted most in my DOS. In parallel with my software design of DOS 4.1 I wanted to create enough documentation for someone else to "come up to speed" and be able to create their "wish list" items for their unique version of an Apple DOS if that is their goal, too. I have no doubt that what I think is a worthy enhancement may not be so worthy to someone else. Someone else may rather use the code space for a different utility or functionality, and that would make their DOS XYZ just as powerful for their software environment and applications. Another one of my DOS design goals centered on how best to display information from many of the command-line command enhancements. I realize there are only 24 lines on an Apple][display, but I found that spacing commands and their output information provides a far better visual presentation. In all of the software programs that I developed for users at Hughes Aircraft Company, I put "Consistency in Design" at the top of my design goals list. I wanted users to be instantly comfortable with all current and future versions of my programs and utilities once they had initially acclimated to any one of my many program or utility menus. In the same fashion I focused my design of Apple DOS to use "Consistency in Design" for each group of related commands in how those commands gather, store, retrieve, and display information.

3. DOS Wish List

I can easily recall at least five DOS 3.3 enhancements aimed to speed up data input and output to a Disk][, even going so far as modifying the soft sector skewing table. All the enhancements performed well, but they were usually at the expense of losing one or more DOS capabilities such as the INIT function, for example. In DOS 3.3 there was no support for file date and time stamping even though many clock cards were already available in the early 1980's. DOS included placeholders for the future support of additional file types, but those features have never been implemented to my knowledge. A diskette's Volume Table Of Contents, or VTOC, was actually designed to support media having up to thirty-two sectors per track, and up to fifty tracks per volume, but those features have never been implemented with any supporting hardware I know of. There was no easy way to manipulate text files or create a simple EXEC file from the Apple command line. For example, one needed sophisticated tools to even display the contents of a volume sector.

Another missing native DOS capability was an Applesoft program CHAIN function where all previous Applesoft variables would be available to the next CHAIN Applesoft program, similar in concept to the DOS CHAIN capability for Integer BASIC programs. An assembly language program was available to provide Applesoft program CHAIN capability, but the program had to reside on each and every application volume in order to support the CHAIN of applications across multiple volumes. Even that software had a major design flaw that could wreak havoc with program variables. DOS did not support lowercase command entry even though Applesoft did support lowercase entry on an Enhanced Apple //e. And, DOS could not "undelete" a file once it was deleted without using special software utilities along with a convoluted set of procedures.

Those early pioneers who wanted to write massive Applesoft applications were mostly out of luck because DOS consumed at least 11 KB of the available 48 KB of memory below memory address 0xC000; only Diversi-DOS was able to relocate DOS to the Language Card, and that actually became very useful to some software application publishers. Of course, it would be far better to have a version of DOS that would boot directly into the Language Card and be totally resident and native in the Language Card as well.

Apple DOS depends on a few ROM routines for initialization, keyboard input, and video output. I do not believe a discussion about an Apple][DOS would be complete without considering the Monitor firmware. The ROM, alone, would be a fascinating subject, but together, the DOS and the ROM complete the Apple][hardware and software architecture. The ROM contains flawed code, functions that should be excluded, and functions that should be included. So, I include exploring the contents of the ROM on my DOS wish list, too.

Yes, the DOS wish list goes on and on, but it also needs to include solutions to all the flawed DOS routines, and the DOS routines that were simply coded incorrectly. I believe DOS 4.1 not only meets the demands of this wish list, but also exceeds it in all expectations as well.

4. DOS 4.1 Software Development

In 1983 most everyone including me who wrote software for Ken Williams at Sierra On-Line used Randall Hyde's Lazer's Interactive Symbolic Assembler, that is, *Lisa* V2.6, for the software development of 6502 assembly language programs. I have taken the time to source *Lisa* in order to add additional capabilities to its repertoire of commands and directives, and to modify and/or eliminate its direct DOS 3.3 dependencies. *Lisa* now uses the variable table interfaces in DOS 4.1 in order to access some necessary DOS 4.1 internal variables and structures. I do all my verification testing on an Enhanced Apple //e having a Super Serial slot card, a clock slot card of my own design and fabrication, a quikLoader slot card, a Rana Disk][Controller slot card, and an Axlon interface slot card connected to a RAM Disk 320. The Super Serial slot card is connected to my Apple G4 dual processor tower using a Keyspan serial to USB adapter. I use Gerard Putter's application Virtual][, Version 7.5.4 (my Apple MacBook Pro uses Version 10.1) to create my software applications and perform the initial, though simulated testing. Once I am satisfied with an application or program running under Virtual][, I connect Virtual]['s A2V2 application to the Super Serial card via the Keyspan, and run the mating application *ADT* on the Apple //e. After I have transferred the volume image to a physical diskette or to the RAM Disk 320 connected to DOS 4.1, I am ready to test the application or program on real hardware. If I make any software changes to modify or enhance the application under test, I can, of course, transfer that modified volume image back to Virtual][and archive the volume image on the G4 or the MacBook Pro. It was absolutely necessary that I use the Disk][and a physical diskette when I tested my version of the DOS RWTS read/write I/O routines, for example. It is unfortunate that Virtual][only emulates the ThunderClock clock card. I designed and built my own clock slot card for my Apple][+, and now use it in my Apple //e. I inherited my mother's Applied Engineering's TimeMaster II clock card from her Apple //e. DOS 4.1 absolutely supports these three clock cards and quite possibly others.

Because I entered the Apple][+ market when the computer had a full 48 KB of memory on its motherboard and 16 KB of memory in the Language Card available then, I never made use of a Master boot disk image: I only created and used Slave boot disk images, even when I was employed at Sierra. Therefore, to my way of thinking, DOS loads to memory address 0x9D00, end of story. Also, DOS 3.3 loads several buffers (catalog, VTOC, and the primary nibble buffer) unnecessarily, and it ignores two sectors on track 0x00 used by and reserved for the Master boot disk image. To my surprise and delight I found that with some clever (okay, a little clever) organization I could fit all of DOS 4.1 onto tracks 0x00 and 0x01, and not even utilize any of the five sectors DOS 3.3 uses on its reserved track 0x02. I cannot tell you all the time I spent in early 1984 designing programs that would modify the VTOC on a diskette so that I could access those eleven unused sectors remaining on track 0x02. Now, I have made all of track 0x02 available for data storage and, as a result, shortened the time for DOS to boot into memory. In the early Apple][market there was initially Integer BASIC in ROM unless you owned a Language Card into which the Applesoft Interpreter could be loaded when that language became available. My Apple][+ contained the Applesoft Autostart ROMs so my Language Card was simply used to load Integer BASIC if I desired, or the Pascal or Fortran languages. Eventually, DOS was enhanced to support both Integer BASIC and Applesoft, and it was able to switch between those two languages. I suppose I used Integer BASIC all of one time in order to watch AppleVision by Bob Bishop. This may not surprise anyone: Sierra did not ever carry one single product in its inventory that required Integer BASIC. And I do not recall any other software-publishing house marketing an Integer BASIC product in the early 1980's. I chose to remove all traces of Integer BASIC support from DOS 4.1. ProDOS does not support Integer BASIC as well.

Over the years a lot of fuss was made concerning the page-zero memory address location Apple chose for the RWTS Input/Output Context Block (IOCB) pointer at 0x48/0x49. Unfortunately, the Apple Monitor, which I believe takes priority, also uses page-zero memory bytes 0x48/0x49 to save the processor and status registers after the processor receives an interrupt. Instead of fixing this problem in DOS, Apple advised programmers to always store a 0x00 byte at memory address 0x48 after using the 0x3D9 vector to call RWTS. Others suggested using the MOTORTIM (RWTS motor on time) memory bytes 0x46/0x47 for the RWTS IOCB pointer and moving the MOTORTIM pointer elsewhere. I chose to do a very careful and thorough study of the Monitor routines and their use of page-zero memory. I modified the MSWAIT routine to use the page-zero memory bytes 0x3C/0x3D for the MOTORTIM bytes. In view of no longer supporting Integer BASIC, DOS 4.1 uses the page-zero bytes 0x4A/0x4B for the RWTS IOCB pointer which were previously used by Integer BASIC. Therefore, the 0x45 to 0x49 page-zero bytes are now untouched by DOS 4.1 and exclusively for use by the Monitor. In the little experience I gained in generating and handling interrupts with my clock card, I realized that the interrupt handling of the Apple Monitor was totally under-realized, under-appreciated, and under-utilized. The RTI instruction is certainly available, it works, and it could be used for some awesome hardware design firmware coupled with the right DOS.

During my review of DOS 3.3 I found that it took less than a handful of instructions to give DOS 4.1 full lowercase support for all commands, and even fewer instructions to allow DOS 4.1 access to all of track 0x00 for data storage. *FID* also required a few easy modifications in order for it to access track 0x00 for data retrieval and data storage as well. I also found that to add date and time stamping to disk volumes and files only required three slight modifications to the volume initialization routine, the closing of files routine, and the routine that updates the disk volume VTOC. By the way, the VTOC also includes enough unused space to hold the DOS Version, Build number, a 24-character Volume Name, a Volume Type showing if it is a bootable or a data storage volume, a Volume Library number, and a flag indicating which location in RAM that DOS 4.1 was occupying when the volume was initialized: DOS 4.1L, L for Low RAM DOS, that is, DOS from 0x9D00 to 0xBFFF, or DOS 4.1H, H for High RAM DOS, or DOS fully located (not relocated) natively in the Language Card.

Before beginning any discussion of a complicated subject like an operating system for the Apple][, it is usually easier to understand each component part of such a system if they are shown as part of a Big Picture. That Big Picture is shown in Table I.4.1. Though certainly not to scale, Table I.4.1 simply shows the memory utilization for the Apple][and where the basic components are found in Main memory. I exclude any discussion of Auxiliary memory as found in the Apple //e in this book. The basic components shown Table I.4.1 are the 6502 microprocessor requirements, the DOS vectors, text pages, graphic pages, DOS file buffers, DOS code, hardware soft switches, peripheral-card memory, Applesoft, and the ROM Monitor. The following pages will discuss the Apple][memory utilization in great detail so it may be helpful to refer to Table I.4.1 occasionally in order to fully understand how those details relate to the entire software and hardware management of the Apple][computer. The Apple][computer is a wonderful machine and it has a magnificent architecture. I hope you find my presentation of DOS 4.1 vis-à-vis the Apple][computer interesting, enlightening, and useful in view of your own hardware and software experiences with this delightful machine.

Memory Page	Description	Description
0x00	Page-zero pointers, special addressing modes	
0x01	Stack for 6502 microprocessor	
0x02	Input buffer, Applesoft interpretation buffer	
0x03	User buffer, DOS vectors	
0x04-0x07	Text or LORES graphics page 1	
0x08-0x0B	Applesoft program start, Text or LORES graphics page 2	
0x0C-0x1F	Free	
0x20-0x3F	HIRES graphics page 1 or free	
0x40-0x5F	HIRES graphics page 2 or free	
0x60-0x95	Free	
0x96-0x9C	DOS 4.1L HIMEM, three DOS 4.1L file buffers	
0x9D-0xBC	DOS 4.1L routines	
0xBE-0xBF	DOS 4.1H HIMEM, DOS 4.1H Language Card interface, DOS 4.1L continuation	
0xC0	Hardware configuration soft switches	
0xC1-0xC7	Peripheral-card ROM memory for slots 1-7	
0xC8-0xCF	Peripheral-card expansion ROM memory	
0xD0-0xDF	Language Card Bank 2, Applesoft, DOS 4.1H routines	Bank 1, DOS 4.1H RWTS and HELP
0xE0-0xEB	Applesoft, DOS 4.1H routines	
0xEC-0xEF	Applesoft, DOS 4.1H file buffers	
0xF0-0xF7	Applesoft, DOS 4.1H file buffers	
0xF8-0xFF	ROM Monitor routines	

Table I.4.1. Apple][Memory Utilization

5. Page-Zero Utilization

The Instruction Set for the 6502 microprocessor (and the 65C02 processor as well) includes special processor instructions that utilize variables located in the first 256 bytes, or page, of addressable memory, that is, locations 0x0000 to 0x00FF. I designate this area of memory "page-zero." When Steve Wozniak designed the Apple Monitor he allocated a number of page-zero locations for its variables and pointers. Similarly, Applesoft, DOS, and virtually all other user assembly language programs use page-zero locations in order to utilize those special instructions. The 6502 microprocessor contains an accumulator, the A-register, and two index registers, the X-register and the Y-register. Page-zero instructions using these registers include load and store instructions, indexed load and store instructions, indexed indirect addressing instructions using the X-register, and indirect indexed addressing instructions using the Y-register. Page-zero wraparound occurs with indexed indirect addressing instructions but not with indirect indexed addressing instructions.

When developing a user assembly language program it is critical to select page-zero locations that do not conflict with the Apple Monitor, Applesoft, or DOS depending on whether those applications are important to the user program. Knowing which page-zero locations are used by or critical to resident applications can greatly simplify the selection of unused or available page-zero locations. Because DOS 3.3 supports Integer BASIC, a few page-zero locations were used to process that file type. DOS 4.1 also uses those same page-zero locations for processing the Applesoft CHAIN command, for example, and other command enhancements. There are definitely obvious page-zero locations that cannot be used except for how they were intended, like the horizontal and vertical cursor locations CH and CV, respectively. Then, there are less obvious, rather dubious page-zero locations that are used by some Applesoft commands from 0x00 to 0x1F. These page-zero locations are fair game for user programs that do not use the Applesoft interpreter or Steve Wozniak's *SWEET16* interpreter. Tables I.5.1 through I.5.4 list all page-zero locations and the applications that use those particular locations according to my references and the best of my ability to decipher the code that uses those locations. Figure I.5.1 summarizes the data in Tables I.5.1 through I.5.4 to show all used and unused page-zero locations. The darker shaded locations in Figure I.5.1 are unused page-zero locations that probably are not used by the Apple //e Monitor or Applesoft, so they are more than likely the better locations to select. Indirect indexed addressing instructions using the Y-register do require a page-zero byte-pair, so it is even more critical that neither address byte is clobbered by software external to the user program.

There are certainly common page-zero locations that all software routines can use for temporary variables and pointers. The 6502 microprocessor is not time-shared and there is no context switching between routines, so if a routine uses some common page-zero locations, it should complete all processing using those locations and not expect to find its results sometime later. Examples of common page-zero locations would be A1L/A1H, A2L/A2H, A3L/A3H, A4L/A4H, OPRND, and DSCTMP (3 bytes). Using these page-zero locations to move or copy data would be safe and not interfere with Monitor, Applesoft, or DOS processing. Actually, some Monitor routines require that some of these locations just mentioned contain your data before using those routines. The Monitor routine MOVE at 0xFE2C is one such example. It is really up to the user to confirm and verify that the selected page-zero memory locations do not interfere with other routines external to and required by the user software.

Addr	Monitor	MiniAsm	C1 ROM	Applesoft	RWTS	DOS 4.1	Description
0x00	LOC0	LOC0	LOC0	LOC0			AS JMP vector
0x01	LOC1		LOC1	LOC1			
0x02			ZPG02	ZPG02			
0x03			ZPG03	ZPG03			AS JMP vector
0x04			ZPG04	ZPG04			
0x05				ZPG05			
0x06							** free **
0x07							** free **
0x08							** free **
0x09							** free **
0x0A				ZPG0A			AS JMP vector
0x0B				ZPG0B			
0x0C				ZPG0C			
0x0D				ZPG0D			AS STRLT2 string utility
0x0E				ZPG0E			AS STRLT2 string utility
0x0F				ZPG0F			
0x10				ZPG10			
0x11				ZPG11			AS flag for last FAC
0x12				ZPG12			
0x13				ZPG13			
0x14				ZPG14			AS subscript flag
0x15				ZPG15			
0x16				ZPG16			AS FP comparison type
0x17				ZPG17			
0x18				ZPG18			
0x19				ZPG19			
0x1A				SHAPE			
0x1B				:			
0x1C				HCOLOR1			
0x1D		INDEX		COUNTH			
0x1E		ADRCNTR					** free **
0x1F			ZPG1F				
0x20	WNDLFT		WNDLFT	WNDLFT			Left column of scroll window
0x21	WNDWDTH		WNDWDTH	WNDWDTH			Width of scroll window
0x22	WNDTOP		WNDTOP	WNDTOP			Top line of scroll window
0x23	WNDBTM		WNDBTM	WNDBTM			Bottom line of scroll window
0x24	CH		CH	CH		CH	Cursor horizontal, WNDLFT
0x25	CV		CV	CV			Cursor vertical, WNDTOP
0x26	BASL			BASL	TEMPZ	BUFRADRZ	LORES plot left end point
0x27	BASH			BASH	TEMP2Z	:	HIRES plot base address
0x28	BASEZ		BASEZ	BASEZ		BASEZ	Memory address of text line
0x29	:		:	:		:	
0x2A	BAS2L		BAS2L	BAS2L	CURTRKZ	ASPTRSAV	Memory address for scrolling
0x2B	BASEH		BASEH	BASEH	SLOT16Z	:	
0x2C	H2			H2	DATAFNDZ	:	Right end point for HLINE
0x2D	V2			V2	SECFNDZ	:	Bottom point for VLINE
0x2E	MASK	MASK	MASK	MASK	TRKFNDZ	:	LORES color mask
0x2F	SIGN	SIGN	SIGN	SIGN	VOLFNDZ	:	
0x30	HMASK			COLOR			LORES color for PLOT
0x31	MODE	MODE					Monitor command processing
0x32	INVFLG		INVFLG	INVFLG			Video format control
0x33	PROMPT	PROMPT		PROMPT		PROMPT	Prompt character
0x34	YSAV	YSAV	YSAV				Monitor command processing
0x35	YSAV1	YSAV1	YSAV1			(DOS 3.3 DRIVNO)	Y-register save for COUT1
0x36	CSWL		CSWL			CSWL	Monitor/DOS output
0x37	CSWH		CSWH			CSWH	
0x38	KSWL		KSWL			KSWL	Monitor/DOS input
0x39	KSWH		KSWH			KSWH	
0x3A	PCL	PCL	PCL				Program counter
0x3B	PCH	PCH	PCH				
0x3C	A1L	A1L	A1L	A1L	MOTORTIM		MiniAsm trace work area
0x3D	A1H	A1H	A1H	A1H	:		
0x3E	A2L	A2L	A2L	A2L	ODDBITSZ	BUFADR2Z	
0x3F	A2H	A2H	A2H	A2H	SECTORZ	:	

Table I.5.1. Page-Zero Memory Locations 0x00-0x3F

Addr	Monitor	MiniAsm	C1 ROM	Applesoft	RWTS	DOS 4.1	Description
0x40	A3L				TRACKZ	FILEBUFZ	
0x41	A3H				VOLUMEZ	:	
0x42	A4L	A4L	A4L			BUFADRZ	
0x43	A4H	A4H	A4H			:	
0x44	OPRND	OPRND	OPRND			DIRINDX	
0x45	AREG						(DOS 3.3 SYNCNT)
0x46	XREG						(DOS 3.3 MONTIME)
0x47	YREG						(:)
0x48	PREG						(DOS 3.3 IOBADR)
0x49	SPNT						(:)
0x4A					IOBADR	IOBADR	(DOS 3.3 INTLOMEM)
0x4B					:	:	(:)
0x4C						DOSPTR	(DOS 3.3 INTHIMEM)
0x4D						:	(:)
0x4E	RNDL		RNDL				
0x4F	RNDH		RNDH				
0x50			ACL	ACL		LINNUM	
0x51			ACH	ACH		:	
0x52				TEMPPT			AS temporary string pointer
0x53				LASTPT			AS last temp string pointer
0x54				EL			HIRES error for HLIN
0x55				STRATCH			AS string scratch name/length
0x56		AREG1		:			
0x57		XREG1		:			
0x58		YREG1		TEMPDSC			AS temp save for DSCTMP
0x59		PREG1		:			
0x5A				:		DOSTEMP1	
0x5B						DOSTEMP2	
0x5C						DOSBUFR	
0x5D						:	
0x5E				INDEX			AS stack for moving strings
0x5F				:			
0x60				P2			
0x61				:			
0x62				LASTMUL			
0x63				:			
0x64				:			
0x65				:			
0x66				:			
0x67				TEXTTAB		ASPGMST	AS program start
0x68				:		:	
0x69				VARTAB		ASVARS	AS simple variables pointer
0x6A				:		:	
0x6B				ARYTAB		ASARYS	AS array pointer
0x6C				:		:	
0x6D			STREND	STREND		ARYEND	AS top of array pointer
0x6E			:	:		:	
0x6F			FRETOP	FRETOP		ASSTRS	AS end of strings pointer
0x70			:	:		:	
0x71				FRESPC			AS temp string storage
0x72				:			
0x73			MEMSIZE	MEMSIZE		ASHIMEM	AS HIMEM
0x74			:	:		:	
0x75				CURLIN			AS current line
0x76				:		ASRUN	
0x77				OLDLIN			AS last line processed
0x78				:			
0x79				TEXTPTR			AS old text pointer
0x7A				:			
0x7B				DATLIN			AS line where data being read
0x7C				:			
0x7D				DATPTR			AS absolute read data address
0x7E				:			
0x7F				SRCPTR			AS current source of input

Table I.5.2. Page-Zero Memory Locations 0x40-0x7F

Addr	Monitor	MiniAsm	C1 ROM	Applesoft	RWTS	DOS 4.1	Description
0x80				:			
0x81				LASTVBL			AS last variable's name
0x82				:			
0x83				VARPNT			AS last variable's value
0x84				:			
0x85				FORPNT			AS general pointer
0x86				:			
0x87				GENTEMP			
0x88				:			
0x89				:			
0x8A				TEMP3			AS FP register
0x8B				:			
0x8C				GENTPTR			
0x8D				:			
0x8E				:			
0x8F				ZPG8F			
0x90				ZPG90			JMP vector
0x91				ZPG91			
0x92				ZPG92			
0x93				TEMP1			AS FP register
0x94			HIGHDS	HIGHDS			Block transfer utility, dest
0x95			:	:			
0x96				HIGHTR			Block transfer utility, end
0x97				:			
0x98				TEMP2			AS FP register
0x99				:			
0x9A				:			
0x9B			LOWTR	LOWTR			AS general purpose register
0x9C			:	:			
0x9D				DSCTMP			AS temp string descriptor
0x9E				:			
0x9F				:			
0xA0				FACMO			AS middle order mantissa
0xA1				FACLO			AS low order mantissa
0xA2				FACSIGN			AS sign of FAC
0xA3				ZPGA3			
0xA4				ZPGA4			
0xA5				ARGEXP			AS secondary FP accumulator
0xA6				ARGMANT			AS 4 byte mantissa
0xA7				:			
0xA8				:			
0xA9				:			
0xAA				ARGSGN			AS sign of ARG
0xAB				STRNG1			AS MOVINS utility
0xAC				:			
0xAD				STRNG2			AS STRLT2 utility
0xAE				:			
0xAF				PRGEND		ASPEND	AS end of program
0xB0				:		:	
0xB1				CHRGET			AS routine, TXTPTR++
0xB2				:			
0xB3				:			
0xB4				:			
0xB5				:			
0xB6				:			
0xB7				CHRGOT			AS routine, no TXTPTR++
0xB8				TXTPTR			AS next program character
0xB9				:			
0xBA				:			
0xBB				:			
0xBC				:			
0xBD				:			
0xBE				:			
0xBF				:			

Table I.5.3. Page-Zero Memory Locations 0x80-0xBF

Addr	Monitor	MiniAsm	C1 ROM	Applesoft	RWTS	DOS 4.1	Description
0xC0				:			
0xC1				:			
0xC2				:			
0xC3				:			
0xC4				:			
0xC5				:			
0xC6				:			
0xC7				:			
0xC8				PTREND			
0xC9				FPRAND			AS FP random number
0xCA				:			
0xCB				:			
0xCC				:			
0xCD				:			
0xCE							** free **
0xCF							** free **
0xD0				ZPGD0			
0xD1				ZPGD1			
0xD2				ZPGD2			
0xD3				ZPGD3			
0xD4				ZPGD4			
0xD5				ZPGD5			
0xD6				MYSTERY		PROTECT	All commands equal RUN
0xD7							** free **
0xD8				ERRFLG		ASONERR	AS error flag
0xD9						RKEYWORD	(DOS 3.3 INTRUN)
0xDA				ERRLIN			AS line where error occurred
0xDB				:			
0xDC				ERRPOS			AS TEXTPTR HNDLERR
0xDD				:			
0xDE				ERRNUM			AS error number or code
0xDF				ERRSTK			AS stack pointer before error
0xE0				HRXCOOR			HIRES X-coordinate
0xE1				:			
0xE2				HRYCOOR			HIRES Y-coordinate
0xE3							** free **
0xE4				HRCOLOR			HIRES color byte
0xE5				HRHZNDX			HIRES horizontal byte index
0xE6				HPAG			HIRES page to plot on
0xE7				SCALE			HIRES scale factor
0xE8			HRSHPTBL	HRSHPTBL			HIRES shape table address
0xE9			:	:			
0xEA				HRCOLCNT			HIRES collision counter
0xEB							** free **
0xEC							** free **
0xED							** free **
0xEE							** free **
0xEF							** free **
0xF0				FIRST			AS first dest of LORES PLOT
0xF1				SPDBYT			Speed control, output/display
0xF2				ZPG92			
0xF3	SIGN			ORMASK			Mask for output control
0xF4	X2			X2			Exponent
0xF5				M2			Mantissa, 3 bytes
0xF6				:			
0xF7				:			
0xF8				REMSTK			AS stack pointer
0xF9				M1			FP accumulator for M1
0xFA							** free **
0xFB							** free **
0xFC							** free **
0xFD							** free **
0xFE							** free **
0xFF			ZPGFF	ZPGFF			

Table I.5.4. Page-Zero Memory Locations 0xC0-0xFF

0x	0	1	2	3	4	5	6	7	8	9	A	B	C	D	E	F
00	1234	134	34	34	34	4					4	4	4	4	4	4
10	4	4	4	4	4	4	4	4	4	4	4	4	4	24	2	3
20	134	134	134	134	1346	134	1456	1456	1346	1346	13456	13456	1456	1456	123456	123456
30	14	12	134	1246	123	123	136	136	136	136	123	123	12345	12345	123456	123456
40	156	156	1236	1236	1236	1	1	1	1	1	56	56	6	6	13	13
50	346	346	4	4	4	4	24	24	24	24	46	6	6	6	4	4
60	4	4	4	4	4	4	4	46	46	46	46	46	46	346	346	346
70	346	4	4	346	346	4	46	4	4	4	4	4	4	4	4	4
80	4	4	4	4	4	4	4	4	4	4	4	4	4	4	4	4
90	4	4	4	4	34	34	4	4	4	4	4	34	34	4	4	4
A0	4	4	4	4	4	4	4	4	4	4	4	4	4	4	4	46
B0	46	4	4	4	4	4	4	4	4	4	4	4	4	4	4	4
C0	4	4	4	4	4	4	4	4	4	4	4	4	4	4		
D0	4	4	4		4	4	46		46	6	4	4	4	4	4	4
E0	4	4	4		4	4	4	4	34	34	4					
F0	4	4	4	14	14	4	4	4	4	4				4		34

Figure I.5.1. Page-Zero Memory Usage Summary

Key

1 – used by the Monitor
2 – used by the Mini Assembler
3 – used by the C1-CF ROM
4 – used by Applesoft
5 – used by RWTS
6 – used by DOS 4.1

13

6. VTOC Structure

How I agonized over how to implement date and time stamping for files and disk volumes. Preferably I only wanted to update a date and time stamp when either a file or the VTOC of a disk volume has changed. I also wanted to date and time stamp a disk volume (or disk image) when that volume was first created. However, creating or updating a date and time stamp is only half the task: the date and time stamp needs to be displayed appropriately. And, when the contents of a volume's Catalog directory are listed the file's date and time stamp needs to be displayed along with its filename. Since the VTOC is basically the heart of the disk volume, it is best to begin there and show its organization and content in DOS 4.1. The VTOC is defined to be located on track 0x11, in sector 0x00. The volume Catalog sectors may be on any other track, but typically they are defined to be on track 0x11 for optimal access speed.

Figure I.6.1 shows the VTOC for a data disk having five sectors available for the volume Catalog, a major change in Build 46. A data disk is defined as volume type D for Data disk. A bootable disk having a DOS 4.1L image or a DOS 4.1H image is defined as volume type B for Boot disk. Table I.6.1 defines each entry in the VTOC, Table I.6.2 defines the free sector bitmap for each track, and Table I.6.3 defines the bytes of the six-byte date and time stamp and the order of those bytes. There is more information in Section I.14 about the free sector bitmap definition as it is used in DOS 4.1.

0x	0	1	2	3	4	5	6	7	8	9	A	B	C	D	E	F
00	00	11	05	41	46	CC	12	C4								
10	Volume Name — 24 characters															
20	Date & Time Volume created							7A	Lib Num		Date & Time VTOC changed					
30	11	01			23	10	00	01	FF	FF	00	00	FF	FF	00	00
40	FF	FF	00	00	FF	FF	00	00	FF	FF	00	00	FF	FF	00	00
50	FF	FF	00	00	FF	FF	00	00	FF	FF	00	00	FF	FF	00	00
60	FF	FF	00	00	FF	FF	00	00	FF	FF	00	00	FF	FF	00	00
70	FF	FF	00	00	FF	FF	00	00	FF	FF	00	00	FF	00	00	00
80	FF	FF	00	00	FF	FF	00	00	FF	FF	00	00	FF	FF	00	00
90	FF	FF	00	00	FF	FF	00	00	FF	FF	00	00	FF	FF	00	00
A0	FF	FF	00	00	FF	FF	00	00	FF	FF	00	00	FF	FF	00	00
B0	FF	FF	00	00	FF	FF	00	00	FF	FF	00	00	FF	FF	00	00
C0	FF	FF	00	00												
D0																
E0																
F0																

Figure I.6.1. DOS 4.1L Data Disk Volume VTOC

In DOS 3.3 much code and valuable data space was dedicated to the manipulation of Volume number beginning with the Command Manager, through the File Manager, and on to RWTS, and then back to the File Manager. Since all positional parameters such as Slot, Drive, and Volume are initialized to 0x00 by the Command Manager after a DOS 4.1 command has been parsed, the default VOLVAL for the Volume number keyword is always 0x00. DOS 4.1 passes Volume number through the File Manager and to RWTS **unchanged**. Therefore, the **default** Volume number that is displayed by DOS

14

4.1 is "000" and not "254" (or 0xFE) as it is by DOS 3.3. The Volume number at byte 0x06 in the VTOC is the **official** Volume number for the volume, not the one RWTS finds encoded in the Address Field header of a diskette sector. Bytes 0x01 and 0x02 of the VTOC are the track and sector number, respectively, for the first Catalog sector. As in DOS 3.3, DOS 4.1 uses byte 0x03 of the VTOC for DOS Version, and uses the unused byte at 0x04 for the DOS Build Number. Byte 0x05 is used to designate which RAM DOS, L (or 0xCC) or H (or 0xC8), was in memory (i.e. DOS 4.1L or DOS 4.1H) when the volume was created, and byte 0x07 is used for the Disk Volume Type, B (or 0xC2) or D (or 0xC4). Bytes 0x08 through 0x1F are used for the 24-character Disk Volume Name or title, bytes 0x20 through 0x25 are used for the Disk Volume Date and Time stamp when the volume was created, and bytes 0x2A through 0x2F are used for the VTOC Date and Time stamp, and this time stamp is updated whenever DOS 4.1 changes the VTOC for any reason. Bytes 0x28 and 0x29 are used for a 16-bit (low/high byte order) Disk Library value. All other VTOC variables are still at their original, DOS 3.3 location. All these new variables are displayed by the DOS 4.1 CATALOG command.

Byte	Name	Value	Description
0x00	VTOCSB	0x00	VTOC Structure Block
0x01	FRSTTRK	0x11	Track number of first catalog sector
0x02	FRSTSEC	0x05	Sector number of first catalog sector
0x03	DOSVRSN	0x41	DOS Version number used to INIT this VTOC
0x04	DOSBUILD	0x46	Build number used to INIT this VTOC
0x05	DOSRAM	0xCC	RAM DOS that initialized this volume (L or H)
0x06	DISKVOL	0x12	Volume number (0x00-0xFF)
0x07	DISKTYPE	0xC4	Volume type (B or D)
0x08-0x1F	DISKNAME	~	Volume name (24 characters)
0x20-0x25	INITIME	~	Date and time when volume was initialized
0x26		0x00	unused
0x27	NUMTSENT	0x7A	Maximum number of T/S pairs in one sector
0x28-0x29	DISKSUBJ	~	Volume Library (subject) (0x0000-0xFFFF) (Lo/Hi)
0x2A-0x2F	VTOCTIME	~	Date and Time VTOC was last changed
0x30	NXTTOALC	0x11	Last track where sectors were allocated
0x31	ALLCDIR	0x01	Direction of track allocation (0x01 or 0xFF)
0x32-0x33		0x00	unused
0x34	NUMTRKS	0x23	Number of tracks in volume
0x35	NUMSECS	0x10	Number of sectors per track
0x36-0x37	BYTPRSEC	0x100	Number of bytes per sector (Lo/Hi)
0x38-0x3B	BITMAP	~	Bitmap of free sectors for track 0
0x3C-0x3F		~	Bitmap of free sectors for track 1
0x40-0xC3		~	Bitmap of free sectors for tracks 2-34
0xC4-0xFF		0x00	reserved for expansion

Table I.6.1. DOS 4.1 VTOC Structure Block Definition

Byte	Sector	Bitmap Order
0	0F-08	FEDCBA98
1	07-00	76543210
2	1F-18	FEDCBA98
3	17-10	76543210

Table I.6.2. Free Sector Bitmap for Each Track

Byte	Value Range	Date and Time Values
0	0x00 – 0x59	second
1	0x00 – 0x59	minute
2	0x00 – 0x23	hour
3	0x00 – 0x99	year
4	0x01 – 0x31	day
5	0x01 – 0x12	month

Table I.6.3. DOS 4.1 Date and Time Definition and Variable Order

0x	0	1	2	3	4	5	6	7	8	9	A	B	C	D	E	F
00		11	04									Trk 1	Sec 1	Type 1	Name 1->	-
10	-	-	-	-	-	-	-	-	-	-	-	-	-	-	-	-
20	-	-	-	-	-	Name <-1	Time 1->	-	Time <-1	Date 1->	-	Trk 2	LenL 1	LenH 1	Trk 2	Sec 2
30	Type 2	Name 2->	-	-	-	-	-	-	-	-	-	-	-	-	-	-
40	-	-	-	-	-	-	-	-	Name <-2	Time 2->	-	Date <-1	Date 2->	-	Date <-2	LenL 2
50	LenH 2	Trk 3	Sec 3	Type 3	Name 3->	-	-	-	-	-	-	-	-	-	-	-
60	-	-	-	-	-	-	-	-	-	-	-	Time <-2	Time 3->	-	Time <-3	Date 3->
70	-	Date <-3	LenL 3	LenH 3	Trk 4	Sec 4	Type 4	Name 4->	-	-	-	-	-	-	-	-
80	-	-	-	-	-	-	-	-	-	-	-	Name <-3	-	-	Name <-4	Time 4->
90	-	Time <-4	Date 4->	-	Date <-4	LenL 4	LenH 4	Trk 5	Sec 5	Type 5	Name 5->	-	-	-	-	-
A0	-	-	-	-	-	-	-	-	-	-	-	-	-	-	-	-
B0	-	Name <-5	Time 5->	-	Time <-5	Date 5->	-	Date <-5	LenL 5	LenH 5	Trk 6	Sec 6	Type 6	Name 6->	-	-
C0	-	-	-	-	-	-	-	-	-	-	-	LenL 6	LenH 6	-	-	-
D0	-	-	-	-	Name <-6	Time 6->	-	Time <-6	Date 6->	-	Date <-6	Date 7->	-	Trk 7	Sec 7	Type 7
E0	Name 7->	-	-	-	-	-	-	-	-	-	-	-	-	-	-	-
F0	-	-	-	-	-	-	-	Name <-7	Time 7->	-	Time <-7	-	-	Date <-7	LenL 7	LenH 7

Figure I.7.1. DOS 4.1 First Volume Catalog Sector

7. DOS 4.1 Catalog

The first volume Catalog sector for DOS 4.1 is shown in Figure I.7.1. Bytes 2 and 3 point to the next catalog sector as they do in the VTOC sector. The last catalog sector, typically sector 0x01 on track 0x11, contains 0x00 for these bytes. Table I.7.1 shows a volume Catalog entry for a file. In this table the track and sector values point to the file's Track/Sector List (or TSL) that contains the track/sector pairs for each sector comprising the contents of that file. The third byte of the catalog entry is the file type and it is followed by the 24-character file name. The 3-byte time and 3-byte date stamp when the file was created or last modified follow the file name. The last two bytes of a catalog entry is the size of the file in sectors including all TSL sectors in low/high byte order. Table I.7.2 shows the volume Catalog data locations for each of the seven files contained in a Catalog sector. Table I.7.3 lists each file type byte, its disk Catalog representation, and its description. DOS 4.1 does not process file type 0x01 (or Integer BASIC) files, and file type 0x40 is used by DOS 4.1 to process *Lisa* files natively (DOS 3.3 referred to these as "B type" files). DOS 4.1 will process "A type" (or 0x20) files as Applesoft files. DOS 4.1 does not process "S type" or "R type" files natively until a suitable definition for those files can be determined. In DOS 4.1 a file is marked "deleted" when the most significant bit (i.e. MSB, or bit 7) of its TSL's track is set, that is, in bytes 0x0B, 0x2E, 0x51, 0x74, 0x97, 0xBA, or 0xDD from Table I.7.2. Furthermore, DOS 4.1 stipulates there will always be less than 64 tracks (or 0x3F or less) on a disk volume, so bit 7, the MSB of the TSL's track is available to signify a file's delete status. That definition also leaves bit 6 of the TSL's track available to signify track 0x00 as 0x40. Using bit 6 of the TSL's track to represent physical track 0x00 allows all of the File Manager logic testing for "last track/sector pair" in a TSL to remain unchanged. I have updated my version of *FID* to include this representation of track 0x00 and how a deleted file is marked.

Item	Offset	Length	Format	Description
Track	0x00	0x01	%DZTT TTTT	'D'elete bit, track 'Z'ero bit, TSL 'T'rack bits
Sector	0x01	0x01	%000S SSSS	TSL 'S'ector bits
Type	0x02	0x01	%LTTT TTTT	'L'ock bit, 'T'ype bits
Name	0x03	0x18	upper ASCII	24-character file name
Time	0x1B	0x03	0xSS MM HH	'S'econds byte, 'M'inute byte, 'H'our byte
Date	0x1E	0x03	0xYY DD MM	'Y'ear byte, 'D'ay byte, 'M'onth byte
Size	0x21	0x02	0xLL HH	2-byte file size in sectors, 'L'ow/'H'igh order

Table I.7.1. DOS 4.1 Volume Catalog Entry

If an attempt is made to load (i.e. LOAD or BLOAD) a nonexistent file into memory when the volume Catalog is full, DOS 3.3 erroneously prints the "DISK FULL" error message rather than the "FILE NOT FOUND" error message. If an attempt is made to save (i.e. SAVE or BSAVE) a file when the volume Catalog is full, DOS 3.3 again erroneously prints the "DISK FULL" error message even when there are sufficient sectors available on the volume. Even though this situation is unusual where the volume Catalog is full, having DOS issue the wrong error message could lead one to make erroneous conclusions. DOS 4.1 provides a default volume Catalog consisting of five sectors that can support up

18

to 35 files. However, the volume Catalog may be made as small as one sector by using the B keyword with the DOS INIT command. If the volume Catalog consists of one or two sectors, the volume Catalog will only support 7 or 14 files, respectively, and this DOS 3.3 erroneous error message can have significant consequences in this instance. I have identified and repaired the flawed DOS 3.3 routines, and DOS 4.1 prints the correct error message "File Not Found" when a file does not exist in a volume Catalog regardless whether the Catalog is full or not full. Also, DOS 4.1 prints the new error message "Catalog Full" when attempting to save a file to a volume whose Catalog is full even if there are sufficient sectors available in the volume for the contents of the file.

File	Track*	Sector	Type**	Name	Time	Date	Size
1	0x0B	0x0C	0x0D	0x0E-0x25	0x26-0x28	0x29-0x2B	0x2C-0x2D
2	0x2E	0x2F	0x30	0x31-0x48	0x49-0x4B	0x4C-0x4E	0x4F-0x50
3	0x51	0x52	0x53	0x54-0x6B	0x6C-0x6E	0x6F-0x71	0x72-0x73
4	0x74	0x75	0x76	0x77-0x8E	0x8F-0x91	0x92-0x94	0x95-0x96
5	0x97	0x98	0x99	0x9A-0xB1	0xB2-0xB4	0xB5-0xB7	0xB8-0xB9
6	0xBA	0xBB	0xBC	0xBD-0xD4	0xD5-0xD7	0xD8-0xDA	0xDB-0xDC
7	0xDD	0xDE	0xDF	0xE0-0xF7	0xF8-0xFA	0xFB-0xFD	0xFE-0xFF

* If MSB is set the file shown is deleted   ** If the MSB is set the file shown is locked

Table I.7.2. DOS 4.1 Catalog Sector Data Offsets for File Entries

File Type	Catalog	Description
0x00	T	Text file
0x01	I	Integer BASIC file (not supported)
0x02	A	Applesoft file
0x04	B	Binary file
0x08	S	S type file (not supported)
0x10	R	Relocatable object file (not supported)
0x20	A	A type file (processed as an Applesoft file)
0x40	L	L (*Lisa*) type file (formally B type)
0x80	*	File lock bit

Table I.7.3. DOS 4.1 File Type Byte Description

At the heart of every file is its Track/Sector List. This list of track/sector pairs is contained in the sector that every catalog entry points to. If a file exceeds 0x7A (NUMTSENT from Table I.6.1) sectors of data, the TSL sector has provisions to point to another sector that contains additional track/sector entries. And, for every increment of 0x7A data sectors, DOS creates a new TSL sector for the file. Figure I.7.2 shows a typical TSL sector and Table I.7.4 defines each entry in the TSL. "Next TSL" at bytes 0x01/0x02 points to the next TSL sector if it exists, otherwise these bytes are 0x00/0x00. "Offset" at bytes 0x05/0x06 is equal to 0x00/0x00 for the first TSL, and "Offset" increases by 0x7A for each successive TSL. Regardless whether the TSL contains track/sector entries from previous file saves, DOS only loads into memory the number of bytes specified by an Applesoft or binary file. The DOS TLOAD command, on the other hand, reads all data sectors for a text file into memory regardless of its actual size. The TSL officially concludes when the next track/sector entry is equal to 0x00/0x00.

0x	0	1	2	3	4	5	6	7	8	9	A	B	C	D	E	F
00	00	Next TSL				Offset							T/S 0x01		T/S 0x02	
10	T/S 0x03		T/S 0x04													
20																
30																
40																
50																
60																
70																
80																
90																
A0																
B0																
C0																
D0																
E0																
F0															T/S 0x7A	

Figure I.7.2. DOS 4.1L TSL Sector

Byte	Name	Value	Description
0x00	TSLSB	0x00	unused, start of TSL structure block
0x01	TSTRKOFF	0x00	Track to next TSL; 0x00 if no more TSLs
0x02	TSSECOFF	0x00	Sector to next TSL; 0x00 if no more TSLs
0x03-0x04		0x00	unused
0x05-0x06	TSRECOFF	0x00	TSL record offset from RELSLAST; 0x00 first TSL
0x07-0x0B		0x00	unused
0x0C-0x0D	TSLTSOFF	~	T/S for data sector 0x01; at least one entry is required
0x0E-0x0F		~	T/S for data sector 0x02; 0x00/0x00 if at end
0x10-0x11		~	T/S for data sector 0x03; 0x00/0x00 if at end
0x12-0xFD		~	T/S for data sectors 0x04-0x79
0xFE-0xFF		~	T/S for data sector 0x7A

Table I.7.4. DOS 4.1 TSL Structure Block Definition

8. Booting DOS 4.1

DOS 4.1L occupies the first two tracks of a disk volume, whereas an additional 10 sectors on track 0x02 are needed for DOS 4.1H, assuming the disk volume has 16 sectors per track. The remaining 6 sectors on track 0x02 are available in the VTOC for data. The disk drive firmware in its slot card ROM always loads the bootstrap code from sector 0x00 on track 0x00 into memory address 0x0800-0x08FF. This starts the Stage 1 boot process and the X-register is always equal to the slot number of the slot card times 16. The first byte of this bootstrap must equal 0x01 for the boot process to continue and read the next sector into memory. Therefore, the Stage 0 boot instructions actually begin at 0x0801 to initialize the Stage 1 boot software. Bytes 0x08FE and 0x08FF are known as BOOTADR and BOOTPGS as shown in Table I.8.1, and they direct the Stage 1 boot software to read in sectors 0x06 to 0x00 on track 0x00 into memory address 0xB900 to 0xBF00 for DOS 4.1L, or sectors 0x0F to 0x02 into memory address 0xD000 to 0xDD00 and sectors 0x01 and 0x00 into memory address 0xBE00 to 0xBF00 for DOS 4.1H.

A 16-byte sector interleave table is available to the Stage 1 boot software as well as to RWTS whose interface is now in memory in page 0xBF for both DOS 4.1L and DOS 4.1H. Transfer of control passes to the Stage 2 boot software, also in memory page 0xBF, that can now use RWTS to access any track and sector. DOS 4.1L loads the remaining 25 sectors in descending order starting with sector 0x0F on track 0x01 and ending with sector 0x07 on track 0x00, in ascending order of memory pages. Similarly, DOS 4.1H loads 26 sectors starting with sector 0x09 on track 0x02 and ending with sector 0x00 on track 0x01, in ascending order of memory pages. The initial RWTS IOCB values are specified in a BOOTCFG structure in memory page 0xBF and used by the routine RWPAGES which is called by Stage 2 to complete the DOS load. A typical DOS 4.1L BOOTCFG table is shown in Table I.8.2. When all of DOS 4.1 is in memory, ROM initialization is done, the main video and character set are selected and XMODE is initialized, a search is made for a clock card, and DOS is cold-started and is now ready to execute the DOS CMDVAL command, a topic that will be discussed further in Section I.9. As an aside, the DOS INIT command also uses the RWPAGES routine to write DOS onto a newly initialized volume in the same order it was read into memory.

Address	Variable	Instruction	Value DOS 4.1L	Value DOS 4.1H
0xBFE2	DISKADRS	7 addresses in table	0xBCD2*7	0xD275*7
0xBFF0	BOOTCFG	8 bytes in table	~	~
0xBFF8	INITDOS	ADR DOSBEGIN	0xBED9	0xBED9
0xBFFA	USERNDX	BYT USEROFF	0x58	0x5A
0xBFFB	DISKTBL	BYT DISKADRS-2	0xE0	0xE0
0xBFFC	BCFGNDX	BYT BOOTCFG	0xF0	0xF0
0xBFFD	NBUF1ADR	HBY NBUF1	0xB8	0xDE
0xBFFE	BOOTADR	HBY RWTSTART	0xB9	0xD0
0xBFFF	BOOTPGS	HBY BOOTEND-RWTSTART	0x06	0x0F

Table I.8.1. DOS 4.1 RWTS Slot Interface Structure Definition

Offset	Variable	Size	Value	Description
0x00	DNUM	0x01	0x01	drive number
0x01	VOLEXPT	0x01	0x00	volume number expected
0x02	TNUM	0x01	0x01	track number
0x03	SNUM	0x01	0x0F	sector number
0x04	DCTADR	0x02	0x0000	DCT address
0x06	USRBUF	0x02	0x9D00	DOS start address

Table I.8.2. DOS 4.1L Boot Configuration Table

DOS 4.1H includes a new DOS command, HELP, that utilizes the remaining memory of the Language Card. It is for this DOS command the boot image of DOS 4.1H requires 8 of the 10 sectors on track 0x02.

Once DOS 4.1 is in memory and has initialized, other I/O disk or disk-emulating devices can easily attach their slot card handler address to DOS 4.1. Table I.8.1 shows where the RWTS disk address table DISKADRS is located in DOS 4.1. By design, this interface structure conveniently resides at the same memory address in both DOS 4.1L and DOS 4.1H. To attach a slot card handler, simply save the byte found at DISKTBL and 0xBF to a page-zero pointer. This address is automatically offset to accommodate slot 0, a slot that is never used for external hardware. Simply double the slot number of the device, transfer that number to the Y-register, and indirectly save the address of the slot card handler in low/high byte order to the DISKADRS disk address table. RWTS will transfer control to the correct slot card handler for the requested I/O based on slot number. Keep in mind that the byte value found at DISKTBL may change but the location of the DISKTBL variable will not change. I have made it a habit to always include this DOS 4.1 connection algorithm in the firmware for the RAM Disk 320, Rana, Sider, and Compact Flash For Apple (CFFA) at 0xCs10, where s is the slot number for the device. And, I have always placed the disconnection vector to DOS 4.1 at 0xCs18. Figure I.8.1 shows an example assembly language routine that attaches the RAM Disk handler to DOS 4.1. The handler's address is RDENTRY, its CX page (or 0xC7 for slot 7) is found in RDPAGECX, and its slot number is found in RDSLOT.

The disk track/sector mapping to memory address for DOS 4.1 is shown in Tables I.8.3 and I.8.4 for DOS 4.1L and for DOS 4.1H, respectively. The file images of DOS 4.1 and how they map to memory are shown in Tables 1.8.5 and 1.8.6. These tables correlate file offset to memory address in pages, and gives the basic function of the code found there, such as DOS Command routine handlers (CMD), DOS File Manager routine handlers (MNGR), Data buffers (DATA), tables and variables (DATA), DOS Read/Write Track/Sector routine handlers (RWTS), and the Stage 0, Stage 1, and Stage 2 boot routines (BOOT). The asterisks in Tables 1.8.4 and 1.8.6 indicate that these DOS 4.1H routines or structures reside in RAM Bank 1 of the Language Card; the CMD and MNGR routines and DATA reside in RAM Bank 2 of the Language Card.

```
:                          :         :
00FA                       5    PTR      epz $FA
0800                       6             enz
BFFB                       7    DISKTBL  equ $BFFB
C020                       8    RDENTRY  equ $C020
C900                       9    RDPAGECX equ $C900
C901                      10    RDSLOT   equ $C901
:                          :         :
0900 AC FB BF             18             ldy DISKTBL
0903 A9 BF                19             lda /DISKTBL
0905 84 FA                20             sty PTR
0907 85 FB                21             sta PTR+1
0909                      22    ;
0909 AD 01 C9             23             lda RDSLOT
090C 0A                   24             asl
090D A8                   25             tay
090E A0 20                26             ldy #RDENTRY
0910 91 FA                27             sta (PTR),Y
0912 C8                   28             iny
0913 AD 00 C9             29             lda RDPAGECX
0916 91 FA                30             sta (PTR),Y
:                          :         :
```

Figure I.8.1. Attaching a Slot Card Handler to DOS 4.1

Track	Sector	Address	Code	Track	Sector	Address	Code
0x00	0x00	0xBF00	BOOT	0x01	0x00	0xAC00	MNGR
0x00	0x01	0xBE00	RWTS	0x01	0x01	0xAB00	MNGR
0x00	0x02	0xBD00	RWTS	0x01	0x02	0xAA00	MNGR
0x00	0x03	0xBC00	RWTS	0x01	0x03	0xA900	MNGR
0x00	0x04	0xBB00	RWTS	0x01	0x04	0xA800	CMD
0x00	0x05	0xBA00	RWTS	0x01	0x05	0xA700	CMD
0x00	0x06	0xB900	RWTS	0x01	0x06	0xA600	CMD
0x00	0x07	0xB500	DATA	0x01	0x07	0xA500	CMD
0x00	0x08	0xB400	DATA	0x01	0x08	0xA400	CMD
0x00	0x09	0xB300	DATA	0x01	0x09	0xA300	CMD
0x00	0x0A	0xB200	DATA	0x01	0x0A	0xA200	CMD
0x00	0x0B	0xB100	MNGR	0x01	0x0B	0xA100	CMD
0x00	0x0C	0xB000	MNGR	0x01	0x0C	0xA000	CMD
0x00	0x0D	0xAF00	MNGR	0x01	0x0D	0x9F00	CMD
0x00	0x0E	0xAE00	MNGR	0x01	0x0E	0x9E00	CMD
0x00	0x0F	0xAD00	MNGR	0x01	0x0F	0x9D00	CMD

Table I.8.3. DOS 4.1L Disk Track/Sector Mapping to Memory Address

Track	Sector	Address	Code	Track	Sector	Address	Code
0x00	0x00	0xBF00	BOOT	0x01	0x05	0xE400	MNGR
0x00	0x01	0xBE00	I/F	0x01	0x06	0xE300	MNGR
0x00	0x02	*0xDD00	HELP	0x01	0x07	0xE200	MNGR
0x00	0x03	*0xDC00	HELP	0x01	0x08	0xE100	MNGR
0x00	0x04	*0xDB00	HELP	0x01	0x09	0xE000	MNGR
0x00	0x05	*0xDA00	HELP	0x01	0x0A	0xDF00	MNGR
0x00	0x06	*0xD900	HELP	0x01	0x0B	0xDE00	MNGR
0x00	0x07	*0xD800	HELP	0x01	0x0C	0xDD00	MNGR
0x00	0x08	*0xD700	HELP	0x01	0x0D	0xDC00	CMD
0x00	0x09	*0xD600	HELP	0x01	0x0E	0xDB00	CMD
0x00	0x0A	*0xD500	RWTS	0x01	0x0F	0xDA00	CMD
0x00	0x0B	*0xD400	RWTS	0x02	0x00	0xD900	CMD
0x00	0x0C	*0xD300	RWTS	0x02	0x01	0xD800	CMD
0x00	0x0D	*0xD200	RWTS	0x02	0x02	0xD700	CMD
0x00	0x0E	*0xD100	RWTS	0x02	0x03	0xD600	CMD
0x00	0x0F	*0xD000	RWTS	0x02	0x04	0xD500	CMD
0x01	0x00	0xE900	DATA	0x02	0x05	0xD400	CMD
0x01	0x01	0xE800	DATA	0x02	0x06	0xD300	CMD
0x01	0x02	0xE700	DATA	0x02	0x07	0xD200	CMD
0x01	0x03	0xE600	DATA	0x02	0x08	0xD100	CMD
0x01	0x04	0xE500	MNGR	0x02	0x09	0xD000	CMD

Table I.8.4. DOS 4.1H Disk Track/Sector Mapping to Memory Address

Offset	Address	Code	Offset	Address	Code
0x0000	0x9D00	CMD	0x1000	0xAD00	MNGR
0x0100	0x9E00	CMD	0x1100	0xAE00	MNGR
0x0200	0x9F00	CMD	0x1200	0xAF00	MNGR
0x0300	0xA000	CMD	0x1300	0xB000	MNGR
0x0400	0xA100	CMD	0x1400	0xB100	MNGR
0x0500	0xA200	CMD	0x1500	0xB200	DATA
0x0600	0xA300	CMD	0x1600	0xB300	DATA
0x0700	0xA400	CMD	0x1700	0xB400	DATA
0x0800	0xA500	CMD	0x1800	0xB500	DATA
0x0900	0xA600	CMD	0x1900	0xB900	RWTS
0x0A00	0xA700	CMD	0x1A00	0xBA00	RWTS
0x0B00	0xA800	CMD	0x1B00	0xBB00	RWTS
0x0C00	0xA900	MNGR	0x1C00	0xBC00	RWTS
0x0D00	0xAA00	MNGR	0x1D00	0xBD00	RWTS
0x0E00	0xAB00	MNGR	0x1E00	0xBE00	RWTS
0x0F00	0xAC00	MNGR	0x1F00	0xBF00	BOOT

Table I.8.5. DOS 4.1L File Image Mapping to Memory Address

Offset	Address	Code	Offset	Address	Code
0x0000	0xD000	CMD	0x1500	0xE500	MNGR
0x0100	0xD100	CMD	0x1600	0xE600	DATA
0x0200	0xD200	CMD	0x1700	0xE700	DATA
0x0300	0xD300	CMD	0x1800	0xE800	DATA
0x0400	0xD400	CMD	0x1900	0xE900	DATA
0x0500	0xD500	CMD	0x1A00	*0xD000	RWTS
0x0600	0xD600	CMD	0x1B00	*0xD100	RWTS
0x0700	0xD700	CMD	0x1C00	*0xD200	RWTS
0x0800	0xD800	CMD	0x1D00	*0xD300	RWTS
0x0900	0xD900	CMD	0x1E00	*0xD400	RWTS
0x0A00	0xDA00	CMD	0x1F00	*0xD500	RWTS
0x0B00	0xDB00	CMD	0x2000	*0xD600	HELP
0x0C00	0xDC00	CMD	0x2100	*0xD700	HELP
0x0D00	0xDD00	MNGR	0x2200	*0xD800	HELP
0x0E00	0xDE00	MNGR	0x2300	*0xD900	HELP
0x0F00	0xDF00	MNGR	0x2400	*0xDA00	HELP
0x1000	0xE000	MNGR	0x2500	*0xDB00	HELP
0x1100	0xE100	MNGR	0x2600	*0xDC00	HELP
0x1200	0xE200	MNGR	0x2700	*0xDD00	HELP
0x1300	0xE300	MNGR	0x2800	0xBE00	I/F
0x1400	0xE400	MNGR	0x2900	0xBF00	BOOT

Table I.8.6. DOS 4.1H File Image Mapping to Memory Address

Having DOS 4.1 as a file image can be very useful. The image could be read into memory from a quikLoader, for example, and placed in memory according to Tables I.8.5 or I.8.6 depending on the DOS RAM. Getting DOS 4.1 started is as easy as using an indirect JMP regardless which DOS 4.1 image is loaded, such as "JMP (INITDOS)". Refer to Table I.8.1 for the address of the variable INITDOS. DOS 4.1 will initialize and then transfer control to Applesoft. If, on the other hand, you do not wish to lose control of DOS 4.1 initialization to Applesoft, there is a DOS 4.1 command that is not part of the normal DOS command repertoire, and this command allows you to initialize DOS and have DOS transfer its control back to your program. This is fully discussed in Section I.9.

The address found at INITDOS shown in Table I.8.1 is also for the DOS 4.1 Initial Address Table shown in Table I.8.7. One should reference the variables of the Initial Address Table indirectly and, therefore, more generally using the address found at INITDOS and the offsets shown in Table I.8.7.

Table I.8.1 also contains the most significant byte of the address for NBUF1. NBUF1 is 256 bytes of memory on a page boundary. This buffer resides in RAM Bank 1 memory in DOS 4.1H. This address byte was included in order to provide easy access to a temporary page of memory as long as RWTS is not invoked, which would overwrite the contents of this buffer. The firmware I developed for the Rana disk drive makes excellent use of the NBUF1ADR address byte in verifying whether DOS 4.1H is resident in memory or not. If DOS 4.1H is resident (NBUF1ADR > 0xC000) the firmware makes extensive use of the NBUF1 buffer in RAM Bank 1. On the other hand, if DOS 4.1L is resident then the firmware makes extensive use of NBUF1 within that DOS.

Offset	Address	Variable	Size	Description
0x00	0xBED9	DOSBEGIN	0x03	Initialize DOS in memory JMP
0x03	0xBEDC	FLNAMADR	0x02	DOS first buffer filename address
0x05	0xBDDE	CMDVLADR	0x02	DOS command variables address
0x07	0xBEE0	KEYVLADR	0x02	DOS keyword variables address
0x09	0xBEE2	FMWAADR	0x02	DOS file manager workarea address
0x0B	0xBEE4	VTOCADR	0x02	DOS VTOC structure memory address
0x0D	0xBEE6	CATSBADR	0x02	DOS catalog structure memory address
0x0F	0xBEE8	WARMADR	0x02	ROM soft entry handler address
0x11	0xBEEA	ERRORADR	0x02	ROM error handler address
0x13	0xBEEC	RESETADR	0x02	ROM set/reset handler address
0x15	0xBEEE	USERADR	0x02	USERCMD handler address
0x17	0xBEF0	CMDVAL	0x01	DOS cold-start command
0x18	0xBEF1	NMAXVAL	0x01	MAXFILES at initialization
0x19	0xBEF2	YEARVAL	0x01	year for ThunderClock clock card
0x1A	0xBEF3	SECVAL	0x01	number of sectors in catalog
0x1B	0xBEF4	ENDTRK	0x01	number of tracks in volume
0x1C	0xBEF5	SUBJCT	0x02	volume library value (subject number)
0x1E	0xBEF7	TRKVAL	0x01	catalog track
0x1F	0xBEF8	VRSN	0x01	DOS version number
0x20	0xBEF9	BLD	0x01	DOS build number
0x21	0xBEFA	RAMTYP	0x01	DOS RAM type
0x22	0xBEFB	TSPARS	0x01	number of T/S pairs per sector
0x23	0xBEFC	ALCTRK	0x01	next sector to allocate
0x24	0xBEFD	ALCDIR	0x01	sector allocation direction
0x25	0xBEFE	ENDSEC	0x01	number of sectors per track
0x26	0xBEFF	SECSIZ	0x01	(bytes per sector) / 256

Table I.8.7. DOS 4.1 Initial Address Table Definition

9. DOS 4.1 Initialization

Software developers of my favorite utilities like *ADT*, *Big Mac*, *FID*, *Lisa*, *PGE*, *GPLE*, and *Sourceror*, made use of the DOS 3.3 initial address table from 0x9D00 to 0x9D0F, 0x9D56 to 0x9D83, and, unfortunately, direct entry points to many other internal DOS variables and routines. I chose to retain this initial address table concept in order to update those tools to DOS 4.1 in a more expeditious fashion. According to Table I.8.7 both DOS 4.1L and DOS 4.1H contain the initialization JMP instruction at 0xBED9, parameter and data structure addresses from 0xBEDC through 0xBEE7, and ROM handler routine addresses from 0xBEE8 through 0xBEED. Furthermore, Table I.8.7 contains the USERADR and DOS initialization values from 0xBEEE through 0xBEFF.

One can simply modify the DOS initialization values to tailor a DOS 4.1 boot image specific to ones needs: CMDVAL specifies the HELLO file type (i.e. 0x06 for RUN, 0x14 for EXEC, and 0x34 for BRUN), NMAXVAL specifies what the initial MAXFILES value will be, and YEARVAL specifies the current year to support the ThunderClock clock card which lacks a year register. SECVAL defines how many sectors will be used for the file catalog, ENDTRK specifies how many tracks are on the volume, and ENDSEC specifies whether a track has 16 or 32 sectors. In order to support hardware providing 40 tracks per volume, simply change ENDTRK to 40 (or 0x28). If hardware supports 32 sectors per track, change ENDSEC to 32 (or 0x20). Modify some or all of these parameters in memory directly or use the INIT keywords and initialize another disk volume with the appropriate HELLO file. A file catalog will be created on this new volume according to the values you specify.

The address variable USERADR is tied to the command CMDUSER and the variable CMDVAL. This special DOS command, CMDUSER has an index value found at USERNDX (see Table I.8.1) for the Command Handler Entry Point Table in the DOS 4.1 source code. Temporarily replace the value at CMDVAL with the value found at USERNDX and save your handler's return entry address at USERADR, and make a direct or indirect call to DOSBEGIN to completely initialize DOS and transfer control back to your program through USERADR. The original address at USERADR is MON, or 0xFF65, and the value at CMDVAL is typically CMDRUN-CMDTBL, or 0x06. When USERADR and CMDVAL are restored, DOS 4.1 for all intents and purposes will appear as if it had just been booted from disk. Once your processing has completed, simply call DOSWARM as shown in Table I.9.1 and control will be transferred to Applesoft. Figure I.9.1 shows an example assembly language routine that sets up USERADR and CMDVAL to execute SPCLCODE after DOS has initialized. DOS initialization is done by indirectly jumping to INITDOS. DOS will then process CMDVAL and indirectly jump to SPCLCODE which returns the default values to USERADR and CMDVAL, do some processing, and jump to DOSWARM.

The EPROM Operating System (*EOS*) I developed for the quikLoader loads either DOS 4.1L or DOS 4.1H from EPROM into memory, and uses USERADR and CMDVAL as described above to initialize DOS and return control back to *EOS* for further processing. It is simple and easy to manipulate DOS 4.1 in this fashion. Begin with INITDOS at 0xBFF8 (see Table I.8.1) and copy the address found there to a page-zero pointer. Then replace the address pointed to using an indirect index of 0x15 in the Y-register for USERADR with the address of your routine that will handle the CMDUSER processing after DOS has initialized. Finally place the value of USEROFF (index of CMDUSER) found at USERNDX, address 0xBFFA, into CMDVAL (see Table I.8.7), using an indirect index of 0x17 in the Y-register. This method depends only on the address found at INITDOS and the value found at USERNDX as shown in Table I.8.1. Using this method eliminates having to know which type of DOS 4.1 has currently been read into memory.

```
       :                 :               :
    00FA              5   PTR         epz  $FA
    0800              6               enz
    0006              7   CMDRUN      equ  $06
    0015              8   USEROFF     equ  $15
    03D0              9   DOSWARM     equ  $3D0
    BFF8             10   INITDOS     equ  $BFF8
    BFFA             11   USERNDX     equ  $BFFA
    FF65             12   MON         equ  $FF65
       :                 :               :
    0900 AC F8 BF    20               ldy  INITDOS
    0903 A9 F9 BF    21               lda  INITDOS+1
    0906 84 FA       22               sty  PTR
    0908 85 FB       23               sta  PTR+1
    090A             24   ;
    090A A0 15       25               ldy  #USEROFF
    090C A9 1E       26               lda  #SPCLCODE
    090E 91 FA       27               sta  (PTR),Y
    0910 C8          28               iny
    0911 A9 09       29               lda  /SPCLCODE
    0913 91 FA       30               sta  (PTR),Y
    0915 C8          31               iny
    0916 AD FA BF    32               lda  USERNDX
    0919 91 FA       33               sta  (PTR),Y
    091B 6C F8 BF    34               jmp  (INITDOS)
       :                 :               :
    091E A0 15       43   SPCLCODE ldy  #USEROFF
    0920 A9 65       44               lda  #MON
    0922 91 FA       45               sta  (PTR),Y
    0924 C8          46               iny
    0925 A9 FF       47               lda  /MON
    0927 91 FA       48               sta  (PTR),Y
    0929 C8          49               iny
    092A A9 06       50               lda  #CMDRUN
    092C 91 FA       51               sta  (PTR),Y
       :                 :               :
    092E 4C D0 03    59               jmp  DOSWARM
       :                 :               :
```

Figure I.9.1. Using USERADR and CMDVAL in DOS 4.1

When DOS 4.1 performs a cold-start it sets MAXFILES equal to NMAXVAL, it initializes the file buffers, it makes EXEC inactive, and it copies the contents of Table I.9.1 into memory at 0x3D0. It is this interface where the important entry addresses of DOS routines are found, such as RWTS and the File Manager. Essentially, this interface is the same as that found in DOS 3.3 in order to maintain compatibility with virtually all previous software, but with some important additions: read DOS version or read clock routine (RDCLKVSN) at 0x3E1, the error printing routine (PRTERROR) at 0x3E8, and the Apple //e DOXFER routine (XFERADR) at 0x3ED. All three routines can be accessed using an indirect JMP instruction such as "JMP (RDCLKVSN)". The two routines GETFMCB and GETIOCB are changed in DOS 4.1, but return the same information: the address of the RWTS I/O Context Block in the Y-register (low byte) and the A-register (high byte), and the address of the File

Manager Context Block in the Y-register and the A-register. These two context blocks are shown in Tables I.9.2 and I.9.5, respectively. The routine RDCLKVSN reads the current DOS version, a 19-byte upper ASCII string (i.e. "DOS4.1.46L 01/01/21" or "DOS4.1.46H 01/01/21"), into a buffer whose address is in the Y- and A-registers with the carry flag set. The routine RDCLKVSN reads the current date and time into a 6-byte buffer as shown in Table I.6.3 whose address is in the Y- and A-registers with the carry flag clear. The routine PRTERROR prints the error message as shown in Table I.9.8 whose index error number is in the X-register. Example code segments to read the current DOS version into a 20-byte zero-filled buffer and the current date and time into a 6-byte buffer are shown in Figures I.9.2 and I.9.3. Figure I.9.4 shows how *Big Mac* prints all of its File Manager error codes.

Variable	Routine	Address	Description
DOSWARM	WARMSTRT	0x3D0	DOS warm-start JMP
DOSCOLD	DOSBEGIN	0x3D3	DOS cold-start JMP
CALLFM	FMHNDLR	0x3D6	File Manager JMP
CALLRWTS	RWTSHNDL	0x3D9	RWTS handler JMP
GETFMCB	LDY #FMVALS	0x3DC	puts File Manager Context Block
	LDA /FMVALS	0x3DE	address in #Y/A
RDCLKVSN	ADR DOCLKVSN	0x3E1	buffer addr in #Y/A, clock clc, version sec
GETIOCB	LDY #TBLTYPE	0x3E3	puts RWTS I/O Context Block
	LDA /TBLTYPE	0x3E5	address in #Y/A
PRTERADR	ADR PRTERROR	0x3E8	prints error message of index error # in X-reg
HOOKDOS	INITPTRS	0x3EA	DOS reconnect JMP
XFERADR	ADR *-*	0x3ED	used for the Apple //e DOXFER routine
AUTOBRK	OLDBRK	0x3EF	ROM break handler JMP
AUTORSET	ADR WARMSTRT	0x3F2	ROM auto-reset routine address
PWRSTATE	BYT 0xA5^(0x3F3)	0x3F4	power up byte
USRAHAND	RPEATCMD	0x3F5	& handler JMP
USRYHAND	AUXMOVE	0x3F8	ctrl-Y handler JMP to 0xC311
NMASKIRQ	MON	0x3FB	non-maskable IRQ JMP to 0xFF65
MASKIRQ	ADR MON	0x3FE	maskable IRQ routine address at 0xFF65

Table I.9.1. DOS 4.1 Page 0x03 Interface Routines

It is worthwhile to note that DOS 4.1 RWTS only supports the Disk][type hardware since there was no other device manufactured that was substantially different. The Device Characteristics Table (DCT) was originally designed so that RWTS could support devices having different stepper motor phases per track in order to support half-tracking for example, or even different motor on-time requirements. I saw no need for DOS 4.1 to support something that simply does not, nor will ever exist. I am aware that the RanaSystems EliteThree is a dual-headed disk drive with the ability to access 80 half-tracks on both sides of a double-sided, double-density diskette. Of course, the DCT for the Rana is different, but the Rana uses its own interface handler with its own PHASEON/PHASEOFF tables for its track stepper motor, and its own number of motor phases to accomplish its half-tracking capabilities. I even developed my own firmware for the Rana that formats a disk with 40 tracks on both sides of a diskette with the first 16 sectors on side 1 and the next 16 sectors on side 2, effectively creating a volume where each track has 32 sectors. I was absolutely successful and, by design, the firmware attached to the DOS 4.1 RWTS Slot Card Interface. I was able to obtain double-sided, double-density 5.25-inch floppy diskettes from floppydisk.com. As a word of caution, double-sided, double-density 5.25-inch floppy diskettes are manufactured with an inner reinforcement ring. Significantly better performance will be achieved from those diskettes whether half-tracking is employed or not. In summary, DOS 4.1 does not utilize the DCT, and it ignores any DCT address found in any RWTS IOCB for a Disk][.

```
   :              :            :
03E1              5     RDCLKVSN equ $3E1
   :              :            :
0900 A0 0C       13              ldy #VSNBUFR
0902 A9 09       14              lda /VSNBUFR
0904 20 08 09    15              jsr READVSN
   :              :            :
0907 60          17              rts
   :              :            :
0908 38          19     READVSN  sec
0909 6C E1 03    20              jmp (RDCLKVSN)
090C             21     VSNBUFR  dfs 20,0
   :              :            :
```

Figure I.9.2. Reading the DOS Version in DOS 4.1

```
   :              :            :
03E1              5     RDCLKVSN equ $3E1
   :              :            :
0900 A0 0C       13              ldy #CLKBUFR
0902 A9 09       14              lda /CLKBUFR
0904 20 08 09    15              jsr READCLK
   :              :            :
0907 60          17              rts
   :              :            :
0908 38          19     READCLK  clr
0909 6C E1 03    20              jmp (RDCLKVSN)
090C             21     CLKBUFR  dfs 6,0
   :              :            :
```

Figure I.9.3. Reading the Date and Time in DOS 4.1

```
:                   :              :
0044               118   A5L        epz $44
0045               119   A5H        epz $45
:                   :              :
0800               215              enz
:                   :              :
03D6               323   CALLFM     equ $3D6
03DC               324   GETFMCB    equ $3DC
03E8               327   PRTERADR   equ $3E8
:                   :              :
D0B0 6C E8 03       14   PRTERROR   jmp (PRTERADR)
:                   :              :
D12D 20 DC 03      131              jsr GETFMCB
D130 84 44         133              sty A5L
D132 85 45         134              sta A5H
:                   :              :
E58A A2 01         316              ldx #1
E58C 20 D6 03      318              jsr CALLFM
E58F               319              bcc HE599
E591 A0 0A         321              ldy #10
E593 B1 44         323              lda (A5L),Y
E595 AA            324              tax
:                   :              :
E5BC 8A            361              txa
E595 48            324              pha
:                   :              :
E5C1 E8            366              inx
E5C2 20 B0 D0      368              jsr PRTERROR
E5C5 68            370              pla
E5C6 AA            371              tax
E5C7 20 B0 D0      373              jsr PRTERROR
E5CA 20 8E FD      374              jsr CROUT
:                   :              :
E599 A2 0E         328   HE599      ldx #$0E
:                   :              :
FD8E A9 8D         253   CROUT      lda #$8D
:                   :              :
```

Figure I.9.4. Big Mac Printing a File Manager Error in DOS 4.1

The DOS 4.1 RWTS interface is very straightforward and simple to use. When you call GETIOCB as shown in Table I.9.1, the Y- and A-registers point to the IOCB within RWTS. You are certainly welcome to use any other address space for an RWTS IOCB as well. Once you have initialized the IOCB with your variables as shown in Table I.9.2, call CALLRWTS with the address of your IOCB, or the address of the IOCB within DOS, in the Y- and A-registers. The RWTS handler pushes the current processor status onto the stack and disables interrupts, and then saves the Y- and A-registers to the IOB address at 0x4A/0x4B. Next, the handler extracts the supplied buffer address from within the IOCB and saves the address to BUFADR2Z at 0x3E/0x3F. The handler also extracts the slot*16 number, copies it to the X-register, saves it to SLOTFND, and calculates the low-order address byte for DISKJMP based on the slot*16 number value divided by eight. The RWTS handler then indirectly

31

jumps to that address in DISKJMP, which is to the routine whose address is located in the disk address table for the specified slot number. The routine now handling the volume's I/O must mask all track values it encounters with TRKMASK, or 0x3F in order to remove the value of TRKZERO, or 0x40. When the routine has completed its processing, it is required to save its results in the supplied IOCB: ERRCODE, VOLFND, and DRVFND. The RWTS handler will restore the original processor status and either clear or set the carry flag based on the return status from the slot handler routine. If interrupts were initially enabled before the call to the RWTS handler, interrupts will be re-enabled when the RWTS handler completes its processing. Table I.9.3 shows the four command codes available to RWTS and Table I.9.4 shows the seven possible error codes generated by RWTS.

Offset	Name	Size	Description
0x00	TBLTYPE	0x01	IOCB structure
0x01	SNUM16	0x01	slot * 16
0x02	DNUM	0x01	drive number
0x03	VOLEXPT	0x01	expected volume number
0x04	TNUM	0x01	track number
0x05	SNUM	0x01	sector number
0x06	DCTADR	0x02	address of Device Characteristics Table
0x08	USRBUF	0x02	data buffer address
0x0A	RWTSPARE	0x01	not used
0x0B	BYTCNT	0x01	bytes to read/write; 0 means 256 bytes
0x0C	CMDCODE	0x01	command
0x0D	ERRCODE	0x01	return error code
0x0E	VOLFND	0x01	return volume found
0x0F	SLOTFND	0x01	return slot found
0x10	DRVFND	0x01	return drive found

Table I.9.2. RWTS I/O Context Block Definition

Command	Value	Description
RWTSSEEK	0x00	seek to track/sector command code
RWTSREAD	0x01	read track/sector command code
RWTSWRIT	0x02	write track/sector command code
RWTSFRMT	0x04	format volume command code

Table I.9.3. RWTS Command Codes

Error	Value	Description
RWNOERR	0x00	RWTS no error
RWINITER	0x08	RWTS initialization error
RWPROTER	0x10	RWTS write protect error
RWVOLERR	0x20	RWTS volume number error
RWSYNERR	0x30	RWTS syntax error (added)
RWDRVERR	0x40	RWTS drive error
RWREADER	0x80	RWTS read error (obsolete)

Table I.9.4. RWTS Error Codes

Offset	Name	Size	Description
0x00	FMOPCOD	0x01	File Manager opcode
0x01	SUBCODE	0x01	File Manager subcode
0x02	RECNUM	0x02	record number
	or FN2ADR	0x02	secondary filename address
0x04	BYTOFFSET	0x02	byte offset
	or VOLUME	0x01	volume number
0x05	DRIVE	0x01	drive number
0x06	BYTRANGE	0x02	byte range
	or SLOT	0x01	slot number
0x07	FILETYPE	0x01	file type or VTOC/Data Flag
0x08	DATADR	0x02	data byte address
	or FNADR	0x02	primary filename address
	or DATABYTE	0x01	data byte
0x0A	RTNCODE	0x01	return code
0x0B	FMSPARE	0x01	not used
0x0C	WBADR	0x02	workarea buffer address
0x0E	TSLTSADR	0x02	track/sector buffer address
0x10	DATASADR	0x02	data buffer address

Table I.9.5. File Manager Context Block Definition

The DOS 4.1 File Manager is not as straightforward as RWTS, and it is somewhat more difficult to use. One look at Table I.9.5 shows how convoluted the File Manager Context Block is. Essentially, the Context Block is completely command dependent and is intended to be used with that in mind. So many of the Context Block entries are overloaded and the entry definition and its usage totally depends on the command in question. Table I.9.6 shows the fourteen command codes available to the File Manager including a new command code in DOS 4.1, FMURMCD. This command code can be used to undelete a file that has been previously deleted from the volume Catalog by the FMDELECD command code. The File Manager Context Block entries are used in the same way for the FMURMCD command as they are used for the FMDELECD command where bytes 8 and 9 contain the address of the filename to be undeleted. The sectors in the file's TSL are marked as used in the VTOC free sector bitmap as well as the TSL sector. It is prudent to always undelete a deleted file before subsequent files use those sectors made available when the file was deleted. A volume can be rendered unusable if a data sector should ever be interpreted as a TSL sector. **There is no harm in undeleting a file that already exists in the file Catalog**.

Command	Value	Description
FMNOERR	0x00	File Manager No Operation code
FMOPENCD	0x01	File Manager OPEN code
FMCLOSCD	0x02	File Manager CLOSE code
FMREADCD	0x03	File Manager READ code
FMWRITCD	0x04	File Manager WRITE code
FMDELECD	0x05	File Manager DELETE code
FMCATACD	0x06	File Manager CATALOG code (modified)
FMLOCKCD	0x07	File Manager LOCK code
FMUNLKCD	0x08	File Manager UNLOCK code
FMRENMCD	0x09	File Manager RENAME code
FMPOSICD	0x0A	File Manager POSITION code
FMINITCD	0x0B	File Manager INIT code (modified)
FMVERICD	0x0C	File Manager VERIFY code
FMURMCD	0x0D	File Manager URM code (added)

Table I.9.6. File Manager Command Codes

Command	Value	Description
FMNOOPSC	0x00	File Manager No Operation subcode
FMRW01SC	0x01	File Manager read/write 1-byte subcode
FMRWNBSC	0x02	File Manager read/write range subcode
FMPOS1SC	0x03	File Manager Position and read/write 1-byte subcode
FMPOSRSC	0x04	File Manager Position and read/write range subcode

Table I.9.7. File Manager Read and Write Command Subcodes

Some File Manager commands require a subcode to specify how the command will be used. Table I.9.7 lists the five subcodes used by the read and write commands FMREADCD and FMWRITCD. A subcode was added to the CATALOG command in order to optionally display what the R keyword provides to the Command Manager. Simply save a non-zero value to the SUBCODE parameter of the File Manager Context Block if that additional CATALOG information is desired. Table I.9.8 shows all the possible error codes reported by DOS and the source or sources of those error codes: Command Manager, File Manager, or RWTS. In DOS 4.1 the File Manager uses a table lookup algorithm to translate an RWTS error code into a File Manager error code reported by DOS. The actual value of the

RWTS error code is shown in parenthesis. An RWTS Initialization Error message "Init Error" was added to the Error and Display Message Text table as well as a "Catalog Full" error message.

There does exist a fifteenth File Manager command code used to implement the DOS 4.1 TS command (read Track/Sector) in order to utilize the error processing capabilities of the File Manager if an error in reading a volume sector should ever occur. This opcode does not utilize the File Manager Context Block sufficiently for external use; rather, a user should always use RWTS to read a volume sector.

Error #	CMD	FM	RWTS	Error Message
0	√	√	√	Ring bell and print two <RTN>
1	√			Clock Not Found
2	√	√		Range Error
3			√ (0x08)	Init Error
4	√		√ (0x10)	Write Protected
5	√	√		End of Data
6		√		File Not Found
7	√		√ (0x20)	Volume Number Error
8			√ (0x40)	I/O Error
9		√		Disk Full
10		√		File Locked
11	√		√ (0x30)	Syntax Error
12	√			No Buffers Error
13	√			File Type Error
14	√			Program Too Large
15	√			Not Direct Command
16		√		Catalog Full

Table I.9.8. DOS 4.1 Error Messages and Sources

The INIT handler in DOS 4.1 specified by the File Manager FMINITCD command has been substantially modified from its DOS 3.3 version. Before the DOS INIT command is even processed, the Command Manager initializes the File Manager Context Block to 0x00 except for the FMOPCOD and SUBCODE values. Then it initializes bytes 0x02/0x03 with the address of the Volume Title (SFNAME). The DOS Flag found in byte 0x01 of the Context Block, or SUBCODE as shown in Table I.9.5, actually has a very useful function in DOS 4.1. To better understand how to use this SUBCODE, Table I.9.9 shows the values that could be assigned to DOS Flag. In order to create a fully bootable DOS B type volume, DOS Flag must have a non-zero value, the signal to the INIT handler to write DOS to the volume.

If DOS Flag is 0x00 the volume will be labeled a D type data volume where all of track 0x00 can be used for data, too. The Volume Title address found in bytes 0x02/0x03, or FN2ADR, is the address where the INIT handler copies a 24-character upper ASCII Volume Title to the VTOC. In the ideal situation the File Manager knows nothing about the Command Manager and the values it parses from the command line keywords. All the information the File Manager requires for processing its commands **must** come from its Context Block and its workarea buffer. And this is particularly true for INIT handler processing. In normal Command Manager INIT handler processing the address in bytes 0x08/0x09 of the Context Block will be 0x00 since the Command Manager has already initialized the filename (FNAME). But if the MSB of byte 0x07 of the Context Block is set (i.e. the VTOC/Data Flag or FILETYPE as shown in Table I.9.5), the INIT handler will use the address found at bytes 0x08/0x09 to copy a 24-character upper ASCII filename to FNAME, the name of the file that will be used to RUN, EXEC, or BRUN when the disk is a B type bootable volume. When the Command Manager calls the File Manager it copies its buffer addresses to bytes 0x0C through 0x11 of the Context Block.

DOS Flag	DOS Installed	Description
0x00	No	Data Disk D, all of track 0x00 is used for data
0x06	Yes	Boot Disk B, RUN command code 0x06 put into CMDVAL
0x14	Yes	Boot Disk B, EXEC command code 0x14 put into CMDVAL
0x34	Yes	Boot Disk B, BRUN command code 0x34 put into CMDVAL
0xN, 0x00≤N≤0x58	Yes	Boot Disk B, any even value valid within the DOS command table is put into CMDVAL

Table I.9.9. File Manager INIT DOS Flags (SUBCODE)

Offset	Name	Size	Range	Description
0x00	SECVAL	0x01	0x01—0x0F	number of sectors in catalog
0x01	ENDTRK	0x01	0x12—0x32	number of tracks in volume
0x02	SUBJCT	0x02	0x0000—0xFFFF	volume library (subject) value

Table I.9.10. File Manager Initialization Data, VTOCVALS

```
  :                  :              :
1300              394    FMVALS:
1300              395    ;
1300 0B           396    OPCODE     byt  INITCMD
1301 06           397    SUBCODE    byt  DOSFLAGS
1302              398    ;
1302 2A 13        399    FN2ADR     adr  VTITLE
1304              400    ;
1304 00           401    VOLUME     hex  00
1305 01           402    DRIVE      hex  01
1306              403    ;
1306 06           404    SLOT       hex  06
1307 80           405    FILETYPE   hex  80
1308              406    ;
1308 12 13        407    FNADR      adr  FNAME
130A              408    ;
130A 00           409    RTNCODE    hex  00
130B              410    ;
130B 00           411    FMSPARE    hex  00
130C              412    ;
130C 0E 13        413    WBADR      adr  SECVAL
130E 07           414    SECVAL     hex  07
130F 23           415    ENDTRK     hex  23
1310 34 12        416    SUBJCT     hex  3412
1312              417    ;
0012              418    FMPLEN     equ  *-FMVALS
1312              419    ;
1312 E8 E5 EC     420    FNAME      asc  "hello"
1315 EC EF
1317              421               dfs  FNLEN-5,SPACE
132A              422    ;
132A D4 E5 F3     423    VTITLE     asc  "Test Disk"
     F4 A0 C4
     E9 F3 EB
1333              424               dfs  FNLEN-9,SPACE
  :                  :              :
```

Figure I.9.5. Using the File Manager Context Block in DOS 4.1

In normal Command Manager `INIT` handler processing the addresses found in bytes `0x0C` through `0x11` in the Context Block are not used. However, for users of the File Manager external to DOS, if the MSB of the `VTOC`/Data Flag (or `FILETYPE`) is set, then `WBADR` must contain an address of a 4-byte data block containing the values for `SECVAL`, `ENDTRK`, and `SUBJCT` as shown in Table I.9.10. Recall that `SECVAL` defines how many sectors will be used for the file catalog, `ENDTRK` specifies the number of tracks in the volume, and `SUBJCT` is the two-byte Volume Library value. If bit-6 of the `VTOC`/Data Flag is set, the volume will be initialized with 32 sectors per track rather than 16 sectors. This logic was different in Build 45 where the MSB of `SECVAL` signaled the initialization of 32 sector tracks. The 4-byte `VTOCVALS` data block and the address for `FNAME` along with DOS Flag and the `VTOC`/Data Flag provide the same information the Command Manager obtains when it parses the `A`, `B`, `L`, and `R` keywords for the DOS `INIT` command. Figure I.9.5 shows an Assembly Language listing of a File Manager Context Block where the VTOC/Data Flag (or FILETYPE) is set to 0x80 and bytes 0x0C/0x0D contain the address of VTOCVALS, located in the following bytes 0x0E through 0x11 of the Context Block beginning with SECVAL, and including ENDTRK and the two-byte variable SUBJCT. Yes, surprise! It's a thoroughly good use of where the Context Block variables TSLTSADR and DATASADR normally reside but are otherwise unused in the INIT command.

The complete list of File Manager commands and the parameters and buffers that are needed by these commands is shown in Figure I.9.6. Understand that the File Manager uses only its own Context Block that resides within DOS memory. GETFMCB can be called to obtain the address of that Context Block so that its individual parameters can be modified, similar to how *FID* uses its File Manager Context Block. *FID* maintains its own copy of the 18-byte Context Block, modifies it as needed, and then copies it in its entirety back into DOS address space before calling CALLFM. Upon return from the File Manager, *FID* again copies the entire Context Block back into its own address space before looking at the return code RTNCODE value. The File Manager Context Block in DOS 4.1H resides in the interface area of DOS address space that is not within the Language Card memory, so bank switching is unnecessary to read and write the DOS 4.1H File Manager Context Block.

It is always the responsibility of the user to utilize the RWTS I/O Context Block and the File Manager Context Block rationally and with great care. If any context block value is not within its normal value range unpredictable results should be expected. By design, the Command Manager always supplies values for these context blocks that are within their normal operational range. But the user carries the full burden of selecting context block values that will provide the intended results. For example, if SECVAL is initialized to 0x00 or any value greater than 0x7F, and the File Manager Context Block OPCODE is set to FMINITCD, the target volume's VTOC will never initialize and DOS will hang. Table I.9.10 shows that setting SECVAL to a value greater than 0x0F is not within its normal range and there may very well be unexpected results. It is always a good policy to test and experiment on disk volumes that are clearly identified as "Test Disk #nnn" when testing new programs whether the program is written in Applesoft, assembly language, Fortran, or Pascal. Even EXEC files should first be tested on volumes that are exclusively used for experimentation. No one is immune to mistakes, but carelessly using these context blocks will surely cause very unwanted results.

It is the job of the Command Manager to supply rational values for either the RWTS I/O Context Block or for the File Manager Context Block. DOS 4.1, like DOS 3.3, does not bother verifying the values it finds in either context block, and uses the context blocks as they are found. Whether the values are within range or out of range for the normal operation of each opcode is simply not confirmed. Hopefully an error will be reported if the opcode fails somewhere in its processing, but that may not always be the case. As mentioned above, using a value of 0x00 for SECVAL will cause the volume initialization opcode to hang, thus preventing the File Manager the ability to even report the error. The RWTS and the File Manager Context Blocks provide the assembly code user the greatest power and flexibility in order to control and mange DOS's volume structure and file Catalog. DOS will do nothing to stop a user from completely trashing the volume structure and file Catalog of any disk volume. Therefore, I say again, it is always the responsibility of the user to utilize these context blocks rationally and with very great care.

Offset	0x00	0x01	0x02	0x03	0x04	0x05	0x06	0x07	0x08	0x09	0x0A	0x0B	0x0C	0x0D	0x0E	0x0F	0x10	0x11
Command	Opcode	Subcode	Record Length Record Number Filename Address		Volume	Drive	Slot	File Type	Filename Address One Byte Data Range Address		Return Code Output	Not Used	Workarea Buffer Address		Track/Sector Buffer Address		Data Sector Buffer Address	
OPEN	0x01		Record Length or 0x0000		V	D	S	File Type	Address of Filename									
CLOSE	0x02																Address of Data Sector Buffer	
READ	0x03	See Table I.9.7	Record Number		Byte Offset		Range Length		One Byte Data or Range Address		Return Code Output		Address of Workarea Buffer		Address of Track/Sector Buffer			
WRITE	0x04		Record Number		Byte Offset		Range Length		One Byte Data or Range Address									
DELETE	0x05				V	D	S		Address of Filename									
CATALOG	0x06	RKEY-WORD Flag			V	D	S											
LOCK	0x07				V	D	S		Address of Filename									
UNLOCK	0x08				V	D	S		Address of Filename						Address of Track/Sector Buffer			
RENAME	0x09		Address of New Filename		V	D	S		Address of Filename									
POSITION	0x0A		Record Number		Byte Offset													
INIT	0x0B	DOS Flag	Address of Volume Title		V	D	S	VTOC SEC32 Flag					Address of VTOCVALS See Table I.9.10		SECVAL value	ENDTRK value	SUBJCT value	
VERIFY	0x0C				V	D	S		Address of Filename				Address of Workarea Buffer		Address of Track/Sector Buffer		Address of Data Sector Buffer	
URM	0x0D				V	D	S											

Figure I.9.6. File Manager Command Parameter List

Offset	Name	Size	Description
\multicolumn{4}{c}{Data and Track/Sector Buffers}			
0x000	DATABUFR	0x100	I/O data buffer
0x100	TSBUFFER	0x100	T/S buffer
\multicolumn{4}{c}{WORKAREA – File Manager Workarea Variables}			
0x200	TSFRSTTS	0x02	T/S of first T/S list
0x202	TSCURRTS	0x02	T/S of current T/S list
0x204	TSCURDAT	0x02	T/S of current data sector
0x206	WAFLAGS	0x01	0x02 = VTOC has changed 0x40 = data buffer has changed 0x80 = T/S buffer has changed
0x207	SECATOFF	0x01	sector offset into catalog
0x208	BYCATOFF	0x01	byte offset into catalog
0x209	MAXTSECR	0x02	maximum entries in T/S list
0x20B	SECFRSTS	0x02	offset of first T/S entry
0x20D	SECLASTS	0x02	offset of last T/S entry
0x20F	SECLSTRD	0x02	relative sector last read
0x211	SECRSIZE	0x02	sector size in bytes
0x213	SECRPOST	0x02	current position in sector
0x215	BYSECOFF	0x01	current sector byte offset
0x216	RECDLNGH	0x02	fixed record length
0x218	RECURNUM	0x02	current record number
0x21A	BYRECOFF	0x02	byte offset into record
0x21C	SECFILEN	0x02	length of file in sectors
0x21E	SECALOTR	0x01	next sector to get on this track
0x21F	CURALOTR	0x01	current track to allocate
0x220	SECFRETR	0x04	bitmap of free sectors on this track
0x224	WAFILTYP	0x01	file type (^0x80 = locked)
0x225	WASLTNUM	0x01	slot number times 16
0x226	WADRVNUM	0x01	drive number
0x227	WAVOLNUM	0x01	volume number
0x228	WATRKNUM	0x01	track number
\multicolumn{4}{c}{Filename Buffer}			
0x229	FILNAMBF	0x18	upper ASCII filename
\multicolumn{4}{c}{Addresses of Buffer Locations}			
0x241	WABUFADR	0x02	address of WORKAREA
0x243	TSBUFADR	0x02	address of TSBUFFER
0x245	DABUFADR	0x02	address of DATABUFR
0x247	NXTFNADR	0x02	address of next FILNAMBF

Table I.10.1. File Manager File Buffer Definition

10. DOS 4.1 Data Structures

The Data Structures, or areas where data is found in DOS 3.3 are spread out between the various managers. Those variables used by the Command Manager are found after the Command Manager. Those variables used by the File Manager are found after the File Manager. The RWTS IOCB is found in the middle of all the RWTS routines. I thought DOS 4.1 should have better organization of the various collections of variables and data structures, and therefore reduce the number of addresses required to access any single variable or data structure if that is what is desired.

The Data Structures in DOS 4.1 reside after the File Manager routines and are followed by the two pages of memory needed for the working VTOC and Catalog buffers, and the page of memory needed for the primary nibble buffer NBUF1. In DOS 4.1L the RWTS routines follow the NBUF1 and NBUF2 buffers and the WRTNIBL and RDNIBL disk nibble translate tables. The five DOS file buffers follow the VTOC and Catalog buffers in DOS 4.1H. Quite a few software tools such as *Big Mac*, *Lisa*, and *PGE* make use of several internal variables from the data structures found after the File Manager routines. *Big Mac* needs the internal values of LOADLEN and DRVAL, and it needs the addresses of what DOS considers to be the true CSWL and KSWL handlers. *Lisa* also needs the internal values of LOADLEN and DRVAL. *PGE* needs the internal value of ADRVAL. There is no telling what other software utilities and programs that exist that need values from these internal data areas and data structures of DOS in order to complete their processing functions. Both DOS 4.1L and DOS 4.1H provide addresses for the internal DOS data structures as shown in Table I.8.7. Caution must be exercised in using the addresses for these data structures in DOS 4.1H because they are addresses in the Language Card memory area, specifically RAM Bank 2. Bank switching code is necessary to access the actual data. There are no data structures in RAM Bank 1 except for the RDNIBL and WRTNIBL data translate tables and the two nibble buffers NBUF1 and NBUF2, conveniently located there for access to all the RWTS routines. Except for RWTS, DOS 4.1 makes no queries into these particular data tables and buffers.

The address found at FLNAMADR (offset 0x03) in Table I.8.7 is for the filename FILNAMBF in the first DOS file buffer. DOS must have at least one file buffer allocated, which is all that *Lisa* actually needs and uses, surprisingly. Even the CATALOG command requires an unused file buffer. Of course, more file buffers can be allocated using the DOS MAXFILES command if they are needed. Table I.10.1 shows the contents of a file buffer which is 585 (or 0x249) bytes in size: one memory page (256 bytes) for the data buffer DATABUFR, one memory page for the track/sector buffer TSBUFFER, 41 bytes for the working variables buffer WORKAREA, 24 bytes for the filename buffer FILNAMBF, and 8 bytes for the addresses of WORKAREA, TSBUFFER, DATABUFR, and NXTFNADR, the address of FILNAMBF for the next (not necessarily following) file buffer, much like a single-direction linked-list address. If the address in NXTFNADR is 0x0000, there are no more next-linked file buffers. Incidentally, the size of a file buffer in DOS 3.3 is 0x250 bytes, or 7 bytes larger due to the larger filename buffer and the resize of the BYSECOFF variable to 1 byte as it should have been.

I have changed the order of some of the variables in the workarea shown in Table I.10.1 from the order found in DOS 3.3. As long as the workarea definition in Table I.10.1 is consistent with the File Manager workarea definition shown in Table I.10.4 there will be no processing problems. I made these changes in order to reduce the number of routines necessary to copy variables to and from a file buffer workarea and the File Manager copy of those workarea variables in its workarea buffer. I also provided *FID* with the same changes to its copy of the WORKAREA structure definition as well.

The address found at CMDVLADR (offset 0x05) in Table I.8.7 points to the data structure called CMDVALS because it contains the variables used by the Command Manager in processing DOS commands as shown in Table I.10.2. Simply transfer the address found at CMDVLADR to a page-zero pointer and index into the structure for the desired variable in order to obtain its value or change its value. Table I.10.2 provides the offset, or index to use for each variable.

Offset	Name	Size	Description
0x00	BUFRADR	0x02	current file buffer address
0x02	CURSTATE	0x01	0x00 = warm-start status 0x01 = READ state status 0x40 = Applesoft RAM (unused) 0x80 = cold-start status
0x03	CSWSTATE	0x01	CSWL intercept state number
0x04	CMDLNIDX	0x01	offset into Apple command line
0x05	CMDINDX	0x01	index of last command * 2
0x06	ASAVE	0x01	A-register save
0x07	XSAVE	0x01	X-register save
0x08	YSAVE	0x01	Y-register save
0x09	SSAVE	0x01	S-register save
0x0A	CSWLSAV	0x02	true CSWL handler address
0x0C	KSWLSAV	0x02	true KSWL handler address
0x0E	EXECFLAG	0x01	EXEC active flag
0x0F	EXECBUFR	0x02	EXEC file buffer address
0x11	TEMP	0x01	scratch variable
0x12	MAXFILES	0x01	MAXFILES value
0x13	MONFLAGS	0x01	0x10 = Output 0x20 = Input 0x40 = Command
0x14	DIRTS	0x02	catalog track and sector values
0x16	FILELAST	0x02	file end address
0x18	FILESTRT	0x02	file start address
0x1A	FILELEN	0x02	file length
0x1C	CLKSLOT	0x01	clock slot
0x1D	CLKINDEX	0x01	index into clock data
0x1E	FIRSTCAT	0x01	number of sectors in catalog
0x1F	LASTRACK	0x01	number of tracks in volume

Table I.10.2. CMDVALS Data Structure Definition

In Build 46 I found it absolutely necessary to add two additional variables to the end of the CMDVALS Data Structure shown in Table I.10.2. These two variables are FIRSTCAT and LASTRACK. At first glance these two variables look exactly like SECVAL and ENDTRK in VTOCVALS shown in Table I.9.10. In the DOS 4.1 source code FIRSTCAT and SECVAL are set to the same value as are

LASTRACK and ENDTRK. SECVAL and ENDTRK are working variables in that their values can be changed by the Command Manager or by a user using the File Manager Context Block. FIRSTCAT and LASTRACK are reference variables in that their values are transferred to SECVAL and ENDTRK, respectively, when the Command Manager determines that the values it finds in the B keyword or in the A keyword is 0x00. Now, the user can set FIRSTCAT and LASTRACK to any default value without having to reassemble DOS 4.1.

Like the address found at CMDVLADR, the address found at KEYVLADR (offset 0x07) in Table I.8.7 points to the data structure called KEYVALS because it contains the keyword variables the Command Manager extracts during DOS command parsing, and those variables are shown in Table I.10.3. Simply transfer the address found at KEYVLADR to a page-zero pointer and index into the structure for the desired variable in order to obtain its value or change its value. Table I.10.3 provides the offset, or index to use for each variable. Before DOS 4.1 begins to parse the keyword variables it initializes the keyword variables from ADRVAL through RUNFLAG to 0x00. This is convenient because now these keywords and the processing flags KYWRDFND, CHNFLAG, and RUNFLAG all begin at a known state. Only when certain DOS commands are selected do CHNFLAG and RUNFLG have any effect on command processing.

Offset	Name	Size	Description
0x00	SLOTVAL	0x02	S keyword, slot value
0x02	DRVAL	0x02	D keyword, drive value
0x04	VOLVAL	0x02	V keyword, volume value
0x06	ADRVAL	0x02	A keyword, address value
0x08	LENVAL	0x02	L keyword, length value
0x0A	RECVAL	0x02	R keyword, record value
0x0C	BYTVAL	0x02	B keyword, byte value
0x0E	LOADLEN	0x02	LOAD and BLOAD length
0x10	MONVAL	0x01	MON/NOMON value
0x11	KYWRDFND	0x01	command-line keyword found
0x12	CHNFLAG	0x01	CHAIN flag
0x13	RUNFLAG	0x01	RUN/LOAD flag
0x14	FNAME	0x18	primary filename buffer
0x2C	SFNAME	0x18	secondary filename buffer

Table I.10.3. KEYVALS Data Structure Definition

Figure I.10.1 shows a sample assembly language program used in *Lisa* to obtain the value of LOADLEN. LOADLEN is the memory load address used by the DOS LOAD or BLOAD command. The routine extracts LOADLEN from the KEYVALS Data Structure simply by starting with the address found at INITDOS and using the offsets found in Tables I.8.6 and I.10.3. KEYVLADR has an offset of 0x07 and is the index value given to the parameter KEYVLNDX. LOADLEN has an offset of 0x0E and is the index value given to the parameter LDLENNDX. First, the address at INITDOS is copied to a page-zero pointer FMT and the offset KEYVLNDX is used to extract the address KEYVLADR. Next, the address at KEYVLADR is copied to the same page-zero pointer FMT and the offset LDLENNDX is used to extract the value of LOADLEN. Finally, LOADLEN is used to adjust the address found in BUFR.

```
    :                    :              :
0002                  5   BUFR      epz  $02
0044                  6   FMT       epz  $44
0800                  7             enz
0007                  8   KEYVLNDX  equ  $07
000E                  9   LDLENNDX  equ  $0E
    :                    :              :
0900 AD F8 BF        18             lda  INITDOS
0903 85 44           19             sta  FMT
0905 AD F9 BF        20             lda  INITDOS+1
0908 85 45           21             sta  FMT+1
090A                 22   ;
090A A0 07           23             ldy  #KEYVLNDX
090C B1 44           24             lda  (FMT),Y
090E 48              25             pha
090F C8              26             iny
0910 B1 44           27             lda  (FMT),Y
0912 85 45           28             sta  FMT+1
0914 68              29             pla
0915 85 44           30             sta  FMT
0917                 31   ;
0917 A0 0E           32             ldy  #LDLENNDX
0919 18              33             clc
091A A5 02           34             lda  BUFR
091C 71 44           35             adc  (FMT),Y
091E 85 02           36             sta  BUFR
0920 C8              37             iny
0921 A5 03           38             lda  BUFR+1
0923 71 44           39             adc  (FMT),Y
0925 85 03           40             sta  BUFR+1
    :                    :              :
```

Figure I.10.1. Lisa Using LOADLEN from KEYVALS in DOS 4.1

The address found at FMWAADR (offset 0x09) in Table I.8.7 points to the Data Structure called FMWORK because it contains the workarea variables used by the File Manager in processing DOS input/output commands. The FMWORK variables are shown in Table I.10.4. Simply transfer the address found at FMWAADR to a page-zero pointer and index into the structure for the desired variable in order to obtain its value or change its value. Table I.10.4 provides the offset, or index to use for each variable. Except for the VTOC and CAT structure blocks, Table I.10.4 maps directly to the WORKAREA shown in Table I.10.1 so that the two buffers can be copied to each other in total as needed. In DOS 4.1H the data areas and structures shown in Tables I.10.2, I.10.3, and I.10.4 all reside in RAM Bank 2.

Offset	Name	Size	Description
0x00	FRTSTRK	0x01	first T/S track
0x01	FRTSSEC	0x01	first T/S sector
0x02	CURTSTRK	0x01	current T/S track
0x03	CURTSSEC	0x01	current T/S sector
0x04	CURDATRK	0x01	current data track
0x05	CURDASEC	0x01	current data sector
0x06	FLAGS	0x01	0x02 = VTOC has changed 0x40 = data buffer has changed 0x80 = T/S buffer has changed
0x07	DIRSECIX	0x01	directory sector index
0x08	DIRBYTIX	0x01	directory byte index
0x09	SECPERTS	0x02	T/S entries in a sector
0x0B	RELSFRST	0x02	relative sector to first sector
0x0D	RELSLAST	0x02	relative sector to last sector
0x0F	RELSLRD	0x02	relative sector to just read sector
0x11	SECTLEN	0x02	sector size in bytes
0x13	FILEPOSN	0x02	current file position
0x15	FILEBYTE	0x01	current file byte
0x16	OPNRCLEN	0x02	file open record length
0x18	RECNUMBR	0x02	current record number
0x1A	BYTEOFFS	0x02	current byte offset
0x1C	SECCNT	0x02	sector count
0x1E	NEXTSECR	0x01	next sector
0x1F	CURTRACK	0x01	current track
0x20	SECBTMAP	0x04	sector bitmap
0x24	FYPTE	0x01	File type (^0x80 = locked)
0x25	SLOT16	0x01	slot * 16
0x26	DRVNUMBR	0x01	drive number
0x27	VOLNUMBR	0x01	volume number
0x28	TRKNUMBR	0x01	track number
0x29	VTOCSB	0x100	VTOC structure block
0x129	CATSB	0x100	Catalog structure block

Table I.10.4. File Manager Workarea Structure Definition

The address found at VTOCADR (offset 0x0B) in Table I.8.7 points to the VTOC structure block and the address found at CATSBADR (offset 0x0D) points to the Catalog structure block. Now, both the VTOC and the Catalog structure blocks can be easily accessed as needed. Refer back to Table I.6.1 for the definition of the VTOC structure block or to Table I.7.2 for the definition of the Catalog structure block. In DOS 4.1H these two structure blocks both reside in RAM Bank 2. It is quite easy to calculate the free space on any volume that has been immediately accessed simply by obtaining the address of the VTOC structure block and processing its free sector bitmap.

Many DOS commands utilize the File Manager to open a file, which is handled by the Common Open routine `CMNOPN`. This routine initializes the File Manager workarea, sets the sector size, checks the `RECNUM` value as shown in Table I.9.5 for `0x0000`, and allocates a file if the requested filename is not found in the Catalog. If DOS 3.3 finds `RECNUM` equal to `0x0000`, it changes the value of `OPNRCLEN` to `0x0001` as shown in Table I.10.4. If DOS 4.1 finds `RECNUM` equal to `0x0000`, it changes the value of `OPNRCELN` to `BYTPRSEC` as shown in Table I.6.1. For sectors that are 256 bytes in size, `BYTPRSEC` would equal `0x0100`. The DOS 4.1 design uses a far better and more logical value to set `OPNRCLEN` if `CMNOPN` finds `RECNUM` equal to `0x0000`.

11. DOS 4.1 Clock Access

As soon as DOS 4.1 is read into memory it attempts to locate a clock card in one of the seven peripheral slot card slots. Fortunately, the clock cards I am acquainted with conform to a convention that can be used to identify a peripheral slot card slot as having a clock slot card. The FINDCLK routine begins checking slot 7, working its way down to slot 1, and it looks for the PHP and SEI signature bytes, the first two bytes of the clock slot card firmware, and the CLKID byte, the last byte of the clock slot card firmware, set to either 0x03 or 0x07. When those conditions have been met, the slot number is saved, a "colon read" command is issued to the clock slot card firmware, and an attempt is made to parse the generated data from the clock slot card. The "colon read" command expects the clock data to be written to the INPUT buffer, or page 0x02 of memory (address 0x200) in the generic format of "mo/dd hh:mi:ss" or "mo/dd/yy hh:mi:ss", where mo is month, dd is day, yy is year, hh is hour, mi is minute, and ss is second. Some clock firmware includes the number of the week's day "w" before the date and time, or some firmware might include a period and a three-digit millisecond suffix to the seconds' data. Both my clock card and the TimeMaster clock card model the "colon read" command after the ThunderClock clock card, except those clock cards produce a year value whereas the ThunderClock clock card does not.

(Why the ThunderClock clock card became the de facto standard is beyond my comprehension. Maybe it was the first clock card marketed for the Apple? So what! Maybe it was well integrated in ProDOS. Again, so what! Not being able to produce a year value was just wrong, and definitely shortsighted.)

In order to evaluate the clock data, an index to the month data must be determined: there must be either no data before the month value or there must be at least one space before the month value. It does not matter what precedes that space, or what the separators are for the date and time values (/, :, ;, or space). Table I.11.1 lists the DOS 4.1 supported clock cards, the raw data string generated when a "colon read" command is issued (where x can be any data), and the index determined for that data. The READCLK routine uses that data index to begin extracting the date and time values, and substituting in YEARVAL (see Table I.8.7) if it is parsing ThunderClock clock card data. If it is not parsing ThunderClock clock card data, READCLK assumes the date data will contain a year value.

Clock Card	Data Index	Raw Data String
ThunderClock card	0	mo/dd hh;mi;ss
unknown clock card	1	mo/dd/yy hh:mi:ss
unknown clock card	2	x mo/dd/yy hh:mi:ss
Philip's clock card	3	"w mo/dd/yy hh:mi:ss
TimeMaster clock card	3	"w mo/dd/yy hh:mi:ss
unknown clock card	4	xxx mo/dd/yy hh:mi:ss
unknown clock card	5	xxxx mo/dd/yy hh:mi:ss

Table I.11.1. Supported Clock Cards in DOS 4.1

The slot number CLKSLOT of the clock slot card and the index into the clock data CLKINDEX are shown in Table I.10.2, and are available as indexed parameters of CMDVALS. If CLKSLOT is 0x00 there is no clock slot card and any value found in CLKINDEX is not valid. If an indirect JMP is made to the address found in RDCLKVSN as shown in Table I.9.1 with the Y-register containing the low byte and the A-register containing the high byte of the address of a 6-byte data buffer, and the carry flag is cleared, READCLK will read the clock, parse the clock data, and put the date and time values obtained in the order shown in Table I.6.3 into the supplied 6-byte data buffer as shown in Figure I.9.3.

The date and time values represent **decimal** data in a **hexadecimal** format, so the data must be printed as hexadecimal values or converted to an equivalent decimal value, if desired. This data encoding format is referred to as Binary Coded Decimal, or BCD. The 6502 (and 65C02) microprocessor can easily add, subtract, and compare BCD values after the microprocessor has executed the SED instruction in order for it to correctly process decimal, or base-10 numbers. Once BCD data processing has completed, the CLD instruction must be executed in order to return the microprocessor to correctly process hexadecimal, or base-16 numbers.

12. DOS 4.1 Error Processing

Whether an Applesoft or Binary program is running, if Applesoft is not running, or if Applesoft is running and the ASONERR (or 0xD8) flag has its MSB **clear**, the first step in DOS 4.1 error processing is to beep the speaker and print the error message text as shown in Table I.9.8. Applesoft is running when ASRUN (or 0x76) is not equal to 0xFF **and** PROMPT (or 0x33) is not equal to the] character. Conversely, Applesoft is not running when ASRUN equals 0xFF or PROMPT equals the] character. If Applesoft is running and the MSB of ASONERR is **set**, the error message is not printed and DOS exits indirectly to 0xD865 by means of ERRORADR (offset 0x11 in Table I.8.7). After the error message is printed, the next step in error processing is started beginning with DOS restoring its keyboard and video intercepts, and exiting indirectly to 0xD43C by means of WARMADR (offset 0x0F in Table I.8.7).

Applesoft programs can handle DOS error processing by using the "ONERR GOTO <*line number*>" command in order to prevent program termination. Assembly language programs need to do a little more work: store 0xFF to ASONERR, 0x00 to ASRUN and PROMPT, and change the address stored at ERRORADR to your own error handler. DOS 4.1 will load the X-register with the appropriate DOS error number as shown in Table I.9.8 before exiting indirectly to ERRORADR (or WARMADR for that matter if Applesoft is **not** running). Calling PRTERADR as shown in Table I.9.1 using an indirect JMP instruction and with the appropriate DOS error number stored in the X-register, will print the corresponding DOS error message text without beeping the speaker and without printing a carriage return after the error message. *Big Mac*, for example, utilizes PRTERADR in printing all error messages when DOS errors are encountered as shown in the assembly language snippet of Figure I.9.4. In that example code the first call to PRTERROR with the X-register set to 0x00 will beep the speaker. Then *Big Mac* calls PRTERROR with the actual error number in the X-register, and is followed by a carriage return. There is absolutely no need to locate the PRTERROR routine in the source code because it is so conveniently located in the Page 0x03 vectors at 0x3E8.

13. DOS 4.1 CHAIN Command

DOS 4.1 does include an actual `CHAIN` command designed specifically for floating point Applesoft. Having a native `CHAIN` command is far more convenient than having to include an assembly language utility on each and every application volume for those programs requiring this capability. However, careful considerations must be made when designing Applesoft programs that `CHAIN` to each other. The purpose of the DOS `CHAIN` command is to move two areas of memory where they reside for the `START` program to where they need to reside for the `CHAIN` program. These two areas of memory include the Simple Variables and the Array Variables, or `SAV`s for short. Figure I.13.1 shows a typical `START` Applesoft Program in memory. In that figure Free Space memory exists when the `START` Program, its `SAV`s, and its Character String Pool memory area do not exceed the value stored in `HIMEM` minus `0x0801`, the address where the `START` Program begins. Also, the `START` Program must never `CHAIN` to a `CHAIN` Program whose size will exceed the available Free Space memory.

Applesoft uses a large number of page-zero memory locations for its use. Many of these locations are to store addresses in low/high byte order that can easily be used as pointers for memory management routines. An Applesoft program loads into memory starting at address `0x0801`, which is the value found in `PRGTAB` at `0x67/0x68`. The DOS `LOAD` command knows the program's size in bytes even before it actually loads the file by reading its first data sector and examining the first two bytes, and it calculates where in memory its end address will be, and stores that information in `PRGEND` at `0xAF/0xB0`. Initially, `VARTAB`, `ARYTAB`, and `STREND` will be initialized to the same value in `PRGEND`, and `FRETOP` will be initialized to the same value in `HIMEM`. Of course, the `MAXFILES` command can be used to change `HIMEM`, and thus `FRETOP`, and this should be done early in the `START` program before any string variables are pushed into the Character String Pool memory area.

As the Applesoft program begins to execute its instructions it will start to create simple variables that include integers, real numbers, and string pointers. These variables and pointers reside in the Simple Variables area of memory as descriptors beginning in `VARTAB` at `0x69/0x6A`, and ending in `ARYTAB` at `0x6B/0x6C`. The definition of the descriptors for these variables and pointers that comprise the content of the Simple Variables is shown in Table I.13.1. As more and more Simple Variable descriptors are added, the Array Variables area is pushed higher and higher up in memory. Simple variables are always seven bytes in size, and depending on the variable type, some of the bytes may not be used. Table I.13.1 shows that real variables require all seven bytes for the variable name, the exponent, and its 4-byte mantissa. Integers require only four bytes for the variable name and its value in **high/low** byte order, leaving the remaining three bytes set to `0x00`. Finally, simple strings require only five bytes for the variable name, the length of the string, and the address where the string resides in low/high byte order, leaving the remaining two bytes set to `0x00`.

The definition of the descriptors for Applesoft Array Variables is shown in Table I.13.2. As seen in Figure I.13.1 the Array Variables area of memory begins in `ARYTAB` and ends in `STREND` at `0x6D/0x6E`. This area of memory contains single and multi-dimensioned arrays of integers, real numbers, and string pointer descriptors. Table I.13.2 shows arrays having two dimensions. Successive array element dimension sizes precede each other with the first dimension size (**high/low** byte order) always coming last. The array variable descriptor grows as the number of dimensions increase in number. The nominal size of an array variable descriptor is seven bytes for a single dimension array. The descriptor increases in size by two bytes for each dimension added. Therefore, the dimension number becomes a critical piece of information that is used to calculate where the array elements begin relative to the address of the array variable descriptor.

50

Pointer Addresses	Start Program	Smaller Program	Problem Program	Bigger Program
	0x0000	0x0000	0x0000	0x0000
PRGTAB – 0x67/0x68	0x0801 START Applesoft Program	0x0801 Small CHAIN Applesoft Program	0x0801 Problem CHAIN Applesoft Program	0x0801 Big CHAIN Applesoft Program
PRGEND – 0xAF/0xB0				
VARTAB – 0x69/0x6A	Simple Variables			
ARYTAB – 0x6B/0x6C	Array Variables			
STREND – 0x6D/0x6E				
	Free Space			
FRETOP – 0x6F/0x70				
	Character String Pool			
HIMEM – 0x73/0x74				
	DOS	DOS	DOS	DOS

Figure I.13.1. Example Applesoft Program Layout in Memory

Using Table I.13.1 as a guide and extracting the two variable name bytes shows that Real elements of a Real array variable are each five bytes, one byte for the exponent and four bytes for the mantissa. Integer elements of an Integer array variable are each two bytes, and the values are in **high/low** byte order. Finally, string elements of a String array variable are each three bytes, one byte for the length of the string and two bytes for the address where the string resides in memory in low/high byte order. As in the case for simple variables, the actual string data referenced by these string elements is pushed into the Character String Pool memory area that begins at HIMEM at 0x73/0x74 and ends at FRETOP at 0x6F/0x70. The Free Space memory is what is left over as the SAVs memory area grows up in memory and the Character String Pool memory area grows down in memory.

Variable Type	Byte Definitions						
	Byte 1	Byte 2	Byte 3	Byte 4	Byte 5	Byte 6	Byte 7
Real Numbers	name1 +ASCII 65	name2 +ASCII 66	Exponent	Mantissa 1	Mantissa 2	Mantissa 3	Mantissa 4
Integer Numbers	name1 -ASCII 195	name2 -ASCII 196	High Value	Low Value	0	0	0
Simple Strings	name1 +ASCII 69	name2 -ASCII 198	String Length	Low Address	High Address	0	0

Table I.13.1. Applesoft Simple Variable Descriptor Definition

Variable Type	Byte Definitions								
	Byte 1	Byte 2	Byte 3	Byte 4	Byte 5	Byte 6	Byte 7	Byte 8	Byte 9
Real Array	name1 +ASCII 65	name2 +ASCII 66	Low Byte Offset	High Byte Offset	Number of Dimensions K	Size of Kth Dim High Byte	Size of Kth Dim Low Byte	Size of K-1 Dim High Byte	Size of K-1 Dim Low Byte
Integer Array	name1 -ASCII 195	name2 -ASCII 196	Low Byte Offset	High Byte Offset	Number of Dimensions K	Size of Kth Dim High Byte	Size of Kth Dim Low Byte	Size of K-1 Dim High Byte	Size of K-1 Dim Low Byte
String Array	name1 +ASCII 69	name2 -ASCII 198	Low Byte Offset	High Byte Offset	Number of Dimensions K	Size of Kth Dim High Byte	Size of Kth Dim Low Byte	Size of K-1 Dim High Byte	Size of K-1 Dim Low Byte

Table I.13.2. Applesoft Array Variable Descriptor Definition

Many times an Applesoft program will contain the text of some string variable. As long as there is no text operation on that string variable such as "A$ = A$ + B$", for example, the text pointer address found in the Simple Variable or in the Array Variable descriptor will point to the actual string text within the contents of the Applesoft program, and therefore the string can never be available to a CHAIN Program. In order for a simple string variable or a string element to be available to a CHAIN Program, the actual string text of the string variable must be located in the Character String Pool memory area. A simple way to force this is to perform some text operation on that string variable, such as "A$ = A$ + """". This particular operation does nothing to string A$ except to cause the actual text of A$ to be copied from within the contents of the Applesoft program and into the Character String Pool memory area.

The purpose of the CHAIN command is to move the SAVs of the START Program to the end of the CHAIN Program, and to update PRGEND, VARTAB, and ARYTAB with their new addresses so that the CHAIN Program may access the variables and strings of the START Program. Because of some required Applesoft calls, even FRETOP needs to be reinitialized. When the CHAIN Program is smaller than the START Program or when the CHAIN Program is larger than the START Program plus the size of the SAVs area, there is no problem copying the SAVs directly to their new location. However, if the end of the CHAIN Program occurs somewhere within the SAVs area of the START Program, there will be disaster if the SAVs are copied directly. Due to the nature of the memory move routine, if the SAVs area of memory is copied in this particular situation, the move routine will begin to overwrite the same area of memory it is attempting to copy. And this will certainly lead to disaster for the CHAIN Program because some of the variable descriptors of the START Program will be overwritten and, therefore, destroyed. Disaster will also occur if the SAVs area is copied in reverse order (high memory to low memory) to the end of a CHAIN Program that is smaller than the START Program. The CHAIN routine can either refuse to perform the CHAIN operation and signal an error message in these situations, or select another alternative algorithm.

One option of another alternative algorithm is to copy the SAVs to the address in STREND and set PRGEND and VARTAB to that address if there is enough Free Space memory. PRGEND does not necessarily have to be exactly the address where the CHAIN Program ends in memory, technically at its triple-nulls. In fact, an Applesoft program may include assembly language subroutines attached to its triple-null ending giving the program a different physical end address. The DOS SAVE command uses PRGTAB and PRGEND to calculate the number of bytes to save, not necessarily the address where the triple-nulls occur in memory minus 0x0801. However, this option does potentially waste a good deal of memory if the SAVs area is sizeable.

The better option would be to always copy the SAVs up in memory to FRETOP and then copy them again down in memory to the new PRGEND. Unfortunately, the first copy would require a negatively-indexed memory move algorithm (the pointers are decremented, not incremented), which is not for the faint of heart due to its difficulty and complexity, and it requires more CPU instructions than a simple positively-indexed memory move algorithm. The second copy would require a straight-forward positively-indexed memory move algorithm. Fortunately, there was enough code space to implement this far superior option. The user can utilize the DOS 4.1 CHAIN command to their heart's content and rest assured that CHAIN will always place the SAVs fully intact precisely where the CHAIN Program ends with the single caveat already mentioned: the START Program must never CHAIN to a CHAIN Program whose size will exceed the available Free Space memory.

If the R keyword is **not** used with the CHAIN command, CHAIN will call the Applesoft ROM routine GARBAG at 0xE484 before it moves the Simple Variable and Array Variable descriptors to their new location at the end of the CHAIN Program. The GARBAG routine utilizes an algorithm similar in concept to a basic bubble sort algorithm to remove all unreferenced string data from the Character String Pool memory area, thus compacting the Character String Pool before CHAIN relocates the SAVs in memory. The processing time for this garbage algorithm to collect all the little bits and pieces of old strings is proportional to the square of the number of strings in use. That is, if there are 100 active strings it will take four times longer to process those strings than if there had been only 50 active strings. Many Garbage Collection algorithms have been previously published that accomplish the same results as GARBAG in far less time, but there can be a number of caveats when using some of these algorithms. For instance, normal Applesoft programs save all string data in lower ASCII, i.e.

with the MSB of each byte cleared to zero. Furthermore, normal Applesoft programs never allow more than one string descriptor to point to the same exact copy of that string in memory. Some Garbage Collection algorithms depend on these constraints. If either constraint is not true, a catastrophe will happen during the course of subsequent Applesoft processing! Of course, if the Applesoft program's string data is normal, there will be no subsequent problems. Only if assembly language appendages to the Applesoft program or other code segments perform exotic manipulations to string descriptors or to Character String Pool data might these constraints be violated, for example. The Applesoft Garbage Collector is discussed in more detail in section II.5.

If an efficient Garbage Collection routine is available, the user should invoke that routine before using the DOS CHAIN command and utilize the R keyword to bypass calling GARBAG from within CHAIN processing. There is always the dilemma in finding that balance between making the Applesoft and CHAIN programs smaller in order to accommodate an external and complex assembly language Garbage Collection routine or enlarging the Applesoft and CHAIN programs, and strategically placing multiple Applesoft "FRE(aexpr)" commands throughout the program.

The "FRE(aexpr)" command calls GARBAG and will process the Character String Pool more efficiently if there are fewer inactive strings and little unreferenced string data. Again, there is always the dilemma in finding that balance for the best strategy in ensuring that memory is used as efficiently as possible.

14. The VTOC Bitmap Definition

The free sector bitmap of a volume is located in the VTOC of a volume starting at byte 0x38 as shown in Figure I.6.1. Four bytes are reserved for each track on a volume whose bits determine whether a sector on that track is utilized or not utilized for a CATALOG sector, a TSL sector, or a data sector. There are two routines where DOS 3.3 uses NUMSECS, the VTOC variable equal to the number of sectors comprising a track: ALLOCSEC and RORBITMP. ALLOCSEC is a routine that will find and allocate a disk track that has an available sector. It uses the VTOC bitmap to locate this track. RORBITMP is a routine used by FREESECT that will set or clear a sector's assigned bit within the 4-byte bitmap of a track. The ramifications of limiting these routines to the value in NUMSECS causes the definition of the bit assigned to sector 0x00 to be different in 16-sector and 32-sector tracks. In DOS 3.3 sector 0x00 is assigned to the first bit in the second byte of the 4-byte bitmap of its track when NUMSECS is equal to 16 as shown in Table I.6.2. When NUMSECS is equal to 32, sector 0x00 is assigned to the first bit in the fourth byte of the 4-byte bitmap of its track as shown in Table I.14.1. Furthermore, *FID* always assumes NUMSECS is equal to 16 and always rotates the bitmap of a track accordingly. *FID*, as published by Apple, cannot copy files onto a volume that contains 32-sector tracks because it does not rotate the bitmap properly for 32-sector tracks.

Here is a confounded situation where the VTOC, designed by Apple, is not fully supported even by Apple designed utilities. I wonder if Apple thought as early as 1979 when Apple published *FID* that there would never be a device that would support 32-sector tracks? Perhaps Apple had given up on DOS 3.3 in preference to ProDOS earlier than anyone suspected. I was never convinced that the Apple][series of computers was necessarily the right platform for the hierarchal directory structures created in ProDOS. I'm even less convinced now.

Byte	Sector	Bitmap
0	1F-18	FEDCBA98
1	17-10	76543210
2	0F-08	FEDCBA98
3	07-00	76543210

Table I.14.1. Free Sector Bitmap for 32 Sector Tracks in DOS 3.3

ALLOCSEC and RORBITMP manipulate the free sector bitmap for each track as shown in Table I.6.2 consistently in DOS 4.1 without regard to the value found in NUMSECS: 32 sectors per track is always assumed even when a volume contains 16-sector tracks. DOS 4.1 only interacts with the VTOC bitmap by means of the variable NEXTSECR exclusively OR'd with the value 0x10 in the routines FREESECT and ALLOCSEC. In other words, the bitmap is manipulated as if it looks like what is shown in Table I.14.1, but the bitmap appears in the VTOC as if it looks like what is shown in Table I.6.2. Whether a volume contains 16-sector or 32-sector tracks does not matter to the DOS 4.1 routines that utilize the bitmap. When the bitmap is manipulated in this fashion, sector 0x00 will always be assigned to the first bit in the second byte of the four-byte bitmap of its track as shown in Table I.6.2.

For volumes having 16-sector tracks, the 4-byte bitmap of such a track having all 16 of its sectors available would be "FF FF 00 00". For volumes having 32-sector tracks the 4-byte bitmap of such a track having all 32 of its sectors available would be "FF FF FF FF". When the 4-byte bitmap of a track is not used consistently for 16-sector and 32-sector volumes, it puts an unnecessary burden on the DOS INIT command routine to determine exactly which bit is assigned to sector 0x00 and which bit is assigned to sector 0x10. Utilizing and manipulating the 4-byte bitmap of a track consistently puts virtually no further throughput burden onto DOS. I have also incorporated the necessary changes into *FID* that model how DOS 4.1 defines the 4-byte bitmap of a track and how the bitmap must be manipulated correctly. As to be expected, DOS 4.1 and DOS 4.1 *FID* can fully read, copy, and write a 16-sector DOS 3.3 volume, or any other volume for that matter, without exception, onto a DOS 4.1 volume whether that volume contains 16-sector or 32-sector tracks.

15. ProDOS Disk I/O Algorithm

I have no idea whether Apple or Axlon, the manufacture of the RAM Disk 320, developed the fast disk read algorithm. As described in section IV.17, the RAM Disk software can transfer the contents of an entire 35-track diskette to one of the RAM Disk drives in seven seconds, the time to make 35 revolutions, one revolution for each track on a Disk][. The Axlon software locates track 0x00 on the Disk][volume, clears a 16 byte "sector read" table, and finds the first sector data header it encounters. The software notes the sector number and proceeds to read the sector data putting the first 86 bytes into a buffer like NBUF2 as shown in Table I.15.1. These 86 bytes contain the lower two bits for the next three groups of data bytes about to be read. The first group of data bytes is comprised of 86 bytes, each byte shifted left two bits and OR'd with its lower two bits obtained from the BITNIBL table indexed by the respective byte from NBUF2, and stored directly into the designated RAM Disk sector. The second group of data bytes is comprised of another 86 bytes, similarly processed, and stored in the designated RAM Disk sector. The last 84 data bytes are similarly processed and stored in the designated RAM Disk sector. The final byte read is the checksum byte. If the checksum is 0x00 then no read error is flagged and the "sector read" table is updated with the sector marked as read. Once the "sector read" table is complete the Axlon software moves to the next Disk][track, clears the "sector read" table, and looks for the first sector data header it encounters. The Axlon software is finished when it has read and processed track 0x34.

Routine, Table, or Buffer	DOS 4.1		ProDOS	
	Bytes	Cycles	Bytes	Cycles
PRENIBL	36	10557	172	6331
POSTNIBL	23	9524	n/a	
READSCTR	84	11207	206	11248
WRITSCTR	128	11419	222	11420
RDNIBL	106		106	
WRTNIBL	64		n/a	
BITNIBL	n/a		256	
NBUF1	256		n/a	
NBUF2	86		86	
Total	783	42707	1048	28999

Table I.15.1. DOS 4.1 and ProDOS RWTS Routines, Tables, and Buffers

The ProDOS version of the fast disk read algorithm is essentially the same as the Axlon version except that ProDOS incorporates the contents of the WRTNIBL table into the unused portion of its BITNIBL table. Since only three of every four bytes are needed for NBUF2 processing, it made sense to utilize the remaining fourth byte for its WRTNIBL table. Axlon did not provide a fast disk write algorithm so there was no need to incorporate the WRTNIBL table in its BITNIBL table. Closer inspection of the two algorithms indicates to me that the Axlon version is a little cleaner programmatically speaking. Perhaps Axlon obtained the ProDOS version and tweaked it some? If I had seen the ProDOS version initially, I would have made the same modifications Axlon did. I cannot imagine the reverse taking place where Apple obtained the Axlon version and purposefully sabotaged it. Whatever the case, the algorithm is clever and it works well, and there is no need for a POSTNIBL routine. However, the READSCTR routine that implements the ProDOS fast disk read algorithm is nearly twice in size as that of the combined DOS 4.1 READSCTR and POSTNIBL routines: 206 bytes versus 107 bytes, respectively. The ProDOS READSCTR routine also takes a few more startup processing cycles than the DOS 4.1 READSCTR routine. ProDOS requires the BITNIBL table and DOS 4.1 requires the NBUF1 buffer for its data processing. Both are the same size, but the BITNIBL table also includes the WRTNIBL table, a table that is a standalone table in DOS 4.1. To read and process a DOS 4.1 sector takes 20731 cycles, or 20.73 milliseconds. ProDOS takes 11.25 milliseconds to read and process a sector. In order for ProDOS to read a block of data it must read two data sectors.

The processing duration of the ProDOS version of the fast disk write algorithm is essentially the same as the DOS 4.1 algorithm, and this is to be expected. Both algorithms must write five 40-microsecond sync bytes, three 32-microsecond prologue bytes, 343 32-microsecond data bytes and checksum, three 32-microsecond epilogue bytes, and a final 32-microsecond sync byte. However, their algorithm sizes are substantially different and that is because NBUF1 begins on a page boundary for DOS 4.1 and the user data buffer may or may not begin on a page boundary for ProDOS. ProDOS must prenibblize user buffer data in the same way that DOS 4.1 prenibblizes user buffer data, and "on the fly" ProDOS must modify its WRITSCTR code: it must determine whether the user data buffer begins on a page boundary, and if not, then which pages contain what portion of the buffer. There is one exception the ProDOS algorithm must also handle, and that is when the user data buffer falls off a page boundary by just one byte. The ProDOS fast disk write algorithm requires 394 bytes for its PRENIBL and WRITSCTR routines, and gets its WRITNIBL table for free. On the other hand, DOS 4.1 requires a mere 164 bytes for its PRENIBL and WRITSCTR routines, but it requires a WRITNIBL table, for a total of 228 bytes which is still 57% the size of the ProDOS memory requirements. To process and write a DOS 4.1 sector requires 21976 cycles, or 21.98 milliseconds. ProDOS requires 17751 cycles to process and write a sector, or 17.75 milliseconds. In order for ProDOS to write a block of data it must write two data sectors.

I have been referring to the data in Table I.15.1 for the information in the above sizing and timing discussion. Overall, the amount of software, table data, and buffer space required for DOS 4.1 to read and write data to and from a diskette is 783 bytes. ProDOS requires 1048 bytes, a difference of 265 bytes, or an additional page of memory plus nine bytes. This difference in bytes amounts to a 25% increase in memory requirements for ProDOS. The time to read and write a sector of data requires 42.71 milliseconds for DOS 4.1 and 29.00 milliseconds for ProDOS. The ProDOS algorithms are 32% faster than the DOS 4.1 algorithms overall. With these results it is obvious that the extensive use of table data and self-modifying code alone cannot account for the visible differences the two operating systems demonstrate when reading and writing files.

ProDOS achieves its significant speed difference by employing a sector interleaving (or skewing) such that only two revolutions are required to read all eight blocks on a track, similar to the same technique Apple Fortran and Apple Pascal use for reading their data diskettes. The sectors on a track are arranged such that there is one sector between each of the sectors that comprise a block, and there is one sector between each successive block. Data blocks are read and written in ascending block number (i.e. "2 ascending" skew) in ProDOS and sectors are read and written in descending sector number (i.e. "2 descending" skew) in DOS 4.1. DOS 4.1 employs a sector interleaving such that it is possible to read all 16 sectors on a track in two revolutions, but typically three revolutions are more realistic. For a more complete discussion on sector interleaving refer to Worth's and Lechner's

Beneath Apple DOS, *Beneath Apple ProDOS*, and *Bag of Tricks*. These references provide the reader with a thorough discussion of this rather complicated subject.

One may ask whether DOS 4.1 could benefit from the disk I/O routines of ProDOS. To test this very question I removed most of the code that supports the HELP command in DOS 4.1H and inserted the ProDOS disk I/O routines in place of the DOS 4.1 disk I/O routines. ProDOS also uses the Language Card memory for its disk I/O routines so I thought this was an ideal match. I was astonished, though I should not have been, to learn there was absolutely **no** benefit to DOS 4.1. Without these ProDOS I/O routines coupled with a "2 ascending" sector interleaving skew table the overall disk I/O throughput did not benefit. DOS 4.1 still uses the "2 descending" sector interleaving skew table from DOS 3.3 to maintain compatibility to that operating system. The DOS 4.1 I/O routines are still perfectly matched to that "2 descending" skew table for the best possible I/O performance.

16. Building and Installing DOS 4.1 Images

The source code for both DOS 4.1L and DOS 4.1H and their object code `SEGnn` files each completely fit on DOS 4.1 data volumes. A separate data Image volume called `DOS4.1.Image` contains the linked images of both versions of DOS 4.1. The *Lisa* `ctrl-P` command is used to create a linked image from several object code files on the source code volume so the complete object code image can be saved to the Image volume. The Image volume also contains several utilities that can install the DOS 4.1 images onto the boot tracks of a volume and to copy the DOS 4.1 images to other volumes. For example, `INSTALL46L` reads the linked DOS 4.1L image `DOS4.1.46L` from the Image volume in disk drive 2 and installs it directly onto the boot tracks of the volume in disk drive 1 as if the DOS image had been written onto those tracks by the DOS `INIT` command. The utility `DOS2TO1` copies the linked DOS images `DOS4.1.46L` and `DOS4.1.46H` from the Image volume in disk drive 2 to a volume in disk drive 1. It is assumed that both disk drives are connected to the disk controller slot card in slot 6. The utility `DOS2TO1.2` does essentially the same thing except the saved file names are shortened to `DOS4.1L` and `DOS4.1H`.

It is quite a simple matter to assemble the DOS 4.1L source code found on the DOS 4.1L Source volume `DOS4.1.SourceL` and to assemble the DOS 4.1H source code found on the DOS 4.1H Source volume `DOS4.1.SourceH`. I imagine it would take some effort to adapt this source code and its directives to another assembler other than *Lisa*. *Lisa* provides all the enhancements and directives necessary as well as the addition of new assembler directives to provide a straightforward assembly: the source code may be sectioned into many input files that are linked using a directive, and the generated object code may be saved into many output files as well. In other words, the entire source code does not need to reside in memory and the generated object code files may be linked together later with the *Lisa* `ctrl-P` command. The `ctrl-P` command is not exactly a Linker as found in a compiler; it merely combines into memory a series of object code files sequentially. As discussed in Section IV.14, *Lisa* uses lower memory above `0x0800` for the object code, the source code, and the complete symbol table for the software that is currently being assembled.

To assemble the DOS 4.1L source code place the DOS 4.1 Tools volume `DOS4.1.ToolsL` in disk drive 1, boot, and start *Lisa*. Enter the `SE` command-line command to select the `SETUP` program in order to verify or set the `Start of Source Code` to `0x2100` and the `End of Source Code` to `0x6000`. Place the DOS 4.1L Source volume `DOS4.1.SourceL` in disk drive 2, load the `DOS4.1L.L` file into memory, and start the assembler by entering either the `A` command-line command or the `Z` command-line command. If a printed version of the screen output is desired, simply preface the `A` or `Z` command with the `P1` command-line command. Four object code files will be generated on the DOS4.1L Source volume: `SEG01` to `SEG04`. The four object code files can be combined in memory sequentially starting at `0x1000` using the `ctrl-P` command. The complete binary image can be saved to the DOS 4.1 Image volume `DOS4.1.Image`, or to any other volume, as `DOS4.1.46L`.

The DOS 4.1H source code is assembled using the same procedure. Place the DOS 4.1H Source volume `DOS4.1.SourceH` in disk drive 2 and load the `DOS4.1H.L` file into memory. Assemble as above and save the complete binary image to the DOS 4.1 Image volume `DOS4.1.Image`, or to any other volume, as `DOS4.1.46H`.

17. Using DOS 4.1 Commands

I have enhanced many of the original DOS 3.3 commands primarily using the R keyword as a command switch since this keyword has very limited usage other than in the commands EXEC, POSITION, and the Random-Access Data file commands READ and WRITE. All DOS commands may be entered in lowercase and/or uppercase in DOS 4.1. Filenames may also be entered in a mixture of lowercase and uppercase, and the filenames are treated as case sensitive. For example, the filenames HELLO and Hello are treated as two different files. In order to make full use of lowercase and uppercase in DOS 4.1, an Apple //e is preferred. DOS 4.1 does function quite nicely on an Apple][or an Apple][+ if its character generator (for example, Dan Paymar's Lowercase Adaptor Interface PROM) can display the complete lowercase and uppercase Latin character set. DOS 4.1 does print error messages in mixed case. The Apple //e ROM also supports lowercase and/or uppercase data entry for Applesoft commands. However, in my opinion this ROM continues to have at least two substantial deficiencies: no native DELETE key utilization and the HLIN drawing algorithm is flawed. Both deficiencies are correctable within the available ROM code space without sacrificing other routines and algorithms. And that's quite an achievement!

There is no consistency in DOS 3.3 in whether no, one, or two carriage returns are printed after completing DOS command processing when the DOS command is issued from the Apple command line. Certainly it would be a mistake to print any additional carriage returns after completing DOS command processing during the execution of an Applesoft program or during the processing of an EXEC file. DOS 4.1 does print one carriage return after completing DOS command processing when the DOS command is issued from the Apple command line. This policy is to ensure that there will be at least one blank line between all DOS commands issued from the Apple command line in order to keep the DOS commands and their output data as legible as possible on the screen. Of course, DOS 4.1 does not print any additional carriage returns after completing DOS command processing during the execution of an Applesoft program or during the processing of an EXEC file. However, DOS commands that are issued from assembly language programs using COUT will appear with the additional carriage return. One way to prevent DOS 4.1 from printing the additional carriage return is to store a 0x00 at the variables ASRUN (or 0x76) and PROMPT (or 0x33). When DOS 4.1 checks these variables after completing DOS command processing, it will appear to DOS 4.1 that Applesoft is running and, therefore, DOS will not print an additional carriage return.

Both DOS 3.3 and DOS 4.1 save files to a disk volume using the TSL resources of the file if the file already exists. For example, if the file TEMP already exists and its TSL contains eight entries, those same track/sector entries will be used to save TEMP again whether TEMP is larger or smaller than its initial size. If TEMP is larger, the File Manager will simply request additional sectors and add them to the file's TSL. If TEMP is smaller, say the program only uses three pages of memory, the first three TSL entries will be used to save the file's content and the last five TSL entries will be unused. In other words, the last five track/sector entries in this example will remain allocated to the file and those data sectors will be unavailable for use by any other file. This inherent resource wastefulness for both DOS 3.3 and DOS 4.1 is perpetuated by programs like *FID*. *FID* uses the File Manager to copy files in total, and it assumes that all track/sector entries in a file's TSL belong to that file. DOS 4.1, Build 46 introduces the new strategy "File Delete/File Save". The DOS 4.1 commands BSAVE, LSAVE, SAVE, and TSAVE can now utilize the B keyword to implement "File Delete/File Save".

II. Apple ROM Modifications

In my version of the Apple //e ROM firmware source code I use the variables KEYMOD and HLINMOD in conditional assembly directives that are used to optionally assemble the original (or flawed) code (or KEYMOD EQU 0) or the modified (or corrected) code (or KEYMOD EQU 1). The object code is located in either a single 128 Kb ROM (or 27128 EPROM) as found in the Enhanced Apple //e or in two 64 Kb ROMs. On the other hand, the Apple //e character generator that defines the pixels of each ASCII character is located in a 32 Kb ROM (or 2732 EPROM). An EPROM burner (or programmer) is needed in order to program a new EPROM having the necessary modifications to replace the Apple //e firmware ROM or ROMs depending on the motherboard version.

1. Apple ROM Modification for Correct HLIN Drawing Algorithm

I have always disliked the unsymmetrical look of a HIRES diagonal line in either the horizontal or the vertical direction ever since acquiring my Apple][+. And this same HLIN code resides in the Apple //e ROM unchanged, which is shameful. When I was assigned to provide all the icons for *HomeWord Speller* at Sierra On-Line I analyzed the HLIN algorithm and found the algorithm does not calculate the delta difference of a line's horizontal and/or vertical end points correctly. It is a simple matter to demonstrate this error before and after installing the code modifications. There are two locations that require a small code adjustment. The first code adjustment is located at 0xF57A.

```
0xF57A:
            .if  HLINMOD
            bcs  HF580              ; branch to 0xF580 if set
            asl                     ; times 2
            jsr  HF465              ; call 0xF465
HF580       clc                     ; prepare for delta, not diff
            lda  ZPGD4              ; 0xD4
            .el
            bcs  HF581              ; branch to 0xF581 if set
            asl                     ; times 2
            jsr  HF465              ; call 0xF465
            sec                     ; prepare for diff, not delta
HF581       lda  ZPGD4              ; 0xD4
            .fi
```

where ZPGD4 is the page-zero location 0xD4 and HF465 is a label for a routine at memory address 0xF465. The second code adjustment is located at 0xF5A5.

63

```
0xF5A5:
        .if HLINMOD
        sec                     ; prepare for diff, not delta
        .el
        clc                     ; prepare for delta, not diff
        .fi
```

You will be simply amazed at how "lovely" and symmetrical diagonal lines are drawn either left to right, right to left, top to bottom, or bottom to top. And I am appalled that the old code passed any sort of testing and/or code review vis-à-vis how trivial this modification is and how elegant the results are.

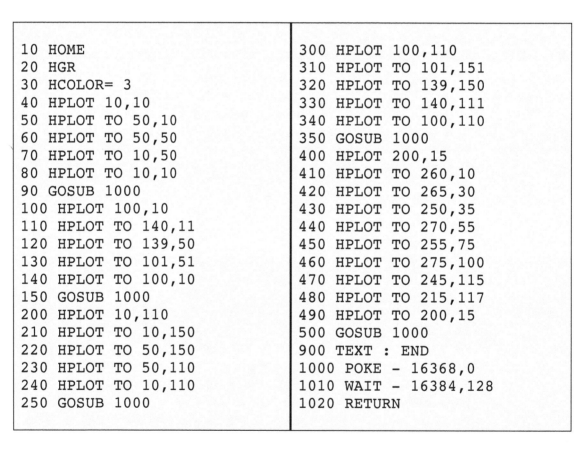

```
10  HOME                        300  HPLOT 100,110
20  HGR                         310  HPLOT TO 101,151
30  HCOLOR= 3                   320  HPLOT TO 139,150
40  HPLOT 10,10                 330  HPLOT TO 140,111
50  HPLOT TO 50,10              340  HPLOT TO 100,110
60  HPLOT TO 50,50              350  GOSUB 1000
70  HPLOT TO 10,50              400  HPLOT 200,15
80  HPLOT TO 10,10              410  HPLOT TO 260,10
90  GOSUB 1000                  420  HPLOT TO 265,30
100 HPLOT 100,10                430  HPLOT TO 250,35
110 HPLOT TO 140,11             440  HPLOT TO 270,55
120 HPLOT TO 139,50             450  HPLOT TO 255,75
130 HPLOT TO 101,51             460  HPLOT TO 275,100
140 HPLOT TO 100,10             470  HPLOT TO 245,115
150 GOSUB 1000                  480  HPLOT TO 215,117
200 HPLOT 10,110                490  HPLOT TO 200,15
210 HPLOT TO 10,150             500  GOSUB 1000
220 HPLOT TO 50,150             900  TEXT : END
230 HPLOT TO 50,110             1000 POKE - 16368,0
240 HPLOT TO 10,110             1010 WAIT - 16384,128
250 GOSUB 1000                  1020 RETURN
```

Figure II.1.1. Applesoft HLIN Demonstration Program

Figure II.1.1 shows an Applesoft program that can be used to demonstrate the difference between the original HLIN drawing algorithm and the modified drawing algorithm. Figure II.1.2 shows what this Applesoft program produces when it runs on an Apple //e without the HLIN modification to its ROM firmware. The two boxes on the left are square boxes that draw perfectly no matter in which direction the lines are drawn. The two middle boxes are nearly square boxes where the horizontal and vertical line end points differ by one pixel, and they show different anomalies depending upon which direction the lines are drawn: the upper box is drawn clockwise and the lower box is drawn counterclockwise. The shape on the right is drawn clockwise and it shows many corner anomalies as the direction and angle of the lines change. Figure II.1.3 shows what this same Applesoft program produces when the program runs on the same Apple //e having the HLIN modification included in its ROM firmware. All corner anomalies disappear and when the lines are drawn diagonally they are segmented equally. It is obvious from Figure II.1.3 that having the HLIN modifications allows one to draw shapes in any direction and in any order without having to worry about corner anomalies and inconsistent line segmentation.

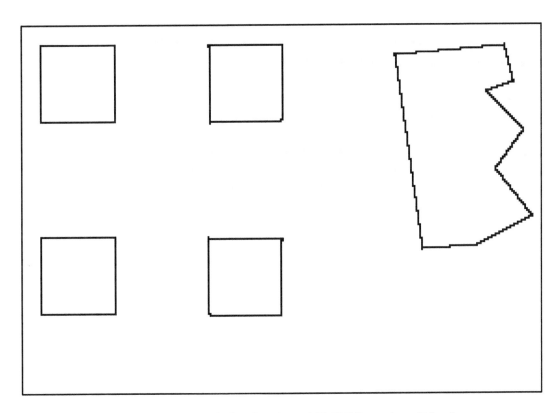

Figure II.1.2. Original ROM HLIN Routine Display

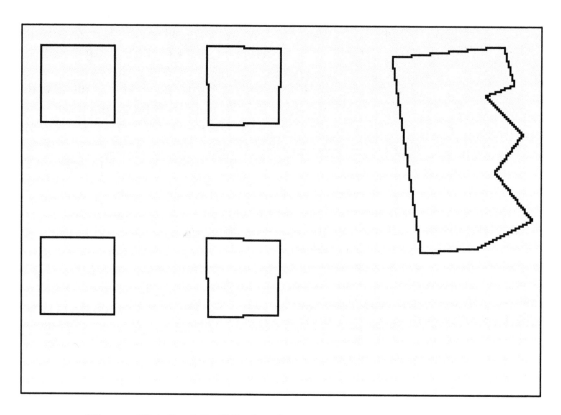

Figure II.1.3. Modified ROM HLIN Routine Display

2. Apple ROM Modification for Delete Key Utilization

In order to have native DELETE key utilization the Apple //e firmware locations 0xC29A and 0xC846 require the following code changes.

```
0xC29A:
            .if KEYMOD
            jsr MODKEY          ; 0xFB0A, check for DELETE
            .el
            sta CLRKEY          ; 0xC010, clear keyboard strobe
            .fi


0xC846:
            .if KEYMOD
            jsr MODKEY          ; 0xFB0A, check for DELETE
            .el
            sta CLRKEY          ; 0xC010, clear keyboard strobe
            .fi
```

The MODKEY routine is placed at 0xFB0A.

```
0xFB0A:
            .if KEYMOD
MODKEY      sta CLRKEY          ; 0xC010, clear keyboard strobe
            cmp #NEGONE         ; 0xFF, is it DELETE
            bne MODKEY2         ; branch if not
            lda #LARROW         ; 0x88, get backspace character
;
MODKEY2     rts                 ; return to caller
;
            .el
            asc "Apple ]["      ; unused data
;
            dfs 2,0             ; add 2 bytes of space
;
            .fi
```

The .el/.fi code in MODKEY replaces ten bytes of unused data that is not accessed by any firmware routine or algorithm. The next section will explain why MODKEY is situated at this particular location.

3. Apple //e 80 Column Text Card and ROM Monitor

My parents purchased their Apple //e while I was working at Sierra On-Line with the understanding that I would set up their system, teach them how to use its capabilities, fix and/or repair any software or hardware problems, and perform any regular maintenance as required. I didn't fully realize what I was getting myself into particularly when I attempted to teach my father how to use *VisiCalc*: his hands were quite large so his fingers were not keyboard-nimble, he had poor close-up vision, and he could not remember key-entry sequences very well. I developed his *VisiCalc* daily expense report (requiring wide paper in their EPSON MX-100 printer) and an Applesoft program to strip his monthly totals from his *VisiCalc* data files in order to create his annual summary *VisiCalc* data file. I provided him detailed instructions on how to begin a *VisiCalc* session and how to enter his data into each row and column. When he made mistakes or skipped instructions he became agitated and blamed the computer for making his errors. My mother would then enter the data for him to keep everyone calm.

My parents purchased their Apple //e early in its availability before the enhanced version was developed. I have no recall if we were even aware of an Enhanced Apple //e while I was at Sierra around 1983 and 1984. Because I was assisting in porting *ScreenWriter* to the Apple //e I became very familiar with the 80-column text card and the routines AUXMOVE and XFER. Also, Ken Williams asked me to extract the database from **the Dic-tio-nary**, the companion spell checker to *ScreenWriter*, for his new product *HomeWord Speller*, the companion spell checker to *HomeWord* he had already released. *HomeWord* and *HomeWord Speller* were both developed in-house. I utilized calls to XFER within a printer driver I wrote for **the Dic-tio-nary**, its only vulnerable access location at 0x300, and my driver sent specific sections of the product's database to Auxiliary memory instead of to a printer. Once I took control of the computer after the data transfer, I was able to copy that database section from Auxiliary memory to Main memory, and then into a file on a disk volume. It is important to note that the XFER starting address is found at 0x3ED and 0x3EE in the Page 0x03 Interface Routines.

I believe the enhanced version of the Apple //e provides MouseText characters in place of the alternate uppercase inverse character set, and it also introduced double-high-resolution graphics. This Apple also provides lowercase input for Applesoft and its new Monitor provides lower ASCII data input to memory, a search command, and the return of the phenomenal Mini-Assembler. The new Monitor also supports a very sophisticated interrupt handler that works in any Apple //e memory configuration. This is done by saving the current memory configuration state at the time of the interrupt onto the stack, placing the Apple in a standard memory configuration before calling the requested interrupt handler, and then restoring the original memory configuration state when the requested interrupt handler is finished. However, in my estimation Apple fell way short in not providing the ability to fully utilize the Mini-Assembler to enter and to display the complete 65C02 Instruction Set particularly in view of the fact that the computer was designed to use and was shipped with a 65C02 processor. What was Apple thinking? Any fool knows that the Mini-Assembler is dynamite when coupled with the Monitor STEP and TRACE commands.

What was Apple thinking when it continues to promote and to support the use of a cassette tape recorder to store and retrieve programs, multi-dimensioned integer and real arrays, and shape tables? I know of no software engineer in my professional career or among my personal friends who ever used a cassette tape recorder with any Apple computer for any reason. I did develop a communication protocol with a programmable keyboard by means of a wire, which was similar to the tape output data to a cassette tape recorder. Other than programming a keyboard using an annunciator, I have never used a cassette tape recorder with any of my Apple computers. I have never used the Applesoft LOAD, RECALL, SAVE, STORE, or SHLOAD commands in any of my Applesoft programs nor have I seen these commands used in any professional or commercial Applesoft programs. And, I have never used the Monitor READ or WRITE commands at any time. Why would I use such a ridiculous and incredibly slow data archiving method when I have the Disk][, the Rana, the RAM Disk 320, the Sider, or the CFFA card to save programs and data in the form of files, visible within its media, and time and date stamped? Honestly, I derive no personal satisfaction in knowing that one can read data into an Apple computer using a cassette tape recorder port. I do have a few suggestions for what could replace the useless Monitor READ and WRITE commands with something rather quite useful.

Address	Access	Name	Description	Notes
0xC000	W	STR80OFF	Disable 80 column store	1
0xC001	W	STR80ON	Enable 80 column store	1
0xC002	W	RAMRDOFF	Read enable Main RAM, 0x0200-0xBFFF	2
0xC003	W	RAMRDON	Read enable Auxiliary RAM, 0x0200-0xBFFF	2
0xC004	W	RAMWROFF	Write enable Main RAM, 0x0200-0xBFFF	2
0xC005	W	RAMWRON	Write enable Auxilary RAM, 0x0200-0xBFFF	2
0xC006	W	CXROMOFF	Enable slot ROMs, slots 1-7, or 0xC100-0xC7FF	3
0xC007	W	CXROMON	Enable internal CX ROM, or 0xC100-0xCFFF	3
0xC008	W	AUXZPOFF	Enable Main ZP, stack, language card, Av1 BSR RAM	4
0xC009	W	AUXZPON	Enable AUX ZP, stack, language card, AV1 BSR RAM	4
0xC00A	W	C3ROMOFF	Enable internal CX3 ROM, 0xC300-0xC3FF	
0xC00B	W	C3ROMON	Enable Slot ROM, 0xC300-0xC3FF	
0xC00C	W	VID80OFF	Disable 80 column video	
0xC00D	W	VID80ON	Enable 80 column video	
0xC00E	W	ALTCHOFF	Enable normal Apple character set	
0xC00F	W	ALTCHON	Enable alternate character set (no flash)	

Table II.3.1. New Memory Management and Video Soft Switches

Address	Access	Name	Description	Clear	Set	Notes
0xC000	R/R7	KEY	Read keyboard input	No key	Yes key	
0xC010	R/R7	CLRKEY	Clear keyboard strobe	No key	Yes key	
0xC011	R7	RDBANK2	Which LC BANK in use	BANK1	BANK2	
0xC012	R7	RDLCRAM	LC RAM or ROM read-enabled	ROM	LC RAM	
0xC013	R7	RDRAMRD	Main, AUX RAM read-enabled	Auxiliary	Main	
0xC014	R7	RDRAMWR	Main, AUX RAM write-enabled	Auxiliary	Main	
0xC015	R7	RDCXROM	Slot or internal ROM enabled	Slot	Internal	
0xC016	R7	RDAUXZP	Which ZP & LC enabled	Main	Auxiliary	
0xC017	R7	RDC3ROM	Slot or CX ROM enabled	Slot ROM	CX3 ROM	
0xC018	R7	RDSTR80	State of STR80 switch	Disabled	Enabled	
0xC019	R7	RDVRTBLK	State of vertical blanking	Yes	No	
0xC01A	R7	RDTEXT	State of TEXT switch	Graphics	Text	
0xC01B	R7	RDMIXED	Read MIXED switch	OFF	ON	
0xC01C	R7	RDPAGE2	State of PAGE2 switch	PAGE1/Main	PAGE2/AUX	
0xC01D	R7	RDHIRES	State of Graphics resolution	LOWRES	HIRES	
0xC01E	R7	RDALTCH	State of Alternate Char. Set	OFF	ON	
0xC01F	R7	RDVID80	State of VID80 video	Disabled	Enabled	
0xC07E	R7	RDIOUDIS	Read IOUDIS switch	DHIRES On	DHIRES Off	5
0xC07F	R7	RDDHIRES	Read DHIRES switch	OFF	ON	5

Table II.3.2. New Soft Switch Status Flags

The Apple //e Main and Auxiliary memory together total 128 KB and each can be controlled by means of an MMU and an IOU device using soft switches. By design, the memory addresses of a 65C02 processor within the Apple //e hardware architecture can be naturally divided into four strategic areas: page-zero and the stack, 0x200 to 0xBFFF, 0xC000 to 0xCFFF, and 0xD000 to 0xFFFF that includes the bank-switched 0xD000 to 0xDFFF space. These memory areas can be individually activated from Main or Auxiliary memory resources using the appropriate soft switches. What is also unique to the Apple //e is that the Monitor firmware has been expanded to include additional ROM firmware that is mapped to the 0xC100 to 0xCFFF address space. This address space is controlled using the appropriate soft switches. If there is a display slot card residing in Slot 3, its firmware can be activated rather than using the internal 80-column text card firmware. Table II.3.1 summarizes the new memory management and video soft switches used to control Main and Auxiliary memory. Some data must be written to all these soft switches in order to invoke their action. It does not matter what that data is. Table II.3.2 summarizes the new soft switch status flags. It is by means of these status flags that one may determine the complete memory and video configuration of the Apple //e.

Address	Access	Name	Description	Notes
0xC020	R	TAPEOUT	Cassette output Toggle	
0xC030	R	SPKRTOGL	Speaker output Toggle	
0xC040	R	UTILTOGL	Utility Strobe; 1 ms pulse Game I/O pin 5	
0xC050	R/W	TEXTOFF	Display Graphics	
0xC051	R/W	TEXTON	Display Text	
0xC052	R/W	MIXEDOFF	Full Screen graphics	6
0xC053	R/W	MIXEDON	Text with graphics	6
0xC054	R/W	PAGE1ON	Display Page 1 or Main video memory	7
0xC055	R/W	PAGE2ON	Display Page 2 or Auxiliary video memory	7
0xC056	R/W	HIRESOFF	Select low resolution Graphics	6
0xC057	R/W	HIRESON	Select high resolution Graphics	6
0xC058	R/W	ANN1OFF	Annunciator 1 OFF (active if IOUDIS ON)	
0xC059	R/W	ANN1ON	Annunciator 1 ON (active if IOUDIS ON)	
0xC05A	R/W	ANN2OFF	Annunciator 2 OFF (active if IOUDIS ON)	
0xC05B	R/W	ANN2ON	Annunciator 2 ON (active if IOUDIS ON)	
0xC05C	R/W	ANN3OFF	Annunciator 3 OFF (active if IOUDIS ON)	
0xC05D	R/W	ANN3ON	Annunciator 3 ON (active if IOUDIS ON)	
0xC05E	R/W	ANN4OFF	Annunciator 4 OFF (active if IOUDIS ON)	
0xC05E	R/W	DHRESON	Double HIRES ON (active if IOUDIS OFF)	
0xC05F	R/W	ANN4ON	Annunciator 4 ON (active if IOUDIS ON)	
0xC05F	R/W	DHRESOFF	Double HIRES OFF (active if IOUDIS OFF)	
0xC060	R	TAPEIN	Cassette input	8
0xC061	R	PB1IN	Push Button 1 input	8
0xC062	R	PB2IN	Push Button 2 input	8
0xC063	R	PB3IN	Push Button 3 input	8
0xC064	R	GC1IN	Game Controller 1 input	9
0xC065	R	GC2IN	Game Controller 2 input	9
0xC066	R	GC3IN	Game Controller 3 input	9
0xC067	R	GC4IN	Game Controller 4 input	9
0xC070	R	GCTOGL	Game Controller Strobe; resets GC1-GC4	
0xC073	W	BANKSEL	RamWorks Bank Select; 64 KB bank select	
0xC07E	W	IODISON	Disable annunciators, enable double HIRES	
0xC07F	W	IODISOFF	Enable annunciators, disable double HIRES	

Table II.3.3. Original Input/Output Control Soft Switches

For completeness I have included Tables II.3.3, II.3.4, and II.3.5 showing the original Input/Output, memory management, and Disk][control soft switches. In all cases the names of each soft switch are those that I use within the *Lisa* assembler because *Lisa* has an eight-character limitation for labels. Figure II.3.1 contains all notes referenced by Tables II.3.1 to II.3.5.

Address	Access		Name	Description	Notes
0xC080	R		RAM2WP	Select Bank 2; write protect RAM	
0xC081	R	RR	ROM2WE	Deselect Bank 2; enable ROM | write enable RAM	
0xC082	R		ROM2WP	Deselect Bank 2; enable ROM; write protect RAM	
0xC083	R	RR	RAM2WE	Select Bank 2 | write enable RAM	
0xC084				See 0xC080	
0xC085				See 0xC081	
0xC086				See 0xC082	
0xC087				See 0xC083	
0xC088	R		RAM1WP	Select Bank 1; write protect RAM	
0xC089	R	RR	ROM1WE	Deselect Bank 1; enable ROM | write enable RAM	
0xC08A	R		ROM1WP	Deselect Bank 1; enable ROM; write protect RAM	
0xC08B	R	RR	RAM1WE	Select Bank 1 | write enable RAM	
0xC08C				See 0xC088	
0xC08D				See 0xC089	
0xC08E				See 0xC08A	
0xC08F				See 0xC08B	

Table II.3.4. Original Memory Management Soft Switches

Address	Access	Name	Description	Notes
0xC080	R	PHAS0OFF	Turns stepper motor phase 1 OFF	
0xC081	R	PHAS0ON	Turns stepper motor phase 1 ON	
0xC082	R	PHAS1OFF	Turns stepper motor phase 2 OFF	
0xC083	R	PHAS1ON	Turns stepper motor phase 2 ON	
0xC084	R	PHAS2OFF	Turns stepper motor phase 3 OFF	
0xC085	R	PHAS2ON	Turns stepper motor phase 3 ON	
0xC086	R	PHAS3OFF	Turns stepper motor phase 4 OFF	
0xC087	R	PHAS3ON	Turns stepper motor phase 4 ON	
0xC088	R	MOTOROFF	Turns motor OFF	
0xC089	R	MOTORON	Turns motor ON	
0xC08A	R	DRV0EN	Selects Drive 1	
0xC08B	R	DRV1EN	Selects Drive 2	
0xC08C	R	STROBE	Strobe data latch for I/O	
0xC08D	R/W	LATCH	Load data latch	
0xC08E	R	DATAIN	Prepare latch for input	10
0xC08F	W	DATAOUT	Prepare latch for output	11

Table II.3.5. Original Disk][Control Soft Switches

1) If STR80OFF, then access PAGE1/PAGE2 and use RAMRD and RAMWR; if STR80ON, then access Main or Auxiliary display page (or 0x400) using PAGE2.
2) If 80STORE is ON these switches do not affect video memory.
3) If INTCXROM is ON, then switch SLOTC3ROM is available; otherwise Main ROM is accessed.
4) Use bank enable and write protect switches to control 0xD000-0xFFFF.
5) Triggers paddle timer and resets VBLINT.
6) This mode is only effective when TEXT switch is OFF.
7) This switch changes function when 80STORE is ON.
8) Data is in MSB only.
9) Read 0xC070 first, then count until MSB is zero.
10) DATAIN with STROBE for Read and DATAIN with LATCH for Sense Write Protect.
11) DATAOUT with STROBE for Write and DATAOUT with LATCH for Load Write Latch.

Figure II.3.1. Notes for Tables II.3.1 to II.3.5

Address	Access	Name	Description
0xC05A	W	ZIPCTRL	4 writes of 0x5A unlocks *Zip Chip*; 0xA5 locks *Zip Chip*
0xC05B	W	ZIPSTATS	Any byte written enables *Zip Chip*
0xC05B	R	ZIPSTATS	Bits 0 and 1 is RAM size: 0 = 8K, 1 = 16K, 2 = 32K, 3 = 64K; bit 3 for memory delay: 0 = fast mode (no delay), 1 = sync mode (delay); bit 4 is ZIP enable: 0 = enabled, 1 = disabled; bit 5 is paddle speed: 0 = fast, 1 = normal; bit 6 is cache update: 0 = NO, 1 = YES; bit 7 is clock pulse every 1.0035 ms
0xC05C	R/W	ZIPSLOTS	read/write speaker/slot 0 = fast, 1 = normal. Bit 0 = speaker, bits 1 to 7 for slots 1 to 7
0xC05D	W	ZIPSPEED	Write speed: bit 2 = clk2/3, bit 3 = clk3/4, bit 4 = clk4/5, bit 5 = clk5/6, bit 6 = clk/2, bit 7 = clk/4
0xC05E	W	ZIPDELAY	Bit 7: 0 = enable delay, 1 = disable and reset delay
0xC05E	R	ZIPDELAY	0 = OFF, 1 = ON: bit 0 = ROMRD, bit 1 = RAMBNK, bit 2 = PAGE2, bit 3 = HIRES, bit 4 = 80STORE, bit 5 = MWR, bit 6 = MRD, bit 7 = ALTZP
0xC05F	W	ZIPCACHE	Bit 6 paddle delay: 0 = disable, 1 = enable; bit 7 language card cache: 0 = enable, 1 = disable

Table II.3.6. Zip Chip Control Soft Switches

Table II.3.6 shows the soft switches that are used to control the *Zip Chip* if it is used in place of the 65C02 processor. The *Zip Chip* includes a 65C02 processor along with cache memory and a cache memory controller in order to execute processor instructions and manage memory data faster. Table II.3.7 shows the soft switches that are used to control the CFFA and Table II.3.8 shows the soft switches that are used to control the quikLoader. Table II.3.9 shows the soft switches that are used to control the Sider, RAM Disk 320, RAM Card, and Rana drives. Typically, the X-register contains the slot number in which the device resides times sixteen and the register is used in combination with the addresses shown in Tables II.3.7, II.3.8, and II.3.9. Or, if speed is critical and the address space where the device driver is writable, the slot number of the device times sixteen is added to the base addresses shown in these tables. In addition to what is shown in Table II.3.9, the Rana controller card also uses the original Disk][control soft switches shown in Table II.3.5. The Rana controller card uses a complicated algorithm using some of the `PHASEON` and `PHASEOFF` control soft switches to select its upper or lower recording head and the `0xC800`/`0xC801` addresses to select drives 1 and 2 or 3 and 4.

Address	Access	Name	Description
0xC080	R/W	ATADATAH	Read or write high data byte register
0xC081	R	SETCSMSK	Disable pre-fetch register
0xC082	R	CLRCSMSK	Enable pre-fetch register
0xC086	W	ATADEVCT	Write device control register
0xC086	R	ATASTAT2	Read alternate status register
0xC088	R/W	ATADATAL	Read or write low data byte register
0xC089	R	ATAERROR	Read error register
0xC08A	W	ATASECCT	Write sector count register
0xC08B	W	ATASECTR	Write LBA3 (07:00) address register
0xC08C	W	ATACYLNL	Write LBA2 (15:08) address register
0xC08D	W	ATACYLNH	Write LBA1 (23:16) address register
0xC08E	W	ATAHEAD	Write drive/head configuration register
0xC08F	W	ATACMD	Write command register
0xC08F	R	ATASTAT	Read primary status register

Table II.3.7. CFFA Control Soft Switches

Address	Access	Name	Description
0xC080	W	QLSELC0	Select banks 0 or 1, ON/OFF, USR, EPROM number
0xC081	W	QLSELC1	Select banks 2 or 3, ON/OFF, USR, EPROM number
0xC082	W	QLSELC2	Select banks 4 or 5, ON/OFF, USR, EPROM number
0xC083	W	QLSELC3	Select banks 6 or 7, ON/OFF, USR, EPROM number

Table II.3.8. quikLoader Control Soft Switches

Address	Access	Name	Description
0xC080	R	SDINPUT	Sider read status
0xC080	W	SDINPUT	Write drive number, DCB data, input data
0xC081	R	SDOUTPUT	Sider read output data
0xC081	W	SDOUTPUT	Write start, flush, and stop commands
0xC080	W	RDSECTR	RAM Disk sector number
0xC081	W	RDTRACK	RAM Disk track number
0xC084	W	RAMCARD	RAM Card on/OFF, track*2, sector/8
0xC800	W	ROMCODE1	Select Rana drive pairs 1 and 2
0xC801	W	ROMCODE2	Select Rana drive pairs 3 and 4

Table II.3.9. Sider, RAM Disk, RAM Card, and Rana Control Soft Switches

The Apple][+ Monitor disabled the STEP and TRACE commands. Now that the Apple //e has additional ROM memory in the CX (or 0xC100 to 0xCFFF) address space, the disabled STEP and TRACE table entry points are now used for the Mini-Assembler command (the ! command) entry and for the SEARCH command (the S command) entry. In my opinion the SEARCH command is pretty lame for it can find at most two consecutive bytes in low/high byte order. And I am still annoyed that the cassette tape recorder READ and WRITE commands were retained in the Apple //e. What disturbs me the most is that the Monitor cannot display the additional opcodes of the 65C02 Instruction Set that pertain to the specific 65C02 processor used in the Apple //e. As an aside, the 65C02 Instruction Set was expanded even further in the Rockwell and WDC versions of the 65C02 processor to include the BBR, BBS, RMB, and SMB mnemonics adding thirty-two additional opcodes. These opcodes are not available in the Apple //e 65C02 processor. Therefore, it makes no sense to me to provide a user with a computer that utilizes a particular processor, and its firmware can only display a subset of its processor's mnemonics. What I would have done is to recommend to Apple to retire the Monitor READ and WRITE commands and reintroduce the Monitor STEP and TRACE commands, and to provide a more useful Monitor command in addition to the SEARCH command if there was sufficient room. And, of course, the Monitor must be able to display all of the useable 65C02 mnemonics. Will retiring the Monitor READ and WRITE commands provide enough room for all my suggestions? Can the Monitor's new lower ASCII data input routine be further enhanced? Let's find out. The Monitor software begins at 0xF800.

I have no doubt that the engineering team that designed the Apple //e ROM firmware, and subsequently the Enhanced Apple //e ROM firmware were given a momentous task. That task was to preserve sixteen "classic" entry points and introduce a few new Monitor entry points in order to support both 40-column and 80-column screen displays, and to support most all previously written software for the Apple][and Apple][+. These "classic" and new entry points include GETFMT, RESET, BASCALC, NEWVW, RDKEY1, KEYIN, RDESC, PICKFIX, IOPRT1, MINIASM, and the screen handling routines HOME, SETWND, VTABZ, CLEOLZ, CLREOP, and SCROLL. Obviously, one can no longer expect to use any Monitor entry point "within" these routines or any other Monitor routine and expect reliable results. For example, the IRQ interrupt vector at 0xFFFE and 0xFFFF no longer uses the old BREAK vector at 0xFA40. The snippet of code left at 0xFA40 only saves the A-register to 0x45 (or AREG) before jumping to the new IRQ interrupt handler at 0xC3FA instead of to the address found at 0x3FE and 0x3FF (usually the address of the Monitor, 0xFF65). This new IRQ handler now pushes all the registers onto the stack and saves the current memory configuration state of the machine as previously explained. It appears that it may be no longer necessary to clear the page-zero 0x48 location after making a call to RWTS if DOS 4.1 is not being utilized.

The RESET routine has undergone a substantial overhaul as well. If the ClosedApple key is held down along with the CONTROL key while pressing and releasing the RESET key, the built-in self-test diagnostics will begin to execute. These diagnostics test page-zero RAM separately from all other writable RAM in Main memory, it repeats these tests for Auxiliary memory, and then it tests the IOU and MMU devices. If an error should occur, the output message simply states an error has occurred in ZP RAM, RAM, IOU, or MMU, and nothing more. The diagnostics simply freeze on the occurrence of the first error it encounters, and does not continue to determine if there are additional memory or device errors. Essentially, the user is left bewildered and confused, and the only course of action is to seek authorized Apple service. If the diagnostics do not find an error, it prints "System OK" and the computer freezes. Only then, if the ClosedApple and OpenApple keys are pressed together will the built-in self-test diagnostics execute again and leave the computer frozen as before. Generally, the computer needs to be powered OFF, then powered ON in order for it to be placed in a normal, useable configuration. These diagnostics consume two pages of address space in the CX ROM from 0xC600 to 0xC7FF, a rather substantial, if not bombastic amount of ROM space. Unfortunately, these tests require them to reside and execute in the ROM address space as they will not execute correctly in any other address space.

It is fair to say that ROM address space is very, very precious. I believe the Apple engineering team did a remarkable job in building a quality 80-column text card software product that performs simply and elegantly. For example, it is so easy to place the cursor or characters anywhere on the screen compared to the difficulty I had with the Videx UltraTerm video display card for the very same task. In order to support the Monitor READ and WRITE commands and the Applesoft commands that depend on those Monitor commands, the Apple team used an entire page of CX ROM from 0xC500 to 0xC5FF. I disabled those Applesoft commands dependent on the Monitor READ and WRITE commands by replacing the nine subroutine calls at 0xD8C0, 0xD8C6, 0xD8CC, 0xD8E3, 0xF3B3, 0xF3B9, 0xF3BF, 0xF3D5, and 0xF77B with a subroutine call to IORTS at 0xFF58, a simple RTS instruction. Now, if any of these Applesoft commands are used on the command line or within a program, the Applesoft command performs no action and it returns immediately without error.

It must be understood and accepted that the location of some data tables in the Monitor is not sacrosanct and these tables may be moved to other locations. For example, there are three unused bytes between the Translate table XLTBL and the Display Register table RTBL. By moving the XLTBL up three bytes in memory will provide sufficient room for MODKEY. The BASCALC routine at 0xFBC1 is repeated in the CX ROM at 0xCABA, and there is even an entry point at 0xC1B6 that is simply not utilized, though incorrectly coded in my opinion. The following code segments show how to code the 0xC1B6 entry point correctly so that both the X-register and Y-register will be preserved.

```
0xFBC1:
BASCALC     sty BASL        ; 0x28, preserve Y-reg
            ldy #2          ; index for XBASCLC routine
            bne GOTOROM     ; 0xFBB4, go to the CX ROM
FMT2        byt %00000000   ; first byte of table at 0xFBC7


0xC1B6:
XBASCLC     ldy BASL        ; 0x28, recover Y-reg
            jsr XBASCALC    ; 0xCABA, do the calculation
            bcc CXEXIT      ; 0xC208, always taken
```

Using the CX ROM BASCALC routine will provide enough room for the new 65C02 16-byte FMT2 table to reside in the Monitor beginning at 0xFBC7. Once the FMT2 table has been relocated there is enough address space starting at 0xF962 for the larger 65C02 FMT1, MNEML, and MNEMR tables leaving 4 unused bytes at 0xFA3C. The INSDS1 routine at 0xF882 needs a little modification in view of the new FMT1 and FMT2 tables, and there is just enough room to detect the relative (or zpage) opcode format (for example, LDA ($A5)). The various FMT2 tables I have seen usually contain the value 0x4B for the relative (or zpage) opcode format. The correct value is 0x49. In addition, this value is still unique among the other FMT2 table entries and using this value highly simplifies the code at 0xF8A5 to adjust the opcode index into the MNEML/MNEMR tables, the calculation of LENGTH, and the search for the correct opcode by the Mini-Assembler. The GETFMT routine is continued in the CX ROM at 0xC1D5 using a Y-register index of 16. The following code segment shows the necessary changes.

```
0xF8A5:
          tax                    ; FMT2 index
          lda FMT2,X             ; 0xFBC7, get opcode format
          cmp #$49               ; is it relative (zpage) format
          bne GETFMT1            ; 0xF8AE, if not this format
          dey                    ; correct the opcode index
;
GETFMT1   tax                    ; preserve opcode format
          sty BAS2L              ; 0x2A, preserve opcode index
          ldy #16                ; index for XGETFMT routine
          jmp GOTOROM            ; 0xFBB4, enter CX ROM

0xC1D5:
XGETFMT   txa                    ; recover opcode format
          sta FORMAT             ; 0x2E, save format
          and #3                 ; mask to extract length
          sta LENGTH             ; 0x2F, save length
          lda BAS2L              ; 0x2A, recover opcode index
          jmp XGETFMT2           ; 0xC5D5, continue processing
```

Some of the new 65C02 opcodes do not follow the general classification rules of the 6502 Instruction Set so they must be processed using a lookup table. This is what the XGETFMT2 code does at 0xC5D5 in combination with tables TBLC and TBLL which I placed at 0xCA71 instead of segmenting the XGETFMT2 code. Table TBLC at 0xCA71 contains the problem opcode index and table TBLL at 0xCA7D contains the new opcode index that indexes into the MNEML and MNEMR tables that contain the actual compressed ASCII of the opcode mnemonics. The Monitor STEP and TRACE commands as well as the GETNSP routine must now fit into the remaining space in the 0xC5 page from 0xC500 through 0xC5D4. Before the TRACE and STEPZ entry points can be restored to their "classic" entry location in the Monitor, the CXOFF1 and CXRTN entry points need to be moved. These four bytes fit nicely at 0xFA3C, just after the MNEMR data table mentioned earlier. The following code segments show the reintroduction of the TRACE and STEPZ entry points and their exit entry point STEPRTN that handles a BRK opcode, a ctrl-C key entry, and when STEP processing has completed. If the space bar is pressed, TRACE will pause until any key is pressed. If the ESC key is pressed during a TRACE pause, TRACE will exit cleanly. Either STEP or TRACE may be resumed after exiting TRACE. STEP and TRACE will now utilize the complete 65C02 Instruction Set.

```
0xFEC2:
TRACE       dec YSAV            ; 0x34, automatically repeat STEP
STEPZ       sta CXROMON         ; 0xC007, turn the CX ROM ON
            jmp CXSTEP          ; 0xC508, enter CXSTEP

0xFCCA:
STEPRTN     sta CXROMOFF        ; 0xC006, turn the CX ROM OFF
            bcs STEPRTN2        ; 0xFC5D, if a BRK occurred
            jmp NXTITM          ; 0xFF73, enter NXTITM

0xFC5D:
STEPRTN2    jmp OLDBRK          ; 0xFA59, enter OLDBRK
```

I know I have used the following Monitor instructions hundreds (or thousands?) of times to either clear memory or to set memory to a particular value.

```
*1000:0                 ; set 0x1000 to zero
*1001<1000.1FFEM        ; copy current data to next byte

*1000:FF                ; set 0x1000 to negative one
*1001<1000.1FFEM        ; copy current data to next byte
```

I do recall only one or two instances when I needed to search memory for certain bytes in order to defeat someone's copy protection algorithm. Now, having the Mini-Assembler in ROM allows me to enter a few lines of code, say at 0x300, to find any number of consecutive bytes in a range of memory either in Main or Auxiliary memory. Unfortunately, the Monitor SEARCH command does not search Auxiliary memory. Now that the STEP and TRACE commands have been fully integrated into the Monitor once again, the S command is taken by the STEP command and the SEARCH command must be either renamed or replaced. I chose to rename the SEARCH command to the X command for "eXamine" memory. Since there is no longer a need for a WRITE command at 0xFECD I believe a memory ZAP command would be the perfect replacement for that command. The ZAP command has the following syntax.

```
*00<1000.1FFFZ          ; change memory to zero
*FF<1000.1FFFZ          ; change memory to negative one
```

The following code can be placed at 0xFECD.

```
0xFECD:
ZAPMEM    lda A4L          ; 0x42, get value to set memory
          sta (A1L),Y      ; 0x3C, change memory
          jsr NXTA1        ; 0xFCBA, increment address
          bcc ZAPMEM       ; 0xFECD, continue if not done
          rts              ; return to 0xFF85
```

After removing the READ command at 0xFEFD and its return code CXOFF2 at 0xFF03, moving the GETNSP routine to 0xC500 where it belongs, and moving TITLE down from 0xFF0A to 0xFF05, the enhanced ASCII data input capability allows one to enter lower **and** upper ASCII data easily into memory. The following lines of Monitor instructions is an example showing how this is done.

```
*300:'A 'B 'C              ; enter 0x41, 0x42, 0x43 to 0x300
*303:"A "B "C              ; enter 0xC1, 0xC2, 0xC3 to 0x303
```

Instead of increasing the size of the CHRTBL table at 0xFFCC and the SUBTBL table at 0xFFE3, the Apple engineers added an additional routine called LOOKASC at 0xFF1B prior to entering DIG at 0xFF8A. This routine essentially accomplishes the ability to add additional commands to the Monitor's repertoire. Because there is now additional code space from 0xFF0F to 0xFF1B, why not enhance the utility and power of lower ASCII data input and modify the Apostrophe command used to enter lower ASCII data by including a QUOTE command to enter **upper** ASCII data? Also, can the LOOKASC routine be leveraged such that it can be used to enter the SEARCH command routine so that the ZAPMEM routine can be accessed by means of the CHRTBL/SUBTBL method like all other Monitor commands? Actually, the ZAPMEM routine must be accessed by means of the CHRTBL/SUBTBL method because it depends on having the Y-register initialized to 0x00 since there is not enough code space for the routine to do this. On the other hand, the SEARCH routine initializes the Y-register to the values it requires. Unfortunately, there is simply not enough code space to accomplish all of these wonderful ideas unless some serious changes are made in a few other Monitor routines.

Both the CX ROM and the 0xF0 ROM share a common routine to change lowercase characters to uppercase characters. There is absolutely no reason why the CX ROM routines cannot use part of the UPMON routine found at 0xFCFD and eliminate the UPRCASE routine found at 0xCE14. That space could be used by the XRDKEY originally found at 0xC2F2 since it only requires ten bytes of code space. Moving the routine XRDKEY to the 0xCE ROM page provides sufficient code space to the 0xC2 ROM page in order to allow an expansion of the XRESET routine originally found at 0xC2B0.

```
0xFCFD:
UPMON       lda INPUT,Y         ; 0x200, get next input character
            iny                 ; increment index
;
UPRCASE     cmp #"a"            ; is it a lowercase value
            bcc UPMON2          ; 0xFD0B, branch if less than
            cmp #"z"+1          ; is it within range
            bcs UPMON2          ; 0xFD0B, branch if out of range
            and #LWRMASK        ; 0xDF, make it uppercase
;
UPMON2      rts                 ; return to caller

0xCE14:
XRDKEY      ldy CH              ; 0x24, get cursor location
            lda (BASL),Y        ; 0x28, get screen character
            bit RDVID80         ; 0xC01F, is 80 column enabled
            bpl INVERT          ; 0xCE26, branch if not
            rts                 ; return to caller
;
            dfs 1,ZERO          ; add 1 byte of space
```

Both the RESET routine at 0xFA62 and the OLDRST routine at 0xFF59 share twelve bytes of common code. The OLDRST routine happens to be midway between the LOOKASC routine and the JMP instruction to LOOKASC at 0xFFBB. If the common code at OLDRST could be partially eliminated there would be sufficient code space to enhance the ASCII data input routine and provide a means to enter the SEARCH command routine. The following code shows how this can be done.

```
0xC2AE:
XRESET      lda ANN1OFF         ; 0xC058, turn annunciator 1 OFF
            lda ANN2OFF         ; 0xC05A, turn annunciator 2 OFF
            lda ANN3ON          ; 0xC05D, turn annunciator 3 ON
            lda ANN4ON          ; 0xC05F, turn annunciator 4 ON
            lda #NEGONE         ; 0xFF, get negative one
            sta XMODE           ; 0x4FB, initialize MODE
            ...
;
;
0xFA62:
RESET       cld                 ; clear decimal
            jsr RSETINIT        ; $FA6A, do the initialization
            ldy #9              ; index for XRESET routine
            bne RESET1          ; $FA78, skip over RSETINIT
;
```

```
RSETINIT   jsr SETNORM          ; 0xFE84, set normal video
           jsr INIT             ; 0xFB2F, init mode and window
           jsr SETVID           ; 0xFE93, init CSWL (or 0x36)
           jmp SETKBD           ; 0xFE89, init KSWL (or 0x38)
           dfs 2,ZERO           ; add 2 bytes of space
;
RESET1     jsr GOTOROM          ; 0xFBB4, enter CX ROM
           lda CLRROM           ; 0xCFFF, disable extension ROM
           bit CLRKEY           ; 0xC010, clear keyboard strobe
           ...
```

Now, working from upper memory to lower memory, the changes to the NXTCHR and OLDRST routines can be better appreciated.

```
0xFFAD:
NXTCHR     jsr UPMON            ; 0xFCFD, get next input char
           eor #"0"             ; extract number
           cmp #10              ; is it a decimal digit
           bcc DIG              ; 0xFF8A, process decimal digit
           adc #$88             ; shift value to get HEX digit
           cmp #$FA             ; is it a HEX digit
           bcs DIG              ; 0xFF8A, process HEX digit
           bcc LOOKASC0         ; 0xFF5F, process command
           ...
;
0xFF59:
OLDRST     jsr RSETINIT         ; 0xFA6A, do the initialization
           jmp MON              ; 0xFF65, enter Monitor
;
LOOKASC0   cmp #$89+$B0^"""     ; 0x9B, is it Quote command
           beq LOOKASC1         ; 0xFF18, process it (carry set)
           bne LOOKASC          ; 0xFF0F, continue
```

This six-byte space in the OLDRST routine area is just enough code space to eliminate the JMP instruction to LOOKASC at 0xFFBB and to provide the first check if there is a QUOTE command. The next two checks determine if there is a SEARCH command or an APOSTROPHE command at LOOKASC.

```
0xFF0F:
LOOKASC    cmp #$89+$B0^"X"        ; 0xF1, is it SEARCH command
           beq SEARCH              ; 0xFED7, process it
           cmp #$89+$B0^"'"        ; 0xA0, is it Apostrophe command
           bne IORTS              ; 0xFF58, branch if not (done)
           clc                    ; make sure carry flag is clear
;
LOOKASC1   php                    ; save processor status
           lda INPUT,Y            ; 0x0200, get the ASCII data
           cmp #RETURN            ; 0x8D, is it a premature end
           beq LOOKASC3          ; 0xFF2A, branch if so (done)
           plp                    ; recall processor status
           bcs LOOKASC2          ; 0xFF25, branch if Quote command
           and #MSBCLR            ; 0x7F, turn MSB OFF
;
LOOKASC2   ldx #7                 ; get ASL counter for NXTBIT
           iny                    ; point to next data byte
           bne NXTBIT             ; 0xFF90, always taken
;
LOOKASC3   plp                    ; recall processor status
           beq GETNUM             ; 0xFFA7, always taken
```

Entering the Monitor SEARCH command routine in this manner is certainly not normal, and its exit must be handled differently than the other CHRTBL/SUBTBL command routines. Also, I found that adding an extra carriage return at the conclusion of the routine's output highlights the addresses the routine finds. There are eight bytes free at 0xFEFD after the CRMON routine at 0xFEF6 and before the TITLE data in upper ASCII at 0xFF05. The return from the Mini-Assembler MINIASM routine fits nicely here, after CRMON where the READ routine used to be.

```
0xFED7:
SEARCH     ldy #1                 ; index to second search address
           lda A4H                ; 0x43, second search data
           beq SEARCH1           ; 0xFEE1, skip if none requested
           cmp (A1L),Y            ; 0x3C, check for match
           bne SEARCH2           ; 0xFEEB, skip if no match
;
SEARCH1    dey                    ; index to first search address
           lda A4L                ; 0x42, first search data
           cmp (A1L),Y            ; 0x3C, check for match
           bne SEARCH2           ; 0xFEEB, skip if no match
           jsr PRA1              ; 0xFD92, print A1H and A1L
;
```

81

```
SEARCH2    jsr NXTA1              ; 0xFCBA, increment address
           bcc SEARCH             ; 0xFED7, still in search range
           jsr CROUT              ; 0xFD8E, print carriage return
           jmp CRMON1             ; 0xFEF9, fix program counter
;
CRMON      jsr BL1                ; 0xFE00, process input SPACE
;
CRMON1     pla                    ; pop stack, low address byte
           pla                    ; pop stack, high address byte
           bne MONZ               ; 0xFF69, enter Monitor
;
MINIASM    ldy #13                ; index for XMINIASM
           jsr GOTOROM            ; 0xFBB4, enter CX ROM
           jmp CRMON              ; 0xFEF6, re-enter Monitor
;
TITLE      asc "Apple //e+"       ; screen title during autostart
           ...
```

This just about completes the changes I made to the Enhanced Apple //e Monitor firmware. One last detail is to integrate the ZAP memory command into the CHRTBL and SUBTBL tables in place of the SEARCH memory command. Once that is accomplished there is little if any unused code space left in the Monitor firmware except for a sum of 19 bytes, all in byte pairs except for one single byte instance. This is certainly not enough address space to get excited about. There are ten bytes of unused address space in the 0xC2 ROM page at 0xC2F6 as a result of moving the XRDKEY routine to 0xCE14.

As an exercise I was able to compact the RESET diagnostic routines residing in CX ROM pages 0xC6 and 0xC7 to gain an additional 34 bytes of address space without compromising the integrity of those routines. That turned out to be more effort than it was actually worth. Finally, I found that the RESET diagnostic routines do not play very well with the *Zip Chip* because the *Zip Chip* handles RESET activities internally before it releases the *INH* line so the MMU and IMU devices can initiate their internal switching. It only staggers the imagination what one could do with two pages of code space in lieu of the virtually useless RESET diagnostic routines that only provide a PASS result if no errors are encountered or a FAIL result when only the first error is encountered. What about subsequent errors?

I came away from my analysis of the CX ROM code realizing I know little if anything about the required ROM entry points that support Pascal processing. The 80-column video firmware residing in page 0xC3 of the CX ROM contains signature bytes at 0xC30B and 0xC30C followed by four offset bytes for the JPINIT, JPREAD, JPWRITE, and JPSTAT entry points. These entry points provide jump instructions for the INIT, READ, WRITE, and STATUS Pascal routines within the 0xC8 and 0xC9 pages of the CX ROM. What I am unclear about are the CX ROM entry points for PXINIT at 0xC800, a jump instruction to PINIT1 located at 0xC9B0, for PXREAD at 0xC84D, a jump instruction to JPREAD located at 0xC350, and for PXWRITE at 0xC9AA, a load and jump instruction to JPWRITE located at 0xC356. The addresses 0xC800, 0xC84D, and 0xC9AA appear to be hard-coded such that other CX ROM routines must span these specific addresses and/or entry points. I wonder if the original designers of the Pascal firmware failed to utilize a common jump-block structure strategy, perhaps at 0xC800, where the jump-block order of jump instructions can remain constant, thus allowing the addresses within the jump-block to change. Both Randall Hyde and Glen Bredon used this technique quite successfully when they designed *Lisa* and *Big Mac*, respectively. Both software engineers put their jump-block structures at the beginning of page 0xE0, the traditional entry point area for ROM software, like Applesoft does for its warm-start and cold-start entry points. If it is so important to support Pascal, then there is little choice but to "dance" around these hard-coded addresses. What I need to ascertain is what was the previous firmware that established the 0xC800, 0xC84D, and 0xC9AA addresses in the first place, and why the Pascal software engineer created these hard-coded addresses that surely would cause future issues.

It is quite straight forward to assemble the source code for the ROM firmware found on the ROM Source volume ROM.SW16.Source. This ROM firmware does not include the TAPEIN and TAPEOUT routines nor does it include the Apple //e Memory Test routines. This ROM firmware does include the Mini-Assembler, the complete 65C02 disassembler, the enhanced ASCII data input, STEP, TRACE, and ZAP commands, and the *SWEET16* Metaprocessor. It would take some effort to adapt this source code and its directives to another assembler other than *Lisa*. *Lisa* provides all the enhancements and directives necessary as well as the addition of new directives to provide a straightforward assembly. As discussed in Section IV.14, *Lisa* uses lower memory above 0x0800 for the object code, the source code, and the complete symbol table for the software that is currently being assembled.

To assemble the ROM.SW16 firmware, place the Image volume ROM.SW16.Image in disk drive 1 and boot the volume. *Lisa* will automatically load. Enter the SE command-line command to select the SETUP program in order to verify or set the Start of Source Code to 0x1A00 and the End of Source Code to 0x4A00. Place the ROM.SW16 Source volume ROM.SW16.Source in disk drive 2, load the ROM2E.L file into memory, and start the assembler by entering either the A command-line command or the Z command-line command. If a printed version of the screen output is desired, simply preface the A or Z command with the P1 command-line command. Four object code files will be generated on the Image volume: C0ROM, D0ROM, E0ROM, and F0ROM. The utility BLDROM can be used to combine the four object code files in memory sequentially starting at 0x1000, and the utility saves the complete ROM.SW16 firmware file SW16ROM and the two half-firmware files SW16ROM.A and SW16ROM.B to the Image volume. Now, the utility *BURNER* can used to program a 27128 EPROM using the firmware file SW16ROM or two 2764 EPROMs using the firmware files SW16ROM.A and SW16ROM.B.

It is beyond the scope of this book to describe and include all of the C language routines and programs I have created in the XQuartz environment that support and process Apple][DOS 4.1 volumes and files. Suffice it to say that ~.dsk files are simple binary files that begin with a 256-byte page of data for track 0x00, sector 0x00 and end with a 256-byte page of data for track 0x22, sector 0x0F. There are no headers that preface each of the 256-byte pages of data that label their track and sector numbers. I found that it was most efficient to read a ~.dsk file into a three-dimensional array defined as "UCHAR Disk[48][32][SECTOR_SIZE]" and base the Track and Sector maximum index values on the size of the ~.dsk file. For example, a ~.dsk file that is exactly 143360 bytes in size when opened will have a maximum of 35 tracks, each track having 16 sectors. A ~.dsk file that is exactly 393216 bytes in size when opened will have a maximum of 48 tracks, each track having 32 sectors. Of course, there are other quite valid algorithms to choose from. My programs can extract files from and insert files onto any DOS 4.1 ~.dsk volume simply by knowing the structure of Apple][files based on filetype and the structure of the DOS 4.1 VTOC and Catalog sectors. Once I extract all the files from an Image volume such as `ROM.SW16.Image`, I can easily create a ROM firmware file for Virtual][, like `APPLE2E.SW16.ROM`. I prefer to use the UNIX `tcsh` C shell environment for processing UNIX command files. Here are the entries in the command file `buildRom`:

```
cat d0rom e0rom f0rom > romA
cat c0rom romA > SW16.ROM
cat zeropage zeropage zeropage slot3 > rom1
cat zeropage zeropage slot6 zeropage > rom2
cat zeropage zeropage zeropage zeropage > rom3
cat rom1 rom2 rom3 rom3 romA > rom4
cat rom4 c0rom romA > APPLE2E.SW16.ROM
rm rom1 rom2 rom3 rom4 romA
```

All that is left to do is to copy the ROM firmware file `APPLE2E.SW16.ROM` to the Virtual][ROM directory found at:

`Users/<username>/Library/Application Support/Virtual ][/ROM`

The directory `Library` must be made visible, of course. Within Virtual][simply pull down the `Machine/Configure/Components/ROM` memory tab and select the button for `Use specific ROM`. The ROM firmware file `APPLE2E.SW16.ROM` can be selected from the ROM files listed. Be sure to save this version of Virtual][appropriately labeled.

Section II.5 discusses the Applesoft Garbage Collector. The source code for the modifications to the ROM firmware that supports my Applesoft garbage collector is found on the `ROM.SW16GC` Source volume `ROM.SW16GC.Source` and Image volume `ROM.SW16GC.Image`. The firmware files `SW16GCROM`, `SW16GCROM.A`, and `SW16GCROM.B` can be created using the same procedures as above. The resulting ROM firmware file `APPLE2E.SW16GC.ROM` can be copied to the `Virtual ][` ROM directory as well.

As mentioned earlier, the Applesoft `LOAD`, `RECALL`, `SAVE`, `STORE`, and `SHLOAD` commands are useless without the cassette tape `TAPEIN` and `TAPEOUT` routines, which were removed from the `0xC500` page in favor of the Mini-Assembler. Instead of replacing the calls to the `TAPEIN` and `TAPEOUT` routines with a call to `IORTS` at `0xFF58` as in the Source volume `ROM.SW16.Source`, I replaced the addresses to the Applesoft `LOAD`, `RECALL`, `SAVE`, `STORE`, and `SHLOAD` commands with a call to `IORTS` in the Source volume `ROM.SW16GC.Source`. Doing this frees a total of `0xAE` bytes for other processing and/or other Applesoft commands. The text of the Applesoft commands is located from `0xD0D0` to `0xD25F`, and the entry addresses of the commands are located from `0xD000` to `0xD0CF`. Table II.3.10 shows the available ROM space and its location when the Applesoft `LOAD`, `RECALL`, `SAVE`, `STORE`, and `SHLOAD` commands are disabled and effectively removed. I have no doubt that I will innovate a terrific use for this ROM memory space in the next development cycle.

84

Start	End	Length	Applesoft Commands
0xD8B0	0xD900	0x51	LOAD and SAVE
0xF39F	0xF3D7	0x39	STORE and RECALL
0xF775	0xF786	0x12	SHLOAD
0xF7D5	0xF7E6	0x12	GETARYPT

Table II.3.10. Disabled Applesoft Commands

4. SWEET16 Metaprocessor

SWEET16 is a "pseudo microprocessor" implemented in 6502 assembly language. Originally conceived and written by Steve "Woz" Wozniak, *SWEET16* and Integer BASIC were included in the ROM firmware of early Apple II computers. *SWEET16* is a really smart and useful extension to a 6502 based computer and it can be ported to other 6502 based systems to provide useful 16-bit functionality. It can be thought of as a virtual machine that gives the 6502 programmer a 16-bit extension to the 8-bit CPU. *SWEET16* utilizes sixteen 16-bit registers/pointers in page-zero and it provides new opcodes to use those registers. Although *SWEET16* instructions are not as fast as native 6502 instructions, they can reduce the code size of programs and ease some programming difficulties.

Steve Wozniak wrote "While writing Apple BASIC for the 6502 microprocessor, I repeatedly encountered a variant of Murphy's Law. Briefly stated, any routine operating on 16-bit data will require at least twice the code that it should. Programs making extensive use of 16-bit pointers such as compilers, editors, and assemblers are included in this category. In my case, even the addition of a few double-byte instructions to the 6502's Instruction Set would have only slightly alleviated the problem. What I really needed was a hybrid of the MOS Technology 6502 and RCA 1800 architectures: a powerful 8-bit data handler complemented by an easy to use processor with an abundance of 16-bit registers and excellent pointer capability. My solution was to implement a non-existent 16-bit "metaprocessor" in software, interpreter style, which I call *SWEET16*. *SWEET16* is based around sixteen 16-bit registers called R0 to R15, which are actually implemented as 32 memory locations. R0 doubles as the *SWEET16* Accumulator (or `ACC`), R15 as the Program Counter (or `PC`), and R14 as the Status Register. R13 holds compare instruction results and R12 is the Subroutine Return stack pointer if *SWEET16* subroutines are used. All other *SWEET16* registers are at the user's unrestricted disposal.

"*SWEET16* instructions fall into register and non-register categories. The register instructions specify one of the sixteen registers to be used as either a data element or as a pointer to data in memory, depending on the specific instruction. For example, the instruction `INR R5` uses R5 as a data register and `ST @R7` uses R7 as a pointer register to data in memory. Except for the `SET` instruction, register instructions require one byte. The non-register instructions are primarily 6502 style branch operations with the second byte specifying a +/- 127-byte displacement relative to the address of the following instruction. If a Prior Register (or `PR`) operation result meets a specified branch condition, the displacement is added to the *SWEET16* Program Counter, thus effecting a branch. *SWEET16* is intended as an enhancement package to the 6502 processor, not as a standalone processor. A 6502 program switches to *SWEET16* mode with a subroutine call, and subsequent code is interpreted as *SWEET16* instructions. The non-register instruction `RTN` returns the user program to the 6502's direct execution mode after restoring the A, X, Y, P, and S internal registers. Even though most opcodes are only one byte long, *SWEET16* runs approximately ten times slower than equivalent 6502 code, so it should be employed only when code is at a premium or execution is not. As an example of its usefulness, I have estimated that about 1K byte could be weeded out of my 5K byte Apple][BASIC interpreter with no observable performance degradation by selectively applying *SWEET16*."

SWEET16 was probably the least used and least understood seed in the original Apple][. In exactly the same sense that the Integer and Applesoft BASICs are languages, *SWEET16* is a language, too. Compared to the BASICs, however, it would be classified as lower level with a strong likeness to conventional 6502 Assembly language. Obviously, to use *SWEET16*, you must learn the language. And according to "Woz", "The opcode list is short and uncomplicated." *SWEET16* was ROM based in every early Apple][from `0xF689` to `0xF7FC`. It uses the `SAVE` and `RESTORE` routines in the Apple's Monitor to preserve the 6502 registers during its use, allowing *SWEET16* to be used as a subroutine. Table II.4.1 lists the *SWEET16* registers and the function of each register. The complete *SWEET16* Instruction Set is shown in Tables II.4.2 and II.4.3 listing each opcode, its mnemonic, and a brief description what the opcode does. Table II.4.2 lists the non-register opcodes and Table II.4.3 lists the register opcodes. In Table II.4.2 "ea" means "effective address."

Register	Description
R0	*SWEET16* Accumulator (ACC)
R1-R11	*SWEET16* user registers
R12	*SWEET16* subroutine return Stack Pointer (SP)
R13	*SWEET16* compare instruction results
R14	*SWEET16* Status Register (PR & carry flag)
R15	*SWEET16* Program Counter (PC)

Table II.4.1. SWEET16 Register Descriptions

Opcode	Mnemonic	Description
0x00	RTN	Return to 6502 mode to process native 6502 instructions
0x01	BR ea	Branch always to PC+ea+2→PC
0x02	BNC ea	Branch if prior operation left carry clear to PC+ea+2→PC
0x03	BC ea	Branch if prior operation left carry set to PC+ea+2→PC
0x04	BP ea	Branch if Prior Register is positive to PC+ea+2→PC
0x05	BM ea	Branch if Prior Register is negative to PC+ea+2→PC
0x06	BZ ea	Branch if Prior Register is zero to PC+ea+2→PC
0x07	BNZ ea	Branch if Prior Register is not zero to PC+ea+2→PC
0x08	BM1 ea	Branch if Prior Register is minus one to PC+ea+2→PC
0x09	BNM1 ea	Branch if Prior Register is not minus one to PC+ea+2→PC
0x0A	SOUT chr	Send character chr to COUT (originally the BK opcode)
0x0B	RS	Return from Subroutine, and POPD @SP→PC, SP=SP-2
0x0C	BS ea	Branch to Subroutine, and PC→STD @SP, SP=SP+2, PC+ea+2→PC
0x0D	RSNS	Return from Subroutine without stack, and SP→PC (originally unassigned opcode)
0x0E	BSNS ea	Branch to Subroutine without stack, and PC→SP, PC+ea+2→PC (originally unassigned opcode)
0x0F	SJMP adr	Jump to 16-bit address adr and adr-1→PC (originally unassigned opcode)

Table II.4.2. SWEET16 Non-Register Opcodes

Opcode	Mnemonic	Description
0x1n	SET Rn,val	Load Rn with 16-bit value `val`
0x2n	LD Rn	Load ACC from Rn, PR=n
0x3n	ST Rn	Store ACC into Rn, PR=n
0x4n	LD @Rn	Load LO ACC indirectly using Rn, HO ACC=0, Rn=Rn+1, PR=0
0x5n	ST @Rn	Store LO ACC indirectly using Rn, Rn=Rn+1, PR=0
0x6n	LDD @Rn	Load ACC indirectly using Rn, Rn=Rn+2, PR=0
0x7n	STD @Rn	Store ACC indirectly using Rn, Rn=Rn+2, PR=0
0x8n	POP @Rn	Rn=Rn-1, load LO ACC indirectly using Rn, HO ACC=0, PR=0
0x9n	STP @Rn	Rn=Rn-1, store LO ACC indirectly using Rn, PR=0
0xAn	ADD Rn	ACC = ACC + Rn, status = carry, PR=0
0xBn	SUB Rn	ACC = ACC – Rn, status = carry, PR=0
0xCn	POPD @Rn	Rn=Rn-2, load ACC indirectly using Rn, PR=0
0xDn	CPR Rn	R13 = ACC – Rn, status = carry, PR=13
0xEn	INR Rn	Rn = Rn + 1, PR=n
0xFn	DCR Rn	Rn = Rn – 1, PR=n

Table II.4.3. SWEET16 Register Opcodes

Glen Bredon utilized *SWEET16* extensively in his *Big Mac* software by incorporating the *SWEET16* interpreter within its source code since the interpreter did not exist in the Apple][+ or Apple //e ROMs. Mr. Bredon re-coded the NUL and BNM1 opcodes to provide other functions specific to his needs. He also did not use the R12 register as a Return from Subroutine stack pointer and he did not use the R14 register for the Prior Register and status. Rather than using a stack pointer at all, he simply saved the Return from Subroutine address at 0xDA/0xDB and the Prior Register and status at 0xFF. I am simply astounded at how easy it is to utilize the *SWEET16* instructions for any task that processes large sets of data, like in an assembler. In fact, the early versions of the S-C Assembler II used *SWEET16* in several locations. The TED/ASM assembler and all of its descendants, including the DOS Tool Kit, TED II+, Merlin, and many others, used *SWEET16* heavily. Several of the programs in the Apple Programmer's Aid ROM used *SWEET16* including the Integer BASIC Renumber/Append programs.

As Tables II.4.2 and II.4.3 show, the *SWEET16* opcode list is short and uncomplicated. Except for relative branch displacements, hand assembly is trivial. All register opcodes are formed by combining two hexadecimal digits, one for the opcode and one to specify a register. For example, opcodes 0x15 and 0x45 both specify register R5 while opcodes 0x23, 0x27, and 0x2B are all LD Rn instructions. Most register instructions are assigned in complementary pairs to facilitate remembering them. Thus, LD Rn and ST Rn are opcodes 0x2n and 0x3n respectively, while LD @Rn and ST @Rn are opcodes 0x4n and 0x5n. Opcodes 0x00 through 0x0F are assigned to the sixteen Non-Register Opcodes and opcodes 0x1n through 0xFn opcodes are assigned to the fifteen Register Opcodes. Except for the opcodes RTN (or 0x00), SOUT (or 0x0A), BS (or 0x0C), BSNS (or 0x0E), and SJMP (or 0x0F), the non-register opcodes are basic 6502 style branches. The second byte of a branch instruction contains a +/- 127-byte displacement value (in two's complement form) relative to the address of the instruction immediately following the branch. The SOUT (or 0x0A) opcode sends its second byte to COUT at 0xFDED. Of course, the SJMP opcode, like the SET opcode, takes its second and third byte to form a 16-bit address, or a 16-bit value in the case of SET. Before the BS/RS opcodes can be used, R12 must be initialized with the address of the stack that is configured to contain the Return from Subroutine addresses. The stack must be a buffer of sufficient size to hold n-levels of subroutine calls. If a specified branch condition is met by the Prior Register instruction result, the displacement is added to the Program Counter effecting a branch. Except for the BR (Branch always) opcode, the BS (Branch to a Subroutine) opcode, and the BSNS (Branch to a Subroutine without stack) opcode, the branch opcodes are assigned in complementary pairs, thus rendering them easily remembered for hand coding. For example, Branch if Plus and Branch if Minus are opcodes 0x04 and 0x05 respectively, while Branch if Zero and Branch if Not Zero are opcodes 0x06 and 0x07.

The original *SWEET16* software left the last three non-register opcodes unassigned, where any of them could be used as a NUL opcode, and the BK (Break, 0x0A) opcode simply executed a 6502 BRK instruction. The Prior Register and the carry status were both combined in the high order (or HO) byte of R14. I chose to separate the Prior Register and carry status into separate bytes of the R14 register in order to reduce the code size and number of execution cycles for all of the non-register operations. Doing this allowed the inclusion of three additional opcodes within the limited, single memory page boundary that must contain all the SW16 routines: Send character to COUT, Branch to Subroutine without stack, Return from Subroutine without stack, and Jump to Address. Incidentally, one can jump to an address using the other *SWEET16* opcodes, but it requires using two of them (SET and ST), and the address must be already decremented by one, or decremented using a third opcode, DCR. The new instruction, SJMP adr, will load the *SWEET16* Program Counter directly with adr-1.

My implementation of *SWEET16* saves the register number (i.e. the Prior Register) of the register receiving the value or change in value into the low order (or LO) byte of R14 when a register opcode is processed. If the register opcode is ADD, SUB, or CPR, I chose to save the state of the carry flag in bit 0 of the HO byte of R14. The reasons for doing this are quite compelling. Originally, the LO byte of R14 was not utilized by the SW16 interpreter, so it was available to the user. Personally, I found that unused byte to be virtually useless. So, if there was a way to transform that byte into a more useful function I was more inclined to adopt that strategy. Each time a non-register opcode is encountered, the original code used nine cycles in five bytes for part of the setup code, and ten additional bytes were used for five of the branch instructions. My implementation requires only eight cycles in five bytes for the setup code, and no additional bytes for the same five branch instructions. This does not seem like very much of a savings, one cycle for every invocation of a non-register opcode, but in data processing loops that execute many, many times, a single cycle of savings adds up. Mr. Bredon chose to use sixteen cycles in seven bytes for the same capability. While on the same subject, the SET command is another place where a few cycles can be saved just by using a different strategy. The original code used thirteen cycles in ten bytes to increment the SW16 Program Counter by two, not including its RTS instruction. My implementation requires only eleven cycles in ten bytes every time the SET command is utilized. Mr. Bredon requires thirty-five cycles in seven bytes for the same functionality. To me, that seems like a lot of overhead just to save three bytes. This simply exemplifies the observable fact that when code is made extremely compact, the price paid is usually slower execution.

As stated above, the original image of *SWEET16* was located in ROM from 0xF689 to 0xF7FC, so it was 372 bytes in size, though the last three bytes of the 0xF7 page were set to 0xFF. My implementation of *SWEET16* is exactly 400 bytes in size, though it includes four additional, and useful opcodes in my opinion. Previously, in Section II.3 I wrote "It only staggers the imagination what one could do with two pages of code space in lieu of the virtually useless RESET diagnostic routines that only provide a PASS result if no errors are encountered or a FAIL result when only the first error is encountered." I believe having the *SWEET16* Metaprocessor in the Apple //e CX ROM rather than the RESET diagnostic routines certainly makes a lot more sense to me. And, what's more, there is more than sufficient room for the interpreter in the CX ROM if, and only if, there is sufficient room for a calling and return location in the 0xF0 Monitor firmware. Having those ten bytes of unused address space in the 0xC2 ROM page at 0xC2F6 certainly does help, too.

I have revised the RESET interface yet again in order to provide a suitable ROM entry point for *SWEET16* at 0xFA72. I increased the entry address by one byte for XRESET to 0xC2AF because I believe a CLD instruction should be added to the DOCMD routine at 0xC22E before it makes a crucial hexadecimal calculation forming the "jump" address to some of the GOTOROM routines. Removing the test for the state of the solid Apple key and the jump to the DIAGS diagnostic routines certainly help in providing enough room for the instructions removed from RESET at 0xFA62 and relocated to 0xC2AF. Now there remains only seven bytes of unused address space in the 0xC2 ROM page at 0xC2F9. It is totally awesome after plugging in a newly programmed EPROM to have the *SWEET16* Metaprocessor at 0xFA72 ready to interpret any and all software routines containing *SWEET16* instructions. There remains the rare opportunity of what to do with the first 0x70 bytes that are still available in the 0xC6 ROM page.

```
0xC2AF:
XRESETX    cld                     ; clear decimal
           jsr RSETINIT            ; 0xFA66, do the initialization
           lda ANN1OFF             ; 0xC058, turn annunciator 1 OFF
           lda ANN2OFF             ; 0xC05A, turn annunciator 2 OFF
           lda ANN3ON              ; 0xC05D, turn annunciator 3 ON
           lda ANN4ON              ; 0xC05F, turn annunciator 4 ON
           lda #NEGONE             ; 0xFF, get negative one
           sta XMODE               ; 0x4FB, initialize MODE
;
;          lda PB2IN               ; 0xC062, get solid Apple key
;          bpl >1                  ; 0xC2C4, skip if not pressed
;          jmp DIAGS               ; 0xC600, go to DIAGS
;
^1         lda PB1IN               ; 0xC061, get open Apple key
           bpl CXRESET             ; 0xC2DF, switch in C3 ROM
           ...
           lda CLRROM              ; 0xCFFF, disable extension ROM
           bit CLRKEY              ; 0xC010, clear keyboard strobe
           rts                     ; return to caller

0xFA62:
RESET      ldy #9                  ; index for XRESET routine
           bne RESET1              ; $FA7E, skip over RSETINIT
;
RSETINIT   jsr SETNORM             ; 0xFE84, set normal video
           jsr INIT                ; 0xFB2F, init mode and window
           jsr SETVID              ; 0xFE93, init CSWL (or 0x36)
```

90

```
            jmp SETKBD              ; 0xFE89, init KSWL (or 0x38)
;
SWEET16     sta CXROMON             ; 0cC007, turn the CX ROM ON
            jmp SW16                ; 0xC670, enter the SWEET16
SW16RTN     sta CXROMOFF            ; 0xC006, turn the CX ROM OFF
            jmp (R15L)              ; 0x1E, return to 6502 user code
;
RESET1      jsr GOTOROM             ; 0xFBB4, enter CX ROM
;
NEWMON      cld                     ; clear decimal
            ...
```

5. Applesoft Garbage Collector

The Applesoft Garbage Collector routine GARBAG is located in ROM from 0xE484 to 0xE597, and that routine moves all currently active string variables up in String Pool memory as far as possible. There are several routines in ROM that rely on the garbage collector, as well as the Applesoft command "FRE(*aexpr*)", to consolidate the Character String Pool when there is not enough Free Space memory as shown in Figure I.13.1 to perform the requested string variable manipulation. When certain conditions are met while these ROM routines process character string data, GARBAG is called, and depending on how many variables are active, the processing time for GARBAG is proportional to the square of the number of active strings currently in use. This processing time may be a few seconds if there are less than fifty active strings, or many minutes if there are hundreds of active strings. It may even appear as if the Applesoft program has literally stopped, or hanged, for no apparent reason. In section I.13 I even suggested that strategically placing multiple Applesoft "FRE(*aexpr*)" commands throughout an Applesoft program may help to alleviate processing delays.

Many years ago Cornelis Bongers of Erasmus University in Rotterdam, Netherlands, published a brilliant Garbage Collector algorithm for Applesoft strings in *Micro* in August, 1982. According to an article in *Apple Assembly Line*, March, 1984, the speed of his program was incredible when compared to the GARBAG algorithm in ROM. And the processing time for his algorithm was directly proportional to the number of active strings, rather than to the number of active strings squared. The only problem with his algorithm was that the magazine that published it owned the algorithm. Worse yet, the algorithm was tied to a program called *Ampersoft*, marketed by Microsparc, then publishers of *Nibble* magazine. It was reported that a license to use Bongers' algorithm was very costly at that time.

Referring back to Table I.13.1 which shows the definition of a simple string variable descriptor as it is found in the Simple Variables memory area and to Table I.13.2 which shows the definition of an array string variable descriptor as it is found in the Array Variables memory area, Bongers introduced the idea of marking active strings located in the Character String Pool memory area: he set the third byte in the string data to an upper ASCII value and swapped in the address of the string descriptor for the first two bytes of the string data. Also during this first pass through the Simple Variables and Array Variables memory area, he saved those first two bytes of the string data safely in the address field of its descriptor or string element. The address previously in the address field would be changed anyway after all the strings are moved up in memory to their final location. The second pass through the Character String Pool memory area moved all active strings as high in memory as they could go, retrieved the first two characters from storage in its descriptor or string element, and updated the address field to the new memory location for that string.

Bongers' algorithm is most efficient when the active strings are a least three bytes in length, so one- and two-character strings require different handling. On the first pass through the Simple Variables and Array Variables memory area, the first byte of string data pointed to by these "short" descriptors is stored in the string length byte of its descriptor. If the string length is two, the second data byte is stored in the low address byte of its descriptor. For one-character strings the low address byte is flagged with an 0xFF byte. The high address byte in all "short" descriptors is flagged with an 0xFF byte since no string can have an address greater than 0xFF00. If "short" strings are found during the first pass, a third pass returns them to the string pool with their descriptors updated to their new memory location. "Short" strings do slow down Bongers' algorithm a little. However, the number of passes is still proportional to the number of active strings, and not to the number of active strings squared. Tables II.5.1 and II.5.2 illustrate Bongers' algorithm during the first pass.

Table II.5.1. Simple Variable Descriptor Processing in Pass 1

ADL/ADH Descriptor Before Pass 1							⇒	ADL/ADH Descriptor After Pass 1						
+AS	−AS	1	LSB	MSB	0	0		+AS	−AS	41	FF	FF	0	0

LSB/MSB Memory Before Pass 1							⇒	LSB/MSB Memory After Pass 1						
41								41						

ADL/ADH Descriptor Before Pass 1							⇒	ADL/ADH Descriptor After Pass 1						
+AS	−AS	2	LSB	MSB	0	0		+AS	−AS	41	42	FF	0	0

LSB/MSB Memory Before Pass 1							⇒	LSB/MSB Memory After Pass 1						
41	42							41	42					

ADL/ADH Descriptor Before Pass 1							⇒	ADL/ADH Descriptor After Pass 1						
+AS	−AS	>2	LSB	MSB	0	0		+AS	−AS	LEN	41	42	0	0

LSB/MSB Memory Before Pass 1							⇒	LSB/MSB Memory After Pass 1						
41	42	43	44	45	46	47		ADL	ADH	C3	44	45	46	47

Table II.5.1. Simple Variable Descriptor Processing in Pass 1

Table II.5.2. Array Variable Element Processing in Pass 1

ADL/ADH Element Before Pass 1			⇒	ADL/ADH Element After Pass 1		
1	LSB	MSB		41	FF	FF

LSB/MSB Memory Before Pass 1			⇒	LSB/MSB Memory After Pass 1		
41				41		

ADL/ADH Element Before Pass 1			⇒	ADL/ADH Element After Pass 1		
2	LSB	MSB		41	42	FF

LSB/MSB Memory Before Pass 1			⇒	LSB/MSB Memory After Pass 1		
41	42			41	42	

ADL/ADH Element Before Pass 1			⇒	ADL/ADH Element After Pass 1		
>2	LSB	MSB		LEN	41	42

LSB/MSB Memory Before Pass 1							⇒	LSB/MSB Memory After Pass 1						
41	42	43	44	45	46	47		ADL	ADH	C3	44	45	46	47

Table II.5.2. Array Variable Element Processing in Pass 1

Pass two in Bongers' algorithm uses only the information in the String Pool to move all currently active string variables up in String Pool memory as far as possible. This is accomplished by initializing a pool pointer and a string pointer to HIMEM and searching down to FRETOP for any upper ASCII bytes. Once an upper ASCII byte has been found, its string descriptor is located at the address found two bytes before the upper ASCII byte. That string descriptor contains the length of the string and the first two ASCII characters of the string. Those two characters may be safely moved back to the string and the upper ASCII byte changed to a lower ASCII byte. Now, the string length can be subtracted from the current string pointer address, the new string address can be copied to the second and third byte in its string descriptor, and the string can be copied to its new string address location. However, the string must be copied from its last character backward to prevent possibly overwriting part of the string if the string were to be copied from its first character forward. Once the pool pointer reaches the original address in FRETOP, the current string pointer address becomes the new address in FRETOP if the "short" descriptors flag is clear.

If the "short" descriptors flag is set then a third pass must be made through the Simple Variables and Array Variables memory area. A memory pointer is initialized to VARTAB and the 0xFF marker is searched for in either the fifth byte of a Simple Variable descriptor or the third byte of an Array Variable element. If there is also an 0xFF marker in the prior byte then the descriptor is for a one-character string, otherwise the descriptor is for a two-character string. The current string pointer is adjusted for one or two characters, the string data is copied from its descriptor to the string pool, and the string pointer address is copied to its string descriptor. Once the memory pointer reaches STREND, the current string pointer address becomes the new address in FRETOP.

It must be emphasized that Bongers' algorithm depends on two important caveats: normal Applesoft programs save all string data in lower ASCII, i.e. with the high-order bit of each data byte cleared to zero, and normal Applesoft programs never allow more than one string descriptor to point to the same exact copy of that string in memory. If a user should program something like "A$ = CHR$(193)", Bongers' algorithm will fail. If an assembly language program should modify two string descriptors to point to the same string in the Character String Pool, Bongers' algorithm will fail. Therefore, reasonable care must be given to creating an Applesoft program and/or assembly language programs that take the above caveats seriously in order to exact the stupendous benefit in using a garbage collector routine located in ROM that is based on Bongers' algorithm.

Armed with only the above information, my attempt to recreate Bongers' algorithm resulted in an assembly language program that was 0x200 bytes in size. This necessitated creating a suitable Applesoft test program that would verify the accuracy of my program and confirm that no character string was altered in length, modified in content, or destroyed. My ultimate goal would be to replace GARBAG in ROM with my version of Bongers' algorithm. GARBAG occupies 0x113 bytes of ROM and there is 0x70 bytes of memory available in the CX ROM from 0xC600 to 0xC66F (0xC670 is where the *SWEET16* program begins). If the CX ROM is used then CX ROM management must also be incorporated. All totaled my garbage routine must fit within 0x183 bytes if it is to be located in ROM. On the other hand, my garbage routine, after some adjustment, could be attached to an Applesoft program and simply called prior to issuing the DOS CHAIN command providing that the R keyword is utilized with CHAIN. At least that would mitigate having GARBAG called in this particular instance. Periodically, the Applesoft program could check the remaining Free Space memory and call its attached garbage routine based on reasonable criteria. There is still much indeterminacy whether a particular character string manipulation will trigger a call to GARBAG. If that should happen Applesoft processing could come to a grinding halt until the Character String Pool has been processed.

In order to compact an assembly language routine certain decisions must be made that, hopefully, will not cause the introduction of more processor cycles than absolutely necessary. Example strategies would be to limit subroutine calls in the inner-most loops and to limit the pushing and popping of variables onto the stack. Sometimes simply reorganizing the order of a number of processing loops can greatly simplify the code and reduce the reinitialization of registers. Keeping a variable's MSB address in a register when addresses are compared can often help simplify and accelerate the code as well. I have no doubt that Mr. Bongers could have condensed his algorithm down to `0x183` bytes (with six bytes required for `CX` ROM management). My initial attempt to condense my garbage routine could not meet the goal of `0x183` bytes unless I removed the flag that signaled whether a third pass was necessary, and so the routine always made a third pass. Many times it is helpful to just take a break from a difficult programming task like this one, and work on something else. Thus, when I returned to my garbage routine I took a fresh look and I found several additional strategies that could condense the code even further allowing the reintroduction of the third pass flag. I was able to fit one segment into the `0x70` bytes located in the `CX` ROM and the other segment into the `0x113` bytes where `GARBAG` resided. All that was left to do was the testing, the timing, and the verification.

As mentioned earlier a verification test must prove that no character string was altered in length, modified in content, or destroyed by the garbage collector routine. The test results of the new routine must be identical to the results obtained using the original `GARBAG` routine. And since there is a DOS 4.1 `DATE` command available, each pass through the string array variables can be easily time stamped. The Applesoft test created three two-dimension character string arrays where both dimensions were set to twenty-six. Each string array element was initialized with a single character that was "forced" into the Character String Pool. On each successive pass another character was added to each element within the dimension that was being processed from one to twenty-six. This caused the utilization of memory to grow larger (or faster) on each successive pass. Before each pass, I monitored the size of Free Space memory. If Free Space memory was less than 15,000 bytes I issued the Applesoft "FRE(*aexpr*)" command forcing the garbage collector to process the String Pool. I obtained identical memory results for each and every pass in my Applesoft test program whether I used the original `GARBAG` routine in ROM or my new garbage collector routine in ROM. The timing results of my test program are shown in Table II.5.3. After the Pass Number, the next three columns summarize the results obtained from the original `GARBAG` routine. The time each pass began is shown in the first column. If the Free Space memory fell below 15,000 bytes another timestamp was recorded after a call to "FRE(*aexpr*)" was made. This timestamp is shown in the middle column. The delta time the routine required for its processing is shown in the next column. The right three columns contain the same information for my new garbage collector routine.

My implementation of Bongers' algorithm shows how amazing this routine is. Table II.5.3 shows only a peek at what this routine can actually do. When I changed the Free Space memory parameter from 15,000 to 5,000 bytes, the Applesoft program calling the original `GARBAG` routine could not complete, even after an hour, so I terminated it. The Applesoft program using my new garbage collector routine completed in 06:54 minutes, and twenty-four of the twenty-six possible passes finished. Table II.5.3 shows that only eighteen of the twenty-six possible passes finished before insufficient memory remained. Finally, I booted DOS 4.1H because it provides far more Free Space memory before `0xC000`, I removed the `HIMEM` command in the Applesoft program, and I removed all Free Space memory size checks. The program completed all twenty-six passes for both the original and my new version of the garbage collector. The program using the original `GARBAG` routine in ROM completed in 01:11:46 hours and the program using my new version of the garbage collector routine in ROM completed in 00:07:40 hours, or 01:04:06 hours faster. My new version of the garbage collector routine was 9.36 times faster than the original GARBAG routine in ROM for this particular test.

Pass Number	Original Garbage Collector			New Garbage Collector		
	Time	<15000	Delta	Time	<15000	Delta
0	00:00			00:00		
1	00:02			00:02		
2	00:05			00:05		
3	00:09			00:09		
4	00:14			00:14		
5	00:21			00:20		
6	00:28			00:28		
7	00:37			00:36		
8	00:47	01:26	00:39	00:46	00:47	00:01
9	02:37			00:58		
10	02:49	04:55	02:06	01:10	01:12	00:02
11	05:11			01:25		
12	05:25	07:57	02:32	01:39	01:41	00:02
13	08:13	11:08	02:55	01:56	01:58	00:02
14	11:29	14:31	03:02	02:15	02:16	00:01
15	14:59	18:12	03:13	02:34	02:36	00:02
16	18:36	21:59	03:23	02:55	02:56	00:01
17	22:27	26:00	03:33	03:17	03:19	00:02
18	30:27	34:14	03:47	03:42	03:43	00:01
	34:40			03:43		

Table II.5.3. Garbage Collector Timing Results

6. Apple Character Generator ROM

Virtual][, Gerard Putter's MacOS application to emulate the Apple][computer, provides the capability to use a personally designed ASCII character set. The character set is defined by a bitmap file that is either a PNG or TIFF file exactly 128 pixels wide and exactly 64 pixels high, and the bitmap depth must be one or eight pixels. Each character in the bitmap file is defined in a character cell that is eight pixels by eight pixels. Because characters displayed on the Apple][are only seven pixels wide, the right most column of the character cell is ignored by Virtual][. The black pixels within a character cell comprise the background of the character; all other pixels comprise the character itself. The location "Users/<username>/Library/Application Support/Virtual][/CharacterSets" must be used for the bitmap file. The Virtual][documentation suggests using the filename MyCharacters.tif for the bitmap file. An XML file called International.plist must also be located in this directory and it defines the name of the bitmap character set file. This XML file may include the name of an icon bitmap file called MyCharSetIcon.tif that can be up to sixteen pixels wide by eleven pixels high. The XML file may also include a keyboard translation table if that is needed as well. The XML file I created is shown in Figure II.6.1 and it includes two character set bitmap files.

I used Xcode to easily create the XML file. Any "Property List Editor" will work as well. To create the TIFF bitmap files I used the MacOS Paintbrush application because it was available for download at no charge. I am not an expert Paintbrush user and I had some difficulties with the application to produce what I wanted easily. Most of my difficulties occurred when I tried to save my work during incremental stages of testing. I found that if I used the Lasso tool to copy the entire bitmap area into the clipboard, I could save the contents of the clipboard into a new bitmap file of the same size, and then discard the original file. I do not know why the "save" or "save as" option failed to save my incremental work to the original file, and why I had to save my work in such a round-about way. I used the Line tool configured for a "stroke" of one to toggle a pixel from black to white or from white to black. Paintbrush saved the bitmap file as a TIFF file having a Color Space of RGB, a Color Profile of Generic RGB Profile, and the Alpha Channel set to Yes. I have no idea what these specifications mean or imply, but Virtual][had no problem reading and utilizing all the TIFF files I created in this manner.

My greatest source of irritation came when I discovered that the "Library" directory specified in the pathname above is a hidden file by default. I lost more time putting the XML and TIFF files in the wrong location because I could not see the hidden Library directory in my personal Users account. Once I realized this directory was hidden, it was extremely easy to unhide it using XQuartz or the Terminal application found in the Utilities directory. Simply launch the Terminal application and enter bash on the command line. This will start the GNU "Bourne-Again SHell." Now, when you enter the UNIX command ls at /Users/<username>, all files, including "." files, hidden files, and directories, will be displayed. Now enter the command "chflags nohidden Library" and have a look at a Finder window of your personal Users account. You should now see a "Library" directory. Once you have properly located all the XML and TIFF files you have created, and then launch Virtual][, select Quick settings>Character Set>My character set. Be sure to save your Virtual][session when you are satisfied with the selected character set bitmap file: it will be loaded and selected every time you launch Virtual][.

Figures II.6.2 and II.6.3 show the MyNewCharacters.tif and MyCharSetIcon.tif files I created for Virtual][. I modified quite a few of the characters to my preference. Once I was satisfied with my character set bitmap, I created a simple tool using LORES graphics that allowed me to create a 4 KB binary character set ROM file. This file must also contain the inverse characters as well as the alternate keyboard characters which are not included as shown in Figure II.6.2. I found it was easier to read the character generator ROM using the PROmGRAMER, display its character data using my LORES tool, and then edit a copy of each character which is displayed to the right of the original character as shown in Figure II.6.4. Once I made all the changes to the character set, I saved the data currently in memory to another binary ROM file and programmed that data into an equivalent sized 2732 EPROM. All my Apple][computers use the character set shown in Figure II.6.2.

Key	Type	Value
▼ Root	Dictionary	(2 items)
▼ My new character set	Dictionary	(3 items)
CharacterSet	String	MyNewCharacters.tif
Icon	String	MyCharSetIcon.tif
▶ KeyboardTranslation	Dictionary	(0 items)
▼ My old character set	Dictionary	(3 items)
CharacterSet	String	MyOldCharacters.tif
Icon	String	MyCharSetIcon.tif
▶ KeyboardTranslation	Dictionary	(0 items)

Figure II.6.1. International XML File

Figure II.6.2. Inverse of New Character Set TIFF Bitmap File

98

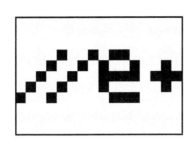

Figure II.6.3. Icon TIFF Bitmap File

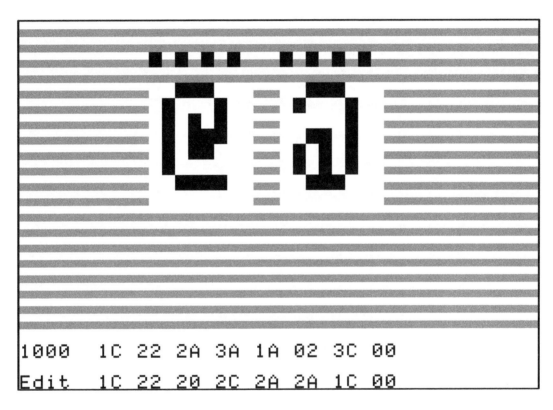

Figure II.6.4. Binary Character Set LORES Editor

7. Peripheral Slot Card Signature Bytes

Most likely Apple Computer designed the concept of Signature Bytes when it first marketed the Disk][floppy disk drive. The first eight bytes of the firmware on the peripheral slot card that connects the Disk][drive to the Apple][computer are defined as the Signature Bytes for this slot card. Other manufactures of peripheral slot cards adopted this scheme so that each slot card could be identified (potentially) by inspecting these first eight bytes. Slot cards that interface disk drives like the Disk][used this scheme developed by Apple Computer. Real time clock cards used the scheme found on the ThunderClock clock card. Similarly, signature byte schemes were developed for printer interface slot cards, serial data interface slot cards, mouse interface slot cards, and display interface slot cards to list a few examples. Each scheme has a general pattern that contains identical portions and unique portions of bytes. Table II.7.1 lists the signature bytes for a number of peripheral slot cards that I happen to own.

All of the odd signature bytes for peripheral slot cards that interface disk drives are the same. This is done purposefully because the Autostart ROM that Apple Computer copyrighted in 1978 checks these four particular bytes during powerup or restart. However, the Autostart routine was modified for the Apple //e Video Firmware, copyrighted in 1981 and in 1984. According to the firmware notes:

```
Check 3 ID bytes instead of 4.  Allows devices
other than Disk II's to be bootable.
```

In other words, only the first three odd signature bytes are checked by the Apple //e Autostart ROM for a bootable disk drive. After analyzing the disk startup firmware that follows the eight signature bytes for the Disk][peripheral slot card shows that upon entry the Y-register must be 0x00, the X-register can be any value from 0x00 to 0x16, and the A-register can be any value. The page-zero location 0x3C is a temporary storage location so any value can be stored there as done in the fourth instruction, "STX $3C". The first instruction, "LDX #$20", does nothing since the third, and critical instruction rewrites the value of the X-register.

Apparently, Applied Engineering used the same signature bytes for their TimeMaster II firmware as found in the ThunderClock firmware. Only the first two bytes are significant as well as the last byte on that firmware page. The last byte, or CLKID for the ThunderClock firmware is 0x07 and the last byte for the TimeMaster II firmware is 0x03. The last byte for my clock card firmware is also 0x03. It is these three bytes, the first two and the last, that DOS 4.1 checks for a valid clock card.

In many cases a peripheral slot card not only must be compatible with DOS, but with possibly ProDOS, CP/M, and Pascal as well. The peripheral-card ROM memory and the peripheral-card expansion ROM memory amounts to only nine pages of code space. Therefore, even the signature bytes must perform a necessary function besides being unique to the particular peripheral slot card. In some cases the signature bytes provide multiple return entry points for input and output data control. If the peripheral slot card supports Pascal, the Pascal initialization, read, write, and status routine offsets closely follow the signature bytes.

Slot Card	0	1	2	3	4	5	6	7
Disk][	LDX	#$20	LDY	#$00	LDX	#$03	STX	$3C
	0xA2	0x20	0xA0	0x00	0xA2	0x03	0x86	0x3C
SCSI][	LDX	#$20	LDX	#$00	LDX	#$03	LDX	#$00
	0xA2	0x20	0xA2	0x00	0xA2	0x03	0xA2	0x00
Rana	LDX	#$20	LDY	#$00	LDX	#$03	LDX	#$3C
	0xA2	0x20	0xA0	0x00	0xA2	0x03	0xA2	0x3C
Sider	LDA	#$20	LDA	#$00	LDA	#$03	LDA	$3C
	0xA9	0x20	0xA9	0x00	0xA9	0x03	0xA9	0x3C
RAM Disk	LDX	#$20	LDY	#$00	LDX	#$03	STY	$3C
	0xA2	0x20	0xA0	0x00	0xA2	0x04	0x84	0x3C
CFFA	LDA	#$20	LDX	#$00	LDA	#$03	LDA	#$00
	0xA9	0x20	0xA2	0x00	0xA9	0x03	0xA9	0x00
ThunderClock	PHP	SEI	PLP	BIT	$FF58		BVS	$Cs0D
	0x08	0x78	0x28	0x2C	0x58	0xFF	0x70	0x05
TimeMaster II	PHP	SEI	PLP	BIT	$FF58		BVS	$Cs0D
	0x08	0x78	0x28	0x2C	0x58	0xFF	0x70	0x05
My Clock	PHP	SEI	BIT	$CFFF		CLR	BCC	$Cs38
	0x08	0x78	0x2C	0xFF	0xCF	0x18	0x90	0x30
SuperSerial	BIT	$FF58		BVS	$Cs11	SEC	BCC	$Cs20
	0x2C	0x58	0xFF	0x70	0x0C	0x38	0x90	0x18
Grappler	CLC	BCS	$Cs3B	BCC	$Cs11	SEC	BCC	$Cs20
	0x18	0xB0	0x38	0x90	0x0C	0x38	0x90	0x18
Mouse	BIT	$FF58		BVS	$Cs20	SEC	BCC	$Cs20
	0x2C	0x58	0xFF	0x70	0x1B	0x38	0x90	0x18
80 Column	BIT	$CE43		BCS	$C317	SEC	BCC	CLC
	0x2C	0x43	0xCE	0x70	0x12	0x38	0x90	0x18

Table II.7.1. Peripheral Slot Card Signature Bytes

The firmware I wrote for the Rana is only dependent on the second signature byte instruction, "LDY #$00", at bootup. The Sider, RAM Disk 320, and CFFA firmware I wrote is not dependent on any of the signature byte instructions. Since the operation of the first signature byte instruction is not used, any of the other ten 6502 Immediate Addressing Mode instructions can be used as a device identifier within the general category of floppy disk drives. Once I realized which were the important and which were the unimportant bytes within the signature byte data, I could design a very simple strategy to quickly identify a Disk][signature byte scheme by checking the first three odd bytes like the Apple //e Autostart ROM does, and use the first instruction byte to select the actual device. Table II.7.2 lists the revised signature bytes for my collection of Disk][, Disk][-like, and disk drive peripheral devices.

Slot Card	0	1	2	3	4	5	6	7
Disk][	LDX	#$20	LDY	#$00	LDX	#$03	STX	$3C
	0xA2	0x20	0xA0	0x00	0xA2	0x03	0x86	0x3C
SCSI][	LDX	#$20	LDX	#$00	LDX	#$03	LDX	#$00
	0xA2	0x20	0xA2	0x00	0xA2	0x03	0xA2	0x00
Rana	ORA	#$20	LDY	#$00	LDX	#$03	STX	$3C
	0x09	0x20	0xA0	0x00	0xA2	0x03	0x86	0x3C
Sider	AND	#$20	LDY	#$00	LDX	#$03	STX	$3C
	0x29	0x20	0xA0	0x00	0xA2	0x03	0x86	0x3C
RAM Disk	EOR	#$20	LDY	#$00	LDX	#$03	STX	$3C
	0x49	0x20	0xA0	0x00	0xA2	0x03	0x86	0x3C
CFFA	ADC	#$20	LDY	#$00	LDX	#$03	STX	$3C
	0x69	0x20	0xA0	0x00	0xA2	0x03	0x86	0x3C
available	LDA	#$20	LDY	#$00	LDX	#$03	STX	$3C
	0xA9	0x20	0xA0	0x00	0xA2	0x03	0x86	0x3C
available	CMP	#$20	LDY	#$00	LDX	#$03	STX	$3C
	0xC9	0x20	0xA0	0x00	0xA2	0x03	0x86	0x3C
available	SBC	#$20	LDY	#$00	LDX	#$03	STX	$3C
	0xE9	0x20	0xA0	0x00	0xA2	0x03	0x86	0x3C
available	LDY	#$20	LDY	#$00	LDX	#$03	STX	$3C
	0xA0	0x20	0xA0	0x00	0xA2	0x03	0x86	0x3C
available	CPY	#$20	LDY	#$00	LDX	#$03	STX	$3C
	0xC0	0x20	0xA0	0x00	0xA2	0x03	0x86	0x3C
available	CPX	#$20	LDY	#$00	LDX	#$03	STX	$3C
	0xE0	0x20	0xA0	0x00	0xA2	0x03	0x86	0x3C

Table II.7.2. Revised Disk Drive Peripheral Slot Card Signature Bytes

III. DOS 4.1 Commands

DOS 4.1 commands comprise a set of commands in addition to the Applesoft ROM commands. As in Applesoft commands, DOS 4.1 commands and keywords may be entered in uppercase and/or lowercase. DOS 4.1 uses a number of data tables in order to process a valid DOS command when it is found in the DOS Command Name Text table. This table consists of the DCI ASCII name for each DOS command in the order of command index value. The Command Valid Keyword table is used to determine which keywords if any are required or may be used in conjunction with each DOS command index. Each command has a two-byte table entry, thus providing 16 possible bit flags indicating which keywords are legal, or if a filename is expected, for example. The bit flag settings for the DOS Command Valid Keywords are defined in Table III.0.1. The legal keywords have been ordered in a more logical and useful way from the order used in DOS 3.3. Before processing a valid DOS 4.1 command, the value of the R keyword is copied to the File Manager SUBCODE variable. This allows users of the external File Manager handler to utilize the SUBCODE in order to simulate the R keyword as in the case of the File Manager FMCATACD command for CATALOG. The DOS INIT command, however, overwrites the SUBCODE variable with DOSFLAGS for its own specific use as shown previously in Figure I.9.5.

Bit	Bit Position	Value	Flag Bit Description
15	%1000 0000 0000 0000	0x8000	Filename legal but optional
14	%0100 0000 0000 0000	0x4000	Command has no positional operands
13	%0010 0000 0000 0000	0x2000	Filename #1 expected
12	%0001 0000 0000 0000	0x1000	Filename #2 expected
11	%0000 1000 0000 0000	0x0800	Slot number positional operand is expected
10	%0000 0100 0000 0000	0x0400	MAXFILES value expected as positional operand
9	%0000 0010 0000 0000	0x0200	Command is only issued from within a program
8	%0000 0001 0000 0000	0x0100	Command creates a new file if the file is not found
7	%0000 0000 1000 0000	0x0080	C, I, O keywords are legal
6	%0000 0000 0100 0000	0x0040	S keyword is legal
5	%0000 0000 0010 0000	0x0020	D keyword is legal
4	%0000 0000 0001 0000	0x0010	V keyword is legal
3	%0000 0000 0000 1000	0x0008	A keyword is legal
2	%0000 0000 0000 0100	0x0004	L keyword is legal
1	%0000 0000 0000 0010	0x0002	R keyword is legal
0	%0000 0000 0000 0001	0x0001	B keyword is legal

Table III.0.1. DOS 4.1 Command Valid Keyword Table

Command Name	Index	ASCII Text	S/W Handler	Keyword
CMDINIT	0x00	INIT	DOINIT	0x317F
CMDLOAD	0x02	LOAD	DOLOAD	0xA072
CMDSAVE	0x04	SAVE	DOSAVE	0xA173
CMDRUN	0x06	RUN	DORUN	0xA074
CMDCHAIN	0x08	CHAIN	DOCHAIN	0x2274
CMDDELET	0x0A	DELETE	DODELETE	0x2070
CMDLOCK	0x0C	LOCK	DOLOCK	0x2070
CMDUNLCK	0x0E	UNLOCK	DOUNLOCK	0x2070
CMDCLOSE	0x10	CLOSE	DOCLOSE	0x6000
CMDREAD	0x12	READ	DOREAD	0x2203
CMDEXEC	0x14	EXEC	DOEXEC	0x2072
CMDWRITE	0x16	WRITE	DOWRITE	0x2203
CMDPOSTN	0x18	POSITION	DOPSTION	0x2202
CMDOPEN	0x1A	OPEN	DOOPENTX	0x2374
CMDAPND	0x1C	APPEND	DOAPND	0x2270
CMDRENAM	0x1E	RENAME	DORENAME	0x3070
CMDCAT	0x20	CATALOG	DOCAT	0x4072
CMDMON	0x22	MON	DOMON	0x4080
CMDNOMAN	0x24	NOMON	DONOMON	0x4080
CMDPRNUM	0x26	PR#	DOPRNUM	0x0800
CMDINNUM	0x28	IN#	DOINNUM	0x0800
CMDMXFLS	0x2A	MAXFILES	DOMXFLS	0x0400
CMDDATE	0x2C	DATE	DODATE	0x4000
CMDLIST	0x2E	LIST	DOLIST	0x2077
CMDBSAVE	0x30	BSAVE	DOBSAVE	0x217F
CMDBLOAD	0x32	BLOAD	DOBLOAD	0x207A
CMDBRUN	0x34	BRUN	DOBRUN	0x2078
CMDVERFY	0x36	VERIFY	DOVERIFY	0x2072
CMDLSAVE	0x38	LSAVE	DOLSAVE	0x217F
CMDLLOAD	0x3A	LLOAD	DOLLOAD	0x207A
CMDTSAVE	0x3C	TSAVE	DOTSAVE	0x2173
CMDTLOAD	0x3E	TLOAD	DOTLOAD	0x207F
CMDDIFF	0x40	DIFF	DODIFF	0x3070
CMDGREP	0x42	GREP	DOGREP	0x3071
CMDMORE	0x44	MORE	DOLIST	0x2077
CMDCAT2	0x46	CAT	DOCAT	0x4072
CMDURM	0x48	URM	DOURM	0x2070
CMDCD	0x4A	CD	DOCD	0x0070
CMDLS	0x4C	LS	DOCAT	0x4072
CMDMV	0x4E	MV	DORENAME	0x3070
CMDRM	0x50	RM	DODELETE	0x2070
CMDSV	0x52	SV	DOSV	0x0008
CMDTS	0x54	TS	DOTS	0x402F
CMDTW	0x56	TW	DOTW	0x2170
CMDHELP	0x58	HELP	DOHELP	0x2000
CMDUSER	0x5A	-	DOUSER	-

Table III.0.2. DOS 4.1 Command Table

Table III.0.2 is a comprehensive listing of all DOS 4.1 commands in processing order showing the command name, index, ASCII text, software handler, and valid keyword value. CMDHELP is only available in DOS 4.1H because there is additional room in RAM Bank 1 where RWTS is located. This additional memory seemed like an ideal location for placing a HELP Command handler in order to provide instant syntactical usage information for all DOS 4.1 commands. DOS 4.1H uses track 0x02 anyway because it needs two additional sectors for its interface and boot pages. Why not use a few more sectors on track 0x02 for something quite useful like the HELP Command handler? Another DOS developer may choose to eliminate the HELP Command handler and utilize the memory and/or the eight disk sectors for something else entirely.

CMDUSER is designed and available to a user who needs to load DOS 4.1 into memory, initialize it, and then have DOS 4.1 return control back to that user instead of to Applesoft. After DOS 4.1 is copied into memory, the user needs to place the address of the user's handler at USERADR, or 0xBEEC, place the value of CMDUSER-CMDTBL found at USERNDX, or 0xBFFA, into CMDVAL, or 0xBEEE, and then initialize DOS using an indirect JMP instruction to DOSBEGIN, or 0xBED7, the address found at INITDOS, or 0xBFF8. USERADR and CMDVAL are located at index byte 0x15 and index byte 0x17, respectively, from the address found at INITDOS. INITDOS is at the same location in both DOS 4.1L and DOS 4.1H, so it makes no difference where USERADR, CMDVAL, and DOSBEGIN are technically located in either DOS 4.1L or DOS 4.1H. Table I.8.7 shows where these variables are currently located. These memory locations are subject to change, but not their index values. Once DOS 4.1 has initialized, the command CMDUSER will be invoked which is simply an indirect JMP instruction to the address found in USERADR. The user's handler should restore the values originally found at USERADR (address of the Monitor routine MON, or 0xFF65) and CMDVAL (i.e. CMDRUN-CMDTBL, or 0x06) so that the DOS that is currently in memory can be used for "pure image" disk initialization, if desired. An example assembly language routine is shown in Figure I.9.1 that illustrates how to set up USERADR and CMDVAL.

DOS 4.1 uses the following four tables to parse valid keywords, ascertain a keyword's bit position, and determine if a keyword is within a minimum and a maximum value: PPARMS, PARMBITS, KWRANGEL, and KWRANGEH. The content of these tables is summarized in Table III.0.3. Unlike DOS 3.3, DOS 4.1 will allow up to 81 drives in order to support CFFA Volume Manager software for up to an 8 GB Compact Flash card, to allow default Volume numbers to be 0x00, and to allow BSAVE and LSAVE to write files greater than 0x7FFF bytes. The Bit Positions for the keywords C, I, O are actually used to generate the MONVAL variable once the MSB of the bit position value is cleared. The other Bit Positions are added to the variable KYWRDFND as each keyword is parsed. It is no accident that the Bit Position of each Keyword in Table III.0.3 is the same as in the lower byte of each command keyword shown in Table III.0.1. When DOS 3.3 checks KYWRDFND against the Keyword of a DOS command as shown in Table III.0.2 in the GETNXT routine, any additional bits found set should immediately signal a Syntax Error as it does in DOS 4.1. Instead, DOS 3.3 jumps to the GETFRST routine which has nothing to do with finding wrong bits set in KYWRDFND.

The syntax of a DOS 4.1 command begins with the command, and is immediately followed by a filename or two if they are required. All parameters whether they are required or optional follow the filename(s) or the command if no filename is required, and usually a comma must delineate each parameter. Optional parameters are contained in square brackets, as in [,Vv]. Commands and keywords are shown in CAPITAL letters and keyword values are shown in lowercase letters for ease of explanation and not how they need to be used or entered on the Apple command line. Table III.0.4 lists all keywords and keyword value items.

105

Keyword Name	Bit Position - Value	Minimum Value	Maximum Value
C	%1100 0000 - 0xC0	-	-
I	%1010 0000 - 0xA0	-	-
O	%1001 0000 - 0x90	-	-
MON/NOMON	%1000 0000 - 0x80	-	-
S	%0100 0000 - 0x40	1 (0x01)	7 (0x0007)
D	%0010 0000 - 0x20	1 (0x01)	81 (0x0051)
V	%0001 0000 - 0x10	0 (0x00)	255 (0x00FF)
A	%0000 1000 - 0x08	0 (0x00)	65535 (0xFFFF)
L	%0000 0100 - 0x04	0 (0x00)	65535 (0xFFFF)
R	%0000 0010 - 0x02	0 (0x00)	32767 (0x7FFF)
B	%0000 0001 - 0x01	0 (0x00)	32767 (0x7FFF)

Table III.0.3. DOS 4.1 Keyword Name and Range Table

Keyword	Name	Description
S	Slot	Keyword followed by slot number
D	Drive	Keyword followed by drive number
V	Volume	Keyword followed by volume number
A	Address	Keyword followed by address number
L	Length	Keyword followed by length number
R	Record	Keyword followed by record number or nothing
B	Byte	Keyword followed by byte number
C	Command	Keyword to display or not to display DOS commands
I	Input	Keyword to display or not to display input data
O	Output	Keyword to display or not to display output data
f	filename	Must begin with a letter and be 1-24 characters in length
f2	2nd filename	Must begin with a letter and be 1-24 characters in length
s	slot number	Slot number of a peripheral slot card, value range 1-7
d	drive number	Initialized to 1, value range 1-81 (for CFFA use)
v	volume number	Initialized to 0, value range 0-255
a	address number	Initialized to 0, value range 0-65535
l	length number	Initialized to 0, value range 0-65535
r	record number	Initialized to 0, value range 0-32767
b	byte number	Initialized to 0, value range 0-32767
n	number	Some numerical value required by some commands

Table III.0.4. DOS 4.1 Keywords and Keyword Value Items

In keeping with the original DOS 3.3 documentation,
DOS 4.1 commands may be grouped into the following six categories.
Remember, the HELP command is a DOS 4.1H command only.

File System Commands

CAT	CATALOG	CD	DATE
DELETE	DIFF	GREP	HELP
INIT	LIST	LOCK	LS
MORE	MV	RENAME	RM
SV	TS	UNLOCK	URM
VERIFY			

System Commands

IN#	MAXFILES	MON	NOMON
PR#			

Applesoft File Commands

CHAIN	LOAD	RUN	SAVE

Binary File Commands

BLOAD	BRUN	BSAVE	LLOAD
LSAVE			

Sequential Text File Commands

APPEND	CLOSE	EXEC	OPEN
POSITION	READ	TLOAD	TSAVE
TW	WRITE		

Random-Access Data File Commands

CLOSE	OPEN	READ	WRITE

Command	Command Syntax
CATALOG	[,Ss][,Dd][Vv][,R]
CAT	[,Ss][,Dd][Vv][,R]
LS	[,Ss][,Dd][Vv][,R]
CD	[,Ss][,Dd][Vv]
DATE	
DELETE	f [,Ss][,Dd][,Vv]
RM	f [,Ss][,Dd][,Vv]
DIFF	f, f2 [,Ss][,Dd][,Vv]
GREP	f, f2 [,Ss][,Dd][,Vv][,Bn]
HELP	c
INIT	f, f2 [,Ss][,Dd][,Vv][,An][,Bn][,Ln][,R[n]]
LIST	f [,Ss][,Dd][,Vv][,Bb][,Ll][,R]
MORE	f [,Ss][,Dd][,Vv][,Bb][,Ll][,R]
LOCK	f [,Ss][,Dd][,Vv]
MV	f, f2 [,Ss][,Dd][,Vv]
RENAME	f, f2 [,Ss][,Dd][,Vv]
SV	An
TS	[,Ss][,Dd][,Vv][,An][,Bn][,L][,R]
UNLOCK	f [,Ss][,Dd][,Vv]
URM	f [,Ss][,Dd][,Vv]
VERIFY	f [,Ss][,Dd][,Vv][,R1]

Table III.1.1. DOS 4.1 File System Commands

1. File System Commands

The DOS 4.1 File System Commands manage the file system of a disk volume and display its contents. The syntax of the File System Commands is shown in Table III.1.1.

```
CATALOG   [,Ss][,Dd][,Vv][,R]
CAT       [,Ss][,Dd][,Vv][,R]          ; short version of CATALOG
LS        [,Ss][,Dd][,Vv][,R]          ; UNIX version of CATALOG

Example:  CATALOG S6,D2
          CAT D1
          LS R
```

This command displays on the screen a wealth of information for the specified volume: the current slot and drive for the volume (S= and D=), the volume number (V=), the remaining free space on the volume (F=), the date and time the VTOC was last modified, and a list of all files on the volume. Each file is displayed with its lock/unlock status, its file type, its size in sectors including its TSL sector(s), the first 14 characters of its filename, and the date and time of the file's creation or last modification. Table I.7.3 lists all file types. Figure III.1.1 shows an example of the CATALOG command and the CAT command. Notice that the asterisk shows that the files DOS4.1.46L and DOS4.1.46H are locked. DOS 4.1 commands may be entered in lowercase.

```
]CATALOG S6,D2

S=6  D=02  V=000  F=0470  01/01/21  08:28:48

*B  034  DOS4.1.46L       01/01/21  08:28:48
*B  044  DOS4.1.46H       01/01/21  08:28:48
 B  003  INSTALL46L       01/01/21  08:28:48
 B  003  INSTALL46H       01/01/21  08:28:48

]cat

S=6  D=02  V=000  F=0470  01/01/21  08:28:48

*B  034  DOS4.1.46L       01/01/21  08:28:48
*B  044  DOS4.1.46H       01/01/21  08:28:48
 B  003  INSTALL46L       01/01/21  08:28:48
 B  003  INSTALL46H       01/01/21  08:28:48

]
```

Figure III.1.1. CATALOG and CAT Command Display

If the R keyword is included with the CATALOG command the screen displays the current version of DOS that is currently in memory (M=), the 24 character volume title (T=), the version and build of the DOS that created this volume (B=), the volume type (i.e. boot or data), the volume library value (L=), and the date and time the volume was created, followed by the information previously shown. The list of files on the volume also includes all deleted files shown by the x character. Without the R keyword each file is displayed as shown in Figure III.1.1. With the R keyword each file is displayed with its sequence number, the track and sector of its first TSL, and all 24 characters of its filename. Figure III.1.2 shows an example the "LS R" command.

```
]LS R

M=DOS4.1.46L T=CATALOG Figure

B=4146L data L=0xF001 01/01/21 08:28:48

S=6 D=02 V=000 F=0470 01/01/21 08:28:48

*001  0x12,0x0F  DOS4.1.46L
*002  0x15,0x0F  DOS4.1.46H
 003  0x18,0x0F  INSTALL46L
 004  0x19,0x0F  INSTALL46H
x005  0x1A,0x0F  DOS2TO1

]
```

Figure III.1.2. LS R Command Display

```
]CD S6,D2,V123

]LS

S=6 D=02 V=123 F=0518 01/01/21 08:28:48

 A 004 HELLO            01/01/21 08:28:48

]CD = S=6 D=02 V=123 123

]*
```

Figure III.1.3. CD Command Display

```
CD          [,Ss][,Dd][,Vv]
```

Example: `CD S6,D2,V3`
            `CD`

This command is new to DOS and it can change the default slot, drive, and volume parameters of the specified volume. If no keywords are used with the `CD` command the current default slot, drive and volume parameters are displayed on the Apple command line after the `CD` command. Figure III.1.3 shows two examples of using the `CD` command. When the `CD` command is used with no keywords, two values are displayed for volume. The first comes from `DISKVOL` as shown in Table I.6.1 and the second comes from `VOLNUMBR` as shown in Table I.10.4. `DISKVOL` is the actual volume number value in the `VTOC` and `VOLNUMBR` is the volume number value used by the File Manager. When these values differ and `VOLNUMBR` is not `000` then the "`Volume Number Error`" message is issued.

`DATE`

Example: `DATE`

This command is new to DOS and it displays on the screen the current date and time as shown in Figure III.1.4. DOS 4.1 supports three known clock cards and possibly others: ThunderClock clock card, TimeMaster clock card, and the clock card I designed and built. The only difference in these clock cards is the index into the output raw data string each card produces where the date and time data begin. Figure III.1.4 also shows an example Applesoft program that displays the raw data string for a ThunderClock clock card residing in slot 4. The index where the date and time data begin for this clock card is `0x00`. My clock card and the TimeMaster clock card both have an index of `0x03`. The indexes for the DOS 4.1 supported clock cards are summarized previously in Table I.11.1. DOS 4.1 can support any clock card having the standard signature bytes and `CLKID`, and a maximum index of `0x05` for its output raw data string where the date and time data begin.

```
]date = 01/01/21 08:28:48

]load read clock

]list

 10  D$ =   CHR$ (4)
 20  SLOT = 4
 30    PRINT D$;"pr#";SLOT
 40    PRINT D$;"in#";SLOT
 50    INPUT ":";A$
 60    PRINT D$;"pr#0"
 70    PRINT D$;"in#0"
 80    PRINT
 90    PRINT A$

]run

01/01 08;28;48.000

]※
```

Figure III.1.4. DATE Command for ThunderClock Clock Card Display

```
*B 034 DOS4.1.46L        01/01/21 08:28:48
 B 002 DOS2TO1           01/01/21 08:28:48

]DELETE DOS2TO1

]CAT R

M=DOS4.1.46L T=DELETE Figure

B=4146L data L=0xF004 01/01/21 08:28:48

S=6 D=02 V=000 F=0520 01/01/21 08:28:49

*001 0x12,0x0F DOS4.1.46L
x002 0x15,0x0F DOS2TO1

]LS

S=6 D=02 V=000 F=0520 01/01/21 08:28:49

*B 034 DOS4.1.46L        01/01/21 08:28:48

]※
```

Figure III.1.5. DELETE Command Display

```
DELETE    f [,Ss][,Dd][,Vv]
RM        f [,Ss][,Dd][,Vv]              ; UNIX version of DELETE
```

Example: DELETE COPYDOS
            RM COPYDOS

This command removes the filename f from the catalog listing in the specified volume if the filename exists by setting the most significant bit of its TSL track byte, and marking the sectors in the file's TSL(s) and the TSL sector(s) as available. Refer to Figure I.7.1 showing a disk catalog sector. Figure III.1.5 shows an example of a file being deleted. It is prudent to undelete a deleted file as soon as possible before the sectors in the file's TSL(s) and the TSL sector(s) are utilized by another file. When a file is deleted, the date and time stamp for the file is not changed but the date and time stamp for the VTOC is updated because the VTOC is changed.


```
DIFF      f, f2 [,Ss][,Dd][,Vv]
```

Example: DIFF TEST1,TEST2

This command is new to DOS and it compares any two files f and f2 in the specified volume up to the end of SECCNT-1 sectors of the second file, f2. The routine will display on the screen the number of bytes compared on the Apple command line, and the location(s) where the files differ and the differing bytes. The two files must reside on the same volume. The location(s) where the files differ are the number of bytes from the beginning of each file. The first differing byte comes from the first file, or file f, and the second differing byte comes from the second file, or file f2. Displayed values are all shown in hexadecimal. Figure III.1.6 shows an example of three pairs of files being compared. The first pair of files are identical and the screen shows that 0x0100 bytes were compared even though the files themselves are only 0x0080 bytes in size. DIFF compares whole sectors. The second pair of files are exactly 0x1000 bytes in size but DIFF compared 0x1100 bytes. Because these are Binary files their address and length bytes occupy the first four bytes of the file making the files actually 0x1004 bytes in length. Again, DIFF compares whole sectors, and the last four bytes of data reside in an additional sector. These files differed at only one location. The third pair of files are 0x300 bytes in size and they differ at five specific locations.

```
]DIFF F1,F2 = 0x0100

]DIFF N1,N2 = 0x1100
0x0F84 = 0x00,0xFF
]DIFF Z1,Z2 = 0x0400
0x0084 = 0x00,0xFF
0x0104 = 0x00,0xFF
0x0184 = 0x00,0xFF
0x0204 = 0x00,0xFF
0x0284 = 0x00,0xFF
]
```

Figure III.1.6. DIFF Command Display

GREP   f, f2 [,Ss][,Dd][,Vv][,Bn]

Example: GREP HELLO,TEST
           GREP HELLO,Manage Test*,B$AA

This command is new to DOS and it searches the file f for the single word ASCII string or the multiple word character-terminated string f2 in the specified volume up to the end of SECCNT-1 sectors of the file. The routine will display on the screen the number of bytes searched on the Apple command line and the location(s) where the string f2 occurs in the file. The location(s) where f2 is found is the number of bytes from the beginning of the file up to the first character of f2. Displayed values are all shown in hexadecimal. Figure III.1.7 shows an example of three files being searched. The first file is an Applesoft file. The second file is a binary file. The third file is the same binary file that uses a multiple word character-terminated string for f2. GREP searches whole sectors, and regardless how many actual bytes are associated with the file in the last sector, the entire last sector of the file is searched. GREP is case sensitive as shown in Figure III.1.7., and GREP masks out the MSB as file f is read so lower ASCII character 0x41 is the same as upper ASCII character 0xC1. DOS 4.1 expects the string contained in f2 to conform to the format and length of a filename, therefore the first character must be an alpha character, otherwise a "?SYNTAX ERROR" will be issued by Applesoft. The maximum length of f2 is 24 characters, which includes the termination character if it is used. Any ASCII character may be used for the termination character as long as it is unique within the

114

characters comprising f2. If a termination character is used it must be defined by the B keyword and equal to its upper ASCII value, that is, with its MSB ON.

```
]GREP HELLO,WINDOW = 0x0300
0x02AB
]GREP VOLMGR,Images,D2 = 0x3C00
0x076D
0x1558
0x183E
0x185D
]grep VOLMGR,Firmware to*,b$aa = 0x3C00
0x00C7
0x159F
] ▒
```

Figure III.1.7. GREP Command Display

HELP   C

Example: HELP HELP
           HELP CATALOG

This command is new to DOS and is only available when DOS 4.1H is booted into memory. In order to port DOS 4.1L to the Language Card I found that it was necessary to create an "interface" page of routines that managed some of the DOS routines vis-à-vis memory bank switching for the Language Card. This implies having to use at least one disk sector on the next track, track 0x02, for the Language Card version of the DOS image. Also, there was a lot of unused memory in RAM Bank 1 where I put all the RWTS routines and nibble buffers. It was an easy decision to utilize the remaining RAM Bank 1 memory for a HELP command and use as much of track 0x02 as I needed. I created the HELP command to provide instant syntactical usage information for all DOS 4.1 commands. Figures III.1.8 through III.1.11 display the command HELP HELP screens. Figure III.1.12 displays an example HELP screen for HELP INIT.

115

```
            HELP Documentation
         File System Commands
   CAT       CATALOG        CD        DATE
  DELETE      DIFF        GREP       HELP
   INIT       LIST        LOCK         LS
   MORE        MV        RENAME        RM
    SV         TS        UNLOCK       URM
  VERIFY


            System Commands

   IN#      MAXFILES       MON       NOMON
   PR#


         Applesoft File Commands

  CHAIN       LOAD         RUN        SAVE


Press any key ... ※
```

Figure III.1.8. HELP HELP Command Display 1

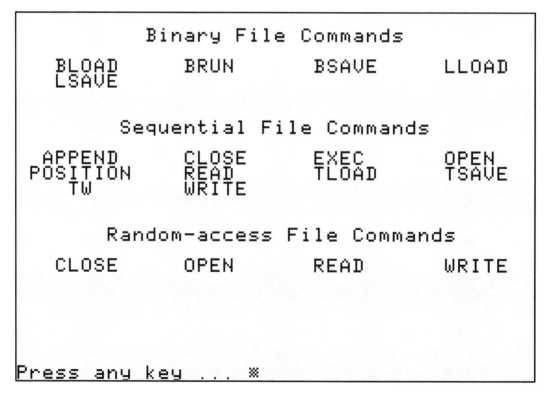

```
         Binary File Commands
  BLOAD       BRUN        BSAVE       LLOAD
  LSAVE


         Sequential File Commands

  APPEND      CLOSE        EXEC       OPEN
 POSITION     READ        TLOAD      TSAVE
    TW        WRITE


         Random-access File Commands

  CLOSE       OPEN         READ       WRITE


Press any key ... ※
```

Figure III.1.9. HELP HELP Command Display 2

```
Key  Name      Description
---  --------  --------------------------
 S   Slot      Slot number follows
 D   Drive     Drive number follows
 V   Volume    Volume number follows
 A   Address   Address number follows
 L   Length    Length number follows
 R   Record    Record number follows
 B   Byte      Byte number follows
 C   Command   Show or not DOS Command
 I   Input     Show or not Input data
 O   Output    Show or not Output data
 f   filename  1-24 characters
 f2  2nd name  1-24 characters
 s   slot #    1-7
 d   drive #   1-81
 v   volume #  0-255
 a   address # 0-65535
 l   length #  0-65535
 r   record #  0-32767
 b   byte #    0-32767
 n   number    required value

Press any key ... ※
```

Figure III.1.10. HELP HELP Command Display 3

```
          Internal Entry Points


*BE00G - RAM bank 2 Monitor Entry
*D000L   (list DOS code)

*BE08G - RAM bank 1 Monitor Entry
*D000L   (list RWTS code)

0xBEB6 - File Manager IOCB
0xBEC8 - RWTS IOCB

0xBED9 - DOS initialization Entry

0xBFF8 - INITDOS
0xBFFA - USERNDX
0xBFFB - DISKTBL
0xBFFC - BCFGNDX
0xBFFD - NBUF1ADR

]&      - Repeat previous Command
]MON    - Enter Monitor

Press any key ... ※
```

Figure III.1.11. HELP HELP Command Display 4

```
INIT f, f2 [,Ss]  [,Dd]  [,Vv]  [,An]
            [,Bn]  [,Ln]  [,R[n]]

INIT HELLO,<Title>,V7,A40        (type B)

INIT HELLO,<Title>,V7,B8,R       (type D)


A = disk tracks
B = disk|catalog sectors
L = subject
R = boot type


] ▒
```

Figure III.1.12. HELP INIT Command Display

INIT   f, f2 [,Ss][,Dd][,Vv][,An][,Bn][,Ln][,R[n]]

Example: INIT HELLO,<title>,V123,L$101   ; creates Volume Type B
           INIT EXECFILE,<title>,V123,R$14   ; creates Volume Type B
           INIT H,<title>,V123,R   ; creates Volume Type D

This command initializes the specified volume with the filename f and writes DOS 4.1 on tracks
0x00 and 0x01 for DOS 4.1L or writes 10 additional sectors on track 0x02 for DOS 4.1H when the
R keyword is **not** included or the value of the R keyword is **not** equal to 0x00 (Volume Type B, or
boot volume) as shown in Figure III.1.13. All initialized disks are titled with the required upper
ASCII string in f2. The parameter v is assigned the volume number if the V keyword is included;
otherwise the disk is initialized with a volume number of 000. If the R keyword is included without a
value or with a value of 0x00, a data disk is initialized with a VTOC and an empty catalog structure,
and all DOS sectors are available for data storage including track 0x00 (Volume Type D, or data
volume) as shown in Figure III.1.14. The upper ASCII string in f2 is still used for the volume Title,
but the filename f is simply a placeholder and not utilized. If the R keyword is included with a
nonzero value, that value is copied to CMDVAL and a disk is initialized having a bootable DOS
(Volume Type B) but no Applesoft boot file is saved to the disk even if there is an Applesoft file in
memory. It is up to the user to copy an Applesoft file for R$06, an EXEC file for R$14, or a Binary
file for R$34 to the disk as its HELLO, or f filename. Other possible values for the R keyword could

be R$10 for CLOSE, R$2C for DATE, and R$2E for LIST, from Table III.0.2. A complete set of initialization values is available from 0xBED7 through 0xBEFF for both DOS 4.1L and DOS 4.1H. These values can be modified directly or with keywords before executing the INIT command in order to tailor a DOS 4.1 volume specific to ones needs and the target hardware. See Table I.8.7 for a list of all of the possible initialization values.

If the A and B keywords are not used or are set to 0x00, the default initialization values for SECVAL and ENDTRK come from FIRSTCAT and LASTRACK, respectively. The default value for ENDSEC is 0x10. The A keyword is used to specify a new ENDTRK, the number of tracks on a Disk][volume. The B keyword is used to specify the number of Catalog sectors from 1 to 15, and to select 16-sector tracks if its MSB is clear or 32-sector tracks if its MSB is set. The L keyword is used to specify a Library Value (or subject value) for the disk volume if it is included, from 0x0000 to 0xFFFF, otherwise the Library Value is set to 0x0000. Once any other initialization parameter has been changed, it remains equal to that value except for SECVAL, ENDTRK, ENDSEC and SUBJCT; that is, there is no reset to "default" settings for NMAXVAL, YEARVAL, TRKVAL, VRSN, BLD, RAMTYP, TSPARS, ALCTRK, ALCDIR, and SECSIZ as shown previously in Table I.8.7. Use common sense when modifying these parameters.

The value in SECVAL determines the number of sectors the catalog will contain not including the VTOC sector. The useable values for SECVAL are 0x00<SECVAL<0x10. If SECVAL is more than fifteen, no more than fifteen Catalog sectors will be created. Table III.1.2 shows the number of available data sectors in a volume based on Volume Type and catalog size for a volume having 35 tracks and 16 sectors per track. A few disk drives, either physical or solid state, were manufactured to access 40 tracks for a volume. Set ENDTRK to 0x28 (or use A$28) to provide access to all 40 tracks, or set ENDTRK to 0x30 (or use A$30) to access 48 tracks if they are available. The VTOC is designed to manage up to 50 tracks per volume as shown previously in Figure I.6.1. Table III.1.3 shows the same information as Table III.1.2 for a volume having 32 sectors per track. Table III.1.4 shows the total number of sectors on a volume having 35, 40, or 48 tracks with 16 or 32 sectors per track.

```
]INIT HELLO,Boot Disk,S6,D2,V123,L$1234
]CAT R
M=DOS4.1.46L T=Boot Disk
B=4146L boot L=0x1234 01/01/21 08:28:48
S=6 D=02 V=123 F=0520 01/01/21 08:28:48
 001 0x12,0x0F HELLO
]▓
```

Figure III.1.13. INIT Command Display 1

```
]init hello,Data Disk,v101,l$4321,r
]cat r
M=DOS4.1.46L T=Data Disk
B=4146L data L=0x4321 01/01/21 08:28:48
S=6 D=02 V=101 F=0554 01/01/21 08:28:48

]
```

Figure III.1.14. INIT Command Display 2

SECVAL	Catalog Sectors	4.1L Data Sectors		4.1H Data Sectors	
		B	D	B	D
0x01	1	526	558	516	558
0x02	2	525	557	515	557
0x03	3	524	556	514	556
0x04	4	523	555	513	555
0x05	5	522	554	512	554
0x06	6	521	553	511	553
0x07	7	520	552	510	552
0x08	8	519	551	509	551
0x09	9	518	550	508	550
0x0A	10	517	549	507	549
0x0B	11	516	548	506	548
0x0C	12	515	547	505	547
0x0D	13	514	546	504	546
0x0E	14	513	545	503	545
0x0F	15	512	544	502	544

Table III.1.2. Initialized Catalog Size for 35 Tracks, 16 Sectors/Track

SECVAL	Catalog Sectors	4.1L Data Sectors		4.1H Data Sectors	
		B	D	B	D
0x01	1	1086	1118	1076	1118
0x02	2	1085	1117	1075	1117
0x03	3	1084	1116	1074	1116
0x04	4	1083	1115	1073	1115
0x05	5	1082	1114	1072	1114
0x06	6	1081	1113	1071	1113
0x07	7	1080	1112	1070	1112
0x08	8	1079	1111	1069	1111
0x09	9	1078	1110	1068	1110
0x0A	10	1077	1109	1067	1109
0x0B	11	1076	1108	1066	1108
0x0C	12	1075	1107	1065	1107
0x0D	13	1074	1106	1064	1106
0x0E	14	1073	1105	1063	1105
0x0F	15	1072	1104	1062	1104

Table III.1.3. Initialized Catalog Size for 35 Tracks, 32 Sectors/Track

Tracks/Volume	Sectors/Track	Total Sectors
35	16	560
35	32	1120
40	16	640
40	32	1280
48	16	768
48	32	1536

Table III.1.4. Total Sectors for Volumes

```
LIST     f [,Ss][,Dd][,Vv][,Bb][,Ll][,R]
MORE     f [,Ss][,Dd][,Vv][,Bb][,Ll][,R]        ; UNIX version of LIST

Example:  LIST EXECFILE,B8,L10,R
```

This command is new to DOS and it displays on the screen the contents of file f in the specified volume in ASCII if the file is a Text type file or in hexadecimal for all other file types. If the R keyword is included, the contents of a Text type file will be displayed in hexadecimal rather than in ASCII. If the B keyword is included, that number of bytes, b, into the file will be skipped. If the L keyword is included, that number of bytes, l, will only be displayed, or until the end of the file, whichever occurs first. LIST displays a complete sector of data at a time, and LIST can be terminated at any time by pressing the ESC key. Figure III.1.15 shows an example of using LIST on a Text type file utilizing the various keywords. First, the entire file is listed. Then the first six bytes of the file are listed. Then, the first nine bytes are skipped and the next seven bytes are listed. Finally, those same seven bytes are displayed in hexadecimal. Hexadecimal pairs of bytes are displayed corresponding to even/odd bytes in the file beginning with zero when counting, so the "L" in "BLOAD" is an odd byte in the file and is skipped, and the second "O" in "FOO" and the carriage return are added. Remember to count the carriage return (or 0x8D) as an ASCII character as well. LIST will not skip over a NULL byte (or 0x00) as found in random-access Data files when displayed in ASCII. These particular files should only be displayed in hexadecimal in order to display the contents of the records contained in those type of data files.

```
]LIST EXECFILE.T

MON CIO
BLOAD FOO
NOMON CIO

]LIST EXECFILE.T,L6

MON CI

]LIST EXECFILE.T,B9,L7

LOAD FO

]LIST EXECFILE.T,B9,L7,R

CFC1 C4A0 C6CF CF8D

]
```

Figure III.1.15. LIST Command Display

```
]CAT

S=6 D=02 V=000 F=0470 01/01/21 08:28:48

 B 034 DOS4.1.46L        01/01/21 08:28:48
 B 044 DOS4.1.46H        01/01/21 08:28:48
 B 003 INSTALL46L        01/01/21 08:28:48
 B 003 INSTALL46H        01/01/21 08:28:48

]LOCK DOS4.1.46L

]CAT

S=6 D=02 V=000 F=0470 01/01/21 08:28:48

*B 034 DOS4.1.46L        01/01/21 08:28:49
 B 044 DOS4.1.46H        01/01/21 08:28:48
 B 003 INSTALL46L        01/01/21 08:28:48
 B 003 INSTALL46H        01/01/21 08:28:48

]
```

Figure III.1.16. LOCK Command Display

```
LOCK        f [,Ss][,Dd][,Vv]

Example:    LOCK TEST
```

This command sets the most significant bit of the Type byte of the file f in the specified volume as shown in Tables I.7.1 through I.7.3. A locked file cannot be deleted or renamed until it is unlocked, and the lock status of a file is indicated in the volume Catalog using an asterisk, *, next to the file's type character as shown in Figure III.1.16. The date and time stamp for the file is also updated but not the date and time stamp for the VTOC because nothing in the VTOC is changed.

```
┌──────────────────────────────────────────────────────────┐
│ ]LS                                                        │
│                                                            │
│ S=6 D=02 V=000 F=0470 01/01/21 08:28:48                    │
│   B 034 DOS4.1.46L        01/01/21 08:28:48                │
│   B 044 DOS4.1.46H        01/01/21 08:28:48                │
│   B 003 INSTALL46L        01/01/21 08:28:48                │
│   B 003 INSTALL46H        01/01/21 08:28:48                │
│ ]RENAME INSTALL46H,INSTALL H DOS                           │
│ ]LS                                                        │
│                                                            │
│ S=6 D=02 V=000 F=0470 01/01/21 08:28:48                    │
│   B 034 DOS4.1.46L        01/01/21 08:28:48                │
│   B 044 DOS4.1.46H        01/01/21 08:28:48                │
│   B 003 INSTALL46L        01/01/21 08:28:48                │
│   B 003 INSTALL H DOS     01/01/21 08:28:49                │
│ ]                                                          │
└──────────────────────────────────────────────────────────┘
```

Figure III.1.17. RENAME Command Display

```
RENAME      f, f2 [,Ss][,Dd][,Vv]
MV          f, f2 [,Ss][,Dd][,Vv]          ; UNIX version of RENAME

Example:    RENAME COPYDOS,COPYDOS.EXEC
```

This command changes the name of the file f to f2 in the specified volume if the file f exists. The time stamp of the renamed file is also updated as shown in Figure III.1.17. A locked file cannot be renamed until it is unlocked. The VTOC time stamp remains unchanged when a file is renamed because nothing in the VTOC is changed.

```
] SV A$1234 = 04660 = 0x1234
] SV A1234 = 01234 = 0x04D2
] sv a0 = 00000 = 0x0000
] sv a$ffff = 65535 = 0xFFFF
]
```

Figure III.1.18. SV Command Display

SV   An

Example: SV A$1234
            SV A1234

This command is new to DOS and it displays on the Apple command line the decimal and hexadecimal value of the A keyword value whether the keyword variable is entered as a decimal or as a hexadecimal value. Figure III.1.18 shows the use of the SV (or Show Value) command. Using the SV command is a convenient way to convert numbers from decimal to hexadecimal or hexadecimal to decimal without having to reach for the calculator.

The DOS 3.3 Print Decimal (i.e. Base-10) routine PRTDEC was severely flawed, and it consumed 37 bytes for its ridiculous implementation. DOS 4.1 needs to convert 16-bit hexadecimal values to decimal and selectively print from one to five zero-prefaced Base-10 digits. The DOS command SV is one example where five zero-prefaced Base-10 digits are printed to the screen. The algorithm I designed for the DOS 4.1 routine PRTDEC is only 32 bytes in size, but it requires five additional bytes for the high-order bytes in the Decimal Table DECTBLH and one additional byte for the low-order bytes in the Decimal Table DECTBLL.

```
0011  0541  46CC  00C4  D2C5  CEC1  CDC5  A0C6
E9E7  F5F2  E5A0  A0A0  A0A0  A0A0  A0A0  A0A0
4828  0821  0101  007A  09F0  4828  0821  0101
1A01  0000  2310  0001  FFFF  0000  FFFF  0000
FFFF  0000  FFFF  0000  FFFF  0000  FFFF  0000
FFFF  0000  FFFF  0000  FFFF  0000  FFFF  0000
FFFF  0000  FFFF  0000  FFFF  0000  FFC0  0000
0000  0000  0000  0000  3FFF  0000  0000  0000
0000  0000  000F  0000  1FFF  0000  1FFF  0000
FFFF  0000  FFFF  0000  FFFF  0000  FFFF  0000
FFFF  0000  FFFF  0000  FFFF  0000  FFFF  0000
FFFF  0000  0000  0000  0000  0000  0000  0000
0000  0000  0000  0000  0000  0000  0000  0000
0000  0000  0000  0000  0000  0000  0000  0000
0000  0000  0000  0000  0000  0000  0000  0000

TS = 0x11,0x00

] ※
```

Figure III.1.19. TS Command of a Data Disk VTOC Display

TS   [,Ss][,Dd][,Vv][,An][,Bn][,L][,R]

Example: TS
            TS A$11,B7
            TS L

This command is new to DOS and it displays on the screen the contents of the specified sector in hexadecimal of the specified track in the specified volume. The A keyword is used to specify a track value and the B keyword is used to specify a sector value, and if not given, their value is 0x00. The value n for these keywords may be entered in decimal or in hexadecimal, and range checking is done against that volume's VTOC parameters NUMTRKS (or number of tracks) and NUMSECS (or number of sectors in a track). It is critical that a relevant DOS command (i.e. CATALOG) has been previously issued to ensure that the volume's VTOC has been read and is currently in memory and NUMTRKS and NUMSECS have relevant values. If the L or R keyword is included then any A or B keyword is ignored if they happen to be included. The R keyword takes precedence over the L keyword if both are included. The L keyword will display the previous sector (i.e. to the Left, or down) and the R keyword

126

will display the next sector (i.e. to the Right, or up). Figure III.1.19 shows a typical TS view of an initialized data disk VTOC: the screen is cleared and the sector data is displayed in hexadecimal byte pairs followed by the TS command and the specified track and sector values given.

UNLOCK   f [,Ss][,Dd][,Vv]

Example: UNLOCK TEST

This command clears the most significant bit of the Type byte of the file f in the specified volume as shown in Tables I.7.1 through I.7.3. The date and time stamp of the file is also updated as shown in Figure III.1.20. A file must be unlocked before it can be deleted or renamed. The date and time stamp for the VTOC is not updated because nothing is changed in the VTOC.

URM   f [,Ss][,Dd][,Vv]

Example: URM MOVEDOS

This command is new to DOS and it restores the file f to the catalog of the specified volume by clearing the most significant bit of its TSL track byte and marking the sectors in the file's TSL(s) and the TSL sector(s) as used. It is prudent to restore a deleted file as soon as possible before the sectors in a file's TSL(s) and the TSL sector(s) are utilized by another file. Even if a file requires multiple TSL sectors, **all** data sectors and **all** TSL sectors are restored with the URM command. **There is no harm in attempting to undelete a file that is already displayed in the volume Catalog.** Figure III.1.21 shows an example of a deleted file being restored using the URM command. Notice the x before the deleted filename is now gone after the file is restored. This command was implemented by adding the URMHNDL handler to the File Manager Subroutine table as shown previously in Table I.9.6. The DOS 4.1 File Manager handles this command much like the DELHNDLR hander. The date and time stamp for the VTOC is updated because the VTOC is changed when a file is restored. The date and time stamp for a file and for the VTOC are both updated even when the URM command is used to restore a file that is already displayed in the volume Catalog.

```
]CAT

S=6 D=02 V=000 F=0470 01/01/21 08:28:48

*B 034 DOS4.1.46L        01/01/21 08:28:48
 B 044 DOS4.1.46H        01/01/21 08:28:48
 B 003 INSTALL46L        01/01/21 08:28:48
 B 003 INSTALL46H        01/01/21 08:28:48

]UNLOCK DOS4.1.46L

]LS

S=6 D=02 V=000 F=0470 01/01/21 08:28:48

 B 034 DOS4.1.46L        01/01/21 08:28:49
 B 044 DOS4.1.46H        01/01/21 08:28:48
 B 003 INSTALL46L        01/01/21 08:28:48
 B 003 INSTALL46H        01/01/21 08:28:48

]
```

Figure III.1.20. UNLOCK Command Display

```
]cat r

M=DOS4.1.46L T=URM Figure

B=4146L data L=0xF00B 01/01/21 08:28:48

S=6 D=02 V=000 F=0520 01/01/21 08:28:48

*001 0x12,0x0F DOS4.1.46L
x002 0x15,0x0F DOS2TO1

]urm DOS2TO1

]ls

S=6 D=02 V=000 F=0518 01/01/21 08:28:49

*B 034 DOS4.1.46L        01/01/21 08:28:48
 B 002 DOS2TO1           01/01/21 08:28:49

]
```

Figure III.1.21. URM Command Display

128

```
VERIFY    f [,Ss][,Dd][,Vv][,R1]
```

Example   `VERIFY DOS4.1,R1`

This command reads into memory each sector listed in the TSL sector(s) of the file f in the specified volume. The read routine in RWTS simply verifies the checksum for each sector read. No data is changed and the date and time stamp of the file is not changed. The TSL sector(s) is indirectly verified since it is read into a DOS buffer and used to obtain the file's track and sector list, but it is not included in the verified sector count. Only when a non-zero R keyword is included will the number of verified sectors be displayed on the Apple command line as shown in Figure III.1.22. If a non-zero R keyword is included with the DOS 4.1 commands SAVE, BSAVE, LSAVE, and TSAVE, not only is the address and length information displayed, but also the number of verified sectors displayed as well. The VTOC time stamp remains unchanged when a file is verified because nothing in the VTOC is changed.

```
]CAT

S=6 D=02 V=000 F=0518 01/01/21 08:28:48

*B 034 DOS4.1.46L       01/01/21 08:28:48
 B 002 DOS2TO1          01/01/21 08:28:48

]VERIFY DOS2TO1

]VERIFY DOS4.1.46L,R1 = 033

]LS

S=6 D=02 V=000 F=0518 01/01/21 08:28:48

*B 034 DOS4.1.46L       01/01/21 08:28:48
 B 002 DOS2TO1          01/01/21 08:28:48

]
```

Figure III.1.22. VERIFY Command Display

Command	Command Syntax
IN#	s
MAXFILES	[n]
MON	[C][,I][,O]
NOMON	[C][,I][,O]
PR#	s

Table III.2.1. DOS 4.1 System Commands

2. System Commands

The DOS 4.1 System Commands manage the Input/Output data streams, the display of commands and data items, and the number of data buffers within DOS 4.1. The syntax of the System Commands is shown in Table III.2.1.

IN#   s

Example: IN#7

This command configures the KSWL interface to receive all subsequent data from the peripheral device residing in the specified slot s instead of from the Apple keyboard. Previously, Figure III.1.4 shows an example of using the IN# command in communicating with the ThunderClock clock card.

MAXFILES [n]

Example: MAXFILES 4
            MAXFILES

This command specifies the number of file buffers n that can be active at any given time up to a maximum of nine buffers for DOS 4.1L and five buffers for DOS 4.1H. When DOS 4.1 boots, the default number of file buffers is configured by the NMAXVAL variable at 0xBEEF as shown in Table I.8.7. This value is set to three in DOS 4.1L and five in DOS 4.1H. Each file buffer requires 585 (or 0x249) bytes of memory. DOS 4.1L builds its file buffers **down** in memory beginning at 0x9D00 whereas DOS 4.1H builds its file buffers **up** in memory beginning at 0xEC00. DOS 4.1H was designed this way such that setting MAXFILES to 3 will allow the MiniAssembler and its associated Monitor to be read into memory at 0xF500 and not perturb any of the DOS file buffers. Apple][memory is very precious, so specifying more file buffers than is absolutely necessary may prevent the

130

development of a very large, complex Applesoft or Binary program. MAXFILES with no parameter n will display the current number of active file buffers on the Apple command line as shown in Figure III.2.1. In Figure III.2.1 the difference of 150,37 (or $9625) and 147,220 (or $93DC) is 2,73, or 585 (or 0x249) bytes. The number of file buffers can never be zero. Even the CATALOG command requires a file buffer. Table III.2.2 shows the memory locations for all file buffers in DOS 4.1L and in DOS 4.1H. Reducing the number of file buffers in DOS 4.1H does **not** provide additional program space because those file buffers reside in the Language Card memory; reducing the number of file buffers to three would only allow the use of the MiniAssembler, for example. Before the MAXFILES command rebuilds the file buffers and allow DOS 4.1 to utilize them, DOS 4.1 terminates any active EXEC file and closes all open files. Therefore, the MAXFILES command should be issued early in a program before any files are opened for data input or data output.

```
]MAXFILES = 3

]PRINT PEEK(116);",";PEEK(115)
150,37

]MAXFILES 4

]PRINT PEEK(116);",";PEEK(115)
147,220

]PRINT ((150-1)-147)*256+((37+256)-220)
585

]MON
*

]NOMON
*▩
```

Figure III.2.1. MAXFILES, MON, and NOMON Command Display

MON   [,C][,I][,O]

Example: MON C,I,O
           MON

This command enables the display of commands, input data, and output data to a volume. If the C keyword is included all programmatically executed DOS Commands are displayed. If the I keyword is included all Input data from a volume is displayed. If the O keyword is included all Output data to a volume is displayed. If no keywords are included the CSWL and KSWL pointers are initialized and DOS enters the Apple Monitor at 0xFF65. Entering a ctrl-C from the Apple Monitor re-enables DOS's control of the CSWL and KSWL pointers as shown in Figure III.2.1.

MAXFILES	DOS 4.1L		DOS 4.1H	
Value	Memory	HIMEM	Memory	HIMEM
1	0x9AB7-0x9CFF	0x9AB7	0xEC00-0xEE48	0xBE00
2	0x986E-0x9AB6	0x986E	0xEE49-0xF091	0xBE00
3	0x9625-0x986D	0x9625	0xF092-0xF2DA	0xBE00
4	0x93DC-0x9624	0x93DC	0xF2DB-0xF523	0xBE00
5	0x9193-0x93DB	0x9193	0xF524-0xF76C	0xBE00
6	0x8F4A-0x9192	0x8F4A	–	–
7	0x8D01-0x8F49	0x8D01	–	–
8	0x8AB8-0x8D00	0x8AB8	–	–
9	0x886F-0x8AB7	0x886F	–	–

Table III.2.2. MAXFILES Memory Locations

```
NOMON      [,C][,I][,O]
```

Example: NOMON C,I,O
            NOMON

This command disables the display of commands, input data, and output data to a volume. If the C keyword is included all programmatically executed DOS Commands are no longer displayed. If the I keyword is included all Input data from a volume is no longer displayed. If the O keyword is included all Output data to a volume is no longer displayed. If no keywords are included the CSWL and KSWL pointers are initialized and DOS enters the Apple Monitor at 0xFF65. Entering a ctrl-C from the Apple Monitor re-enables DOS's control of the CSWL and KSWL pointers as shown in Figure III.2.1.

PR#   s

Example: PR#7

This command configures the CSWL interface to send all subsequent data to the peripheral device residing in the specified slot s instead of to the Apple display. Previously, Figure III.1.4 shows an example of using the PR# command in communicating with the ThunderClock clock card.

Command	Command Syntax
CHAIN	f [,Ss][,Dd][,Vv][,Ll][,R]
LOAD	f [,Ss][,Dd][,Vv][,R]
RUN	f [,Ss][,Dd][,Vv][,Ll]
SAVE	f [,Ss][,Dd][,Vv][,R[1]][,B]

Table III.3.1. DOS 4.1 Applesoft File Commands

3. Applesoft File Commands

The DOS 4.1 Applesoft File Commands manage Applesoft files. The syntax of the Applesoft File Commands is shown in Table III.3.1.

CHAIN   f [,Ss][,Dd][,Vv][,Ll][,R]

Example: CHAIN TESTPART2, D2

This command is new to DOS and is used only from within an Applesoft program. It LOADs and RUNs the Applesoft file f in the specified volume. It does not clear the value(s) of any previous variable so that file f can use the data and the results of the previous program(s), and can provide data and results for any following CHAIN program. If the L keyword is included, processing will begin at that line number only if that line number exists in program f, otherwise an error is reported and Applesoft processing terminates. This capability opens up a myriad of programming possibilities. If the R keyword is **not** used CHAIN calls the Applesoft ROM routine GARBAG at 0xE484 before moving the Simple Variables and Array Variables descriptors to their new location at the end of program f. This allows a user to either invoke the "FRE(*aexpr*)" Applesoft command or utilize another method of string garbage collection before or after using the CHAIN command. It is critical that simple string variables and string array variables that will be used in the next CHAIN program be moved to the Character String Pool memory area where string data is stored. See section I.13 for a more thorough discussion of the DOS CHAIN command.

Table I.13.1 shows the definition of the descriptor for the simple variables used in Applesoft programs. The string descriptor consists of only the first two ASCII characters of the string name (so care must be given in naming variables), the string length, the address in low/high byte order where the string resides in memory, and two NULL filler bytes. String descriptors for array variables are shown in Table I.13.2 and each string element contains the string length and the address in low/high byte order where the string resides in memory. The address in the string descriptor or string element will initially be the location where the actual string data exists within the contents of a program. Once the next CHAIN file f replaces that Applesoft program, the actual string data will be overwritten and lost, and its address will become invalid. Therefore, caution must be exercised when using string variables and CHAIN if the string variables are not moved to the Character String Pool memory area.

Figure III.3.1 shows two Applesoft programs called START and PROGRAM2. START defines four simple variables D$, AB, CD%, and EF$. The string variable EF$ is defined in such a way as to force Applesoft to move it immediately into the Character String Pool memory area where string data is stored. Applesoft will also move the variable D$ to the Character String Pool memory area before it is used with the CHAIN command. All four variables will be available to the CHAIN program PROGRAM2 as shown in Figure III.3.2 when the program START is RUN.

```
] load START

] list

 10  D$  =   CHR$ (4):AB = 123:CD% =
     456:EF$ = "Test Chain" + ""
 20  PRINT : PRINT "This is the S
     TART program to test CHAIN":
     PRINT
 30  PRINT "AB = ";AB;", CD% = ";
     CD%;", EF$ = ";EF$: PRINT
 40  PRINT D$;"CHAIN PROGRAM2"

] load PROGRAM2

] list

 10  PRINT : PRINT "Now running p
     rogram PROGRAM2": PRINT
 20  PRINT "AB = ";AB;", CD% = ";
     CD%;", EF$ = ";EF$
 30  PRINT D$;"CATALOG": PRINT

] ※
```

Figure III.3.1. Listing of START and PROGRAM2 Programs Display

134

```
]run START
This is the START program to test CHAIN
AB = 123, CD% = 456, EF$ = Test Chain

Now running program PROGRAM2
AB = 123, CD% = 456, EF$ = Test Chain

S=6 D=02 V=000 F=0550 02/14/19 08:28:50
 A 002 START              02/14/19 08:28:48
 A 002 PROGRAM2           02/14/19 08:28:49
]
```

Figure III.3.2. Output of Programs START and PROGRAM2 Display

```
]CATALOG
S=6 D=02 V=000 F=0518 01/01/21 08:28:48
 A 004 HELLO              01/01/21 08:28:48
]LOAD HELLO
]LOAD HELLO,R
A$0801,L$02A7
]SAVE HELLO2
]SAVE HELLO2,R
A$0801,L$02A7
]SAVE HELLO2,R1
A$0801,L$02A7 = 003
]
```

Figure III.3.3. LOAD and SAVE Commands Display

```
LOAD       f [,Ss][,Dd][,Vv][,R]

Example    LOAD HELLO
           LOAD HELLO,R
```

This command reads into memory at 0x0801 the Applesoft file f in the specified volume. Applesoft program files are file type 0x02 as shown in Table I.7.3. This command will also process A type files (or 0x20) as an Applesoft file similarly as in DOS 3.3. If the R keyword is included the memory load address (i.e. 0x0801) and the number of bytes loaded (i.e. 0x02A7) are displayed as shown in Figure III.3.3.

```
RUN        f [,Ss][,Dd][,Vv][,Ll]

Example:   RUN START
```

This command reads into memory at 0x0801 the Applesoft file f in the specified volume and begins program execution. DOS pointers are first initialized, then DOS calls 0xD665 in ROM to clear Applesoft variables, it clears the prompt and ONERR flags, and finally it calls 0xD7D2 in ROM to begin program execution. If the L keyword is included processing will begin at that line number only if that line number exists in program f, otherwise an error is reported and Applesoft processing terminates. An example of the use of the RUN command was shown previously in Figure III.3.2.

```
SAVE       f [,Ss][,Dd][,Vv][,R[1]][,B]

Example:   SAVE HELLO2
           SAVE HELLO2,R
           SAVE HELLO2,R1
```

This command saves the Applesoft file f to the specified volume. If the R keyword is included the save address (or 0x0801) and the number of bytes saved (or 0x02A7) are displayed as shown in Figure III.3.3. If a non-zero R keyword is included, the number of verified sectors is also displayed as shown in Figure III.3.3. The B keyword can be used to implement the "File Delete/File Save" strategy. That is, the Applesoft file f will be deleted from the volume Catalog and then saved to the volume in order to ensure that the file's TSL contains the exact number of track/sector entries that are required.

Command	Command Syntax
BLOAD	f [,Ss][,Dd][,Vv][,Aa][,R]
BRUN	f [,Ss][,Dd][,Vv][,Aa]
BSAVE	f [,Ss][,Dd][,Vv][,Aa][,Ll][,R[1]][B]
LLOAD	f [,Ss][,Dd][,Vv][,Aa][,R]
LSAVE	f [,Ss][,Dd][,Vv][,Aa][,Ll][,R[1]][B]

Table III.4.1. DOS 4.1 Binary File Commands

4. Binary File Commands

The DOS 4.1 Binary File Commands manage Binary, or assembly language files. The syntax of the Binary File Commands is shown in Table III.4.1.

BLOAD   f [,Ss][,Dd][,Vv][,Aa][,R]

Example: BLOAD RD
           BLOAD RD,R
           BLOAD RD,A$1000,R

This command reads into memory at address a if the A keyword is included, the Binary file f in the specified volume. If the A keyword is not included the file is read into memory at the address the file was originally saved. Binary files are file type 0x04 as shown in Table I.7.3. If the R keyword is included the memory load address and the number of bytes read into memory are displayed as shown in Figure III.4.1.

BRUN   f [,Ss][,Dd][,Vv][,Aa]

Example: BRUN INSTALLL
           BRUN INSTALLL,A$1000

This command reads the Binary file f in the specified volume into memory at address a if the A keyword is included, and begins program execution at that address. If the A keyword is not included, the Binary file f is loaded into memory at the address the file was originally saved and execution begins at that address. In DOS 4.1 the DOSWARM address is pushed onto the stack before executing an indirect JMP to ADRVAL, the Binary file memory load address, to guarantee that DOS will be in control after the Binary program exits. An example of the BRUN command is shown in Figure III.4.2.

137

```
]BLOAD RD,R
A$4000,L$1700
]BLOAD RD,A$1000,R
A$1000,L$1700
]BSAVE RD2
]BSAVE RD2,R
A$1000,L$1700
]BSAVE RD3,A$4000,L$1700,R1
A$4000,L$1700 = 024
]DIFF RD,RD3 = 0x1800

]
```

Figure III.4.1. BLOAD and BSAVE Commands Display

```
]BRUN INSTALL46L

Reading DOS 4.1.46L image into memory.

DOS 4.1.46L image now in memory.

Insert diskette into Slot 6, Drive 1.
Press any key to continue.

Installing DOS 4.1.46L.

.................................

Installation of DOS 4.1.46L is complete.

]
```

Figure III.4.2. BRUN Command Display

```
BSAVE    f [,Ss][,Dd][,Vv][,Aa][,Ll][,R[1]][,B]
```

Example: BSAVE RD2
         BSAVE RD2,R
         BSAVE RD3,A$4000,L$1C00,R1

This command saves the Binary file f to the specified volume using the memory address a and length
l in bytes if the A and L keywords are included. In DOS 4.1 these keywords are optional, but if they
are included they are both required. If the A and L keywords are not included, the address a and length
l of the previous BLOAD or BSAVE command are used. If the R keyword is included the memory save
address and the number of bytes saved are displayed as shown previously in Figure III.4.1. If a non-
zero R keyword is included, the number of verified sectors is also displayed as shown in Figure III.4.1.
Also shown in Figure III.4.1 is a byte comparison of the two files RD and RD3 using the DOS DIFF
command. The DIFF command proves that both files are identical. The B keyword can be used to
implement the "File Delete/File Save" strategy. That is, the Binary file f will be deleted from the
volume Catalog and then saved to the volume in order to ensure that the file's TSL contains the exact
number of track/sector entries that are required.

```
]LLOAD README.L,R
A$2100,L$07E6
]LLOAD README.L,A$1000,R
A$1000,L$07E6
]LSAVE README2.L
]LSAVE README2.L,R
A$1000,L$07E6
]LSAVE README3.L,A$2100,L$7E6,R1
A$2100,L$07E6 = 008
]DIFF README.L,README3.L = 0x0800

]
```

Figure III.4.3. LLOAD and LSAVE Commands Display

```
LLOAD     f [,Ss][,Dd][,Vv][,Aa][,R]
```

Example: `LLOAD  README.L`
           `LLOAD  README.L,R`
           `LLOAD  README.L,A$1000,R`

This command is new to DOS and it reads into memory the *Lisa* Binary file f in the specified volume at address a if the A keyword is included. If the A keyword is not included the *Lisa* file is read into memory at the address the file was originally saved. *Lisa* files are file type 0x40 as shown in Table I.7.3. If the R keyword is included the memory load address and the number of bytes read are displayed as shown in Figure III.4.3.

```
LSAVE     f [,Ss][,Dd][,Vv][,Aa][,Ll][,R[1]][,B]
```

Example: `LSAVE  README2.L`
           `LSAVE  README2.L,R`
           `LSAVE  README3.L,A$2100,L$CED,R1`

This command is new to DOS and it saves the *Lisa* Binary file f to the specified volume using the address a and length l if the A and L keywords are included. In DOS 4.1 these keywords are optional, but if they are included they are both required. If the A and L keywords are not included, the address a and length l of the previous LLOAD or LSAVE command are used. If the R keyword is included the memory save address and the number of bytes saved are displayed as shown in Figure III.4.3. If a non-zero R keyword is included, the number of verified sectors is also displayed as shown in Figure III.4.3. Also shown in Figure III.4.3 is a byte comparison of the two files README.L and README3.L using the DOS DIFF command. The DIFF command proves that both files are identical. The B keyword can be used to implement the "File Delete/File Save" strategy. That is, the *Lisa* Binary file f will be deleted from the volume Catalog and then saved to the volume in order to ensure that the file's TSL contains the exact number of track/sector entries that are required.

Command	Command Syntax
APPEND*	f [,Ss][,Dd][,Vv]
CLOSE	[f]
EXEC	f [,Ss][,Dd][,Vv][,Rr]
OPEN*	f [,Ss][,Dd][,Vv]
POSITION*	f [,Rr]
READ*	f [,Bb]
TLOAD	f [,Ss][,Dd][,Vv][,A][,Bb][,Ll][,R]
TSAVE	f [,Ss][,Dd][,Vv][,R[1]][B]
TW	f [,Ss][,Dd][,Vv]
WRITE*	f [,Bb]

Table III.5.1. DOS 4.1 Sequential Text File Commands

5. Sequential Text File Commands

The DOS 4.1 Sequential Text File Commands manage sequential Text files. The syntax of the Sequential Text File Commands is shown in Table III.5.1. The commands shown with an asterisk cannot be used on the Apple command line, whereas the other sequential Text file commands are allowed to be used on the Apple command line. Sequential Text files are composed of sequential fields of ASCII characters where a RETURN (or 0x8D) character terminates each field, and a NULL (or 0x00) character terminates the file. DOS 4.1 differentiates between sequential Text files and random-access Data files in how the file is opened. If the L keyword is **not** included with the OPEN command the file is treated as a sequential Text file, and the READ and WRITE commands **must not use** the R keyword as shown in Table III.5.1.

Data may be read from or saved to a sequential Text file immediately after the file is opened, after the file pointer has been positioned to a particular byte location, or after the file pointer has been positioned to a particular field. If the B keyword is included with the READ or WRITE command, it will take precedence over any previous POSITION command. That is, even though the file pointer may be at the beginning of the rth field specified by a previous POSITION command, the B keyword, if it is included with a subsequent READ or WRITE command, will force the file pointer to be recalculated to point to the bth byte relative to the beginning of the file.

APPEND   f [,Ss][,Dd][,Vv]

Example: APPEND STEST.T

This command will open the sequential Text file f in the specified volume if it is not already open. The APPEND command must be followed by a WRITE command to file f. The APPEND command will read the entire file f and position the file pointer to the first NULL (or 0x00) character found in the file. All subsequent input data will be saved to the file beginning at that location. Figure III.5.1

141

shows an example Applesoft program that uses the OPEN, WRITE, and CLOSE commands in order to create the sequential Text file STEST.T. Figure III.5.2 is similar in that it shows an example Applesoft program that uses the APPEND command to add more information to the file STEST.T.

The APPEND command was flawed in several locations in DOS 3.3 requiring patches in how the internal variable BYTOFFST and the File Manager Context Block variable RECNUM were manipulated. DOS 4.1 manipulates these variables correctly within the File Manager driver routine FMDRVR, in the Common Open routine CMNOPN as described in Section I.10, and in the Calculate Position routine CALPOSN. The original DOS 3.3 Calculate Position routine failed to ensure that the carry flag was clear before manipulating its variables in order to calculate the desired file position.

```
]LOAD STEST
]LIST

 10 D$ =   CHR$ (4):F$ = "STEST.T"
    : ONERR  GOTO 100
 20  PRINT D$;"OPEN ";F$
 30  PRINT D$;"WRITE ";F$
 40  PRINT "This is a sequential
    TEXT file."
 50  PRINT D$;"CLOSE ";F$
 100  END
]RUN

]LIST STEST.T
This is a sequential TEXT file.

]
```

Figure III.5.1. OPEN, WRITE, and CLOSE Commands Display

CLOSE   [f]

Example: CLOSE
           CLOSE STEST.T

This command will de-allocate the file buffer associated with the sequential Text file f, thereby closing the file from further data input or data output. If a filename is not supplied with the CLOSE command, all open files regardless of their file type will be closed except for an open EXEC file. If a file f was open for data input, a CLOSE command will cause all remaining data in its file buffer to be saved to the file and then the file f will be closed. Figures III.5.1 and III.5.2 show examples of using the CLOSE command in an Applesoft program.

```
]LOAD STEST2

]LIST

 10 D$ =   CHR$ (4):F$ = "STEST.T"
     : ONERR  GOTO 100
 20   PRINT D$;"OPEN ";F$
 30   PRINT D$;"APPEND ";F$
 40   PRINT D$;"WRITE ";F$
 50   PRINT "This is an appended l
     ine."
 60   PRINT D$;"CLOSE ";F$
 100   END

]RUN

]LIST STEST.T

This is a sequential TEXT file.
This is an appended line.

]※
```

Figure III.5.2. APPEND Command Display

EXEC   f [,Ss][,Dd][,Vv][,Rr]

Example: EXEC ETEST.T
            EXEC ETEST.T,R3

This command opens the file f in the specified volume with the expectation of reading either Applesoft or DOS 4.1 commands as if the commands had been issued from the Apple command line. There can be only one active EXEC file, but an EXEC file may transfer control to another EXEC file. If the R keyword is included the file pointer is positioned that number of fields r from the beginning of the file. A field is a sequence of characters terminated by a RETURN (or 0x8D) character. Figure III.5.3 shows an example of an EXEC file in operation. In Figure III.5.4 the file pointer is positioned at the first character after counting three RETURN characters, thus ignoring those fields, and issuing all subsequent commands contained in that file. Notice that the first three commands in the EXEC file ETEST.T are skipped.

If MAXFILES is used in an EXEC file, the EXEC command processing will terminate and close the executing EXEC file. In both Figures III.5.3 and III.5.4 command-line spacing is set to single spacing while an EXEC file is open. Once the EXEC file is closed DOS 4.1 will return to double spacing for displaying successive Apple command lines.

```
]LIST ETEST.T

print "This is ETEST running."
mon c
brun BTEST
date

]EXEC ETEST.T
]
This is ETEST running.

]

]
This is an example Binary program.
Clock data:  01/01/21 08:28:48
End of Binary program.

] = 01/01/21 08:28:48
]※
```

Figure III.5.3. EXEC Command Display

OPEN   f [,Ss][,Dd][,Vv]

Example: OPEN STEST.T

This command will allocate one of the available file buffers, which is 585 (or 0x249) bytes in size, for the sequential Text file f in the specified volume. This file buffer will be initialized to read from or write to the beginning of this file. If this file does not exist in the specified volume, the file is created and an entry is made in the volume Catalog. If this file is already open, the file is flushed so any remaining data in its file buffer is saved to the file, the file is closed, and the specified file is again opened. Figures III.5.1 and III.5.2 show examples of using the sequential Text file OPEN command in an Applesoft program. The L keyword **must not** be included with the OPEN command when reading and writing sequential Text files.

144

```
]LIST ETEST.T

print "This is ETEST running."
mon c
brun BTEST
date

]EXEC ETEST.T,R3
] = 01/01/21 08:28:48
]※
```

Figure III.5.4. EXEC,Rr Command Display

```
]LIST STEST.T

This is a sequential TEXT file.
This is an appended line.

]LOAD STEST3

]LIST

 10  D$ =  CHR$ (4):F$ = "STEST.T"
      : ONERR  GOTO 100
 20   PRINT D$;"OPEN ";F$
 30   PRINT D$;"POSITION ";F$;",R1
      "
 40   PRINT D$;"READ ";F$
 50   INPUT A$: PRINT A$
 60   GOTO 50
 100   PRINT D$;"CLOSE ";F$: END

]RUN
This is an appended line.

]※
```

Figure III.5.5. POSITION and READ Commands Display

POSITION f [,Rr]

Example: POSITION STEST.T,R1

This command will position the file pointer in the file f that number of fields r ahead relative to the current file pointer position. A field is a sequence of ASCII characters terminated by a RETURN (or 0x8D) character. Figure III.5.5 shows an example Applesoft program where the file pointer is positioned at the first character after counting one RETURN character relative to the beginning of the file STEST.T since this POSITION command follows an OPEN command. Otherwise, the file pointer would be positioned ahead relative to the current file pointer position.

READ   f [,Bb]

Example: READ STEST.T

This command will configure the sequential Text file buffer for file f such that all data will come from that file. If the B keyword is included the file pointer position will be located that many actual bytes b from the beginning of the file before any data is read from the file. Figure III.5.6 shows an example Applesoft program that uses the sequential Text file READ command with a byte b offset. Any previous POSITION command will be ignored if the B keyword is included with the READ command.

TLOAD   f [,Ss][,Dd][,Vv][,A][,Bb][,Ll][,R]

Example: TLOAD ETEST.T,L31
           TLOAD STEST,A,R
           TLOAD ETEST.T,A,B31

This command is new to DOS and it will read into memory the sequential Text file f in the specified volume to memory address 0x0900. If the A keyword is included in a subsequent TLOAD command, that sequential Text file f will be appended to the sequential Text file(s) already in memory as long as the internal variable FILELAST+1 is not 0x00; that is, a sequential Text file must already be in memory. If the B keyword is included, that number of bytes b will be skipped before reading the file into memory. If the L keyword is included, that number of bytes l will be read into memory, or until the end of the file if that should occur first. If the R keyword is included the start address and total number of bytes of text data currently in memory is displayed once the TLOAD command completes.

```
]LIST STEST.T

This is a sequential TEXT file.
This is an appended line.


]LOAD STEST4

]LIST

 10 D$ =  CHR$ (4):F$ = "STEST.T"
    : ONERR  GOTO 100
 20  PRINT D$;"OPEN ";F$
 30  PRINT D$;"READ ";F$;",B3"
 40  INPUT A$: PRINT A$
 50  GOTO 40
 100  PRINT D$;"CLOSE ";F$: END

]RUN
s is a sequential TEXT file.
This is an appended line.

]
```

Figure III.5.6. READ,Bb Command Display

```
]TLOAD ETEST.T,L31

]TLOAD STEST.T,A,R

A$0900,L$0059

]TLOAD ETEST.T,A,B31

]TSAVE TOTAL.T,R1

A$0900,L$006F = 001

]LIST TOTAL.T

print "This is ETEST running."
This is a sequential TEXT file.
This is an appended line.
mon c
brun BTEST
date

]
```

Figure III.5.7. TLOAD and TSAVE Command Display

147

In Figure III.5.7 the first 31 bytes of the file ETEST.T are read into memory at memory address 0x0900. The entire contents of the file STEST.T is read into memory next and appended to the previous Text data already in memory because the A keyword was specified. The total Text data now in memory is shown to be 89 (or 0x59) bytes. Finally, the first 31 bytes of the file ETEST.T are skipped and the remaining contents of the file ETEST.T is appended to all the previous Text data already in memory. The complete sequential Text file data is saved to the file TOTAL.T, and the entire file is displayed using the DOS 4.1 LIST command. It is quite apparent that a complete sequential Text file may be easily created from extracting pieces of other sequential Text files using the TLOAD command and its keywords.

```
]LIST TEST.T

PRINT "This is TEST.T running."
PRINT "Ready to run BTEST."
BRUN BTEST


]TW TEST.T

>DATE
>

]LIST TEST.T

PRINT "This is TEST.T running."
PRINT "Ready to run BTEST."
BRUN BTEST
DATE


]
```

Figure III.5.8. TW Display

TSAVE   f [,Ss][,Dd][,Vv][,R[1]][B]

Example: TSAVE TOTAL.T,R
           TSAVE TOTAL2.T,R1

This command is new to DOS and it will save the sequential Text file data currently in memory to the file f in the specified volume. The start address and total number of bytes of Text data currently in memory is internal to DOS 4.1. If the R keyword is included the start address and total number of bytes of sequential Text file data currently in memory is displayed as shown in Figure III.5.7 once the

`TSAVE` command completes. If a non-zero R keyword is included, the number of verified sectors is also displayed. The B keyword can be used to implement the "File Delete/File Save" strategy. That is, the Text file `f` will be deleted from the volume Catalog and then saved to the volume in order to ensure that the file's `TSL` contains the exact number of track/sector entries that are required.

```
TW        f [,Ss][,Dd][,Vv]
```

Example: `TW ETEST`

This command is new to DOS and it will record all keystrokes typed on the Apple command line into the sequential Text file `f` in the specified volume. If the file does not exist it is created, otherwise the file is always opened in `APPEND` mode. The file is flushed and closed when the `ESC` key is pressed; that is, all buffered data is saved to file `f`, and then the file is closed. No line editing is provided and all keystrokes including arrow keystrokes (quasi editing) are recorded to the file as well. The `TW` (or Text Write) command provides a convenient and expeditious way to create or append an `EXEC` file as the example shows in Figure III.5.8.

```
WRITE     f [,Bb]
```

Example: `WRITE STEST.TXT`

This command will configure the sequential Text file buffer for file `f` such that all data will be saved to that file. If the B keyword is included the file pointer position will be located that many actual bytes b from the beginning of the file before any data is saved to the file. Figures III.5.1 and III.5.2 show examples of using the sequential Text file `WRITE` command in an Applesoft program. Any previous `POSITION` command will be ignored if the B keyword is included with the WRITE command.

Command	Command Syntax
CLOSE	[f]
OPEN*	f, Ll [,Ss][,Dd][,Vv]
READ*	f, Rr [,Bb]
WRITE*	f, Rr [,Bb]

Table III.6.1. DOS 4.1 Random-Access Data File Commands

6. Random-Access Data File Commands

The DOS 4.1 Random-Access Data File Commands manage random-access Data files. The syntax of the Random-Access Data File Commands is shown in Table III.6.1. The commands shown with an asterisk, or OPEN, READ, and WRITE, cannot be used on the Apple command line, whereas the CLOSE command is allowed to be used on the Apple command line. Random-access Data files are composed of specified sized records. A record may be comprised of Text fields, numerical data fields, or both, and they can be as small as one byte or as large as 65535 (or 0xFFFF) bytes in size. The record size is established by the OPEN command. A Text field is any number of sequential ASCII characters terminated with a RETURN (or 0x8D) character. A numerical field may be any number of digits, either integer or floating point, in decimal or hexadecimal, or expressed in scientific notation in the case of real and imaginary numbers. All fields must reside within the specified record size. All records comprising a file f do not necessarily have to contain the same number or order of fields; however, all records must be the same size within file f. DOS 4.1 allows the R keyword r value to be specified up to 32767 (or 0x7FFF), thus permitting up to 32768 records in a single file f. DOS 4.1 differentiates sequential Text files and random-access Data files by how the file is opened. If the L keyword is **included** with the OPEN command the file is treated as a random-access Data file and the READ and WRITE commands **must use** the R keyword as shown in Table III.6.1. All programs that access a random-access Data file must open this file with the same record size l, otherwise the results will be unpredictable and quite possibly disastrous as the file is processed.

Data sectors are created as necessary when a random-access Data file record is supplied with data. The file pointer value is calculated based on record size l and record number r. Using the file pointer value, the necessary TSL index can be determined, and if there is no track/sector entry for the respective data sector, a data sector is obtained from the volume Catalog and an entry is made in the TSL sector. Any numerical remainder from the TSL index calculation plus any b index value determines the byte offset within the data sector where the record data is written. If the complete record requires additional sectors, those sectors will be obtained from the volume Catalog and added to the TSL sector.

CLOSE   [f]

Example: CLOSE RTEST.T

This command will de-allocate the file buffer associated with the random-address Data file f, thereby closing the file from further data input or data output. If a filename is not supplied with the CLOSE command, all open files regardless of their file type will be closed except for an open EXEC file. If a file f was open for data input, a CLOSE will cause all remaining data in its file buffer to be saved to the file. Figure III.6.1 shows an example of using the CLOSE command in an Applesoft program.

```
OPEN      f, Ll [,Ss][,Dd][,Vv]
```

```
Example:  OPEN RTEST.T, L32
```

This command will allocate one of the available file buffers, which is 585 (or `0x249`) bytes in size, for the random-access Data file `f` in the specified volume, and set the record length to the number of bytes `l` specified by the `L` keyword. If this file does not exist in the specified volume, the file is created and an entry is made in the volume Catalog. If this file is already open, the file is flushed so any remaining data in its file buffer is saved to the file, the file is closed, and the specified file is again opened. Figures III.6.1 and III.6.3 show examples of using the random-access Data file `OPEN` command in an Applesoft program. The `L` keyword **must** be included with the `OPEN` command when reading data from and writing data to random-access Data files.

```
READ      f, Rr [,Bb]
```

```
Example:  READ RTEST.T, R1, B12
```

This command will configure the random-access Data file buffer for the file `f` such that all data will come from that file. Data will be read from the specified Record `r`, one field at a time. If the `R` keyword is not included no error will be generated and the file pointer will simply be positioned at the beginning of the file. DOS 4.1 does not check for the presence or absence of the R keyword; it simply utilizes its value. However, even though the R keyword is initialized to `0x00` before a DOS command is parsed, the practice of not using the R keyword with the random-access Data file `READ` command is not advised. If the `B` keyword is included the file pointer will be positioned that many bytes `b` from the beginning of the specified Record `r` before any data is read from the file.

Figure III.6.2 shows a hexadecimal list of the contents of `RTEST.T` using the DOS `LIST` command with the R keyword. Each record is 32 bytes in size from byte 0 to byte 31. There is no data in the first record, Record 0, data in Record 1 begins on byte 12, data in Record 2 begins on byte 6, and data in Record 3 begins on byte 0. Figure III.6.3 shows an example of using the random-access Data file `READ` command in an Applesoft program. The file records may be specified and they can be read from the file in any order, hence the descriptive term 'random-access'. Figure III.6.3 also shows the results of running the `RTEST2` Applesoft program.

```
]LOAD RTEST

]LIST

 10  D$ =  CHR$ (4):F$ = "RTEST.T"
     :L = 32: ONERR  GOTO 60
 20   PRINT D$;"OPEN ";F$;", L";L
 30   PRINT D$;"WRITE ";F$;", R3"
 35   PRINT "This is Record 3."
 40   PRINT D$;"WRITE ";F$;", R2,
     B6"
 45   PRINT "This is Record 2."
 50   PRINT D$;"WRITE ";F$;", R1,
     B12"
 55   PRINT "This is Record 1."
 60   PRINT D$;"CLOSE ";F$: END

]RUN

]
```

Figure III.6.1. OPEN, WRITE, and CLOSE Commands Display

```
]LIST RTEST.T,R

0000 0000 0000 0000 0000 0000 0000 0000
0000 0000 0000 0000 0000 0000 0000 0000
0000 0000 0000 0000 0000 0000 D4E8 E9F3
A0E9 F3A0 D2E5 E3EF F2E4 A0B1 AE8D 0000
0000 0000 0000 D4E8 E9F3 A0E9 F3A0 D2E5
E3EF F2E4 A0B2 AE8D 0000 0000 0000 0000
D4E8 E9F3 A0E9 F3A0 D2E5 E3EF F2E4 A0B3
AE8D 0000 0000 0000 0000 0000 0000 0000
0000 0000 0000 0000 0000 0000 0000 0000
0000 0000 0000 0000 0000 0000 0000 0000
0000 0000 0000 0000 0000 0000 0000 0000
0000 0000 0000 0000 0000 0000 0000 0000
0000 0000 0000 0000 0000 0000 0000 0000
0000 0000 0000 0000 0000 0000 0000 0000
0000 0000 0000 0000 0000 0000 0000 0000

※
```

Figure III.6.2. Contents of RTEST.T Display

152

```
]LOAD RTEST2

]LIST

 10 D$ =  CHR$ (4):F$ = "RTEST.T"
    :L = 32: ONERR  GOTO 60
 20  PRINT D$;"OPEN ";F$;", L";L
 30  PRINT D$;"READ ";F$;", R2, B
    6": INPUT D2$
 40  PRINT D$;"READ ";F$;", R3": INPUT
    D3$
 50  PRINT D$;"READ ";F$;", R1, B
    12": INPUT D1$
 60  PRINT D$;"CLOSE ";F$
 70  PRINT : PRINT D1$: PRINT D2$
    : PRINT D3$: END

]RUN

This is Record 1.
This is Record 2.
This is Record 3.

]
```

Figure III.6.3. READ and RUN Command Display

WRITE   f, Rr [,Bb]

Example: WRITE RTEST.T, R1, B12

This command will configure the random-access Data file buffer for file f such that all data will be
saved to that file. Data will be saved to the specified Record r, one field at a time. If the R keyword is
not included no error will be generated and the file pointer will simply be positioned at the beginning
of the file. The practice of not using the R keyword with the random-access Data file WRITE
command is not advised. If the B keyword is included the file pointer will be positioned that many
bytes b from the beginning of the specified Record r before any data is saved to the file. Figure III.6.1
shows an example of using the random-access Data file WRITE command in an Applesoft program.
The file records may be specified and they can be saved to the file in any order, hence the descriptive
term 'random-access'.

153

7. Analysis of Using a Random-Access Data File in a Program

Denis Molony, a citizen of Australia and author of *DiskBrowser*, provided me with an excellent example of an Applesoft program that creates a random-access Data file that will quickly become useless after a few records are saved to the file. Figure III.7.1 shows Molony's Applesoft program. His program certainly looks simple enough until you realize that the program writes to the last possible record permitted by DOS 4.1, record 32767 (or 0x7FFF), or the 32768th record. When DOS first creates a random-access Data file only the first TSL sector is created as in line 400 and the value of the L keyword, 467 in this example, is saved in the file's workarea in the RECDLNGH variable as shown in Table I.10.1 at offset 0x216. When this file is reopened sometime in the future, the file must be opened with the same L keyword value in order to accurately locate the desired records. When Molony's program writes to record 32767 in line 600 a file pointer is calculated and sufficient TSL sectors are created in order to save that particular record to its rightful data sector.

```
]LOAD CREATE
]LIST

 100  D$ =  CHR$ (4)
 200  F$ = "BIGFILE"
 300  L = 467
 400   PRINT D$;"OPEN ";F$;",L";L
 500  R = 32767
 600   PRINT D$;"WRITE ";F$;",R";R

 700   PRINT "RECORD ";R
 800   PRINT D$;"CLOSE ";F$: END

]RUN

]LS

S=6 D=02 V=000 F=0061 01/01/21 08:28:48

 A 002 CREATE           01/01/21 08:28:48
 T 491 BIGFILE          01/01/21 08:28:48

]
```

Figure III.7.1. Example Random-Access Data File CREATE

How many TSL sectors are created may seem puzzling at first, though easy to determine. Each TSL sector contains 122 (or 0x7A) track/sector entries. These entries are for sectors of data, not for records of data. Each sector of data contains 256 (or 0x100) bytes. Including record 0, therefore,

{ (467 bytes/record * 32768 records) / 256 bytes/sector } / 122 sectors/TSL

   = 490 TSLs

154

When the data is actually written to the file in line 700, an entry is made in the 490th TSL sector for the sector that is created to contain the provided data. The data is not necessarily written to the first byte of the sector, but in this instance to byte 46, which comes at the end of record 32766, or the 32767th record. The entire record of 467 bytes is **not** written to the file but only the data provided in the Applesoft PRINT statement in line 700. This byte offset into the data sector is the remainder from the file pointer calculation:

(467 bytes/record * 32767 records) / 256 bytes/sector

= 59,774 sectors + 45 bytes

Figure III.7.1 shows that BIGFILE is 491 sectors in size, currently composed of 490 TSL sectors and one data sector. There are only sixty-one sectors free on this DOS 4.1 data volume which originally contained 554 sectors when it was first initialized. Why has DOS created all these TSL sectors? It seems rather ludicrous, because 59,774 sectors are required to contain all the data for all the previous 32767 records if every record of 467 bytes contained data and all these records had been written to this file. But that would require a volume having at least 3,736 additional disk tracks. At the very least DOS has created the minimum number of required linked-list TSL sectors in order to write record 32767. It is rather obvious that the file BIGFILE is not at all suitable to contain all the data the program CREATE intended. Therefore, it is critical that random-access Data files are properly sized to the volumes on which they are stored.

Family Roots by Stephen C. Vorenberg and marketed by Quinsept, Inc., utilizes sequential Text files and random-access Data files for the *Family Roots* data base. Each data volume contains three files: CONTROL, NAMELIST, and FAMILY. The random-access Data file NAMELIST uses 26 sectors. The sequential Text file CONTROL uses two sectors, and it contains the Start and End record numbers that exist in the random-access Data file FAMILY whose records have been pre-initialized with a 256-byte empty buffer. The CONTROL file also contains the size of the FAMILY file records, and a few other operating parameters, so that the file FAMILY is always opened with the correct value 1 for the L keyword. Essentially, each FAMILY file contains 224 records, and each record can be utilized up to a maximum of 512 bytes. The equations required to verify whether there is sufficient disk space for this random-access Data file when all of its records are completely filled with data can be expressed as follows:

(224 records * 512 bytes/record) / 256 bytes/sector = 448 sectors

448 sectors / 122 sectors/TSL = 4 TSLs

Since *Family Roots* utilizes the DOS 3.3 disk operating system, tracks 0x00, 0x01, and 0x02 are not available for data (reserved for DOS 3.3), and the VTOC and Catalog combined require sixteen sectors. This leaves 496 sectors for data in a volume having thirty-five tracks. Using the above results, each data volume for *Family Roots* requires 26 + 2 + 448 + 4 = 480 sectors. Therefore, at least sixteen sectors should be left available in each data volume that could be used for additional files. A few data volumes did contain one or two additional files: LASTID and DATE. These files were only two sectors each in size and they appeared transitory. Vorenberg sized his data files such that 96.8% of each data volume is utilized giving the program *Family Roots* a little safety margin.

These two examples demonstrate how important it is to consider whether a single data volume can provide sufficient room to store the contents of a particular random-access Data file, or whether several volumes would be required to store all the generated data when using multiple random-access Data files. Performing the file sizing analysis upfront certainly saves much grief later on when and if a random-access Data file should exceed its storage media capacity. Certainly, a random-access Data file cannot grow endlessly and it must have limits built into its design. Given R for the number of records, L for the size of each record in bytes, and S for the number of available sectors where each sector contains 256 bytes, the general sizing equations incorporating TSL sector overhead can be expressed as follows:

```
S = ( R * L * 123 ) / ( 256 * 122 )                  (always round up)

R = ( S * 256 * 122 ) / ( L * 123 )                  (always round down)

L = ( S * 256 * 122 ) / ( R * 123 )                  (always round down)
```

Inserting Vorenberg's parameters where R = 224 and L = 512:

```
S = ( 224 * 512 * 123 ) / ( 256 * 122 ) = 451.67 => 452 sectors
```

This is precisely the same value obtained above:

```
480 data sectors + 4 TSL sectors = 452 sectors
```

For Molony's example program, the required number of sectors for his random-access Data file is:

```
S = ( 32768 * 467 * 123 ) / ( 256 * 122 ) => 60,266 sectors
```

A single, 35-track volume is hardly the appropriate media for this random-access Data file. Assuming Molony's Data file can be spread over several 35-track volumes each providing 570 sectors when using DOS 4.1, the number of records on each volume would be:

```
R = ( 570 * 256 * 122 ) / ( 467 * 123 ) => 309 records          (round down)
```

And, the number of volumes required would be:

```
32768 records / 309 records/volume => 106 volumes          (round up)
```

A database of this magnitude would require quite a substantial programing effort, but easily managed on the CFFA using DOS 4.1 and the *VOLMGR*. Vorenberg strongly recommended using the Sider with *Family Roots* and that is precisely the hard drive my mother utilized with *Family Roots* in order to digitize the rather extensive size of our family tree.

156

IV. DOS 4.1 Operational Environment

DOS 4.1 provides a far more advanced operational environment for programming tools and utilities particularly when they make full use of its open architecture. I have developed my own programming tools and utilities such as *Applesoft Formatter*, Binary File Installation (*BFI*), *Real Time Clock* (my own hardware, too), *Disk Window*, EPROM Operating System (*EOS*), Volume Manager for the CFFA Card (*VOLMGR, BOOTVOL, BOOTDOS*), and VTOC Manager (*VMGR*), or I have created source files for commercial programs that include Asynchronous Data Transfer (*ADT*), *Big Mac*, PROmGRAMER, CFFA Card firmware, File Developer (*FID*), Lazer's Interactive Symbolic Assembler (*Lisa*), Program Global Editor (*PGE*), Global Program Line Editor (*GPLE*), RAM Disk 320 firmware, RanaSystems EliteThree firmware, The Sider firmware, and *Sourceror* to utilize the features of DOS 4.1.

Because so much time has passed since these commercial programs were published, I did not consider it necessary to request permission from the authors of this software, or object code, to "source" their software: sadly, many of the authors have already passed on. My intent from these programs was to learn their internal dependencies on DOS 3.3. Collectively, these dependencies partially drove my design of DOS 4.1 to best provide enough visibility into the DOS 4.1 processing internals and data structures these authors required.

As is said, "The proof is in the pudding." I have successfully modified all the above-mentioned commercial programming tools, utilities, and firmware to be fully DOS 4.1 compliant as if DOS 4.1 is some black box with a few special access points: there should be no need to directly access any of the DOS 4.1 internal routines. I created these source code files for my own intellectual edification and for my own use. I am simply showing the effort and time I have invested to modify what I consider to be valuable software programs written by other brilliant Apple][software programmers to function successfully within the operational environment of DOS 4.1, Build 46.

1. Applesoft Formatter

After about six months of writing test and demonstration Applesoft programs on my new Apple][+, I began thinking about writing a serious Applesoft program. Binary File Installation was that program, but it became a hybrid program because it included attached assembly language routines as described in section IV.2. I also thought I was now capable of writing a standalone assembly language program. How an Applesoft program appeared on the screen when listed or printed by a printer appalled me and I was determined to use assembly language to design and write an *Applesoft Formatter* program. Along with aligning program line numbers and spacing all parentheses consistently, two inherent features of this program were to optionally split multiple Applesoft commands on one line to appear on separate lines and to optionally indent Applesoft commands within a FOR/NEXT loop no matter how nested they became. Since I owned an Epson MX100 printer I could easily print up to 120 characters on each line if I used wide paper. Basically, this was an exercise in parsing Applesoft tokens, keeping track of FOR/NEXT loops, and counting quotes. As an interesting aside, I wrote this software to execute at any memory address. It was certainly an intriguing exercise.

```
]LOAD TEST
]LIST

 10 MN = 1:MX = 10: PRINT
 20 I = 0: FOR I = MN TO MX: IF I
    = 5 THEN  GOSUB 100
 30 S$ = "Entry #" +  STR$ (I):J =
    I + 7
 40 T$ = S$ +  STR$ (J): NEXT
 50  END
 100  PRINT "I = ";I;", J = ";J;"
    , S$ = ";S$: RETURN
]RUN

I = 5, J = 11, S$ = Entry #4
]*
```

Figure IV.1.1. Applesoft Program Listing

A very simple, unimaginative test Applesoft program is shown in Figure IV.1.1 along with some results when RUN. I have purposefully put several Applesoft commands on the same line and embedded the FOR/NEXT loop within those lines. Even when this program is listed to a printer it appears just as awkward and difficult to read. Needless to say a program many times this size would be exceedingly difficult to read, debug, and analyze. I am sure there must have been at least one utility if not more available in the early 1980's (i.e. Roger Wagner's *Apple-Doc*) that could format Applesoft programs with multiple formatting options. And I am sure those programs did their task magnificently, too. But that was not my intention, to purchase someone else's labors.

I wanted to understand how to parse Applesoft tokens within Applesoft programs, and how to separate those command tokens from the variable names and the embedded ASCII text. So this exercise would require me to do some research, study, and hard work. Figure IV.1.2 shows the output of *Applesoft Formatter* when the split line and indent line options are enabled. Seriously, this listing is totally easy to read, debug, and analyze now that the Applesoft program has been formatted in an appealing and precise way. I also gained an exceptional understanding in assembly language programming for the 6502 microprocessor, how to best use an assembler, and how to write relocatable software. Obviously, the lessons learned in writing *Applesoft Formatter* were forever invaluable to me.

To assemble the *ASLIST* source code place the DOS 4.1 Tools volume `DOS4.1.ToolsL` in disk drive 1, boot, and start *Lisa*. Enter the `SE` command-line command to select the `SETUP` program in order to verify or set the `Start of Source Code` to `0x2100` and the `End of Source Code` to `0x6000`. Place the ASLIST Source volume `ASLIST.Source` in disk drive 2, load the `ASLIST.L` file into memory, and start the assembler by entering either the `A` command-line command or the `Z` command-line command. If a printed version of the screen output is desired, simply preface the `A` or `Z` command with the `P1` command-line command. The complete binary image will be saved to the ASLIST Source volume as `ASLIST`.

```
Maximum Characters/Line (<161):   31
Split Line (Y,N):   Y
Indent (Y,N):   Y
Echo to Screen (Y,N):   Y
    10    MN = 1
          MX = 10
          PRINT
    20    I = 0
          FOR I = MN TO MX
            IF I = 5 THEN GOSUB 100
    30      S$ = "Entry #" + STR$( I )
            J = I + 7
    40      T$ = S$ + STR$( J )
          NEXT
    50    END
   100    PRINT "I = "; I; ", J = "; J;
          ", S$ = "; S$
          RETURN
] ▓
```

Figure IV.1.2. Applesoft Program Programmatically Formatted

159

2. Binary File Installation (BFI)

Binary File Installation was the first totally useful Applesoft program I wrote on my Apple][+. I began writing Applesoft programs initially, but soon explored assembly language for various sort algorithms and disk I/O routines. If I wrote the sort algorithms and disk I/O routines such that they could execute at any memory address then I could attach their binary code to the end of an Applesoft program, modify some page-zero pointers, and save the composite, albeit hybrid program. Whenever I ran the Applesoft program, the program logic would obtain its program size from page-zero locations and then calculate the addresses of the sort algorithm and the disk I/O routines knowing their lengths in bytes, or so many bytes before the end of the program. A CALL could then be made directly to the address of the sort algorithm or the disk I/O routine from any place within the Applesoft program.

I learned I could even pass parameters to an assembly language routine and also have variables returned to the Applesoft program. Any number of relocatable routines could be attached to the end of an Applesoft program and CALLed as long as their location in memory could be precisely determined. I thought a utility could more easily handle this attachment process, so I created Binary File Installation to do just that. The user tells *BFI* which Applesoft program to select that would receive the binary file attachment(s) and all the relocatable binary files to attach. *BFI* then modifies the size of the Applesoft program on disk (its first two bytes in the file) and calls the File Manager to append the binary files to the end of the program on disk after its last three null bytes: simple, clean, and efficient. Once the attachment is done, *BFI* prints the order and the size of all the binary files it attached. The Applesoft program can be edited at any time using the Apple command line and cursor move routines. However, if a tool such as *GPLE* or *PGE* is used to edit the Applesoft program, any attached binary files will be stripped from the program when it is saved to disk. I have yet to explore how to repair this feature in *GPLE* and *PGE*.

I have modified *BFI* a number of times as I increased my knowledge of the VTOC and RWTS, and the HIRES screen and HIRES drawing routines. Sierra's *ScreenWriter* used a HIRES screen font that I adapted for *BFI*, and *BFI* uses an adaptation of the HIRES icon drawing routine I developed for Sierra's *HomeWord Speller* product. I even wrote the icon development and edit tool that I use to create and generate the "shape table" data for all screen icons used in *BFI*. After the initial splash screen shown in Figure IV.2.1, the Main Menu screen is displayed as shown in Figure IV.2.2. Selecting the Hardware icon shown in Figure IV.2.2 displays the Peripheral Selection screen as shown in Figure IV.2.3. Selecting the actual Install icon shown in Figure IV.2.2 begins the binary file installation process.

BFI displays the results of the binary file installation when it completes its processing, and the user can selectively print this report as well. Figure IV.2.4 shows the report that is generated when attaching all the binary files required by the Applesoft code comprising *BFI*. I probably learned more about my Apple from this single program at a very early stage in my computer programming self-education after having been recently graduated with a bachelor's degree in Electrical Engineering.

Binary File Installation

Copyright (c) 2021 by

Walland Philip Vrbancic, Jr.

Figure IV.2.1. BFI Splash Screen

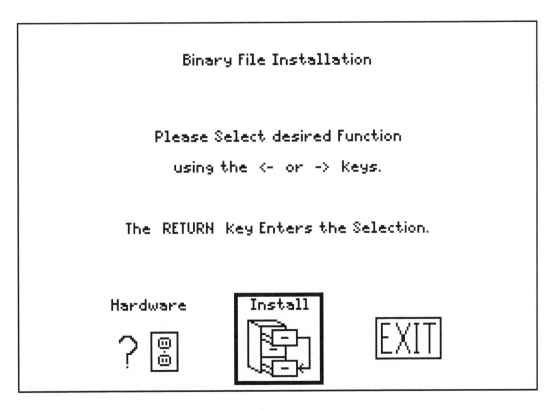

Figure IV.2.2. BFI Main Menu

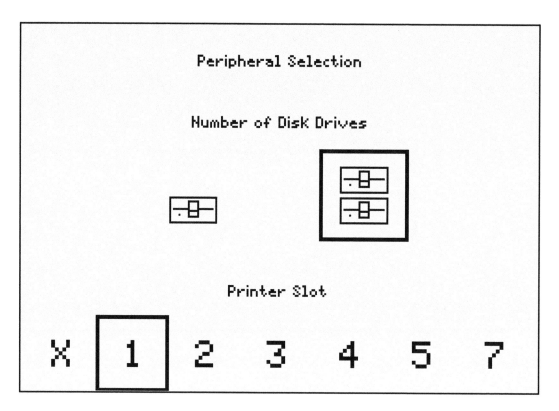

Figure IV.2.3. BFI Peripheral Selection

```
                Binary File Installation Report

*** Applesoft File ***                          Length in Bytes
BFI                                                    6337

*** Binary Files ***
CR                                                      453
SS                                                      336
RW                                                      178
FA                                                      129
MM                                                       93
FS                                                       78
IC                                                       33
DI                                                     1486
SD                                                     1115

                                   Total:             10238
```

Figure IV.2.4. BFI Installation Report on BFI

To assemble the *BFI* assembly language source code routines place the DOS 4.1 Tools volume `DOS4.1.ToolsL` in disk drive 1, boot, and start *Lisa*. Enter the `SE` command-line command to select the `SETUP` program in order to verify or set the `Start of Source Code` to `0x2100` and the `End of Source Code` to `0x6000`. Place the BFI Source volume `BFI.Source` in disk drive 2, load a *Lisa* source code file into memory, and start the assembler by entering either the `A` command-line command or the `Z` command-line command. If a printed version of the screen output is desired, simply preface the `A` or `Z` command with the `P1` command-line command. The object code (i.e. binary file) will be saved to the BFI Source volume. Continue to assemble all the *BFI* assembly language source code routines until all the routines have been assembled. Place the BFI Source volume `BFI.Source` in disk drive 1 and run `BFI`. Select a single drive installation and whatever slot the printer interface slot card resides in. Select `BFI.RAW` for the Applesoft program. Successively select the binary files shown in Figure IV.2.4. Binary files from other volumes may be selected as well. Perform the installation and print the Binary File Installation Report if desired.

Alternatively, place the BFI Source volume `BFI.Source` in disk drive 1 and run `BFI`. Select a double drive installation and whatever slot the printer interface slot card resides in. Place the volume containing the target Applesoft program in disk drive 1 and the volume containing the binary files in disk drive 2. Select the Applesoft program and the necessary binary files to install, perform the installation, and print the Binary File Installation Report if desired.

3. Apple][+ Memory Upgrade

Now that I was an Electrical Engineering graduate student in the early 1980's, I certainly wanted to use my Apple][+ as an opportunity to make some practical hardware modifications. First and foremost I wanted to incorporate a shift key modification, add in keyboard repeat logic, and provide an "alt" key circuit to the keyboard that would set or clear specific bits in the keyboard data in order to generate all the other ASCII characters the Apple][+ keyboard could not generate. This encouraged me to program my own character generator EPROM that included lowercase characters, rather similar to what Dan Paymar was selling as his Lowercase Adaptor Interface. Then I fixed the "glitch" I noticed when switching modes from TEXT, LOWRES, and HIRES using a couple of additional logic gates: it was all a matter of timing in order to alter an inherent logic delay when the display mode was enabled. I reached a level of competence when I decided to remove all twenty-four 16 Kb DRAM chips from the motherboard and replaced them with eight 64 Kb DRAM chips. This required cutting some foil traces, rerouting power, and building a satellite circuit board that would generate an additional DRAM row/column address line. The satellite circuit even included logic to model the Language Card in order to emulate the action of certain addresses that act as soft switches. In theory it all worked perfectly in my head, of course. The satellite circuit I developed is shown in Figure IV.3.1. I paused a very long moment before applying power to my modified motherboard the first time. I was pleased, if not absolutely delighted to find that my 48 KB Apple][+ was fully 64 KB functional as if a Language Card resided in Slot 0. There was no blue smoke. Wow! Even today I marvel at how gutsy I was to implement this drastic modification to the motherboard of my beloved Apple][+.

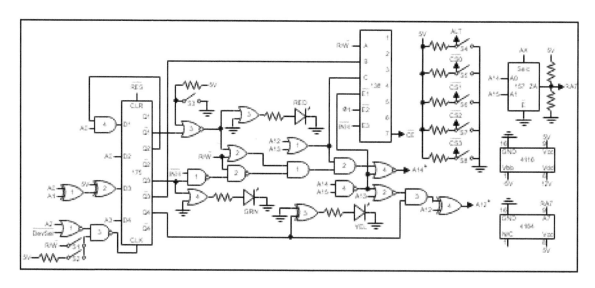

Figure IV.3.1. Apple][+ Satellite Circuit Diagram

The satellite circuit contains the eight logic chips shown in Figure IV.3.1, three LED's, eight DIP switches, and a 26-pin connector for the signals shown in Table IV.3.1 along with power and ground. Either DIP switch 1 or 2 must be closed, but not both. If DIP switch 1 is closed then the 74LS175 configuration register is clocked only with a read to 0xC08n, where n can be 0x0 to 0xF. If DIP switch 2 is closed then the configuration register is clocked with either a read or a write to 0xC08n. Language Card RAM is enabled if 0xC080, 0xC083, 0xC088, or 0xC08B is read, and the green

LED glows. If RAM bank 1 is enabled (i.e. `0xC088` to `0xC08F` is read) the yellow LED glows. RAM is write-enabled if `0xC081`, `0xC083`, `0xC089`, or `0xC08B` is read twice and DIP switch 3 is closed, then the red LED glows. Opening DIP switch 3 will absolutely write-protect Language Card RAM electrically.

Signal	Location	Signal	Location
ø1	B1,6 (74LS175)	A12	H4,3 (8T97)
AX	C2,14 (74LS195)	A13	H5,3 (8T97)
DevSel	H2,15 (74LS138, Slot 0)	A14	J1,9 (74LS257)
INH	F3,18 (ROM-E8)	A15	J1,12 (74LS257)
RES	A7,3 (keyboard socket)	A12*	to C1,3 (74LS157)
R/W	H5,5 (8T97)	A14*	to F2,14 (74LS139)
A0	H5,11 (8T97)	RA7	to all 4164,9
A1	H4,5 (8T97)	CE	to all EPROM's *CE*
A2	H5,7 (8T97)	ALT	to all EPROM's A14
A3	H5,9 (8T97)	*CS0–CS3*	to each EPROM *CS*

Table IV.3.1. Apple][+ Satellite Circuit Board Connections

A 27128 EPROM is the minimum size that will hold the ROM firmware from `0xD000` to `0xFFFF`, although the first 32 KB of the EPROM is not addressed. When a 27256 EPROM is used to contain two ROM firmware images, DIP switch 4 (to pin 27, `A14`) can be used to select the desired image. If DIP switch 4 is closed, the lower image is selected. DIP switches 5, 6, 7, and 8 select one of four possible EPROMs on the Apple][+ motherboard. I removed all six 24-pin ROM sockets and installed four 28-pin EPROM sockets making sure pins 1, 2, 27, and 28 were electrically isolated from the motherboard. Only one of these four DIP switches should be closed, otherwise multiple EPROMs will be enabled simultaneously. Honestly, I ended up preparing and programming only a single EPROM containing two ROM images. Providing access to three more similar EPROMs never became necessary and was slightly over-kill. Better to have too much than too little EPROM expansion capabilities!

Table IV.3.1 lists all the signals I required and the location on the Apple][+ motherboard where I obtained that signal. In order to provide two banks of Language Card RAM for the `0xD000` to `0xDFFF` range, address lines `A12*` and `A14*` must be derived from the outputs of the circuit's 74LS175 configuration register, from the `A12` and `A13` address lines, and from the `A14` and `A15` address lines. The `A14` and `A15` address lines are from a 74LS257 at motherboard location J1, and they also support memory data access and memory refresh. These two derived address lines are connected directly to the pins of C1,3 and F2,14. Memory refresh for the 4164 chips is accomplished using the current `RA0` through `RA6` signals on the motherboard without regard to `RA7`. The derived `RA7` signal simply provides the eighth row and eighth column address in order to access the full 64 Kb of each 4164 DRAM chip. Tables IV.3.2 and IV.3.3 provide the details of the operation of the Apple][+ Satellite Circuit Board vis-á-vis input address, the state of each LED, whether RAM is read-enabled or write-enabled, whether ROM is read-enabled, and the effective address generated for all other motherboard logic.

Input to 74LS175 Latch	Input Address Bus	Red LED State	Grn LED State	Yel LED State	Final A12* State	RAM Enabled		ROM Read Enable	Output Address Bus RAM/ROM
						R	W		
0xC080 RAM2 WP %0100	<0xC000	0	1	0	A12	1	1	0	<0xC000
	0xCnnn	0	1	0	0	0	0	0	0xCnnn
	0xDnnn	0	1	0	1	1	0	0	0xDnnn
	0xEnnn	0	1	0	0	1	0	0	0xEnnn
	0xFnnn	0	1	0	1	1	0	0	0xFnnn
0xC081 ROM2 WP %0010	<0xC000	0	0	0	A12	1	1	0	<0xC000
	0xCnnn	0	0	0	0	0	0	0	0xCnnn
	0xDnnn	0	0	0	1	0	0	1	0xDnnn
	0xEnnn	0	0	0	0	0	0	1	0xEnnn
	0xFnnn	0	0	0	1	0	0	1	0xFnnn
0xC081 0xC081 ROM2 WE %0011	<0xC000	1	0	0	A12	1	1	0	<0xC000
	0xCnnn	1	0	0	0	0	0	0	0xCnnn
	0xDnnn	1	0	0	1	0	1	1	0xDnnn
	0xEnnn	1	0	0	0	0	1	1	0xEnnn
	0xFnnn	1	0	0	1	0	1	1	0xFnnn
0xC082 ROM2 WP %0000	<0xC000	0	0	0	A12	1	1	0	<0xC000
	0xCnnn	0	0	0	0	0	0	0	0xCnnn
	0xDnnn	0	0	0	1	0	0	1	0xDnnn
	0xEnnn	0	0	0	0	0	0	1	0xEnnn
	0xFnnn	0	0	0	1	0	0	1	0xFnnn
0xC083 RAM2 WP %0110	<0xC000	0	1	0	A12	1	1	0	<0xC000
	0xCnnn	0	1	0	0	0	0	0	0xCnnn
	0xDnnn	0	1	0	1	1	0	0	0xDnnn
	0xEnnn	0	1	0	0	1	0	0	0xEnnn
	0xFnnn	0	1	0	1	1	0	0	0xFnnn
0xC083 0xC083 RAM2 WE %0111	<0xC000	1	1	0	A12	1	1	0	<0xC000
	0xCnnn	1	1	0	0	0	0	0	0xCnnn
	0xDnnn	1	1	0	1	1	1	0	0xDnnn
	0xEnnn	1	1	0	0	1	1	0	0xEnnn
	0xFnnn	1	1	0	1	1	1	0	0xFnnn
%0001	This configuration is not possible to select, so it is not valid.								
%0101	This configuration is not possible to select, so it is not valid.								

Table IV.3.2. Apple][+ Satellite Circuit Board Operation Part 1

Input to 74LS175 Latch	Input Address Bus	Red LED State	Grn LED State	Yel LED State	Final A12* State	RAM Enabled R	RAM Enabled W	ROM Read Enable	Output Address Bus RAM/ROM
0xC088	<0xC000	0	1	1	A12	1	1	0	<0xC000
RAM1	0xCnnn	0	1	1	1	0	0	0	0xDnnn
WP	0xDnnn	0	1	1	0	1	0	0	0xCnnn
	0xEnnn	0	1	1	0	1	0	0	0xEnnn
%1100	0xFnnn	0	1	1	1	1	0	0	0xFnnn
0xC089	<0xC000	0	0	1	A12	1	1	0	<0xC000
ROM1	0xCnnn	0	0	1	1	0	0	0	0xDnnn
WP	0xDnnn	0	0	1	0	0	0	1	0xCnnn
	0xEnnn	0	0	1	0	0	0	1	0xEnnn
%1010	0xFnnn	0	0	1	1	0	0	1	0xFnnn
0xC089	<0xC000	1	0	1	A12	1	1	0	<0xC000
0xC089	0xCnnn	1	0	1	1	0	0	0	0xDnnn
ROM1	0xDnnn	1	0	1	0	0	1	1	0xCnnn
WE	0xEnnn	1	0	1	0	0	1	1	0xEnnn
%1011	0xFnnn	1	0	1	1	0	1	1	0xFnnn
0xC08A	<0xC000	0	0	1	A12	1	1	0	<0xC000
ROM1	0xCnnn	0	0	1	1	0	0	0	0xDnnn
WP	0xDnnn	0	0	1	0	0	0	1	0xCnnn
	0xEnnn	0	0	1	0	0	0	1	0xEnnn
%1000	0xFnnn	0	0	1	1	0	0	1	0xFnnn
0xC08B	<0xC000	0	1	1	A12	1	1	0	<0xC000
RAM1	0xCnnn	0	1	1	1	0	0	0	0xDnnn
WP	0xDnnn	0	1	1	0	1	0	0	0xCnnn
	0xEnnn	0	1	1	0	1	0	0	0xEnnn
%1110	0xFnnn	0	1	1	1	1	0	0	0xFnnn
0xC08B	<0xC000	1	1	1	A12	1	1	0	<0xC000
0xC08B	0xCnnn	1	1	1	1	0	0	0	0xDnnn
RAM1	0xDnnn	1	1	1	0	1	1	0	0xCnnn
WE	0xEnnn	1	1	1	0	1	1	0	0xEnnn
%1111	0xFnnn	1	1	1	1	1	1	0	0xFnnn
%1001	This configuration is not possible to select, so it is not valid.								
%1101	This configuration is not possible to select, so it is not valid.								

Table IV.3.3. Apple][+ Satellite Circuit Board Operation Part 2

4. Real Time Clock Card

The experience I gained in building the memory upgrade for my Apple][+ led me to design and build my own *Real Time Clock* peripheral slot card. I had to learn some new skills in order to build a peripheral slot card that would fit within the dimensions allowed for a slot card in the Apple][+. I had never etched a double-sided copper clad board that large nor had I thought about how to place TTL components in terms of organization, data and signal flow, wire length, and clean power. I also had to include circuitry to charge the onboard rechargeable batteries. All these ideas mattered one way or another I am sure, but honestly, I didn't have much of a clue. In hindsight I should have taken a class in TTL circuit board design and layout before I was graduated with my degree in Electrical Engineering. My garage was my ultimate laboratory and workshop! But most importantly I wanted the hardware design to provide a simple, elegant, and thoroughly elementary software interface.

I wanted to design my *Real Time Clock* card around the SaRonix RTC58321 real time clock module, which I probably obtained from Jameco Electronics in the mid 1980's. The RTC58321 incorporated an internal quartz crystal in a single 16-pin DIP package thereby eliminating the need for an external crystal and timing circuit. This clock module provided me with everything I needed: read and write for date and time values and an external *BUSY* signal. I wanted the software interface to be as simple as possible so I put a lot of effort into the design of the hardware logic so the hardware would negotiate with the RTC58321's data and address setup time requirements. Unfortunately, the 6502-clock read/write period happened to be far too short for the required data and address setup time needed for the RTC58321. Initially, I used a breadboard for the TTL logic components to figure out how to negotiate with the RTC58321 using a full 6502-clock period by utilizing a flip-flop. Then I wrote the slot interface firmware for the onboard 2732 EPROM. I modeled my general user Applesoft interface from the Applied Engineering TimeMaster II Applesoft interface. Whatever commands the TimeMaster firmware could handle, I made sure my clock card firmware could handle in addition to all the other commands and capabilities I could devise and had room for in the EPROM. And I figured out how to make use of the standard signals generated by the RTC58321 to pull the IRQ and/or NMI line low in order to initiate a hardware interrupt. Once I had the schematic drawn and the components organized, I drilled all the necessary holes for chip sockets and components, and etched the copper for the power, ground, and some circuit lines. I hand-wired and soldered the remaining connections for the interface board slot finger, chip sockets, transistors, batteries, LEDs, configuration block, resistors, and capacitors. My *Real Time Clock* card is fully operational today as it was over 30 years ago. I have only had to replace the rechargeable batteries a couple of times! Figure IV.4.1 shows the complete circuit diagram for my *Real Time Clock* card that I had originally drawn on March 20, 1988.

Only four of the sixteen peripheral-card I/O memory locations are used for clock configuration, clock address, clock status, clock register, clock data, and interrupt clear and set. Table IV.4.1 shows the description of those memory locations where s is equals to eight plus the slot number of the *Real Time Clock* card. Only Memory Address bits A0 and A1 are captured so it does not matter what is used for Memory Address bits A2 and A3. Addresses 0xC0s4, 0xC0s8, and 0xC0sC are all valid for 0xC0s0 in order to read and write the *Real Time Clock* configuration register. Table IV.4.2 shows the description of the configuration register bits. This register retains its configuration until it is changed by another write to 0xC0s0 or when RESET is pressed. When RESET is pressed the register is cleared to zero. Before loading the clock data registers it is important to stop the clock by setting the STOP Enable bit to one. Once the clock is loaded its previous configuration data can be restored.

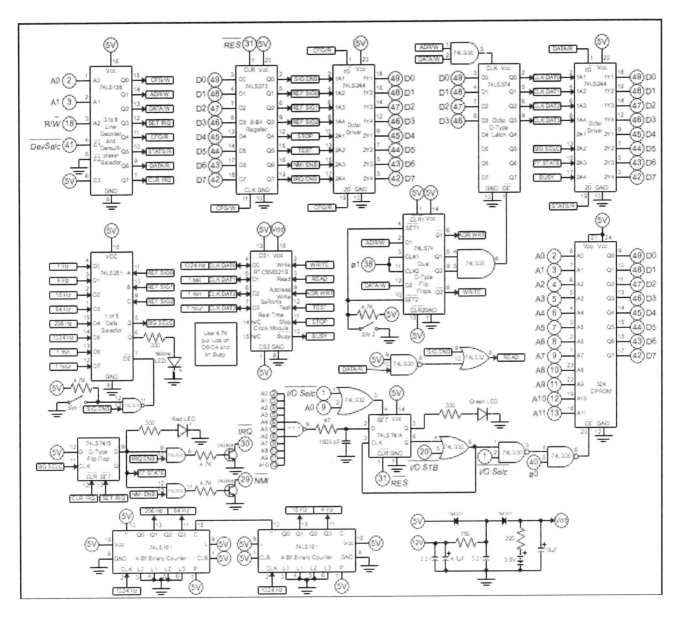

Figure IV.4.1. Real Time Clock Circuit Diagram

Address	Operation	Description
0xC0s0	read	Read configuration register
0xC0s0	write	Write configuration register
0xC0s1	read	Read status register
0xC0s1	write	Write clock register number
0xC0s2	read	Read clock data register
0xC0s2	write	Write clock data register
0xC0s3	read	Clear interrupt flip-flop
0xC0s3	write	Set interrupt flip-flop

Table IV.4.1. Real Time Clock Peripheral-Card I/O Addresses

Bit	Description
0	Interrupt enable, 0 = OFF
1	Interrupt rate select A
2	Interrupt rate select B
3	Interrupt rate select C
4	STOP enable, 0 = RUN
5	TEST enable, 0 = normal operation
6	NMI enable, 0 = OFF
7	IRQ enable, 0 = OFF

Table IV.4.2. Real Time Clock Configuration Register

C	B	A	Description
0	0	0	1 Hz interrupt rate
0	0	1	4 Hz interrupt rate
0	1	0	16 Hz interrupt rate
0	1	1	64 Hz interrupt rate
1	0	0	256 Hz interrupt rate
1	0	1	1024 Hz interrupt rate
1	1	0	1 minute interrupt rate
1	1	1	1 hour interrupt rate

Table IV.4.3. Interrupt Rate Selection

Table IV.4.3 shows the description of the eight interrupt rates that are available for the generation of IRQ and/or NMI interrupts. The selected interrupt rate is made active by setting the Interrupt Enable bit to one as shown in Table IV.4.2. In order for interrupts to be generated either the IRQ Enable bit and/or the NMI Enable bit must be set to one.

Table IV.4.4 lists the sixteen clock registers available in the RTC58321. Any time when clock register 14 or 15 is latched the clock module is put into its idle state and the standard signals are available at its data ports when the READ port of the RTC58321 is set to one. Setting the READ port of the RTC58321 to one is accomplished by setting the Interrupt Enable bit in the configuration register to one as shown in Table IV.4.2. The 1024 Hz signal is divided by two 74LS161 binary counters to obtain the remaining interrupt rates that can be selected by the configuration register. Even though the *Real Time Clock* card can also generate NMI interrupts, the EPROM software only has provisions to generate and handle IRQ interrupts. Nevertheless, software can easily be written to utilize an NMI interrupt if there is an occasion for such an interrupt to be generated. The configuration register also provides control of the TEST enable port of the RTC58321. I no longer can locate any documentation that describes how to test the RTC58321 using the TEST enable port.

Setting data bit D3 in clock register 5 of the RTC58321 will select 24-hour mode. Doing this will clear bit D2 of the same register. If 12-hour mode is selected then bit D2 will select PM if that bit is set to one. The RTC58321 divides the 10-year digit in clock register 12 by 4 in order to determine leap year. The remainder of this division is saved to bits D2 and D3 of clock register 8. If the remainder is zero then leap year is selected. The RTC58321 may be reset by latching clock register 13 and writing any data to that same register. This sets the WRITE port of the RTC58321 to one. The EPROM firmware does not reset the RTC58321.

Reg	D3	D2	D1	D0	Name	D3	D2	D1	D0	Count	Notes
0	0	0	0	0	S1	s8	s4	s2	s1	0 to 9	1-second digit
1	0	0	0	1	S10	-	s40	s20	s10	0 to 5	10-second digit
2	0	0	1	0	MI1	mi8	mi4	mi2	mi1	0 to 9	1-minute digit
3	0	0	1	1	MI10	-	mi40	mi20	mi10	0 to 5	10-minute digit
4	0	1	0	0	H1	h8	h4	h2	h1	0 to 9	1-hour digit
5	0	1	0	1	H10	24/12	PM/AM	h20	h10	0 to 2 / 0 to 1	10-hour digit
6	0	1	1	0	W	-	w4	w2	w1	0 to 6	week digit
7	0	1	1	1	D1	d8	d4	d2	d1	0 to 9	1-day digit
8	1	0	0	0	D10	leap year		d20	d10	0 to 3	10-day digit
9	1	0	0	1	MO1	mo8	mo4	mo2	mo1	0 to 9	1-month digit
10	1	0	1	0	MO10	-	-	-	mo10	0 to 1	10-month digit
11	1	0	1	1	Y1	y8	y4	y2	y1	0 to 9	1-year digit
12	1	1	0	0	Y10	y80	y40	y20	y10	0 to 9	10-year digit
13	1	1	0	1	reset	-	-	-	-		reset register
14	1	1	1	0	idle	1 hour	1 min.	1 sec.	1024 Hz		standard signal register
15	1	1	1	1	idle						

Table IV.4.4. Real Time Clock Registers

The *Real Time Clock* card utilizes two switches to control its function. Closing Switch 1 disables the frequency data selector module and blocks the output of the selected interrupt rate. Therefore, the clock card cannot generate an interrupt even if the IRQ enable bit or the NMI enable bit is set to one in the configuration register. Closing Switch 2 will disable the Address Write and Data Write flip-flops. Therefore, the data in the clock module cannot be changed rendering the RTC58321 write protected.

The clock card utilizes three LEDs to indicate what function the clock card is performing. The Green LED lights whenever the 2732 EPROM is accessed. The Yellow LED lights at the same frequency as the selected interrupt rate if the frequency data selector module is enabled by the Interrupt Enable bit of the configuration register and if Switch 1 is open. The Red LED lights whenever the output of the Interrupt Flip-Flop is set to one regardless whether the IRQ enable bit or the NMI enable bit is set to one in the configuration register. If either bit is set the base of a 2N3904 general purpose transistor is pulled high thereby allowing its collector-emitter junction to conduct and pull the respective interrupt line safely to ground. I placed an R/C network between the output of the 74LS133 and the data input to the EPROM enable flip-flop in order to shift (i.e. delay) the derived CLRROM signal slightly because of the slight delay inherent in the clock pulse to that flip-flop.

171

Offset	Name	Description
0x00	MAINSELC	PHP instruction, DOS PR# and IN# command handler
0x01		SEI instruction
0x02		Issues CLRROM, branches to INITCLK
0x08	WRITSELC	Issues CLRROM, branches to LOADCLK
0x10	READSELC	Issues CLRROM, branches to READCLK
0x18	MODESELC	Issues CLRROM, branches to SETMODE
0x20	IRQSELC	Issues CLRROM, branches to SETIRQ
0x28	STRTSELLC	Issues CLRROM, branches to STRTCLK
0x30	STOPSECL	Issues CLRROM, branches to STOPCLK
0x38	INITCLK	Saves registers, branches to HNDLINIT
0x3F	LOADCLK	Saves registers, branches to HNDLLOAD
0x46	READCLK	Saves registers, branches to HNDLREAD
0x4D	SETMODE	Saves registers, branches to HNDLMODE
0x54	SETIRQ	Saves registers, branches to HNDLIRQ
0x5B	STRTCLK	Saves registers, branches to HNDLSTRT
0x62	STOPCLK	Saves registers, branches to HNDLSTOP
0x69	WRITCLK	Issues CLRROM, branches to HNDLWRIT
0x71	SETRTN	Issues CLRROM, branches to HNDLRTN
0x79	IRQHNDLR	Issues CLRROM, branches to EXECIRQ
0x80	EXIT	Restores registers, issues CLRROM, returns to caller
0x8A	HNDLINIT	Gets slot, processes input command
0x93	HNDLLOAD	Gets slot, writes clock buffer at 0x2F0-0x2FC to clock
0x9C	HNDLREAD	Gets slot, reads clock to clock buffer at 0x2F0-0x2FC
0xA5	HNDLMODE	Gets slot, stores mode value 0x21-0x3E to MODE, 0x478
0xAE	HNDLIRQ	Gets slot, sets IRQ 0-7, clears IRQBUF, 0x2FD-0x2FF
0xB7	HNDLSTRT	Gets slot, updates clock config, puts SETRTN address in KSWL
0xC0	HNDLSTOP	Gets slot, stops clock, puts SETRTN address in KSWL
0xC9	HNDLWRIT	Saves registers, gets slot, stop CLK, write CLK register, start CLK
0xD7	HNDLRTN	Saves registers, gets slot, puts <RTN> at 0x200-0x201
0xE5	EXECIRQ	Saves registers, gets slot, updates IRQBUF, restores registers, issues CLRROM, returns with RTI instruction
0xFA	VERSION	upper ASCII "41"
0xFC	CLKNAME	upper ASCII "RTC"
0xFF	CLKID	0x03

Table IV.4.5. Clock Firmware Entry Points

The first half of the 2732 EPROM is used for eight copies of the same interface software for the peripheral-card ROM address space, one copy for each possible slot in which the Clock card could reside. The second half of the EPROM maps into the peripheral-card expansion ROM address space. Whenever the 6502 microprocessor fetches an instruction only in the first half of the peripheral-card ROM memory, 0xCs00 to 0xCs7F, where s is the slot number of the Clock card, the peripheral-card expansion ROM memory, 0xC800 to 0xCFFF, is enabled. This allows the CLRROM address,

0xCFFF, to disable the expansion ROM memory when CLRROM is used in the second half of the peripheral-card ROM memory, a hardware design trick I learned from the hardware design of the RAM Disk 320 peripheral slot card. Table IV.4.5 shows all the entry points in the EPROM slot firmware for the *Real Time Clock* card. This firmware conforms to the clock card protocol where the first two instructions are PHP and SEI, and the last byte, the clock ID, is 0x03. Clock ID 0x07 can also be used. DOS 4.1 accepts either value as valid.

The program *Set Clock* utilizes some of the special features I designed into the *Real Time Clock* card. Its primary purpose is to set the clock card with the current date and time, of course. The program also displays the current date and time that is stored in its registers, and those values may be automatically selected or new values entered for each of the registers. The surprising feature of this program is that it utilizes an interrupt handler. The clock card is configured to generate an IRQ interrupt every second. Every time the interrupt handler executes it reads the clock card and displays its date and time data. Once the correct date and time data is displayed that data can be written to the clock card. The interrupt handler will continue to display the current date and time data of the clock card while the real time clock continues to update its internal registers. Before the *Set Clock* program exits it restores the data originally found at MASKIRQ (or 0x3FE) as shown in Table I.9.1. and sets the clock card configuration register as shown in Table IV.4.2. to 0x00.

The *Set Clock* program first issues the SEI instruction to the 6502 microprocessor to inhibit all interrupts. During initialization it copies the address found at MASKIRQ to a safe location and sets MASKIRQ to the address of the interrupt handler in *Set Clock*. *Set Clock* then sets the clock card configuration register to #%10000001 in order to enable interrupts and to enable the IRQ interrupt specifically. Once the initialization routine issues the CLI instruction to the 6502 microprocessor, the *Set Clock* interrupt handler will be able to field all IRQ interrupts while the user is setting the various values for the date and time. When the interrupt handler is invoked it first issues the CLD instruction to the 6502 microprocessor, pushes the X- and Y-registers onto the stack, clears the IRQ interrupt on the *Real Time Clock* card, reads the *Real Time Clock* card, displays the current date and time data, restores the X- and Y-registers from the stack, restores the A-register from the page-zero location 0x45, and issues the RTI instruction to the 6502 microprocessor. It is amazing to me how simple it is to use interrupts for this program. Of course, the well thought out hardware design of the *Real Time Clock* card makes utilizing interrupts on the Apple][computer so easy and so much fun!

To assemble the *Real Time Clock* EPROM firmware source code, place the DOS 4.1 Tools volume DOS4.1.ToolsL in disk drive 1, boot, and start *Lisa*. Enter the SE command-line command to select the SETUP program in order to verify or set the Start of Source Code to 0x2100 and the End of Source Code to 0x5800. Place the Real Time Clock Source volume CLOCK.Source in disk drive 2, load the CLOCK.L file into memory, and start the assembler by entering either the A command-line command or the Z command-line command. If a printed version of the screen output is desired, simply preface the A or Z command with the P1 command-line command. The complete binary image will be saved to the Real Time Clock Source volume as CLOCK.

To assemble the *Set Clock* source code follow the same procedure as above, load the SETCLOCK.L file into memory and start the assembler. The complete binary image will be saved to the Real Time Clock Source volume as SETCLOCK.

5. Disk Window

I have no doubt Don Worth and Pieter Lechner inspired thousands of computer hobbyists with their Example Programs found in their book *Beneath Apple DOS*, for these authors certainly inspired me. The learning curve was a bit steep if I recall, diskettes were expensive at that time, and I had some preconceived notion that I would destroy something precious, be it hardware or software, if I started messing around with RWTS. Patience was certainly a virtue, and when one is examining the sectors and tracks of a diskette, it was like peering through some sort of digital microscope. The idea of reading a specific sector on a diskette and displaying that data was awe-inspiring. Furthermore, having a utility that could edit those data bytes and write those edits back to that same sector, or to any other sector for that matter, was totally mind blowing: what can of worms would that capability open? Worth's and Lechner's utility Zap did inspire me to design *Disk Window*, what I call my fancy zap program. It is like having a digital window focused on any device, track, sector, or Logical Block Address (LBA) of my choosing.

The current version of *Disk Window* now supports the reading and writing of any valid LBA sector on a CFFA card. If a CFFA card is detected in the selected slot, LBA mode will be used for reading and writing block data. If a Disk][interface or similar slot card is detected in the selected slot, track-sector mode will be used for reading and writing sector data. Regardless of which mode is used to read and write volume data, the appropriate LBA for the selected volume-track-sector will be displayed according to the conversion algorithm I developed. The startup screen for *Disk Window* is displayed as shown in Figure IV.5.1. The four commands at the bottom of the screen Configure, Select LBA, Select D/V, and Select T/S utilize the respective variables at the top of the screen. The commands Forward and Backward simply increment or decrement the track/sector if in track-sector mode or LBA if in LBA mode. The commands Edit, Write, and Print display a respective screen for their function.

Figure IV.5.2 shows the display of the VTOC data for the diskette in a Disk][whose interface card resides in Slot 6, and Drive 2 is selected. The data is displayed both in hexadecimal and in ASCII, unless it is a control character. The hexadecimal values from 0x00 to 0x1F and 0x80 to 0x9F are displayed as a period. Lower ASCII values from 0x20 to 0x7F are displayed in inverse text and upper ASCII values from 0xA0 to 0xFF are displayed in normal text. If Edit is selected the same VTOC data is displayed as shown in Figure IV.5.3, where the cursor is initially placed on row 0x70 and column 0x07. After all edits have been applied the Write command will write the sector data to the selected sector or to any other sector (or LBA) as shown in Figure IV.5.4.

It must be noted that LBA blocks are 512 bytes in size. Page 0 refers to the first 256 bytes and Page 1 refers to the second 256 bytes. Thus, CFFA sectors 0x00-0x0F reside on Page 0 and CFFA sectors 0x10-0x1F reside on Page 1. The 256-byte sector data may be saved to any available LBA, either on Page 0 or on Page 1. Page 0 is selected by pressing the L key and Page 1 is selected by pressing the H key. The contents of the screen can also be printed using the Print command as shown in Figure IV.5.5. The command Configure in Figure IV.5.5 allows the user to change the Printer Slot value if desired without having to return to the main menu screen as shown in Figure IV.5.1. If an RWTS error should occur it is prominently displayed in the center of the hexadecimal data display window as shown in Figure IV.5.6. I purposefully opened the Disk][door for drive 2 to cause a disk drive error. According to Table I.9.4 an error value of 0x40 is an RWTS Drive error. The error message will remain until any key is pressed on the keyboard.

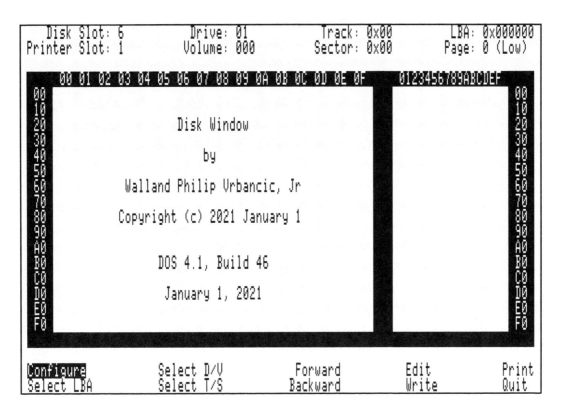

Figure IV.5.1. Disk Window Startup Screen

```
   Disk Slot: 6          Drive: 02          Track: 0x11      LBA: 0x030210
Printer Slot: 1          Volume: 000        Sector: 0x00     Page: 0 (Low)
```

```
      00 01 02 03 04 05 06 07 08 09 0A 0B 0C 0D 0E 0F    0123456789ABCDEF
   00 00 11 05 41 46 CC 00 C4 C4 E9 F3 EB A0 D7 E9 EE    ...AFL.DDisk Win   00
   10 E4 EF F7 A0 D3 EF F5 F2 E3 E5 A0 C3 EF E4 E5 A0    dow Source Code    10
   20 48 28 08 21 01 01 00 7A 20 20 48 28 08 21 01 01    H(.!...z  H(.!..    20
   30 20 01 00 00 23 10 00 01 00 00 00 00 00 00 00 00    ...#............   30
   40 00 00 00 00 00 00 00 00 00 FF 00 00 FF FF 00 00    ................   40
   50 FF FF 00 00 FF FF 00 00 FF FF 00 00 FF FF 00 00    ................   50
   60 FF FF 00 00 FF FF 00 00 FF FF 00 00 FF FF 00 00    ................   60
   70 FF FF 00 00 FF FF 00 00 FF FF 00 00 FF C0 00 00    ...............@   70
   80 00 0F 00 00 00 00 00 00 00 00 00 00 00 00 00 00    ................   80
   90 00 00 00 00 00 03 00 00 00 FF 00 00 00 FF 00 00    ................   90
   A0 07 FF 00 00 0F FF 00 00 1F FF 00 00 00 00 00 00    ................   A0
   B0 01 FF 00 00 7F FF 00 00 7F FF 00 00 FF FF 00 00    ................   B0
   C0 FF FF 00 00 00 00 00 00 00 00 00 00 00 00 00 00    ................   C0
   D0 00 00 00 00 00 00 00 00 00 00 00 00 00 00 00 00    ................   D0
   E0 00 00 00 00 00 00 00 00 00 00 00 00 00 00 00 00    ................   E0
   F0 00 00 00 00 00 00 00 00 00 00 00 00 00 00 00 00    ................   F0
```

```
Configure        Select D/V        Forward          Edit          Print
Select LBA       Select T/S        Backward         Write         Quit
```

Figure IV.5.2. Select T/S Mode

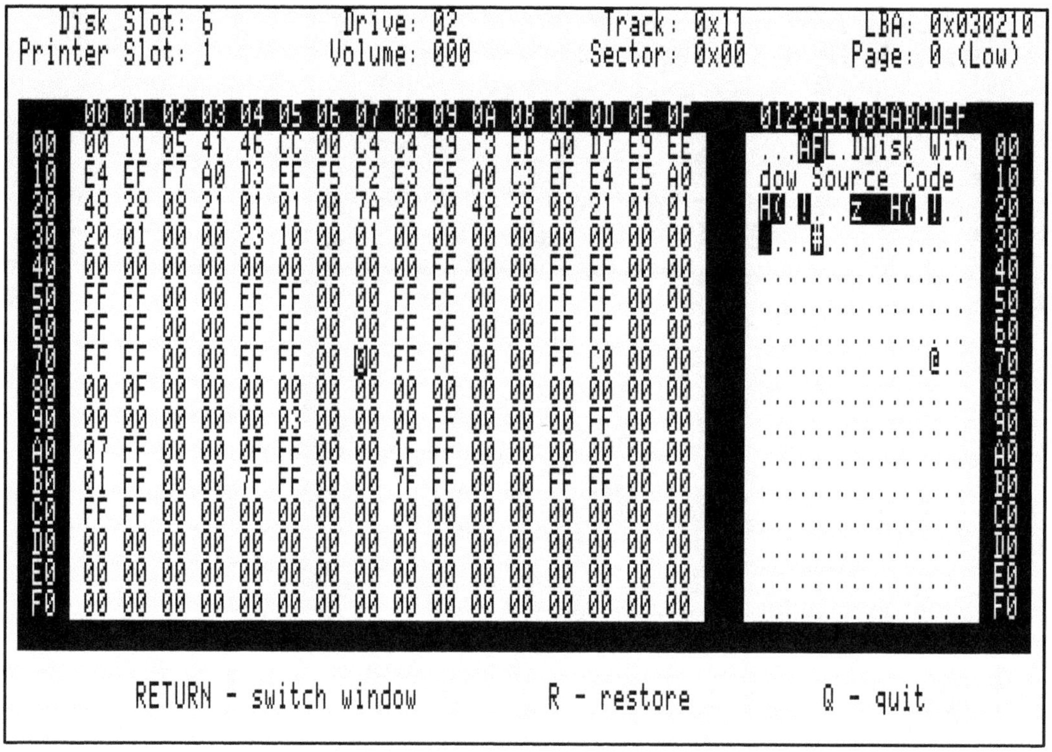

```
     00 01 02 03 04 05 06 07 08 09 0A 0B 0C 0D 0E 0F     0123456789ABCDEF
00   00 11 05 41 46 CC 00 C4 C4 E9 F3 EB A0 D7 E9 EE     ...AFL.DDisk Win    00
10   E4 EF F7 A0 D3 EF F5 F2 E3 E5 A0 C3 EF E4 E5 A0     dow Source Code     10
20   48 28 08 21 01 01 00 7A 20 20 48 28 08 21 01 01     H(.!...z  H(.!..    20
30   20 01 00 00 23 10 00 01 00 00 00 00 00 00 00 00     ...#............    30
40   00 00 00 00 00 00 00 00 00 FF 00 00 FF FF 00 00                         40
50   FF FF 00 00 FF FF 00 00 FF FF 00 00 FF FF 00 00                         50
60   FF FF 00 00 FF FF 00 00 FF FF 00 00 FF FF 00 00                         60
70   FF FF 00 00 FF FF 00 00 FF FF 00 00 FF C0 00 00                     @.  70
80   00 0F 00 00 00 00 00 00 00 00 00 00 00 00 00 00                         80
90   00 00 00 00 00 03 00 00 00 FF 00 00 00 FF 00 00                         90
A0   07 FF 00 00 0F FF 00 00 1F FF 00 00 00 00 00 00                         A0
B0   01 FF 00 00 7F FF 00 00 7F FF 00 00 FF FF 00 00                         B0
C0   FF FF 00 00 00 00 00 00 00 00 00 00 00 00 00 00                         C0
D0   00 00 00 00 00 00 00 00 00 00 00 00 00 00 00 00                         D0
E0   00 00 00 00 00 00 00 00 00 00 00 00 00 00 00 00                         E0
F0   00 00 00 00 00 00 00 00 00 00 00 00 00 00 00 00                         F0
```

RETURN - switch window   R - restore   Q - quit

Figure IV.5.3. Edit Data Screen

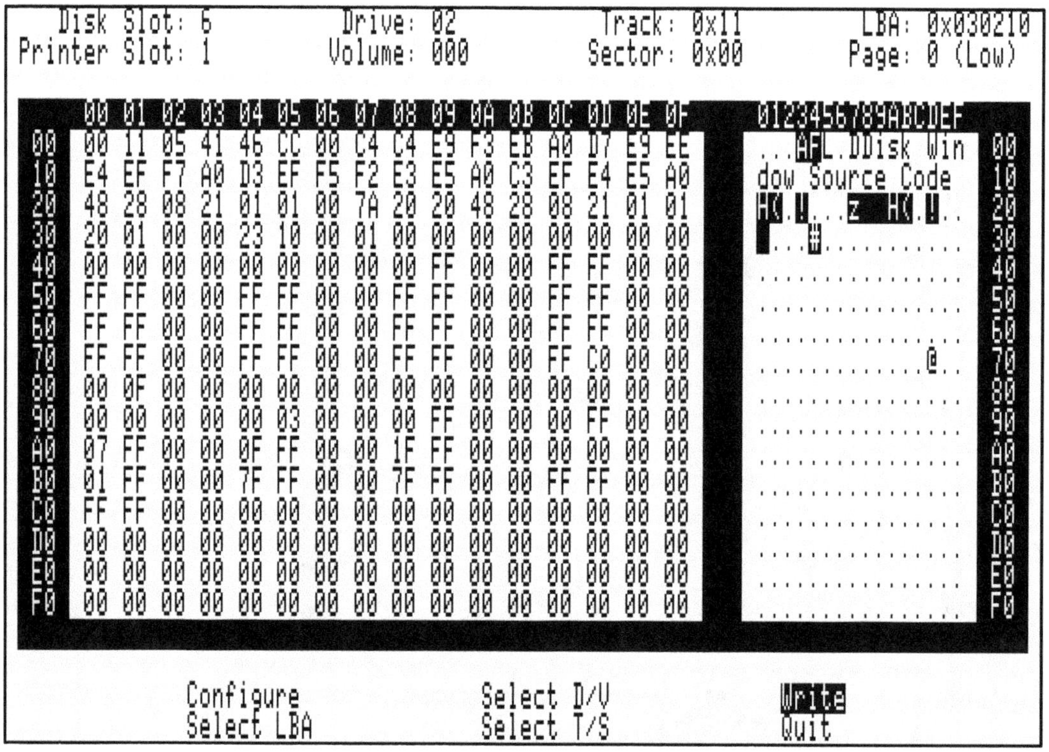

Disk Slot: 6   Drive: 02   Track: 0x11   LBA: 0x030210
Printer Slot: 1   Volume: 000   Sector: 0x00   Page: 0 (Low)

```
     00 01 02 03 04 05 06 07 08 09 0A 0B 0C 0D 0E 0F     0123456789ABCDEF
00   00 11 05 41 46 CC 00 C4 C4 E9 F3 EB A0 D7 E9 EE     ...AFL.DDisk Win    00
10   E4 EF F7 A0 D3 EF F5 F2 E3 E5 A0 C3 EF E4 E5 A0     dow Source Code     10
20   48 28 08 21 01 01 00 7A 20 20 48 28 08 21 01 01     H(.!...z  H(.!..    20
30   20 01 00 00 23 10 00 01 00 00 00 00 00 00 00 00     ...#............    30
40   00 00 00 00 00 00 00 00 00 FF 00 00 FF FF 00 00                         40
50   FF FF 00 00 FF FF 00 00 FF FF 00 00 FF FF 00 00                         50
60   FF FF 00 00 FF FF 00 00 FF FF 00 00 FF FF 00 00                         60
70   FF FF 00 00 FF FF 00 00 FF FF 00 00 FF C0 00 00                     @.  70
80   00 0F 00 00 00 00 00 00 00 00 00 00 00 00 00 00                         80
90   00 00 00 00 00 03 00 00 00 FF 00 00 00 FF 00 00                         90
A0   07 FF 00 00 0F FF 00 00 1F FF 00 00 00 00 00 00                         A0
B0   01 FF 00 00 7F FF 00 00 7F FF 00 00 FF FF 00 00                         B0
C0   FF FF 00 00 00 00 00 00 00 00 00 00 00 00 00 00                         C0
D0   00 00 00 00 00 00 00 00 00 00 00 00 00 00 00 00                         D0
E0   00 00 00 00 00 00 00 00 00 00 00 00 00 00 00 00                         E0
F0   00 00 00 00 00 00 00 00 00 00 00 00 00 00 00 00                         F0
```

Configure   Select D/V   Write
Select LBA   Select T/S   Quit

Figure IV.5.4. Write Sector Data Screen

```
 Disk Slot: 6          Drive: 02        Track: 0x11       LBA: 0x030210
 Printer Slot: 1       Volume: 000      Sector: 0x00      Page: 0 (Low)

       00 01 02 03 04 05 06 07 08 09 0A 0B 0C 0D 0E 0F   0123456789ABCDEF
   00  00 11 05 41 46 CC 00 C4 C4 E9 F3 EB A0 D7 E9 EE   ...AFL.DDisk Win  00
   10  E4 EF F7 A0 D3 EF F5 F2 E3 E5 A0 C3 EF E4 E5 A0   dow Source Code   10
   20  48 28 08 21 01 01 00 7A 20 20 48 28 08 21 01 01   H(.!...z  H(.!..   20
   30  20 01 00 00 23 10 00 01 00 00 00 00 00 00 00 00    ...#..........    30
   40  00 00 00 00 00 00 00 00 00 FF 00 00 FF FF 00 00   ...............   40
   50  FF FF 00 00 FF FF 00 00 FF FF 00 00 FF FF 00 00   ...............   50
   60  FF FF 00 00 FF FF 00 00 FF FF 00 00 FF FF 00 00   ...............   60
   70  FF FF 00 00 FF FF 00 00 FF FF 00 00 FF C0 00 00   ..............@.. 70
   80  00 0F 00 00 00 00 00 00 00 00 00 00 00 00 00 00   ...............   80
   90  00 00 00 00 00 03 00 00 00 FF 00 00 00 FF 00 00   ...............   90
   A0  07 FF 00 00 0F FF 00 00 1F FF 00 00 00 00 00 00   ...............   A0
   B0  01 FF 00 00 7F FF 00 00 7F FF 00 00 FF FF 00 00   ...............   B0
   C0  FF FF 00 00 00 00 00 00 00 00 00 00 00 00 00 00   ...............   C0
   D0  00 00 00 00 00 00 00 00 00 00 00 00 00 00 00 00   ...............   D0
   E0  00 00 00 00 00 00 00 00 00 00 00 00 00 00 00 00   ...............   E0
   F0  00 00 00 00 00 00 00 00 00 00 00 00 00 00 00 00   ...............   F0

              Configure              Print              Quit
```

Figure IV.5.5. Print Sector Data Screen

```
 Disk Slot: 6          Drive: 02        Track: 0x11       LBA: 0x030210
 Printer Slot: 1       Volume: 000      Sector: 0x00      Page: 0 (Low)

       00 01 02 03 04 05 06 07 08 09 0A 0B 0C 0D 0E 0F   0123456789ABCDEF
   00  00 11 05 41 46 CC 00 C4 C4 E9 F3 EB A0 D7 E9 EE   ...AFL.DDisk Win  00
   10  E4 EF F7 A0 D3 EF F5 F2 E3 E5 A0 C3 EF E4 E5 A0   dow Source Code   10
   20  48 28 08 21 01 01 00 7A 20 20 48 28 08 21 01 01   H(.!...z  H(.!..   20
   30  20 01 00 00 23 10 00 01 00 00 00 00 00 00 00 00    ...#..........    30
   40  00 00 00 00 00 00 00 00 00 FF 00 00 FF FF 00 00   ...............   40
   50  FF FF 00 00 FF FF 00 00 FF FF 00 00 FF FF 00 00   ...............   50
   60  FF FF 00 00                            FF FF 00 00 ...............   60
   70  FF FF 00 00   Return error:    0x40   FF C0 00 00 ..............@.. 70
   80  00 0F 00 00                            00 00 00 00 ...............   80
   90  00 00 00 00 00 03 00 00 00 FF 00 00 00 FF 00 00   ...............   90
   A0  07 FF 00 00 0F FF 00 00 1F FF 00 00 00 00 00 00   ...............   A0
   B0  01 FF 00 00 7F FF 00 00 7F FF 00 00 FF FF 00 00   ...............   B0
   C0  FF FF 00 00 00 00 00 00 00 00 00 00 00 00 00 00   ...............   C0
   D0  00 00 00 00 00 00 00 00 00 00 00 00 00 00 00 00   ...............   D0
   E0  00 00 00 00 00 00 00 00 00 00 00 00 00 00 00 00   ...............   E0
   F0  00 00 00 00 00 00 00 00 00 00 00 00 00 00 00 00   ...............   F0

   Configure         Select D/V        Forward        Edit        Print
   Select LBA        Select T/S        Backward       Write       Quit
```

Figure IV.5.6. Disk Window Error Message Display

Disk Window is certainly a giant leap from Worth's and Lechner's utility Zap, but they are the giants whose shoulders I stood on in utilizing their insight and their enthusiasm for everything Apple][.

To assemble the *Disk Window* source code place the DOS 4.1 Tools volume `DOS4.1.ToolsL` in disk drive 1, boot, and start *Lisa*. Enter the `SE` command-line command to select the `SETUP` program in order to verify or set the `Start of Source Code` to `0x2100` and the `End of Source Code` to `0x6000`. Place the Disk Window Source volume `DISKWINDOW.Source` in disk drive 2, load the `DW.L` file into memory, and start the assembler by entering either the `A` command-line command or the `Z` command-line command. If a printed version of the screen output is desired, simply preface the `A` or `Z` command with the `P1` command-line command. Five object code files will be generated on the Disk Window Source volume: `SEG01` to `SEG05`. The five object code files can be combined in memory sequentially starting at `0x0900` using the `ctrl-P` command. The complete binary image can be saved to the Disk Window Source volume, or to any other volume, as `DW`.

6. EPROM Operating System (EOS) for quikLoader

Southern California Research Group's (SCRG) quikLoader as well as their PROmGRAMER were must-have peripheral slot cards when they first appeared in the early 1980's. Without question, data can be read many, many times faster from the Disk][than data read from cassette tape. But data can be read many, many times faster from a quikLoader EPROM than data read from the Disk][. Literally in a fraction of a second DOS can be read into memory from a quikLoader EPROM and begin its command-line processing.

I attended a Los Angeles computer convention where I bought the quikLoader after seeing several demonstrations in what it could do. Essentially, it is a very simple, though elegant peripheral slot card that can hold up to eight 2716 to 27512 EPROMs. The card has some hardware logic that maps the selected quikLoader EPROM to the 0xC100 to 0xFFFF address space.

The software SCRG provided with the quikLoader resides in the first EPROM, or EPROM 0, and this EPROM has room for a few additional programs as well. The SCRG documentation explained how to organize the contents of other programs and utilities in an EPROM and how to build a catalog for those contents. Once an EPROM was programmed with its catalog and its program contents, and seated in the quikLoader, a selected Primary program would be read into memory after pressing its EPROM number followed by the RESET key. The EPROM Catalog was displayed when the letter Q followed by RESET was pressed. I built several quikLoader EPROMs using the SCRG software interface, but I found the process to be tedious and cumbersome, and I thought I might be able to design a better interface. Once I sourced the SCRG EPROM control code, I realized their software interface could have been perhaps better thought out. And I saw there was absolutely no way to programmatically access any of the quikLoader EPROM contents using the current SCRG hardware unless I included a substantial amount of their EPROM control code within my software. The EPROM control code was not actually published, so that made accessing quikLoader contents even more tenuous.

Peripheral slot cards for the Apple][typically incorporate and utilize firmware code in its peripheral-card ROM memory, that is, 0xCs00 to 0xCsFF where s is the slot number of the peripheral slot card. Also, a peripheral slot card can use its peripheral-card expansion ROM memory, 0xC800 to 0xCFFF, for additional firmware code when the slot card is enabled. As an aside, putting 0xCFFF (or CLRROM) onto the address bus should turn off all peripheral-card expansion ROMs. Doing so will allow another peripheral slot card, enabled by accessing its peripheral-card ROM memory, to utilize its peripheral-card expansion ROM. This protocol will prevent memory contention with other peripheral slot cards. The quikLoader hardware did not have the ability to utilize its peripheral-card ROM memory and, therefore, could not utilize any peripheral-card expansion ROM memory for any of its interface software. This inability is simply a hardware design choice, but I viewed it as a hardware design deficiency.

I did find one unused 74LS08 AND gate on the quikLoader. That single AND gate allowed me to modify the quikLoader hardware logic such that it was now possible to access its peripheral-card ROM memory that was mapped to a single page of quikLoader EPROM data. Now I had something physical I could work with, and this led me to develop the EPROM Operating System, or *EOS*. In addition to this very minor hardware logic modification, I added an LED to glow when the quikLoader was enabled and an SPDT switch to logically disable the quikLoader without having to physically remove it from its slot in the computer. The complete circuit diagram of the quikLoader with my modifications is shown in Figure IV.6.1.

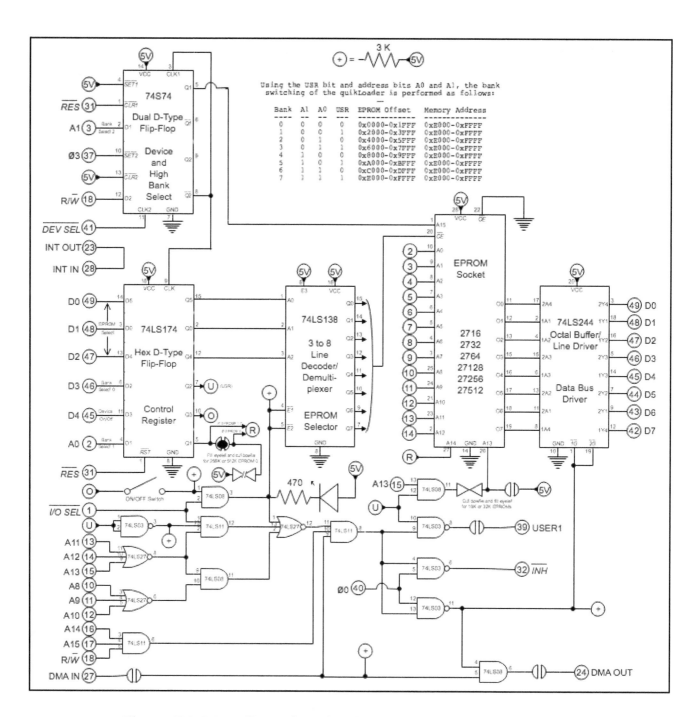

Figure IV.6.1 quikLoader Circuit Diagram with Modifications

Fortunately, I had acquired the "improved" quikLoader, the model capable of addressing a 27512 EPROM. A 74LS74 dual D flip-flop was added to capture the state of the 6502 A1 address line when writing to the quikLoader's 74LS174 control register, and to ever so slightly delay the 6502 clock edge for latching quikLoader EPROM data. The control register data byte can be written to any of the sixteen I/O memory locations dedicated to the quikLoader's slot: 0xC0n0 through 0xC0nF, where n is equal to the slot number of the quikLoader plus eight. However, only the first four address locations (or their relatives) do anything different since the control register only latches the state of address line A0 while the added 74LS74 latches the state of address line A1. The state of address lines A2 and A3

180

are not latched, so their values are not utilized. Data lines D0, D1, and D2 are latched by the control register and they select one of eight quikLoader EPROMs. Data line D3 is latched for the USR bit and data line D4 is latched to turn the quikLoader ON or OFF. If data line D4 is zero the quikLoader is turned ON. The state of data lines D5, D6, and D7 are not utilized.

The SCRG documentation describes how an area of quikLoader EPROM memory at a given offset is mapped to the Apple][′s 0xC100 to 0xFFFF address space, but I found using the first half of this address space strange and confusing, and not very amenable to programmatic utilization. Rather, I found that I could access an entire 27512 EPROM by using eight 8-KByte banks, where each bank uses the upper 0xE000 to 0xFFFF address space. The described function of the USR bit was also strange and confusing, as well as the role it was to perform according to the SCRG documentation. The USR bit was intended to be used as a master/slave flag when multiple quikLoaders are used in the same computer. For the moment I have quite a few programs that I routinely use, and those programs and *EOS* fit comfortably into three 27512 EPROMs. I cannot imagine needing more than one quikLoader in my computer, so my vision of *EOS* became even more tailored when I limited *EOS* to manage a single quikLoader and utilize the USR bit for bank selection. Table IV.6.1 lists the six EPROM sizes the quikLoader can address, their associated memory banks, and the latched control register data values necessary for USR (or D3), A0, and A1 to access those banks.

Bank	EPROM	EPROM Offset	Memory Access	A1	A0	USR
0	2716	0x0000-0x07FF	0xF800-0xFFFF	0	0	0
0	2732	0x0000-0x0FFF	0xF000-0xFFFF	0	0	0
0	2764	0x0000-0x1FFF	0xE000-0xFFFF	0	0	0
0	27128	0x0000-0x1FFF	0xE000-0xFFFF	0	0	0
1		0x2000-0x3FFF	0xE000-0xFFFF	0	0	1
0	27256	0x0000-0x1FFF	0xE000-0xFFFF	0	0	0
1		0x2000-0x3FFF	0xE000-0xFFFF	0	0	1
2		0x4000-0x5FFF	0xE000-0xFFFF	0	1	0
3		0x6000-0x7FFF	0xE000-0xFFFF	0	1	1
0	27512	0x0000-0x1FFF	0xE000-0xFFFF	0	0	0
1		0x2000-0x3FFF	0xE000-0xFFFF	0	0	1
2		0x4000-0x5FFF	0xE000-0xFFFF	0	1	0
3		0x6000-0x7FFF	0xE000-0xFFFF	0	1	1
4		0x8000-0x9FFF	0xE000-0xFFFF	1	0	0
5		0xA000-0xBFFF	0xE000-0xFFFF	1	0	1
6		0xC000-0xDFFF	0xE000-0xFFFF	1	1	0
7		0xE000-0xFFFF	0xE000-0xFFFF	1	1	1

Table IV.6.1. quikLoader Bank Switching

Offset	Name	Description
0x00	QLASEOS	Applesoft interface entry, parses command variables
0x5F	EXIT10	Return unknown command error, 0x10
0x62	EXIT20	Return wrong number of parameters error, 0x20
0x65	EXIT30	Return search range invalid error, 0x30
0x68	EXIT40	Return file not found error, 0x40
0x6B	EXIT00	Return no error, 0x00
0xA6	QLEXIT	If ZipChip present flush cache and enable it, fall into QLEXIT2
0xC2	QLEXIT2	Turn quikLoader OFF, jump to QBMEXIT at 0x0118
0xD0	QLUSER1	Return from DOS USERCMD, entry #1
0xD8	QLUSER2	Return from DOS USERCMD, entry #2
0xE0	QLBINEOS	Turn quikLoader on, load QBMCODE, jump to BINEOS
0xF0	QLEOS	Turn quikLoader on, jump to *EOS* at 0xE800
0xF8	QLBINTXT	ASCII QLBINEOS used to find the slot number for a quikLoader

Table IV.6.2. quikLoader Firmware Entry Points

Bank	Offset	Memory	Size	Contents
0	0x0000	0xE000	0x0004	Sync bytes
	0x0004	0xE004	0x00FC	Catalog
	0x0100	0xE100	0x0100	Slot 1 ASEOS/BINEOS interface
	0x0200	0xE200	0x0100	Slot 2 ASEOS/BINEOS interface
	0x0300	0xE300	0x0100	Slot 3 ASEOS/BINEOS interface
	0x0400	0xE400	0x0100	Slot 4 ASEOS/BINEOS interface
	0x0500	0xE500	0x0100	Slot 5 ASEOS/BINEOS interface
	0x0600	0xE600	0x0100	Slot 6 ASEOS/BINEOS interface
	0x0700	0xE700	0x0100	Slot 7 ASEOS/BINEOS interface
	0x0800	0xE800	0x17FA	*EOS* software
	0x1FFA	0xFFFA	0x0002	NMI vector, address of *EOS*
	0x1FFC	0xFFFC	0x0002	RESET vector, address of *EOS*
	0x1FFE	0xFFFE	0x0002	IRQ/BRK vector, address of *EOS*
1	0x2000	0xE000	0x2000	DOS4.1L
2	0x4000	0xE000	0x2A00	DOS4.1H
3	0x6A00	0xEA00	0x3000	*Lisa* 1 code segment
4	0x9A00	0xFA00	0x1000	*Lisa* 2 code segment
5	0xAA00	0xEA00	0x08D0	LED code segment
	0xB2D0	0xF2D0	0x1900	RAM Disk
6	0xCBD0	0xEBD0	0x12B8	*FID*
	0xDE88	0xFE88	0x0DAD	*ADT2*
7	0xEC35	0xEC35	0x0418	*Volume Copy*
	0xF04D	0xF04D	0x0647	*Set Clock*
	0xF694	0xF694	0x096C	unused

Table IV.6.3. EPROM 0 Containing EOS and Programs

When RESET is pressed the 74LS174 and 74LS74 data control registers are cleared in order to select EPROM 0, force Bank 0 to be mapped into memory from 0xE000 to 0xFFFF, and turn the quikLoader ON. The 6502 microprocessor automatically loads the RESET vector at 0xFFFC/0xFFFD into the program counter and continues fetching instructions from there. As an aside, the NMI vector is at 0xFFFA/0xFFFB and the IRQ/BRK vector is at 0xFFFE/0xFFFF. These three vectors point to the start of *EOS* which begins at 0xE800 in Bank 0. Therefore, *EOS* must reside within the remaining 0x17FA bytes of memory in Bank 0 of a 2764 EPROM, at a minimum, otherwise some sort of bank switching would need to be utilized in order to extend *EOS* processing into another EPROM bank, an option I did not wish to employ. Table IV.6.2 shows the firmware entry points of one of seven copies of the firmware that is mapped to the peripheral-card ROM address space of the quikLoader by incorporating that single, unused 74LS08 AND gate as shown in Figure IV.6.1.

Fortunately, there is enough room for *EOS* to process the 26 commands shown in Figure IV.6.2. There is even room for the EPROM Catalog function, the Applesoft interface (or ASEOS), the assembly language interface (or BINEOS), the ZipChip configuration software to support a ZipChip if one is present, and the software to manage Primary files. Unlike the SCRG interface, *EOS* does not capture the state of the keyboard at the moment the RESET key is pressed. Instead, *EOS* displays an "EOS Main Menu", and any of the displayed options may be selected. I simply chose those programs and utilities I liked best to display in the "EOS Main Menu". Someone else may display a different set of favorite utilities. The way I have organized EPROM 0 is so simple that all one needs to do is model their EPROM 0 after mine. The remaining seven banks on EPROM 0, a 27512, contain DOS 4.1L and DOS 4.1H, ROM Copy, *Set Clock*, *Volume Copy*, *Lisa* and LED, RAM Disk Installation, *FID*, and *ADT2*. Table IV.6.3 shows the contents of EPROM 0 that contains *EOS*. Both *Disk Window* and CFFA Volume Manager software (*VOLMGR*, *BOOTVOL*, and *BOOTDOS*) reside on other EPROMs. *EOS* uses the power and flexibility of BINEOS to load and run those utilities without regard to a specific EPROM number. An example *EOS* Catalog screen is shown in Figures IV.6.3 and IV.6.4.

Later in the discussion concerning the ASEOS interface, Table IV.6.4 shows the definition of the file types used in *EOS*, how each file type is displayed in the *EOS* Catalog screen, and the hexadecimal value of each file type. Notice in Figure IV.6.3 that DOS.4.1.46H is file type S having a value of 0x5C. This value is derived from the logical OR of Binary file (Main memory), Binary file (Bank 1), Binary file (Bank 2), and System file because parts of DOS.4.1.46H reside in all these memory locations. Mathematically, the file type for the DOS.4.1.46H file is:

FILETYPE = 0x04 ∨ 0x08 ∨ 0x10 ∨ 0x40 = <u>0x5C</u>

EOS provides Applesoft users with three commands when using the Applesoft, or ASEOS interface: LOAD file, RUN file, and CATALOG. In order to access ASEOS, the quikLoader control register must be initially configured to quikLoader EPROM 0, Bank 0, and turned OFF. For example, if the quikLoader resides in slot 4, the program must "POKE 49344, 16" (i.e. save 0x10 to 0xC0C0) to initially configure the quikLoader hardware before making the CALL to ASEOS. That will bring *EOS* into focus. In this example "CALL 50176" (i.e. execute the code at 0xC400) will begin ASEOS processing. The CALL command must be followed by some required arguments, and there are some optional arguments as well. These arguments must be presented in the order given and they **must be** integer variables, integer arrays, ASCII strings, or ASCII string arrays where indicated. Real variables and real arrays **must never** be used in an ASEOS CALL statement because those numbers are floating point values and they are not supported by the ASEOS routines.

```
┌─────────────────────────────────────────────┐
│            EOS Main Menu                      │
├─────────────────────────────────────────────┤
│                                               │
│A DOS4.1L Boot        N Copy ROM->RAM          │
│B DOS4.1H Boot        O ->RAM Monitor          │
│C Coldstart DOS       P ->RAM Reset            │
│D Warmstart DOS       Q ->ROM Monitor          │
│E EOS Catalog         R ->ROM Reset            │
│F Select SDV          S Run HELLO (SDV)        │
│G  Boot  Slot S       T  CATALOG  (SDV)        │
│H  Hook  Slot S       U  VTOC  Manager         │
│I Unhook Slot S       V Volume Manager         │
│J FID                 W Volume Copy            │
│K ADT                 X Disk Window            │
│L Lisa                Y  Clock  Config         │
│M RamDisk Init        Z ZipChip Config         │
│                                               │
│                    SDV S=7 D=01 V=000         │
│  ZipChip State                                │
│   -> Out <-        RTN Toggle ZipChip         │
│                                               │
│Enter Selection:                               │
│                                               │
└─────────────────────────────────────────────┘
```

Figure IV.6.2. EOS Commands at RESET

```
┌─────────────────────────────────────────────┐
│         quikLoader EOS Catalog                │
│           Slot 4        EPROM 0               │
│                                               │
│     B 0x04 >RamDisk  Install                  │
│                                               │
│     B 0x04  FID                               │
│                                               │
│     B 0x04  ADT2                              │
│                                               │
│     B 0x04  Volume Copy                       │
│                                               │
│     S 0x44  DOS4.1.46L                        │
│                                               │
│     S 0x5C  DOS4.1.46H                        │
│                                               │
│     S 0x48  LISA 1                            │
│                                               │
│     S 0x50  LISA 2                            │
│                                               │
│     RTN - File Info        (L)oad             │
│     SPC - Next EPROM       (R)un              │
│     0-7 - Select EPROM     (Q)uit             │
└─────────────────────────────────────────────┘
```

Figure IV.6.3. EOS Catalog for EPROM 0, Part 1

```
            quikLoader EOS Catalog
               Slot 4        EPROM 0


      S 0x44    DOS4.1.46L

      S 0x5C    DOS4.1.46H

      S 0x48    LISA 1

      S 0x50    LISA 2

      S 0x44    LISA LED

      B 0x04    Set Clock

      R 0x20    ROM Copy

      R 0x20   >Catalog Sync


      RTN - File Info           (L)oad
      SPC - Next EPROM          (R)un
      0-7 - Select EPROM        (Q)uit
```

Figure IV.6.4. EOS Catalog for EPROM 0, Part 2

Value	File Type	Description
0x01	T	Text file, NULL terminated, like an EXEC file
0x02	A	Applesoft file
0x04	B	Binary file, Main memory
0x08	B	Binary file, Language Card Bank 1 memory
0x10	B	Binary file, Language Card Bank 2 memory
0x20	R	Reserved file
0x40	S	System file
0x80	P	Primary file

Table IV.6.4. EOS File Types Used in Optional Parameter Array

The following shows how to use the ASEOS interface for the LOAD, RUN, and CATALOG commands:

1) LOAD file. This command loads a file into memory from a quikLoader EPROM using ASEOS:

```
QL    = quikLoader slot number
OFF   = 16                            ; 0x10
DEV   = QL * 16 + 49280               ; QL * 0x10 + 0xC080
EOS   = QL * 256 + 49152              ; QL * 0x100 + 0xC000
C%    = 1                             ; LOAD file command
```

185

```
S%    = -1                                      ; set Status to ERROR
E%    = EPROM search range
F$    = Filename (1 to 24 upper ASCII characters)
[A%]  = Alternate load address (optional)

POKE DEV, OFF
CALL EOS, C%, S%, E%, F$ [, A%]
```

2) RUN file. This command loads a file into memory from a quikLoader EPROM and runs that file using ASEOS:

```
QL    = quikLoader slot number
OFF   = 16                           ; 0x10
DEV   = QL * 16 + 49280               ; QL * 0x10 + 0xC080
EOS   = QL * 256 + 49152              ; QL * 0x100 + 0xC000
C%    = 2                             ; RUN file command
S%    = -1                            ; set Status to ERROR
E%    = EPROM search range
F$    = Filename (1 to 24 upper ASCII characters)
[A%]  = Alternate load address (optional)

POKE DEV, OFF
CALL EOS, C%, S%, E%, F$ [, A%]
```

3) CATALOG files. This command catalogs the quikLoader EPROMs using ASEOS:

```
QL          = quikLoader slot number
OFF         = 16                           ; 0x10
M%          = Maximum number of anticipated entries
DEV         = QL * 16 + 49280              ; QL * 0x10 + 0xC080
EOS         = QL * 256 + 49152             ; QL * 0x100 + 0xC000
C%          = 3                            ; CATALOG command
S%          = -1                           ; set Status to ERROR
E%          = EPROM search range
N%          = Number of entries returned (not initialized)
F$(N%)      = Filename array (1 to 24 upper ASCII characters)
[P%(0,N%)]= Parameter Array returned (optional)

DIM F$(M%), P%(4,M%)
POKE DEV, OFF
N% = 0                                     ; start index
CALL EOS, C%, S%, E%, N%, F$(N%) [, P%(0,N%)]
```

EPROM search range for all commands:

```
E% = 0-7 for a single, specific quikLoader EPROM
E% = 0-7:0-7, or ( last EPROM ) * 16 + ( start EPROM )
```

Returned Status values for all commands:

```
S% = 0     No Error
S% = -1    Number of Parameters Exceeded    ; 0xFF
S% = 16    Unknown Command                  ; 0x10
S% = 32    Number of Parameters Invalid     ; 0x20
S% = 48    Search Range Invalid             ; 0x30
S% = 64    File Not Found                   ; 0x40
```

Optional Parameter Array returned:

```
P%(0,N%) = EPROM number
P%(1,N%) = file type
P%(2,N%) = EPROM offset
P%(3,N%) = file size in bytes
P%(4,N%) = destination memory address
```

EOS file types are shown in Table IV.6.4 with their value and their display designation in the *EOS* Catalog function. *EOS* currently uses two Reserved type files: the ROM code from 0xD000 to 0xFFFF and the four Catalog sync bytes. Primary files are Binary files that can use the BINEOS interface, and they may be activated directly by the quikLoader *EOS* Catalog function in order to LOAD or RUN System files. The quikLoader *EOS* Catalog function **cannot** directly load or run System files. System files may be Text, Applesoft, or other Binary files. System files may be attached to a Primary file, or LOADed or RUN by activating its associated Primary file either using the quikLoader *EOS* Catalog function, ASEOS, or BINEOS. *EOS* is not designed to handle Integer BASIC type files because DOS 4.1 does not support Integer BASIC type files. A DOS image and the software tool SOURCEROR are examples of System type files. The program that loads SOURCEROR into memory for execution is an example of a Primary file. System and Primary files used in *EOS* are different in function and concept than those files used in the SCRG interface.

Offset	Length	Variable	Description
0	1	FILETYPE	File type as defined in Table IV.6.4
1	2	SRCVAL	EPROM source address (EPROM offset)
3	2	LENVAL	File length or size in bytes
5	2	DSTVAL	Destination memory address (Apple][memory)
7	1-24	FILENAME	Filename, 1 to 24 ASCII bytes (DCI format)

Table IV.6.5. EOS Catalog File Entry Structure

A quikLoader EPROM Catalog for the files contained in that EPROM is prefaced with four sync bytes, 0xC4, 0xB8, 0x90, and 0xED. The actual catalog begins at offset 0x0004 and it may contain any

187

number of entries, where each entry is a variable size depending on the length in bytes for its filename. An EPROM Catalog filename is a character string that uses lower ASCII for all of its bytes except for the last byte in the string which is in upper ASCII. The *Lisa* assembler calls the utilization of lower and upper ASCII for strings in this manner the DCI format. The catalog is terminated with a NULL (or 0x00) character. An example catalog file entry structure is shown in Table IV.6.5.

EOS provides assembly language users with three commands when using the assembly language, or BINEOS interface: LOAD file, RUN file, and CATALOG. An eight-byte Data Context Block, or DCB is used for the input variables and returned status. The structure of the DCB is command specific. Any assembly language program like Primary files can use QLBINEOS to LOAD and RUN System files. QLBINEOS is located at the 0xE0th byte in the peripheral-card ROM memory of the quikLoader as shown in Table IV.6.2. For example, if the quikLoader resides in slot 4, QLBINEOS is at memory address 0xC4E0. The following code in Figure IV.6.5 shows how to utilize the BINEOS interface.

```
0800            1              ttl "QLBINEOS Utilization, QLBINEOS.L"
0800            2    ;
0800            3    ;
0800            4    ; QLBINEOS.L
0800            5    ;
0800            6    ;
002A            7    SRCPTR    epz $2A
002E            8    DSTPTR    epz $2E
0800            9    ;
0000           10    ZERO      equ $00
00FF           11    NEGONE    equ $FF
0800           12    ;
0000           13    QLON      equ $00
0010           14    QLOFF     equ $10
0800           15    ;
0020           16    CHKNUM    equ $20
0800           17    ;
C080           18    QLSELC    equ $C080
0800           19    ;
C0E0           20    QLBINEOS equ $C0E0
C0F8           21    QLBINTXT equ $C0F8
0800           22    ;
C700           23    PAGEC7    equ $C700
E700           24    PAGEE7    equ $E700
0800           25    ;
CFFF           26    CLRROM    equ $CFFF
0800           27    ;
0800           28    ;
0800           29              org $800
0800           30              obj $800
0800           31              usr
0800           32    ;
0800           33    ;
0800 20 0C 08  34              jsr FINDQL         ; find quikLoader
0803 B0 07     35              bcs FINDERR
0805           36    ;
0805 A0 71     37              ldy #EOSDCBL       ; address of
0807 A9 08     38              lda /EOSDCBL       ;  Load DCB
0809           39    ;
```

```
0809  20 63 08    40              jsr QLBINJMP       ; Load the file
080C              41    ;
080C              42    ;           :::
080C              43    ;
080C              44    FINDERR:
080C              45    ;           :::
080C              46    ;
080C              47    ;
080C              48    FINDQL:
080C  A0 00       49              ldy #PAGEC7        ; get address
080E  A9 C7       50              lda /PAGEC7        ;  of 0xC700
0810              51    ;
0810  84 2A       52              sty SRCPTR         ; store address at
0812  85 2B       53              sta SRCPTR+1       ;  source pointer
0814              54    ;
0814  A9 E7       55              lda /PAGEE7        ; bank 0 slot address
0816              56    ;
0816  84 2E       57              sty DSTPTR         ; store address at
0818  85 2F       58              sta DSTPTR+1       ;  destination pointer
081A              59    ;
081A  A9 07       60              lda #7             ; initialize
081C  8D 66 08    61              sta QLSLOT         ;  for slot 7
081F              62    ;
081F  AD 66 08    63    ^1         lda QLSLOT         ; get slot number
0822              64    ;
0822  0A          65              asl                ; multiply by 16
0823  0A          66              asl
0824  0A          67              asl
0825  0A          68              asl
0826              69    ;
0826  AA          70              tax                ; use as index
0827              71    ;
0827  A9 00       72              lda #QLON          ; turn quikLoader ON
0829  9D 80 C0    73              sta QLSELC,X
082C              74    ;
082C  2C FF CF    75              bit CLRROM         ; detach expansion ROM memory
082F              76    ;
082F  A0 20       77              ldy #CHKNUM        ; initialize index
0831              78    ;
0831  B1 2A       79    ^2         lda (SRCPTR),Y     ; compare slot memory
0833  D1 2E       80              cmp (DSTPTR),Y     ;  and EPROM bank 0
0835  D0 1E       81              bne >4
0837              82    ;
0837  88          83              dey
0838  D0 F7       84              bne <2
083A              85    ;
083A  A9 10       86              lda #QLOFF         ; turn quikLoader OFF
083C  9D 80 C0    87              sta QLSELC,X
083F              88    ;
083F  A0 F8       89              ldy #QLBINTXT      ; point to QLBIN text
0841              90    ;
0841  B1 2A       91    ^3         lda (SRCPTR),Y     ; compare slot memory
0843  D9 71 07    92              cmp QLTEXT-NEGONE&QLBINTXT,Y ;  and text
0846  D0 0D       93              bne >4
0848              94    ;
0848  C8          95              iny
0849  D0 F6       96              bne <3
084B              97    ;
084B  A5 2B       98              lda SRCPTR+1       ; get slot memory address
084D  8D 68 08    99              sta QLBINADR+1     ; save to vector
0850             100    ;
```

189

```
0850 2C FF CF   101           bit CLRROM       ; detach expansion ROM memory
0853            102 ;
0853 18         103           clc              ; quikLoader found
0854            104 ;
0854 60         105           rts
0855            106 ;
0855 C6 2B      107 ^4        dec SRCPTR+1     ; next slot memory
0857 C6 2F      108           dec DSTPTR+1     ; next EOS slot
0859            109 ;
0859 CE 66 08   110           dec QLSLOT       ; next slot
085C D0 C1      111           bne <1
085E            112 ;
085E 2C FF CF   113           bit CLRROM       ; detach expansion ROM memory
0861            114 ;
0861 38         115           sec              ; no quikLoader
0862            116 ;
0862 60         117           rts
0863            118 ;
0863            119 ;
0863 6C 67 08   120 QLBINJMP  jmp (QLBINADR)
0866            121 ;
0866            122 ;
0866            123 QLSLOT    dfs 1,ZERO
0867            124 ;
0867 E0 C0      125 QLBINADR  adr QLBINEOS
0869            126 ;
0869 D1 CC C2   127 QLTEXT    asc "QLBINEOS"
086C C9 CE C5
086F CF D3
0871            128 ;
0871            129 ;
0871            130 EOSDCBL   equ *
0871            131 ;
0871 01         132 DCBLCMD   hex 01           ; Load command
0872 07         133 DCBLEP    hex 70           ; search all EPROMs
0873 00 00      134 DCBLOAD   hex 0000         ; no alternate Load address
0875 FF         135 DCBLSTAT  hex FF           ; return status
0876 0F         136 DCBLFLEN  byt FILENDL-FILNAML ; filename length
0877 79 08      137 DCBLFADR  adr FILNAML      ; filename address
0879            138 ;
0879 C1 F0 F0   139 FILNAML   asc "Apple File List"
087C EC E5 A0
087F C6 E9 EC
0882 E5 A0 CC
0885 E9 F3 F4
0888            140 FILENDL   equ *
0888            141 ;
0888            142 ;

BSAVE QLBINEOS,A$0800,L$0088
0888            143           usr QLBINEOS
0888            144 ;
0888            145 ;
0888            146           end 000

*** End of Assembly
```

Figure IV.6.5. QLBINEOS Utilization Example

1) LOAD file. This DCB loads a file into memory from a quikLoader EPROM using BINEOS:

```
EOSDCBL    equ *                        ; LOAD file DCB
DCBCMDL    hex 01                       ; LOAD command
DCBEPNL    hex 70                       ; search all EPROMs
DCBFALTL   hex 0000                     ; no alternate address
DCBSTATL   hex FF                       ; return status
DCBFLENL   byt FILENDL-FILNAML          ; filename length
DCBFADRL   adr FILNAML                  ; filename address

FILNAML    asc "Applesoft File List"
FILENDL    equ *
```

1) RUN file. This DCB loads a file into memory from a quikLoader EPROM and RUNs that file using BINEOS:

```
EOSDCBR    equ *                        ; RUN file DCB
DCBCMDR    hex 02                       ; RUN command
DCBEPNR    hex 70                       ; search all EPROMs
DCBFALTR   hex 0000                     ; no alternate address
DCBSTATR   hex FF                       ; return status
DCBFLENR   byt FILENDR-FILNAMR          ; filename length
DCBFADRR   adr FILNAMR                  ; filename address

FILNAMR    asc "Volume Copy"
FILENDR    equ *
```

1) CATALOG files. This DCB catalogs the quikLoader EPROMs using BINEOS:

```
EOSDCBC    equ *                        ; CATALOG EPROMs DCB
DCBCMDC    hex 03                       ; CATALOG command
DCBEPNC    hex 70                       ; CATALOG all EPROMs
DCBCALT    hex 0000                     ; not used
DCBSTATC   hex FF                       ; return status
DCBCNUM    hex 00                       ; CATALOG entries number
DCBCADR    adr CATBUFR                  ; CATALOG buffer address

CATBUFR    dfs 32*n,ZERO                ; n 32-byte entries
```

The call to QLBINEOS will return one of the following Status values:

```
0x00 = No Error
0x10 = Unknown Command
0x20 = Filename Length Invalid
0x30 = Search Range Invalid
0x40 = Buffer/Filename Address Error
```

Offset	Length	Variable	Description
0	1	FILEPNUM	EPROM number containing this file
1	1	FILETYPE	File type
2	2	SRCVAL	EPROM source address (EPROM offset)
4	2	LENVAL	File length or size in bytes
6	2	DSTVAL	Destination memory address (Apple][memory)
8	24	FILENAME	Filename, space padded, upper ASCII

Table IV.6.6. BINEOS Catalog File Entry

The quikLoader EPROM search range and file types are the same in BINEOS as they are in ASEOS. The Catalog buffer will contain the number of entries given by DCBCNUM. Each Catalog entry will be thirty-two bytes in size regardless of the length of the filename in bytes. The filename will be converted to upper ASCII and padded with the upper ASCII SPACE (or 0xA0) character to be exactly twenty-four characters in length. A BINEOS Catalog file entry is structured as shown in Table IV.6.6.

EOS makes extensive use of the 6502 microprocessor stack page from 0x110 to 0x19F for the QBMCODE consisting of the routines QLJMP, QLCONFIG, QLMOVE, QLJSR, QLRTN, and QLEXEC. When *EOS* is activated it initializes the stack pointer to 0xFF to ensure that these temporary stack page routines are safe while *EOS* is active. And, it is extremely unlikely that the ASEOS interface will load these stack routines over a stack pointer in this memory region because Applesoft tightly controls this pointer. The same argument can be made for software using the BINEOS interface as long as that software is mindful of the stack pointer location and where the QBMCODE routines reside. *EOS* also makes extensive use of the text INPUT page from 0x0280 to 0x02EF. It is extremely unlikely that a lengthy Applesoft statement or DOS command will ever be issued during ASEOS or BINEOS processing. However, an Applesoft user should be aware that *EOS* does use the upper half of the INPUT page. *EOS* uses the stack and INPUT pages so that the memory page from 0x0300 to 0x03CF is still left available for program loaders. The loader (a Primary file) for SOURCEROR (a System File) is one example of a very short binary program that uses 0x300 to 0x32C to load SOURCEROR from a quikLoader EPROM to memory address 0x8900 using a LOAD DCB. The possibilities are virtually endless in how *EOS* can be utilized to obtain information and data programmatically from an EPROM or from all EPROMs residing in a quikLoader.

To assemble the *EOS* source code place the DOS 4.1 Tools volume DOS4.1.ToolsL in disk drive 1, boot, and start *Lisa*. Enter the SE command-line command to select the SETUP program in order to verify or set the Start of Source Code to 0x5000 and the End of Source Code to 0x7000. Place the EOS Binaries volume EOS.512.Binaries in disk drive 1. Place the EOS Source volume EOS.512.Source in disk drive 2, load the EOS.L file into memory, and start the assembler by entering either the A command-line command or the Z command-line command. If a printed version of the screen output is desired, simply preface the A or Z command with the P1 command-line command. Eight object code files will be generated on the EOS Binaries volume: SEG01 to SEG08. Place the EOS Image volume EOS.512.Image in disk drive 2, load the MOVE.L file into memory from the EOS Binaries volume, and start the assembler using the Z command-line command. The eight object code files will be copied from the EOS Binaries volume to the EOS Image volume. The first four object code files on the EOS Image volume can be combined in memory sequentially starting at `0x1000` using the `ctrl-P` command. The complete binary image can be saved to the EOS Image volume as `EOS1` as shown in Figure IV.14.5. The last four object code files on the EOS Image volume can be combined in memory sequentially starting at `0x1000` using the `ctrl-P` command. The complete binary image can be saved to the EOS Image volume as `EOS2` as shown in Figure IV.14.6. I also place a copy of the utility *BURNER* on the EOS Image volume before I transfer the volume to an Apple //e using A2V2 on the MacBook and *ADT2* on the Apple //e. Now, the utility *BURNER* can easily program a 27512 EPROM using the `EOS1` and `EOS2` binary images as binary source files. `EOS1` must be programmed to the first half of the EPROM and `EOS2` must be programmed to the second half of the EPROM.

To assemble the PGM1 source code with *Lisa* already running, place the PGM1 Binaries volume `PGM1.512.Binaries` in disk drive 1. Place the PGM1 Source volume `PGM1.512.Source` in disk drive 2, load the `PGM.L` file into memory, and start the assembler using either the `A` command-line command or the `Z` command-line command. If a printed version of the screen output is desired, simply preface the `A` or `Z` command with the `P1` command-line command. Eight object code files will be generated on the PGM1 Source volume: `SEG01` to `SEG08`. Place the PGM1 Image volume `PGM1.512.Image` in disk drive 1, load the `MOVE.L` file into memory from the PGM1 Source volume, and start the assembler using the `Z` command-line command. The eight object code files will be copied from the PGM1 Source volume to the PGM1 Image volume. The first four object code files on the PGM1 Image volume can be combined in memory sequentially starting at `0x1000` using the `ctrl-P` command. The complete binary image can be saved to the PGM1 Image volume as `PGM1`. The last four object code files on the PGM1 Image volume can be combined in memory sequentially starting at `0x1000` using the `ctrl-P` command. The complete binary image can be saved to the PGM1 Image volume as `PGM2`. I also place a copy of the utility *BURNER* on the PGM1 Image volume before I transfer the volume to an Apple //e using A2V2 on the MacBook and *ADT2* on the Apple //e. Now, the utility *BURNER* can easily program a 27512 EPROM using the `PGM1` and `PGM2` binary images as binary source files. `PGM1` must be programmed to the first half of the EPROM and `PGM2` must be programmed to the second half of the EPROM.

To assemble the PGM2 source code with *Lisa* already running, place the PGM2 Source volume `PGM2.256.Source` in disk drive 2, load the `PGM.L` file in memory, and start the assembler using either the `A` command-line command or the `Z` command-line command. If a printed version of the screen output is desired, simply preface the `A` or `Z` command with the `P1` command-line command. Four object code files will be generated on the PGM2 Source volume: `SEG01` to `SEG04`. These four object code files can be combined in memory sequentially starting at `0x1000` using the `ctrl-P` command. The complete binary image can be saved to the PGM2 Source volume as `PGM1`. I also place a copy of the utility *BURNER* on the PGM2 Source volume before I transfer the volume to an Apple //e using A2V2 on the MacBook and *ADT2* on the Apple //e. Now, the utility *BURNER* can easily program a 27256 or a 27512 EPROM using the `PGM1` binary image as the binary source file. `PGM1` must be programmed to the first half of a 27512 EPROM if that EPROM size is used.

Seat all three 27512 EPROMs in a quikLoader being mindful that the EPROM containing *EOS* must be seated in Socket 0. Plug the quikLoader into an available slot and power the Apple //e `ON`. The `EOS Main Menu` as shown in Figure IV.6.2 will be displayed.

7. VTOC Manager (VMGR)

The Volume Table of Contents (VTOC) Manager, or *VMGR*, is a utility I developed while I was designing the enhancements to the DOS 4.1 VTOC and Catalog. *VMGR* provides the user the ability to display and change the contents of a volume's VTOC for any given slot, drive, and volume number. Figure IV.7.1 displays the Option Menu for *VMGR*. When the program first starts, it displays the current slot, drive, and volume number values. You can change those values using Option 1. Option 2 reads the VTOC for the selected slot, drive, and volume number as shown in Figure IV.7.2. Option 3 displays the same VTOC contents as in Figure IV.7.2 except that you can edit, or change the information. Great harm can easily be done to a volume, even making the volume unusable, if the VTOC information is changed inappropriately. It is critical that you understand the effect of any change you make to the VTOC and accept the consequences. Options 4 and 5 show and edit the sector bitmap, respectively. Figure IV.7.3 displays the sector bitmap contents for the same volume.

Each track of a DOS 4.1 volume may contain either 16 or 32 sectors depending on the hardware media. The VTOC can support up to 50 tracks. Figure I.6.1 shows the complete sector bitmap that begins at byte 0x38 in the VTOC. The sector bitmap allocates four bytes, or 32 bits, for every track to determine if a sector in that track is available or not. If a sector is available its respective bit is set to 1. Table I.6.2 shows the sector order from left to right: sectors 0x0F to 0x00 for the left two bytes followed by sectors 0x1F to 0x10 for the right two bytes. DOS 4.1 indirectly interacts with the VTOC bitmap by means of the variable NEXTSECR exclusively OR'd with the value 0x10. Therefore, if a volume only supports 16 sectors per track, the right two bytes will be set to 0x00. In Figure IV.7.3, for example, track 24 contains five free sectors and track 28 contains sixteen free sectors.

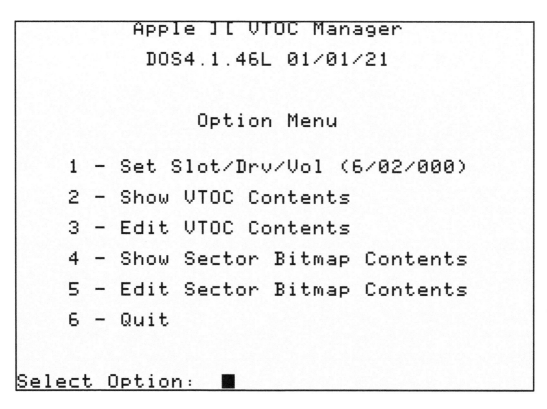

Figure IV.7.1. VMGR Option Menu

194

```
            VTOC Contents


1st Cat T/S    - 0x11/0x05
DOS Version    - 4.1
DOS Build      - 46
DOS RAM        - L (Low RAM)

Volm Number    - 0x00 (000)
Volm Type      - D (Data Disk)
Volm Subject   - 0x50A0 (20640)
Volm DiskName  - VTOC Manager Source Code
Volm DateTime  - 01/01/21 08:28:48
VTOC DateTime  - 01/01/21 08:28:48

T/S Pairs      - 0x7A (122)
Next Track     - 0x1B (27)
Direction      - 0x01 (forward)
Volume Tracks  - 0x23 (35)
Track Sectors  - 0x10 (16)
Sector Bytes   - 0x100 (256)


            Press Any Key
```

Figure IV.7.2. VTOC Contents

```
        Sector Bitmap Contents

             35 Tracks


Trk|FB73FB73  FB73FB73  FB73FB73  FB73FB73
Num|C840C840  C840C840  C840C840  C840C840
---------------------------------------
 00|00000000  00000000  00000000  00000000
 04|3FFF0000  FFFF0000  FFFF0000  FFFF0000
 08|FFFF0000  FFFF0000  FFFF0000  FFFF0000
 0C|FFFF0000  FFFF0000  FFFF0000  FFFF0000
 10|FFFF0000  FFC00000  001F0000  00000000
 14|00000000  00000000  003F0000  07FF0000
 18|001F0000  07FF0000  1FFF0000  00000000
 1C|FFFF0000  FFFF0000  FFFF0000  FFFF0000
 20|FFFF0000  FFFF0000  FFFF0000



            Press Any Key
```

Figure IV.7.3. VTOC Sector Bitmap Contents

To assemble the *VMGR* source code place the DOS 4.1 Tools volume `DOS4.1.ToolsL` in disk drive 1, boot, and start *Lisa*. Enter the `SE` command-line command to select the `SETUP` program in order to verify or set the `Start of Source Code` to `0x2100` and the `End of Source Code` to `0x6000`. Place the VMGR Source volume `VMGR.Source` in disk drive 2, load the `VMGR.L` file into memory, and start the assembler by entering either the `A` command-line command or the `Z` command-line command. If a printed version of the screen output is desired, simply preface the `A` or `Z` command with the `P1` command-line command. Four object code files will be generated on the VMGR Source volume: `SEG01` to `SEG04`. The four object code files can be combined in memory sequentially starting at `0x900` using the `ctrl-P` command. The complete binary image can be saved to the VMGR Source volume, or to any other volume, as `VMGR`.

8. Asynchronous Data Transfer (ADT)

I have done a serious amount of software development for the Apple][using a MacBook Pro running the Virtual][emulation program by Gerard Putter. Virtual][can launch a utility called A2V2 that can transfer a 140 KB diskette image to and from an Apple][that is concurrently running a program called Asynchronous Data Transfer, or *ADT* by Paul Guertin and enhanced by Gerard Putter. My Apple //e uses a Super Serial slot card connected to a Keyspan serial to USB adapter that is connected to the MacBook Pro using a USB cable. Only 140 KB disk images are currently permitted. Because the RAM Disk 320 supports up to 40 tracks and I typically use it to receive disk images, I would like to see the 140 KB restriction removed from A2V2 and *ADT*. I would even like to have Virtual][support 48 track diskettes, but Mr. Putter has rejected that request. Regardless, I did source *ADT* so I could add an Update command to its command repertoire as shown in Figure IV.8.1. After configuring *ADT2*, Update will save *ADT2* with its new configuration set as its default. The *ADT2* Configuration screen is shown in Figure IV.8.2, which uses lowercase characters to assist in making the Apple screen text easier for me to read in my opinion. If and when 160 KB and 200 KB disk images are supported I will be ready. But let's not stop there! My RanaSystems EliteThree drive can support 40 tracks with each track having 32 sectors, so 320 KB disk images are possible, too. In order to process 320 KB disk images *ADT2* may need to utilize an 80-column display. Finally, a CFFA volume having 48 32-sector tracks would require a 400 KB disk image. Now, that would be a seriously fun project: using an 80-colum display to show the transfer of volumes having up to 48 32-sector tracks.

The "?" command displays credits to Paul Guertin, Gerard Putter, and myself for adding enhancements to *ADT2* as shown in Figure IV.8.3.

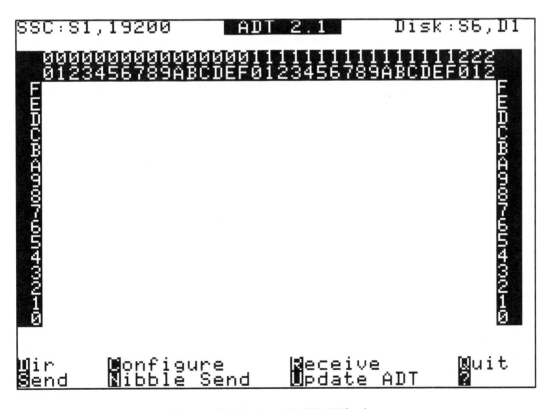

Figure IV.8.1. ADT2 Window

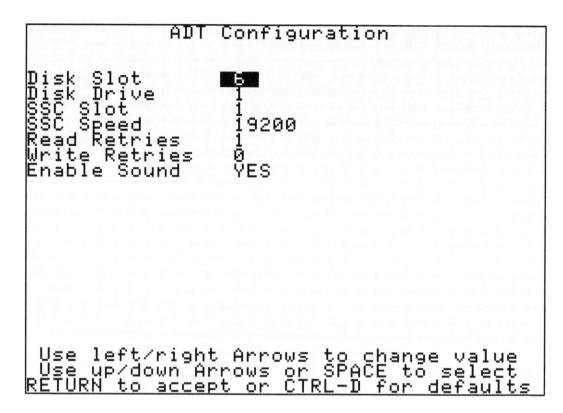

Figure IV.8.2. ADT2 Configuration

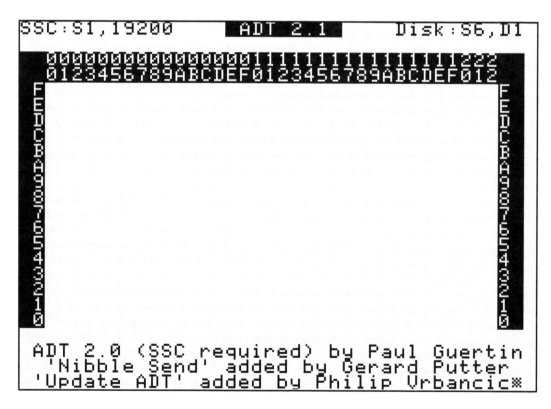

Figure IV.8.3. ADT2 Software Credits

To assemble the *ADT2* source code place the DOS 4.1 Tools volume `DOS4.1.ToolsL` in disk drive 1, boot, and start *Lisa*. Enter the `SE` command-line command to select the `SETUP` program in order to verify or set the `Start of Source Code` to `0x2100` and the `End of Source Code` to `0x6000`. Place the ADT2 Source volume `ADT2.Source` in disk drive 2, load the `ADT2.L` file into memory, and start the assembler by entering either the `A` command-line command or the `Z` command-line command. If a printed version of the screen output is desired, simply preface the `A` or `Z` command with the `P1` command-line command. The complete binary image will be saved to the ADT2 Source volume as `ADT2`.

9. Big Mac

I first started using *Big Mac* by Glen E. Bredon on my Apple][+ as soon as I took an interest in writing assembly language programs. Also, *Sourceror* was designed as a subsidiary tool to *Big Mac* that created *Big Mac* source files from assembly language object code. The main menu for *Big Mac* is shown in Figure IV.9.1 and this is another example where I have used lowercase characters to assist in making the Apple][screen text easier for me to read. When I started working at Sierra On-Line the programmers there only used *Lisa*, and not *Big Mac*. But whenever I used *Sourceror* I was still dependent on *Big Mac* to edit *Sourceror*'s output source files into files resembling *Lisa* source files using the ED/ASM mode, and then saving those files as TEXT files. *Lisa* was able to EXEC the *Big Mac* TEXT files into its format quickly. And this is precisely the procedure I still use today.

```
                  BIG MAC
              By: G. Bredon


  C  :Catalog
  L  :Load source
  S  :Save source
  A  :Append file
  R  :Read text file
  W  :Write text file
  D  :Drive change
  E  :Enter ED/ASM
  O  :Save object code
  Z  :Zero tabs
  Q  :Quit

                  Source: A$0901,L$0000

  Drive: 1

  :
```

Figure IV.9.1. Big Mac Main Menu

Big Mac made frequent use of DOS 3.3 internal routines so it was not at all compatible with DOS 4.1. I needed to know every instance where *Big Mac* utilized DOS 3.3 internals, and then modify those dependencies to use the DOS 4.1 interface. *Big Mac* was certainly a challenge because it packed a huge wallop of a program into the limited space of the Language Card. Creating source code for *Big Mac* that could be modified required a huge effort. It is one thing to have source code that assembles to object code which compares perfectly to the original object code. It is quite another thing to turn that source code into routines whose addresses may change as some code is modified, deleted, and added, and still assemble into a working program. I did remove the ASSEM re-entry command because DOS 4.1 provides no visibility into its commands, their handler addresses, and the companion keyword table. (A seasoned *Big Mac* user may wish to re-install the ASSEM command in DOS 4.1 in lieu of one

200

of the other DOS commands, assemble this unique version of DOS 4.1, and create a bootable *Big Mac* volume having that version of DOS 4.1.) DOS 4.1 does provide access to structures for drive number, start address, and file length, though. I am satisfied that my sourced and modified version of *Big Mac* is fully DOS 4.1L compliant and, as a utility, *Big Mac* is still providing me with a terrific interface between *Sourceror* and *Lisa*.

Sourceror is able to source object files that use 6502, 65C02, and *SWEET16* instructions. Unfortunately, *Big Mac* is only able to assemble source files having just 6502 and *SWEET16* instructions. *Big Mac* cannot assemble the new 65C02 instructions. Furthermore, *Big Mac*'s Monitor can only display 6502 instructions and not 65C02 instructions. The task to update *Big Mac*'s Monitor was easy compared to updating its ability to parse, process, and assemble the new 65C02 instructions. The *Big Mac* tables from `0xF339` to `0xF4DD` contain the addresses and rules for parsing 6502 instructions, and the support code using these tables is exceedingly dense. I slowly began to understand how Mr. Bredon designed his Instruction Set processor and I began adding in the remaining 65C02 instructions. Recognizing the new instructions was one thing; checking the addressing mode for each added instruction was difficult and tedious. Eventually, I was able to fit the additional logic I required within the limited space. However, in order to add the `STZ`, `TRB`, and `TSB` instructions to the end of the table data starting at `0xF481`, I had to move two ASCII tables. One table was at `0xF4E8` and the other was at `0xF4EF`. Combined, they were 15 bytes and I needed 12 bytes for the three new instructions. Fortunately, I had an 18-byte gap in the code at `0xE407` and this where I moved those two ASCII tables. The 10-byte table at `0xF4DE` simply moved down to `0xF4EA`.

To the best of my ability I have verified that *Big Mac* can assemble all 65C02 instructions and increment its program counter correctly for all addressing modes. Furthermore, the *Big Mac* Monitor can display all 65C02 instructions correctly with opcode, value, address, and displacement.

To assemble the *Big Mac* source code place the DOS 4.1 Tools volume `DOS4.1.ToolsL` in disk drive 1, boot, and start *Lisa*. Enter the `SE` command-line command to select the `SETUP` program in order to verify or set the `Start of Source Code` to `0x2100` and the `End of Source Code` to `0x5800`. Place the Big Mac Source volume `BIGMAC.Source` in disk drive 2, load the `BIGMAC.L` file into memory, and start the assembler by entering either the `A` command-line command or the `Z` command-line command. If a printed version of the screen output is desired, simply preface the `A` or `Z` command with the `P1` command-line command. Six object code files will be generated on the Big Mac Source volume: `SEG01` to `SEG06`. The six object code files can be combined in memory sequentially starting at `0x1000` using the `ctrl-P` command. The complete binary image can be saved to the Big Mac Source volume, or to any other volume, as `BIGMAC`.

10. PROmGRAMER

The SCRG quikLoader is of little value without a means to easily program (or burn) EPROMs. So SCRG also marketed the PROmGRAMER, designed by Bob Brice, which can program EPROMs for the quikLoader, the character generator ROM, and the Apple firmware ROMs, for example. The PROmGRAMER is designed to be configurable using DIP switches in order to access 2716, 2716A, 2732, 2732A, 2764, 27128, 27128A, 27256, and 27512 type EPROMs. The PROmGRAMER software by Bob Sander-Cederlof resides in memory beginning at 0x0803, and the program cannot extend beyond 0x0FFF because the desired EPROM image start address is set to be 0x1000. This is necessary particularly in order to program a 27256 or a 27512 EPROM. For a 27256 EPROM its entire 0x8000 byte image must reside in memory for convenience, and if 0x1000 is its start address, then 0x8FFF will be its end address, and that is very close to the beginning of the third DOS file buffer. When MAXFILES is 3, HIMEM is set to 0x9625. To program a 27512 EPROM a 0x10000 byte image must be divided into two or more parts, and the EPROM must be programmed in two or more sessions. It is for this reason that I highly recommend finding the midpoint for the contents of a 27512 EPROM so it can be programmed in only two programming sessions where each session programs 0x8000 bytes. Certainly, a 0x10000 byte image can be divided into two unequal parts and the PROmGRAMER can be used to program the entire 27512 EPROM. In this case the command parameters to program the EPROM would have to be entered manually because the default command parameters assume that the 0x10000 byte image has been divided into two equal parts.

In my discussion of *EOS* as shown in Table IV.6.3, the 27512 EPROM image needs to be split at the 0x8000 byte halfway point. The source code is designed to have the *Lisa* assembler do all the work of splitting the image at the correct place. Therefore, only two programming sessions will be required. The software Mr. Sander-Cederlof provided for the PROmGRAMER allowed the user to enter a command such as F (for Fast program) and the default parameters would be entered and used to program a 27256 or the first half of a 27512 EPROM. There was no command with default parameters to program the second half of a 27512 EPROM image, so the parameters had to be entered manually. I found this to be unfortunate after I ruined one too many 27512 EPROM programming sessions when I mistakenly entered the wrong parameters while attempting to program the second half. So I sourced the PROmGRAMER software and I added all the additional commands that I thought would support a 27512 EPROM.

Figure IV.10.1 shows the PROmGRAMER software being configured and Figure IV.10.2 shows the available commands to the user that fully support the 27512 EPROM with the added S, T, G, and A commands. I had to heavily modify the original code in order for it and the additional code that supports the new commands to fit within the required space. It works. I'm happy.

To assemble the *BURNER* source code place the DOS 4.1 Tools volume DOS4.1.ToolsL in disk drive 1, boot, and start *Lisa*. Enter the SE command-line command to select the SETUP program in order to verify or set the Start of Source Code to 0x2100 and the End of Source Code to 0x6000. Place the BURNER Source volume BURNER.Source in disk drive 2, load the BURNER.L file into memory, and start the assembler by entering either the A command-line command or the Z command-line command. If a printed version of the screen output is desired, simply preface the A or Z command with the P1 command-line command. The complete binary image will be saved to the BURNER Source volume as BURNER.

```
             S.C.R.G. PROmGRAMER

Enter Slot number (1-7):   5


              EPROM Selection

       1 -- 2716          5 -- 27128
       2 -- 2732          6 -- 27128A
       3 -- 2732A         7 -- 27256
       4 -- 2764          8 -- 27512

Enter selection:  ※
```

Figure IV.10.1. PROmGRAMER Configuration

```
Working with a 27512 in Slot 5

              Command Menu

    Start End Offset
R   1000 8FFF  0000    Read EPROM
B   1000 8FFF  0000    Burn EPROM
F   1000 8FFF  0000    Fast Burn & Compare
C   1000 8FFF  0000    Compare RAM/EPROM
S   1000 8FFF  8000    Read EPROM
T   1000 8FFF  8000    Burn EPROM
G   1000 8FFF  8000    Fast Burn & Compare
A   1000 8FFF  8000    Compare RAM/EPROM
D   1000 8FFF         Display RAM
E   0000 FFFF         Erase Check EPROM
H                     Help (Command Menu)
Z                     Restart PROmGRAMER
M                     Exit to Monitor
Q                     Exit to DOS

Enter command:  ※
```

Figure IV.10.2. PROmGRAMER Command Menu

203

11. CFFA Card

The CompactFlash For Apple, or CFFA card is an Apple II peripheral slot card that is able to read from and write to a CompactFlash memory card seated in an on-board CF card socket, or to a hard drive by means of a 40-pin IDE header socket. This slot card is able to present the onboard flash storage as either a hard drive or as a stack of floppy disks when using Disk][emulation firmware. Richard Dreher of R&D Automation created the CFFA card, and the first production run was released in 2002. I purchased my card in 2006, CFFA Version 2.0, revision B. It is my understanding that the CFFA card was most likely designed to be more compatible with ProDOS. Unfortunately, I never participated in the ProDOS movement when my software interests became redirected to UNIX based high-end professional workstations manufactured by SGI (running IRIX) and SUN (running SunOS). In view of my recent development of DOS 4.1 I began working on my own Disk][emulation firmware for the CFFA card. I simply want a means to archive my hundreds of 5.25-inch diskettes, and the CFFA card is the ideal platform.

It is my understanding, however, that Mr. Dreher has enhanced (or changed its interfaces) the CFFA card in many ways since my purchase in 2006. I have no idea if the hardware interface of the current version of the CFFA card resembles that of the past hardware interface, and whether or not my firmware will even function on the current version of the CFFA hardware. I strongly suspect my CFFA card firmware will function on the current hardware design just fine.

Table IV.11.1 shows the entry points of the firmware interface I developed for the CFFA card that is mapped to the peripheral-card ROM address space for the CFFA card.

Offset	Name	Description
0x00	CFBOOT	Entry point for DOS PR# command to boot selected DOS
0x10	ROMHOOK	Entry point to connect the CFFA to DOS 3.3 or DOS 4.1
0x18	ROMUHOOK	Entry point to disconnect the CFFA from DOS 3.3 or DOS 4.1
0x20	USRBOOT	Boot selected DOS image
0x30	VOLBOOT	Boot selected volume DOS image
0x3B	DISKRWTS	DOS 3.3 RWTS entry if DOS 3.3 is active
0x4B	CFRWTS	DOS 4.1 RWTS entry if DOS 4.1 is active
0x5C	VOLBOOT2	Simulate Disk][entry point for Boot Stage 1 code at 0x0801
0x64	CFRWTS2	Convert DVTS to LBA to seek, read, write, and format CF volumes
0xF3	MODOS3	Entry point to modify DOS 3.3 during Boot Stage 2 for CFFA use
0xFE/FF	VERSION	Version number for CF firmware (0x14): Version 1, Build 4

Table IV.11.1. CFFA Card Firmware Entry Points

The CFFA firmware interface allows access to each of the 512-byte blocks on a CompactFlash memory card up to eight GBs in size. Each block has a Logical Block Address (LBA) that is 24-bits in size, divided into three bytes, and saved to three of the sixteen peripheral-card I/O memory locations. Even the Master Boot Record (MBR) can be read and saved. Only three processing commands are necessary to utilize the CFFA: ID, READ, and WRITE. The ID command reads the IDENTIFY

DEVICE block of the CompactFlash card. That block provides the card's serial number, model number, and capacity in LBA addressable blocks as well as other useful information. I approached my design of the CFFA firmware interface as a way to communicate with a massive data storage device. In that end, I devised an equation to convert Drive/Volume/Track/Sector (DVTS) to LBA and an algorithm to perform the reverse conversion. The range allowed for the variables Drive, Volume, Track, and Sector are shown in Table IV.11.2.

Parameter	Range	Description
Drive	1 – 81	in order to support an 8 GB CF card
Volume	0 – 255	supported by the DOS 4.1 VTOC
Track	0 – 47	supported by the DOS 4.1 VTOC
Sector	0 – 31	supported by the DOS 4.1 VTOC

Table IV.11.2. CFFA Firmware DVTS Variable Range

The equations to convert DVTS to LBA is given by:

```
    block = Sector & 0x0F        (value:  0 — 15)
     page = Sector & 0x10        (value:  0 or 16)
 offset1 = 0x100

    LBA = ( ( Drive-1 ) * 0x30000 ) + ( Volume * 0x300 ) +
          ( Track * 0x10 ) + block + offset1
```

These equations imply that each Drive contains 0x30000 LBA blocks and each Volume contains 0x300 LBA blocks. A Volume can consist of up to a maximum of 48 Tracks and each Track has 16 LBA blocks. Since an LBA block contains 512 bytes, the block is partitioned by the page variable such that DOS sectors 0x00 to 0x0F reside on page 0 (the lower half of the LBA block) and DOS sectors 0x10 to 0x1F reside on page 1 (the upper half of the LBA block). I agree that forcing a Volume to be 768 LBA blocks (or 1536 Disk][sectors) in size rather than 560 Disk][sectors in size is wasting a lot of space on the CompactFlash card. DOS 4.1 has the potential to utilize a volume having up to 50 tracks in size, but I considered 48 to be the better upper limit for mathematical reasons and for ease of calculation. Because the VTOC can support 32 sectors per track and an LBA block is 512 bytes in size, it makes sense to me to split an LBA block into a lower 256-byte Disk][sector and an upper 256-byte Disk][sector. The algorithm to calculate an LBA for a given DVTS using the above equation is very fast because all the multiplication is done by using the addition of values obtained from three lookup tables.

The complete firmware interface fits comfortably in the peripheral-card ROM memory and expansion ROM address space of the CFFA card. The peripheral-card ROM memory has the normal slot boot entry at byte 0x00, a CFFA unique byte, my standard DOS 3.3 and DOS 4.1 connection ON/OFF at bytes 0x10 and 0x18, respectively, a user boot entry at byte 0x20, and a volume boot entry at byte 0x30. The user can boot one of six versions of DOS where 32 LBA blocks are provided for each DOS image. The first three DOS images include DOS 3.3, DOS 4.1L, and DOS 4.1H. Thus, there is room for three User Defined DOS images that may be installed. Additionally, the CFFA firmware can boot any bootable volume on any drive within the CF whether the boot tracks contain DOS 3.3 or DOS 4.1.

Connecting the CFFA to DOS 4.1 is trivial because DOS 4.1 contains a reserved address location for each slot that contains a peripheral slot card that is a Disk][-like I/O device that has an RWTS interface address. When the CFFA is booted with an installed default DOS, DOS 4.1L for example, Boot Stage 1 is monitored for ROMSECTR to become 0x00 and for BOOTPGS to become negative. Unlike DOS 3.3, Boot Stage 1 in DOS 4.1 reads sectors 0x06 to 0x00 on track 0x00 in descending order into memory from 0xB900 to 0xBF00 in ascending order. After sector 0x00 is read into memory at 0xBF00, all of DOS 4.1 RWTS is now available to read into memory the remaining pages of DOS 4.1. Normally, a Disk][-like I/O device only boots from drive 1 of two possible drives (or four in the case of the Rana Interface card) regardless of the volume's volume number. However, the CFFA must be able to boot from any of its bootable volumes and from any of its drives, so this puts a special burden on monitoring the Boot Stage 1 process.

In addition to the boot variables BOOTADR and BOOTPGS common to all varieties of DOS, and the DOS 4.1 disk address table shown in Table I.8.1, there is a variable called BCFGNDX that is an index on page 0xBF00. This index points to the BOOTCFG table of variables that is used to initialize the RWTS IOCB and used by the routine RWPAGES which is called during Boot Stage 2. It is at this time when Boot Stage 1 completes, but before Boot Stage 2 begins, that the BOOTCFG table must be updated with the current CF drive and volume that is currently booting. The values for DNUM and VOLEXPT will be utilized by Boot Stage 2 and pushed onto the CFRWTS interface using the RWTS IOCB so that the correct LBA will be calculated from the booting DVTS. Unfortunately, the situation for a booting DOS 3.3 volume is a horrible nightmare and a mess for any firmware, and the CFFA firmware is no exception, but certainly not impossible to monitor and to manage correctly.

Boot Stage 1 for DOS 3.3 reads sectors 0x09 to 0x00 on track 0x00 in descending order to memory from 0xBF00 to 0xB600 in descending order. After sector 0x00 is read into memory at 0xB600, all of DOS 3.3 RWTS is now available to read into memory the remaining pages of DOS 3.3. During Boot Stage 2 DOS 3.3 initializes the RWTS IOCB with DNUM=0x01 and VOLEXPT=0x00, which allows any volume to boot in disk drive 1. These values must be overwritten in order for the CF firmware to calculate the correct LBA from the booting DVTS. Once the routine RWPAGES has read in the remaining pages of DOS from the correct drive and volume, the DOS 3.3 code must be patched yet again in order for it to function properly within the CF environment. The prime issue with DOS 3.3 is how DOS 3.3 manages (or mismanages in my opinion) volume number.

In the CF environment volume number cannot be ascertained from a sector header because there are no sector headers to read. Therefore, a DOS 3.3 routine such as CATHNDLR that handles the DOS CATALOG command must not presuppose any value for volume number. Similarly, the SETDFLTS routine must not initialize or change the current value for volume number so that other DOS 3.3 commands will work properly when the V keyword is not included with a DOS 3.3 command. In order for DOS 3.3 to read into memory any DOS 4.1 file, the filename length must be adjusted to 24. Before any CF volume is initialized with DOS 3.3 all patches like the ones just described probably should be removed. A simple tool can do this, of course, but in order for DOS 3.3 to communicate with the CF firmware and perform volume initialization, its CALLRWTS routine must remain patched. I believe a better solution is to leave DOS 3.3 patched and totally useable in the CF environment, initialize a CF volume as desired, and overwrite the DOS image on tracks 0x00, 0x01, and 0x02 with whatever "pure" DOS 3.3 image you wish knowing full well that it may not boot or function properly in the CF environment. There may be other equally viable solutions. Table IV.11.3 documents all the patches that are applied to DOS 3.3 before and after Boot Stage 2 by the CF firmware.

Address	Old	New	Boot Stage 2	Description
0xB707	0x01	drive	before	update for DNUM
0xB7EB	0x00	volume	before	update for VOLEXPT
0xB748	0x84	#modos3	before	replace address of DOSSTRT with
0xB749	0x9D	cfpage	before	MODOS3 at 0xB748/0xB749
0xAA66	VOLVAL	volume	after	update for VOLVAL
0xB7EB	VOLEXPT	volume	after	update for VOLEXPT
0xA0DA	0x66	0x65	after	bypass initialization of VOLVAL
0xA95B	0x02	cfmaxdrv	after	update KWRANGE for DRIVE
0xAD9E	0xF9	0xFE	after	bypass setting VOLNUMBR to 0xFF in CATHNDLR
0xB203	0x1E	0x18	after	compare 24 character filenames
0xB707	drive	0x01	after	restore original value
0xB748	#modos3	0x84	after	restore address of DOSSTRT at
0xB749	cfpage	0x9D	after	0xB748/0xB749

Table IV.11.3. DOS 3.3 Patches for CFFA

Referring to Table IV.11.3 all variables listed that are in lowercase reside in CF firmware. The uppercase variables reside in DOS 3.3 source code. The first four substitutions are made just after Boot Stage 1 completes. The address for the entry point MODOS3 shown in Table IV.11.1 is used to replace the address for DOSSTRT, or 0x9D84, at 0xB748/0xB749. Once Boot Stage 2 completes DOS 3.3 will enter the CF firmware to install the remaining patches and code replacements for DOS 3.3. After the patches have been made the CF firmware simply jumps to the intended DOSSTRT address at this time. I fondly recall meeting many software engineers, particularly at Sierra Online, who I refer to as "DOS 3.3 Purists." "Thou shalt not modify DOS 3.3." Only when it was demonstrated to Ken Williams that we were able to make DOS 3.3 smarter, faster, and safer did Ken remove the DOS 3.3 Purity Shield. Now, from my current vantage point, I see that DOS 3.3 contained a lot of crappy code based on some very silly ideas, like how volume number was handled, and mishandled, and complimented, and substituted. Hopefully, DOS 4.1 will demonstrate how simple and powerful using volume number in the CF environment can be; that is, using volume number like any other number including slot number, drive number, track number, and sector number.

To assemble the CFFA Firmware source code place the DOS 4.1 Tools volume DOS4.1.ToolsL in disk drive 1, boot, and start *Lisa*. Enter the SE command-line command to select the SETUP program in order to verify or set the Start of Source Code to 0x2100 and the End of Source Code to 0x6000. Place the CFFA Firmware volume CFFA.Firmware in disk drive 2, load the CFFA.L file into memory, and start the assembler by entering either the A command-line command or the Z command-line command. If a printed version of the screen output is desired, simply preface the A or Z command with the `P1` command-line command. The binary images will be saved to the CFFA Firmware volume as `CFFA_SLOT_BUILD14` and `CFFA_ROM_BUILD14`. The utility `COPYCFFA` can be used to copy these two binary files to the CFFA Programs volume `CFFA.Programs`. Simply follow the directions on the screen and press any key to begin the copy.

The CFFA Tools volume `CFFA.Tools` contains the utilities *DOS3.3_TOOLS* and *DOS4.1_TOOLS* to process the DOS binary files `DOS3.3`, `DOS4.1.46L`, and `DOS4.1.46H`. Using the `DOS3.3` binary file, *DOS3.3_TOOLS* creates the binary files `DOS3.3-4.1 IMAGE` and `DOS3.3 IMAGE`. Using the `DOS4.1.46L` and the `DOS4.1.46H` binary files, *DOS4.1_TOOLS* creates the binary files `DOS4.1L IMAGE` and `DOS4.1H IMAGE`. The utility *INSTALL33* can install `DOS3.3` (a pure DOS 3.3 image), `DOS3.3-4.1` (a patched image of DOS 3.3 suitable to work with DOS 4.1 files), or `DOS3.3 IMAGE` (a patched image of DOS 3.3 suitable to work with files on the CFFA), onto tracks `0x00`, `0x01`, and `0x02` of a volume in disk drive 1. The utility *INSTALL46L* can install `DOS4.1.46L` (a pure DOS 4.1L image) or `DOS4.1L IMAGE` (a patched image of DOS 4.1L suitable to work with the files on the CFFA) onto tracks `0x00` and `0x01` of a volume in disk drive 1. Similarly, the utility *INSTALL46H* can install `DOS4.1.46H` (a pure DOS 4.1H image) or `DOS4.1H IMAGE` (a patched image of DOS 4.1H suitable to work with files on the CFFA) onto tracks `0x00`, `0x01`, and `0x02` of a volume in disk drive 1.

To assemble the CFFA Tools source code with *Lisa* already running, place the CFFA Tools volume `CFFA.Tools` in disk drive 2. Load each *Lisa* file into memory, and start the assembler using either the `A` command-line command or the `Z` command-line command. If a printed version of the screen output is desired, simply preface the `A` or `Z` command with the `P1` command-line command. The complete binary image for each *Lisa* file will be saved to the CFFA Tools volume. The utility *COPYTOOLS* can be used to copy all the utilities and DOS images from the CFFA Tools volume `CFFA.Tools` to the CFFA Programs volume `CFFA.Programs`. Simply follow the directions on the screen and press any key to begin the copy.

Along with the CFFA Firmware object code files and the CFFA Tools utilities and DOS images, the CFFA Programs volume `CFFA.Programs` contains the executable object code for *VOLMGR*, *BOOTVOL*, and *BOOTDOS*. The next section introduces and discusses these programs. It is the CFFA Programs volume that I transfer from my MacBook Pro to a diskette in an Apple //e Disk][drive using A2V2 on the MacBook and *ADT2* on the Apple //e since the CFFA card in resident in the Apple //e, not in the MacBook. Now, *VOLMGR* can easily install the new CFFA firmware image and all three DOS images. There is sufficient disk space remaining on the CFFA Programs volume for additional DOS images.

12. Volume Manager (VOLMGR)

The Volume Manager is a utility I developed to manage the CFFA firmware interface, manage the CFFA CompactFlash card utilization and identity, manage the CF Drives, manage the CF Volumes of a CF Drive, and manage the CF User DOS Images. The following eight figures, Figures IV.12.1 to IV.12.8 show a few menu screens from *VOLMGR* as well as an example display of the Device Identity contents of a CompactFlash card. Additionally, the utilities *BOOTDOS* and *BOOTVOL* can be used to boot any of the six DOS images on the CF card or boot any bootable volume on any of the CF volumes and drives.

Boot Stage 1 and Boot Stage 2 cannot be monitored when loading any of the six selectable DOS images. Therefore, the DOS image must be modified before it is saved to CF DOS Image memory in at least two locations: CMDVAL (a boot initialization value) and SNUM16 (located in the IOCB for RWTS). I prefer to use the CLOSE command (i.e. 0x10) in place of the RUN command for CMDVAL and 0x50 in place of 0x60 for SNUM16 since my CFFA card typically resides in slot 5. These modifications are simply for convenience for my particular installation. In the previous section the utilities DOS3.3_TOOLS and DOS4.1_TOOLS performed this function.

VOLMGR will detect a previously unmodified CFFA card by inspecting the first eight firmware bytes known as the signature bytes, and continue processing. This will allow the user to save the current CFFA firmware to a file on a disk volume and to install the new CFFA firmware to the CFFA card. After *VOLMGR* installs the new CFFA firmware those signature bytes will be changed to those listed for the CFFA card in Table II.7.2.

```
        CFFA Volume Manager

         DOS 4.1, Build 46

      Copyright (c) 2021 January 1

                  by

       Walland Philip Vrbancic Jr


      Use this CompactFlash For Apple
        installer and the accompanying
    software programs at your own risk.

   You are responsible for any damage or
   loss of productivity this installer or
    the accompanying software may cause.

       If you agree to these terms
        press any key to continue, or
    press ESC to exit this program now.
```

Figure IV.12.1. VOLMGR Product Warning Screen

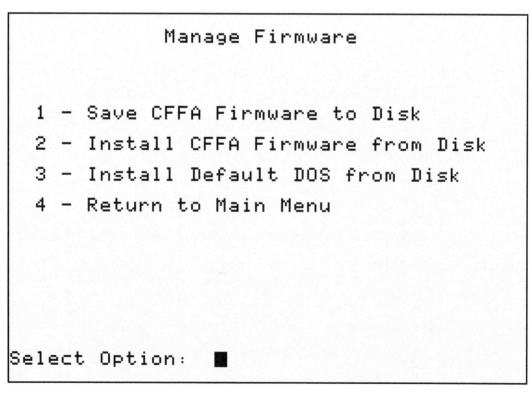

```
          CFFA Volume Manager Main Menu


     1 - Manage Firmware

     2 - Manage CompactFlash

     3 - Manage Drives

     4 - Manage Volumes

     5 - Manage User DOS Images

     6 - Exit Volume Manager



Select Option:  █
```

Figure IV.12.2. VOLMGR Command Menu

```
                 Manage Firmware



     1 - Save CFFA Firmware to Disk

     2 - Install CFFA Firmware from Disk

     3 - Install Default DOS from Disk

     4 - Return to Main Menu






Select Option:  █
```

Figure IV.12.3. VOLMGR Manage Firmware Menu

```
+---------------------------------------------------+
|           Manage CompactFlash                     |
|                                                   |
|                                                   |
|    1 - Display CF Memory Utilization              |
|    2 - Display Device Identity Contents           |
|    3 - Save Device Identity to Disk               |
|    4 - Save Selected LBA to Disk                  |
|    5 - Restore Selected LBA from Disk             |
|    6 - Clear Selected LBA Range                   |
|    7 - Return to Main Menu                        |
|                                                   |
|                                                   |
| Select Option:   ■                                |
+---------------------------------------------------+
```

Figure IV.12.4. VOLMGR Manage CompactFlash Menu

```
+---------------------------------------------------+
|         Display Device Identity Contents          |
|                                                   |
|                                                   |
|       Cylinders - 0007C2                          |
|           Heads - 000010                          |
| Sectors/Track - 00003F                            |
|    Maximum LBA - 1E8BE0                            |
| Serial Number - 020805J2806R5550                  |
|        Firmware - HDX 4.03                         |
|           Model - SanDisk SDCFB-1024              |
|                                                   |
|                                                   |
| Status:  Okay, press any key                      |
+---------------------------------------------------+
```

Figure IV.12.5. VOLMGR Device Identity Contents

```
┌─────────────────────────────────────────────┐
│              Manage Drives                    │
│                                               │
│                                               │
│   1 - List All Drives                         │
│   2 - Display Drive Information               │
│   3 - Change Drive Information                │
│   4 - Return to Main Menu                     │
│                                               │
│                                               │
│                                               │
│                                               │
│                                               │
│ Select Option:   ▊                            │
│                                               │
└─────────────────────────────────────────────┘
```

Figure IV.12.6. VOLMGR Manage Drives Menu

```
┌─────────────────────────────────────────────┐
│              Manage Volumes                   │
│                                               │
│                                               │
│   1 - Display Initialized Volumes on a        │
│       Drive                                   │
│   2 - Display Volume VTOC Information          │
│   3 - Display Sector Bitmap Information        │
│   4 - Initialize a CF Volume                  │
│   5 - Boot a CF Volume                        │
│   6 - Return to Main Menu                     │
│                                               │
│                                               │
│ Select Option:   ▊                            │
│                                               │
└─────────────────────────────────────────────┘
```

Figure IV.12.7. VOLMGR Manage Volumes Menu

212

```
┌─────────────────────────────────────────────────────────┐
│                                                           │
│          Manage User DOS Images                           │
│                                                           │
│                                                           │
│      1 - List Installed DOS Images                        │
│      2 - Display Selected DOS Image                       │
│      3 - Build User DOS Image                             │
│      4 - Select DOS Image for Boot                        │
│      5 - Return to Main Menu                              │
│                                                           │
│                                                           │
│                                                           │
│   Select Option:   ■                                      │
│                                                           │
└─────────────────────────────────────────────────────────┘
```

Figure IV.12.8. VOLMGR Manage User DOS Images Menu

To assemble the *VOLMGR* source code place the DOS 4.1 Tools volume DOS4.1.ToolsL in disk drive 1, boot, and start *Lisa*. Enter the SE command-line command to select the SETUP program in order to verify or set the Start of Source Code to 0x2100 and the End of Source Code to 0x6000. Place the VOLMGR Source volume VOLMGR.Source in disk drive 2, load the VOLMGR.L file into memory, and start the assembler by entering either the A command-line command or the Z command-line command. If a printed version of the screen output is desired, simply preface the A or Z command with the P1 command-line command. Five object code files will be generated on the VOLMGR Source volume: SEG01 to SEG05. The five object code files can be combined in memory sequentially starting at 0x0900 using the ctrl-P command. The complete binary image can be saved to the VOLMGR Source volume, or to any other volume, as VOLMGR.

To assemble the *BOOTVOL* and the *BOOTDOS* source code with *Lisa* already running, load each *Lisa* file into memory, and start the assembler using either the A command-line command or the Z command-line command. If a printed version of the screen output is desired, simply preface the A or Z command with the P1 command-line command. The complete binary image for each *Lisa* file will be saved to the VOLMGR Source volume. The utility COPYVOLMGR can be used to copy *VOLMGR*, *BOOTVOL*, and *BOOTDOS* from the VOLMGR Source volume to the CFFA Programs volume CFFA.Programs. Simply follow the directions on the screen and press any key to begin the copy.

213

13. File Developer (FID)

File Developer (i.e. *FID*) was an original Apple][assembly language utility found on the DOS 3.3 System Master diskette I received with my Apple][+. I suspect it was the most widely used DOS utility of all time. Instead of writing my own similar utility for DOS 4.1 having Volume number included as an input parameter, I decided to source *FID* and add what I needed to that software. Anytime I start tearing into someone else's software I find it to be a real, sometimes rare educational experience. *FID* utilizes `RWTS` and the File Manager interfaces as noted elsewhere in this book, which gave me a good insight in how the "Apple Experts" made use of those interfaces. I received the most grief from *FID*'s hardcoded insistence that track `0x00` could never be used for data storage, that it was a track never to be utilized except for booting DOS. There were several locations in the *FID* software where I had to insert the parameter `TRKZERO` (or `0x40`) so that *FID* would accommodate track `0x00` properly, as a data track, as it is accommodated properly in DOS 4.1.

```
***********************************************
*        Apple ][ File Developer          *
*     Version N with DOS 4.1, Build 46     *
*                                          *
*    Copyright 1979 Apple Computer Inc.    *
***********************************************


    Choose One of the Following Options

        <1>     Copy Files
        <2>     Catalog
        <3>     Space on Disk
        <4>     Unlock Files
        <5>     Lock Files
        <6>     Delete Files
        <7>     Reset Slot, Drive, Volume
        <8>     Verify Files
        <9>     Undelete Files
        <Q>     Quit


Which Option would you like:   ※
```

Figure IV.13.1. FID Main Menu

The most essential task was to implant the use of Volume number because I wanted *FID* to work with the CFFA hardware whose Disk][emulation firmware can access up to 81 Drives (for an 8 GB CompactFlash card) each having 256 Volumes. Actually, I derived this dependency on Volume number from the Sider firmware that utilized Volume number to calculate the Logical Block Address for the start of each DOS 3.3 volume on its hard drive. And, of course, I wanted *FID* to include my new DOS `URM` command in order to undelete files because that capability exists in DOS 4.1 by means of the File Manager. *FID* also makes use of the Catalog command's `SUBCODE` to display the current list of files on a volume with or without listing the deleted files as well. Finally, *FID* had to use the free sector bitmap in the VTOC properly, as it is used properly in DOS 4.1, and not how it is used improperly in DOS 3.3. The main menu for *FID* modified for DOS 4.1 is shown in Figure IV.13.1.

Because *FID* uses the File Manager to copy files from one volume to another, there are certain limitations that one needs to be aware of. Whatever sectors that are associated with a file that are listed in a file's TSL are copied from the source volume to the destination volume. The File Manager has no idea whether all or some of those sectors are actually being used by that file. For example, if a Binary file is created with the DOS "BSAVE TEST1,A$1000,L$6000" command, a file having 98 sectors will be created, 97 sectors for the data sectors and one sector for the TSL sector. Then, if the DOS "BSAVE TEST1,A$1000,L$1000" command is issued, the DOS catalog will still show 98 sectors and *FID* will blindly copy all 97 data sectors even though only the first 17 data sectors have valid data. This same situation can occur with Applesoft files as well. If the original Applesoft file utilizes 41 sectors, then edited to nearly half its size and saved, the Applesoft file will continue to utilize 41 sectors and not, say, 25 sectors unless the file is saved with a new name. There is no way for *FID* to know whether a file uses all or some of the sectors listed in its TSL. If disk space is a premium then *FID* should not be used to copy files; the files should be copied manually.

Why does DOS potentially waste valuable disk space when one is saving less data to a file that already exists? There are probably many reasons, some of which are valid and some are merely cosmetic. I believe the most valid reason is safety. In order to guarantee that a file only uses the disk space it truly requires when that file already exists would be to first delete the existing file, create a new file with the same name, and finally save the requested data to the new file. But would this procedure be entirely safe? What if something causes an error after the file was deleted but before the new file was created or before the requested data could be saved? Is having a DOS URM command enough insurance if such a problem like this should ever occur? Perhaps the requested data should be saved to a XXTEMPXX file first, then the original file could be safely deleted before the XXTEMPXX file is renamed? There may not be enough disk space to have two copies of the file or there may not be enough room in the Catalog for an additional file entry. This procedure would also rearrange the order of files in the Catalog which may not be appealing to some. I believe the best alternative is to save the requested data to an existing file using that file's TSL entries, and if there are more entries in the TSL than needed, those entries should be marked as unused sectors in the volume's VTOC. Of course I would only use this algorithm for the DOS SAVE, BSAVE, LSAVE, and TSAVE commands. It would be a moderately interesting exercise to implement this algorithm, and certainly cause for the release of yet another DOS 4.1 build.

To assemble the *FID* source code place the DOS 4.1 Tools volume DOS4.1.ToolsL in disk drive 1, boot, and start *Lisa*. Enter the SE command-line command to select the SETUP program in order to verify or set the Start of Source Code to 0x2100 and the End of Source Code to 0x6000. Place the FID Source volume FID.Source in disk drive 2, load the FID.L file into memory, and start the assembler by entering either the A command-line command or the Z command-line command. If a printed version of the screen output is desired, simply preface the A or Z command with the P1 command-line command. The complete binary image will be saved to the FID Source volume as FID.

14. Lazer's Interactive Symbolic Assembler (Lisa)

I have to say that I have spent a considerable amount of time adjusting and fine tuning Lazer's Interactive Symbolic Assembler (*Lisa*) to my every whim and need. It truly has been a joy. First and foremost my task was to modify *Lisa* to use the DOS 4.1 interface in order for *Lisa* to obtain various parameters it required for some of its special functions. Next, I wanted to eliminate the need for *Lisa* to save the first file of a multiple-file program as .TEMP before it completed its Pass 1 processing. That task required adding a new directive. I wanted the sort algorithm used to build and optionally print the Symbol Table to be part of *Lisa*. I wanted to add an additional new directive to define the text for a Symbol Table title. I wanted LED to be an integral part of *Lisa* and always be included whenever *Lisa* was activated. I wanted an easier way to enter a PR# and a ctrl-D command. I wanted an additional command-line command besides A to assemble source code that forces the PRNTFLAG to be OFF as if the NLS directive was the first directive in the source code. I wanted *Lisa* to obtain the date and time from DOS 4.1. And I wanted to fix some of the quirkiness *Lisa* sometimes displayed. I also found a few coding errors in *Lisa*.

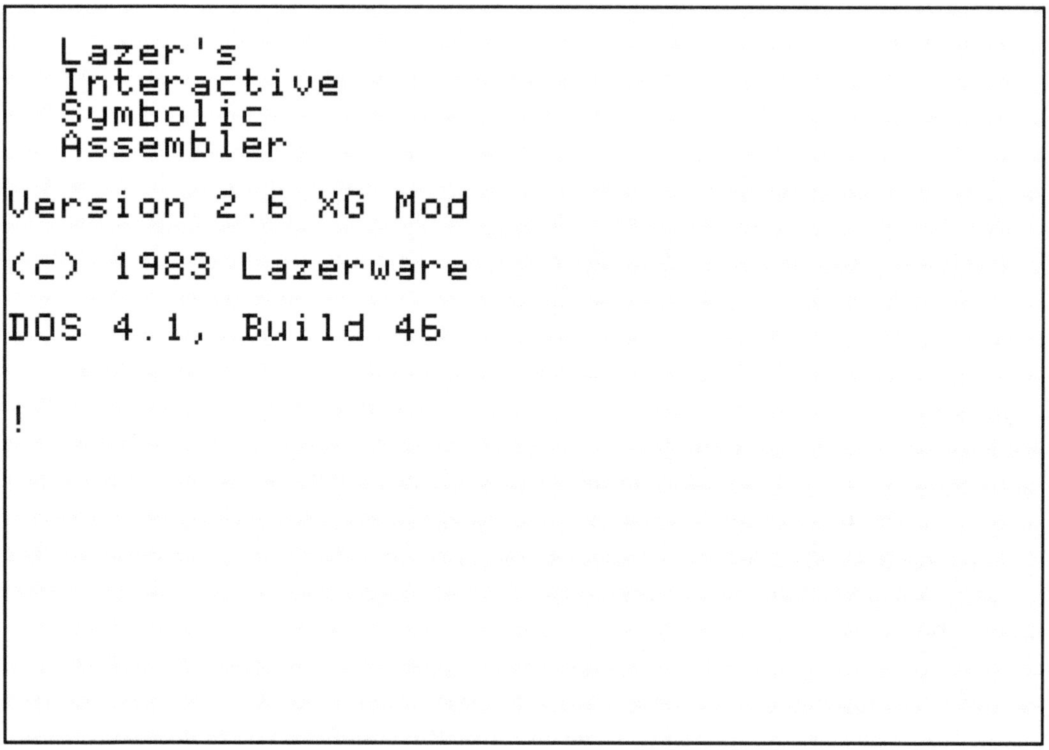

```
Lazer's
Interactive
Symbolic
Assembler

Version 2.6 XG Mod

(c) 1983 Lazerware

DOS 4.1, Build 46


!
```

Figure IV.14.1. Lisa Startup Screen

As in the case for *Big Mac*, *Lisa* fills the entire Language Card memory (both banks, actually) and LED, written by Bob Rosen of RSQ Software Products, occupies the address space below DOS from 0x91E0 to 0x9AB0. *Lisa* uses only one DOS buffer. The momentous task of sourcing *Lisa* took many hours, not just for the conversion of the assembly language object to source code, but the laborious task of understanding the idiosyncrasies of how Randall Hyde designs and writes software.

The optimal desire is to understand the newly generated source code so that 1) it assembles and perfectly matches the original, and 2) it can be modified and all structures and tables and their lengths and sizes will remain unaffected. Quite frequently an author may pass the address of a structure or data table in a register or two, or as an index into a table of addresses, and initially the source code appears like that address or that table of addresses is hardcoded. What needs to be done is to assign a variable to the structure or data table so that if the structure or table shifts up or down in memory, the registers will always contain the variable's correct address location. It is necessary to find all such occurrences in order to reach that optimal state of perfectly sourced code. *Sourceror* can only do so much! Figure IV.14.1 shows the *Lisa* initial startup screen.

Command	Context	Description
USR	after OBJ $$	uses OBJ address to save start address for BSAVE
USR FN	end of code	will BSAVE current code to file FN; follow with another USR
USR .FN	BLOAD file	will BLOAD the file FN to the current object code pointer

Table IV.14.1. Lisa USR Command

```
        L.I.S.A.  Setup Utility


Current values are:

1) Start of Source Code   - 0x2100
2)   End of Source Code   - 0x6000
3) Number of Lines/Page   - 68
4)   Print Title on Page  - YES
5)   End of Symbol Table  - 0x91D0
6) Lower Case Mnemonics   - YES
7)   Console Slot Number  - 00

8) Screen Editing Definitions

9) Quit

Enter option:   ■
```

Figure IV.14.2. Lisa Setup Utility

I give full credit to Robert Heitman who I met at Sierra On-Line for the USR and ctrl-P routines contained in both User (or 0xDF00) pages of *Lisa*. I may have adjusted them slightly for my own

217

particular needs, but essentially the USR functionalities are Heitman's. The USR directive has a number of important uses depending on how it is utilized and which arguments are used with the directive. Its syntax is shown in Table IV.14.1. The combination of "ORG $$/OBJ $$/USR/some code/USR FN" is a very powerful set of directives. The first use of USR, alone, at the top of a program after the ORG and OBJ directives, saves the current address of the object code pointer set by the OBJ $$ directive, where $$ is some hexadecimal address. After some source code has been assembled, the generated object code can be saved to some FileName using the "USR FN" directive. "USR FN" uses the beginning address saved by the first USR, calculates the length of the code segment knowing the current address in the object code pointer, and constructs a DOS BSAVE command. The "USR .FN" (that is, 'period' + FN) directive is useful in order to read a Binary file into memory at the current address in the object code pointer. The object code pointer then needs to be incremented using the DFS directive, for example, knowing the size of the included file. I use the "USR .FN" directive chiefly when I build an EPROM image in order to BLOAD into memory every object file that is to be contained in that image.

Source code for programs such as *Big Mac* or *Lisa* or DOS 4.1 cannot possibly fit in the Apple][memory along with its generated object code, its symbol table, DOS, and the assembler. Large software programs need to be segmented into manageable sizes and their assembled outputs saved to multiple object code files that will be ultimately linked to form the complete executable program. *Lisa*, DOS, and some program source code with its complete symbol table must reside in memory at a minimum. Therefore, judicious values must be chosen for the beginning address of the symbol table memory area so that it is large enough to hold all the variable names and parameters along with their values, the beginning address of the source code memory area, and the beginning address of the object code memory area. It is amazing what can be accomplished in such a small amount of memory as found in the Apple computer. *Lisa* utilizes a utility called SETUP that can be used to set these memory area addresses as shown in Figure IV.14.2. The settings shown provide about 63 pages or disk sectors for source code, room for about 1060 variables and parameters, and about 25 pages or disk sectors for object code. Of course, not every source code segment will require this much memory.

The source code files that comprise DOS 4.1H are shown in Figure IV.14.3. Several source files are processed before their collective object code is saved to a file. The convention used to name these object code files is to begin the filename with a SEG prefix and end the filename with a two digit number suffix beginning with 01. The reason will become apparent shortly. It makes no difference how many SEG files are created; remembering, of course, that each file created also requires an additional disk sector for its TSL. In the case of DOS 4.1H there are only three volume sectors remaining, so there is little volume space left to make any substantial changes to this source code. When all the SEG files are sequentially read into memory the entire image for DOS 4.1H will be created. I have the convention, if not the habit, to begin the load of an object code file at address 0x1000. Loading the first SEG file is easy, as in "BLOAD SEG01,A$1000". To what address is SEG02 loaded next? If the R keyword is used with the BLOAD command the length of SEG01 will be given, and one can simply "BLOAD SEG02" at "0x1000 + length" and so forth. There is an easier method built into *Lisa*: a ctrl-P user function that will sequentially load SEG files.

Lisa provides software hooks to the two 0xDF00 pages where a user can add any routine(s) of their choosing. The USR function mentioned earlier is found at 0xDF00 when Bank 2 is selected using the command "BIT 0xC080". The ctrl-P user function is also found at 0xDF00 when Bank 1 is selected using the command "BIT 0xC088".

```
CATALOG

S=6 D=02 V=000 F=0003 01/01/21  08:28:48

  L  004  DOS4.1H.L        01/01/21  08:28:48
  L  020  INCL.L           01/01/21  08:28:48
  L  045  CMD1.L           01/01/21  08:28:48
  L  057  CMD2.L           01/01/21  08:28:48
  L  055  CMD3.L           01/01/21  08:28:48
  L  060  MNGR1.L          01/01/21  08:28:48
  L  056  MNGR2.L          01/01/21  08:28:48
  L  044  DATA1.L          01/01/21  08:28:48
  L  023  DATA2.L          01/01/21  08:28:48
  L  010  BUFR.L           01/01/21  08:28:48
  L  062  RWTS.L           01/01/21  08:28:48
  L  038  HELP.L           01/01/21  08:28:48
  L  031  BOOT.L           01/01/21  08:28:48
  B  014  SEG01            01/01/21  08:28:48
  B  011  SEG02            01/01/21  08:28:48
  B  005  SEG03            01/01/21  08:28:48
  B  018  SEG04            01/01/21  08:28:48

!■
```

Figure IV.14.3. DOS 4.1H Source Code Volume

```
!fc
CATALOG

S=6  D=02  V=000  F=0012 01/01/21  08:28:48

  B  034  SEG01            01/01/21  08:28:48
  B  034  SEG02            01/01/21  08:28:48
  B  044  SEG03            01/01/21  08:28:48
  B  024  SEG04            01/01/21  08:28:48
  B  028  SEG05            01/01/21  08:28:48
  B  026  SEG06            01/01/21  08:28:48
  B  046  SEG07            01/01/21  08:28:48
  B  035  SEG08            01/01/21  08:28:48
  B  131  EOS1             01/01/21  08:28:48
  B  131  EOS2             01/01/21  08:28:48
  B  009  BURNER           01/01/21  08:28:48

!■
```

Figure IV.14.4. EOS Image Segment Files

```
 Segments = #4
First Seg = #1
  Address = $1000
BLOAD SEG01,A$1000
BLOAD SEG02,A$3000
BLOAD SEG03,A$5000
BLOAD SEG04,A$7A00

Load end = $9000
Save file = EOS1
BSAVE EOS1,A$1000,L$8000

!■
```

Figure IV.14.5. EOS1 Image Creation

```
 Segments = #4
First Seg = #5
  Address = $1000
BLOAD SEG05,A$1000
BLOAD SEG06,A$2A00
BLOAD SEG07,A$42D0
BLOAD SEG08,A$6F57

Load end = $9000
Save file = EOS2
BSAVE EOS2,A$1000,L$8000

!
```

Figure IV.14.6. EOS2 Image Creation

The `ctrl-P` function allows the user to enter the number of segments to be loaded, the segment start number, the object code start address, and optionally the filename to save the composite image comprised of all the object code segments. If the filename is not entered, the length of the image and its final memory address are displayed. Figure IV.14.4 shows all the `SEG` files that were created when the *EOS* source code was assembled. These `SEG` files need to be linked into two `0x8000` byte files that will be used to program a 27512 EPROM. In order to do that most efficiently, `SEG` files 1 to 4 are linked into one file and `SEG` files 5 to 8 are linked into the second file. The `ctrl-P` user function is the perfect way to perform this linking function. Figure IV.14.5 shows how `SEG` files 1 to 4 are linked into the first *EOS* image, `EOS1`, and Figure IV.14.6 shows how `SEG` files 5 to 8 are linked into the second *EOS* image, `EOS2`. Now, the two binary image files `EOS1` and `EOS2` are ready to be programmed into a blank 27512 EPROM. In fact, the utility *BURNER* is conveniently located on the same volume as these two image files. This makes the process of preparing and programming an EPROM very simple, very reliable, and very accurate.

Lisa makes three passes through all source code files for its input in order to create object code files for its output. The first pass can be terminated using the `ENZ` directive, or "ENd of page-Zero" parameter definitions. Pass 2 and Pass 3 must process all source code. In order to return to the first, or initial file when an `ICL`, or InCLude, directive is encountered, *Lisa* has always saved the initial file as an additional file named `.TEMP` so that processing can begin with a known first file for the next pass. Certainly this method is the easiest to implement but comes with an unfortunate price: it wastes some valuable disk space. In the example above for the volume containing the DOS 4.1H source code, Figure IV.14.3, there is no disk space for a `.TEMP` file having the same contents, thus the same size as the file `DOS4.1H.L`. *Lisa* had a few unused opcodes available, so I added the `SRC` directive that requires a filename. The complete syntax is "`SRC 'filename'`". I gave `LED` some additional memory at its beginning where I moved the `.TEMP` filename, and that is where the `SRC` directive copies its filename. Naturally, if the `SRC` directive is not used and there is at least one use of the `ICL` directive, *Lisa* will create a `.TEMP` file as usual. The filename specified in the `SRC` directive should be the filename of the file the directive is found in, but this does not necessarily have to be the case. Referring to Figure IV.14.3, if the `SRC` directive in the `DOS4.1H.L` file was "`SRC INCL.L`", the file `DOS4.1H.L` would not be processed during Pass 2 and Pass 3, thus saving some processing time, but at the expense of not including the `DOS4.1H.L` file as part of the complete print listing, if such a listing is desired. Personally, I like to place the `SRC` directive on line 2, right after the `TTL` directive, in the very first file when there are several source code files comprising a program. Even if all the source code resides in a single file, using the `SRC` directive will do no harm.

I challenged myself to make room in *Lisa* to include the sort algorithm and the code used in the program called `SYMBOLS`. If `SYMBOLS` were activated immediately after *Lisa* processes some source code, it would print out the complete symbol table alphabetized, and then again with the symbols ordered by value. I liked what `SYMBOLS` did but not well enough to fumble around locating a copy of it, even if I did have it in EPROM on the quikLoader, especially after processing a huge project like `DOS4.1H`. Fortunately, `SYMBOLS` is a little program and it did not take much effort to source. Now I had some idea how much room I needed within *Lisa*. Of course, I could always make `LED` larger, thus rob memory from the symbol table, source, and object code memory areas. I know Randall Hyde used good sense when he developed his routines for each opcode for the Pass 2 implementation and separately for the Pass 3 implementation. Regardless of good sense, I studied those routines and found a number of ways to compact a rather large amount of code giving me more than enough code space for `SYMBOLS`. Now that *Lisa* was headed down this path I thought it would be exemplary to provide a means to give the symbol table listing a name in the page titles. I replaced the rarely utilized `CSP` directive with the STT directive (Symbol Table Title) whose syntax is "STT 'title'". This directive copies the string title to the buffer currently used by the TTL directive during Pass 3. If the symbol table is printed its pages contain the new title. If this directive is not used the symbol table pages are printed with the same title from the TTL directive.

To complete this challenge required one further modification, and that was to the END directive. This directive provided the perfect location to control which of three symbol tables to print after the assembled code listing: no symbol tables, unsorted symbols, alphabetically sorted symbols, and numerically sorted symbols. Regardless which if any listings are desired, if at least one is selected the listing includes the memory address where the symbol table begins and where the symbol table ends. From Figure IV.14.2 the absolute physical end of the symbol table is set at 0x91D0. If there is substantial memory not used from the End of Symbol Table as reported in the assembled code listing and 0x91D0, the End of Source Code in Figure IV.14.2 could be adjusted to allow for larger source code files. It's always good to have visibility in how effectively *Lisa* is configured particularly when problems due to source code file size begin to generate errors during assembly. Therefore, to sum up this discussion, the END directive now allows a three-digit binary parameter to control which of the three symbol tables to list in the order stated above. The syntax for the directive is "END nnn" where n can be a 0 or a 1 for OFF and ON, respectively.

I prefer to keep the default setting of the PRNTFLAG variable ON during Pass 3 in order to obtain a printed listing of the assembly, particularly when I am using Virtual][. Rarely do I use the LST and NLS directives anymore. However, when I am debugging software using real Apple][hardware and the RAM Disk 320, leaving the PRNTFLAG variable ON greatly impacts assembly throughput, even with the ZipChip enabled. And it is a nuisance having to insert and then delete the NLS directive in the source code during the debugging process. So I added the Z command-line command to *Lisa* that functions like the A command-line command to start the assembly process, except the Z command sets the PRNTFLAG variable to OFF instead of to ON as if a NLS directive is the first directive in the source code.

Many times it is necessary to enter a DOS command directly on the *Lisa* command line. In order to do so a ctrl-D must precede the command so that *Lisa* will know to send the command to DOS rather than parsing the command for itself. I found it cumbersome for me to enter a ctrl-D before a DOS command every time I needed some information from DOS. So I added another *Lisa* command-line command, "/", which is so much easier for me to enter before a DOS command. For example, to display the contents of the VTOC sector, the following can be entered on the *Lisa* command line:

    !/TS A17

In Figure IV.14.2 the E, F, and G options select the clock slot number, its 0xCs05 value, and its 0xCs07 value, respectively, where s is the clock slot number. However, when *Lisa* is running on Virtual][, *Lisa* obtains the date and time information similarly in how DOS 4.1 obtains that information, so *Lisa* also requires a value for the current year because the ThunderClock clock card lacks a year register. Instead of having a duplicate date and time routine and a duplicate YEARVAL variable to manage in *Lisa*, I removed the date and time routine and YEARVAL variable from *Lisa* and utilized the DOS 4.1 RDCLKVSN vector at 0x3E1 shown in Figure I.9.1. I placed the CLKBUFF buffer conveniently at 0x3C8. Whenever *Lisa* requires the current date and time it requests that information from DOS 4.1. The utility SETUP no longer configures the clock slot, its 0xCs05 value, or its `0xCs07` value since *Lisa* no longer requires that information.

It is always an unspoken goal whenever sourcing someone else's software to never introduce new and unwanted problems. On the other hand, there is always a very good chance of finding and repairing someone else's mistakes because of the intensity of concentration required to understand each and every line of code. I suspect there might be some mistakes in *Lisa* that I have yet to uncover, but for the moment *Lisa* is rock solid stable and it is providing me with object code output files true to their source code input files. Whether the source code input files are necessarily perfect is quite another story.

To assemble the *Lisa* source code place the DOS 4.1 Tools volume `DOS4.1.ToolsL` in disk drive 1, boot, and start *Lisa*. Enter the `SE` command-line command to select the `SETUP` program in order to verify or set the `Start of Source Code` to `0x2100` and the `End of Source Code` to `0x6000`. Place the Lisa Source volume `LISA.Source` in disk drive 2, load the `LISA.L` file into memory, and start the assembler by entering either the `A` command-line command or the `Z` command-line command. If a printed version of the screen output is desired, simply preface the `A` or `Z` command with the `P1` command-line command. Three `SEG` object code files will be generated on the Lisa Source volume: `SEG01` to `SEG03` along with the `LISA.2` and `LED` object code files. The three `SEG` object code files can be combined in memory sequentially starting at `0x1000` using the `ctrl-P` command. The complete binary image can be saved to the DOS 4.1 Tools volume, or to any other volume, as `LISA.1`. The `LISA.2` and `LED` object code files need to be copied to the DOS 4.1 Tools volume as well. The utility `LISA1TO2` can be used to copy the three object code files `LISA.1`, `LISA.2`, and `LED` to another volume in disk drive 2.

15. Program Global Editor (PGE)

When I received my Apple][+ in the early 1980's, I spent my first few months writing Applesoft programs. I was fortunate to obtain the Program Global Editor (*PGE*) written by C. A. Greathouse and Garry Reinhardt. *PGE* certainly made programming Applesoft much easier when one has excellent tools at their disposal. I have to say that there is one particular problem when writing Applesoft programs, and that is dealing with program line numbers. So many commands depend on program line numbers making them essentially a highly critical part of any Applesoft program. There are not many ways to partition an Applesoft program into functions and subroutines except by using large, incrementing sections of program line numbers or by using many "REM ***" statements, but they consume program line numbers as well as memory, which impacts program execution. Here is where *PGE*'s forte provided me the most assistance: *PGE* had a program line renumbering capability. Upon initialization *PGE* remaps the ampersand vector to its "READY [" prompt. The renumber command R requires four parameters for start number, end number, new start number, and increment. *PGE* scours the entire Applesoft program and changes every occurrence of every program line number within the specified range to the new program line number based on the new start number and some program line number increment, say 5 or 10 or 100. To say the results were marvelous would be an understatement. As one's Applesoft programming capabilities mature, better choices for line numbers are usually made, and it becomes easier to create sections of code that resemble a function or a subroutine. In these instances being able to renumber a small section of code is quite powerful.

PGE requires the ability to modify the WARMADR and RESETADR vectors, and to obtain the value found at ADRVAL within DOS. *PGE* simply modified those vectors and read the ADRVAL parameter directly knowing the location for these vectors and parameter within DOS 3.3. DOS 4.1 has these vectors and parameter, of course, and a set procedure to read and write them. As shown in Table I.8.1 the address of INITDOS is 0xBFF8. The address at 0xBFF8 points to the table of address vectors shown in Table I.8.7. KEYVLADR, at offset 0x07, points to the table of KEYVALS shown in Table I.10.3 where ADRVAL is found at offset 0x06. In the same table where KEYVLADR is found, Table I.8.1, the vectors WARMADR at offset 0x0F and RESETADR at offset 0x13 are also found. This procedure of finding vectors and parameters is the same in both DOS 4.1L and DOS 4.1H. Naturally, the vector addresses are different in each of these versions of DOS, but their offsets and contents and the procedure to locate their values are the same. As long as a program like *PGE* does not utilize the Language Card for any purpose it may safely employ these procedures under DOS 4.1H. After I adjusted the *PGE* software to locate the vectors and parameters it needed from DOS 4.1 using the procedures just outlined, *PGE* executes its commands flawlessly under both DOS 4.1L and DOS 4.1H.

To assemble the *PGE* source code place the DOS 4.1 Tools volume DOS4.1.ToolsL in disk drive 1, boot, and start *Lisa*. Enter the SE command-line command to select the SETUP program in order to verify or set the Start of Source Code to 0x2100 and the End of Source Code to 0x6000. Place the PGE Source volume PGE.Source in disk drive 2, load the PGE.L file into memory, and start the assembler by entering either the A command-line command or the Z command-line command. If a printed version of the screen output is desired, simply preface the A or Z command with the P1 command-line command. The complete binary image will be saved to the PGE Source volume as PGE. Also, the *LOADPGE* source code is assembled using the same procedure.

16. Global Program Line Editor (GPLE)

Another invaluable Applesoft editing tool that I was fortunate enough to obtain was Global Program Line Editor (*GPLE*). Neil Konzen published *GPLE* in 1982, and I obtained version V3.4. *GPLE* uses the entire Bank 1 of the Language Card beginning at 0xD000, so it is obviously not compatible with DOS 4.1H. *GPLE* does not utilize any vectors or parameters within DOS so I did not have to adjust *GPLE* whatsoever in order for it to execute under DOS 4.1L. What I liked about *GPLE* was that it worked very much like a word processor for Applesoft programming. It had the ability to globally search and replace any variable, word, or character with any other variable, word, or character within an Applesoft program. And *GPLE* does its work extremely fast.

The *GPLE* loader first verified that the Apple][computer contains 48 KB of memory and that a Language Card is available. Then the loader write-enables Bank 1 of the Language Card and issues a DOS BLOAD command to load *GPLE* to memory address 0xD000. Finally, the *GPLE* loader copies a set of routines comprised of the ctrl-Y entry location, the ampersand entry location, the KSWL entry location, and the CSWL entry location to 0xB6B3, a small, unused area within DOS 3.3, up to 0xB6F9. These routines also control the bank switching of the Language Card as well as providing the entry location for a modifiable JSR instruction used in *GPLE* processing. Of course, DOS 4.1 does not have 70 bytes free at 0xB6B3, or 70 bytes free at any other address, for these routines. I chose to leave these routines where they were on Page 0x03, just after the upper ASCII data of the *GPLE* loader, and just before the DOS vectors at 0x3D0. I modified the *GPLE* code to utilize the Page 0x03 location for these routines instead of using the Page 0xB6 location. There was a total of six addresses comprising the Page 0xB6 routines that I needed to change to Page 0x03. As long as *GPLE* is used to edit an Applesoft program, using Page 0x03 for *GPLE* processing possess no problems whatsoever. However, if the Applesoft program is tested using the RUN command and if the program loads a small routine into Page 0x03, the KSWL/CSWL handlers for *GPLE* will be destroyed. This is the only downside in using *GPLE* with DOS 4.1L.

To assemble the *GPLE* source code place the DOS 4.1 Tools volume DOS4.1.ToolsL in disk drive 1, boot, and start *Lisa*. Enter the SE command-line command to select the SETUP program in order to verify or set the "Start of Source Code to 0x2100 and the End of Source Code to 0x6000. Place the GPLE Source volume GPLE.Source in disk drive 2, load the GPLE.L file into memory, and start the assembler by entering either the A command-line command or the Z command-line command. If a printed version of the screen output is desired, simply preface the A or Z command with the P1 command-line command. The complete binary image will be saved to the GPLE Source volume as GPLE. Also, the *LOADGPLE* source code is assembled using the same procedure.

17. RAM Disk 320

I first became aware of the Axlon RAM Disk 320 when I was self-employed and working under contract for Sierra On-Line around 1985. Living in Oakhurst, California, was really fabulous, and being able to work at home was even better. Except when the thunderstorms came and electrical power was temporarily interrupted, otherwise it was heavenly to live and work in Oakhurst. Uninterrupted Power Supplies, or UPS battery backups were not easy to obtain and they were not very affordable at that time. But when I was in the middle of a massive software development session and the power went out, and I lost hours of work, the cost of a UPS seemed trivial in that moment. That was the time when I decided to purchase a RAM Disk. Actually, I purchased two because a friend of mine wanted a RAM Disk, too. The RAM Disk emulates two 40-track disk drives using DRAM memory, and it has its own built-in power supply and backup lead-acid battery. As long as a power outage did not last more than four hours, all my files were safe on the RAM Disk. My software development pace vastly improved as well because files were assembled from RAM, not diskette. And when the RAM Disk was mated with the ZipChip, large projects could be assembled and linked in seconds rather than in many, many minutes.

Axlon provided excellent software utilities with the RAM Disk. Their RAM Disk initialization software could transfer an entire diskette to one of the RAM drives in the time it took the Disk][(revolving at 300 rpm) to make 35 revolutions, one revolution per track, in 35 * (60 / 300) = 7 seconds. That is impressive. From their software and from the hardware design of their peripheral slot card I truly learned the importance of reading the `CLRROM` address in order to detach expansion ROM memory. Whenever the 6502 microprocessor fetches an instruction in the peripheral-card ROM memory, `0xCs00` to `0xCsFF`, where `s` is the slot number of the peripheral slot card, the peripheral slot card typically enables its peripheral-card expansion ROM address space, `0xC800` to `0xCFFF`. And that is true for the RAM Disk peripheral slot card only in the address range `0xCs00` to `0xCs7F`. Interesting. Software residing in the upper half of its peripheral-card ROM memory can read the `CLRROM` address without re-enabling its expansion ROM address space. That was indeed a very, very impressive design. I made good use of that hardware design in all my versions of RAM Disk firmware while I employed DOS 3.3. Another interesting design of the RAM Disk peripheral slot card was their use of a static RAM chip, a 6116, for their firmware. The static RAM chip had to be initialized only once when power was first turned `ON`, and regardless how many times the Apple][was powered `OFF` and back `ON`, the static RAM chip retained its data because it derived its operating power from the RAM Disk, not the Apple][. One of the static RAM chip pages was mapped to the peripheral-card ROM memory address space, or `0xCs00` to `0xCsFF`, the `0xC800` page was mapped to the selected page of RAM Disk DRAM, and the remaining static RAM chip pages were mapped to the peripheral-card expansion ROM address range, or `0xC900` to `0xCFFF`. I made use of the idea for utilizing a static RAM chip instead of an EPROM when I was testing my new firmware for the Sider peripheral slot card. It was amazing how much easier it was to test different software algorithms for the Sider without having to program yet another, and another EPROM.

I no longer remember when and where I became an owner of a 128K RAM peripheral slot card, or RAM Card. It may have been left inside a used Apple //e I purchased at a garage sale. Regardless, I have no idea who manufactured this RAM Card either. This RAM Card is designed to operate like a Language Card in any peripheral slot card slot in an Apple][+ or in an Apple //e, and it can be easily configured as one of eight Language Card blocks. Since Address Bit `A02` is ignored when configuring the Language Card using its soft switches, the RAM Card utilizes Address Bit `A02` to select a Language Card block. Table IV.17.1 shows the memory management soft switches used by the RAM

Card. Simply reading address `0xC084` selects RAM Card block 1 or reading address `0xC08D` selects RAM Card block 6.

Address	Access	Name	Description
0xC080	R	RAM2WP	Select Bank 2; write protect RAM
0xC081	R ‖ RR	ROM2WE	Deselect Bank 2; enable ROM ‖ write enable RAM
0xC082	R	ROM2WP	Deselect Bank 2; enable ROM; write protect RAM
0xC083	R ‖ RR	RAM2WE	Select Bank 2 ‖ write enable RAM
0xC084	R	RCBLK1	Select RAM Card block 1
0xC085	R	RCBLK2	Select RAM Card block 2
0xC086	R	RCBLK3	Select RAM Card block 3
0xC087	R	RCBLK4	Select RAM Card block 4
0xC088	R	RAM1WP	Select Bank 1; write protect RAM
0xC089	R ‖ RR	ROM1WE	Deselect Bank 1; enable ROM ‖ write enable RAM
0xC08A	R	ROM1WP	Deselect Bank 1; enable ROM; write protect RAM
0xC08B	R ‖ RR	RAM1WE	Select Bank 1 ‖ write enable RAM
0xC08C	R	RCBLK5	Select RAM Card block 5
0xC08D	R	RCBLK6	Select RAM Card block 6
0xC08E	R	RCBLK7	Select RAM Card block 7
0xC08F	R	RCBLK8	Select RAM Card block 8

Table IV.17.1. RAM Card Memory Configuration Soft Switches

The hardware circuit of the RAM Card is shown in Figure IV.17.1. The circuit utilizes an Intel 3242 address multiplexer and refresh counter in order to periodically refresh the sixteen dynamic RAM chips on board. This address multiplexer is designed to refresh 16K dynamic RAMs, not 64K dynamic RAMs like those found on this RAM Card. Therefore, the RAM Card circuit derives Row Address 7 from the selected RAM Card block number. Data that is read from or written to the RAM Card is latched in the `0xD000` to `0xFFFF` memory address range so the RAM Card must pull the *INH* line low in order to disable the Apple ROMs appropriately according to the memory configuration soft switches shown in Table IV.17.1. In order to utilize the RAM Card for anything useful software must be specifically designed to access the RAM Card as eight individual Language Cards, or an interface driver must reside somewhere else in memory to provide RAM Card memory access. Neither of these ideas appealed to me, and I wanted to use the 128K memory of the RAM Card in a more generic fashion.

The hardware of the RAM Disk responds only to the first two of the sixteen peripheral-card I/O address space locations dedicated to the RAM Disk's slot number in order to select sector and track, so Address Bit `A02` will always be low. The RAM Card is designed to latch Address Bits `A00`, `A01`, and `A03` only when Address Bit `A02` of its sixteen peripheral-card I/O address space locations is high. Thus, the active peripheral-card I/O address space locations for the RAM Disk and the RAM Card are mutually exclusive in selecting RAM Disk sector and track versus RAM Card block number. For example, if the RAM Disk resides in slot 7, sector number is saved to `0xC0F0` and track number is saved to `0xC0F1`. If the RAM Card resides in slot 7, block number is selected by reading `0xC0F4` to `0xC0F7` or `0xC0FC` to `0xC0FF`. Once I understood the hardware circuit of the RAM Card in view of its software utilization, I thought perhaps the circuit could be easily re-engineered. I also had plenty of room for additional software within the RAM Disk peripheral-card expansion ROM address space and some room left within the RAM Disk peripheral-card ROM memory address space. From within the RAM Disk peripheral-card ROM memory address space, I knew I could turn `OFF` the RAM Disk peripheral-card expansion ROM address space and use that address space to possibly access eight continuous pages of the RAM Card. Therefore, instead of accessing RAM Card data in the `0xD000` to `0xFFFF` memory address range, RAM Card data would be accessed in the peripheral-card expansion ROM address space from `0xC800` to `0xCFFF`.

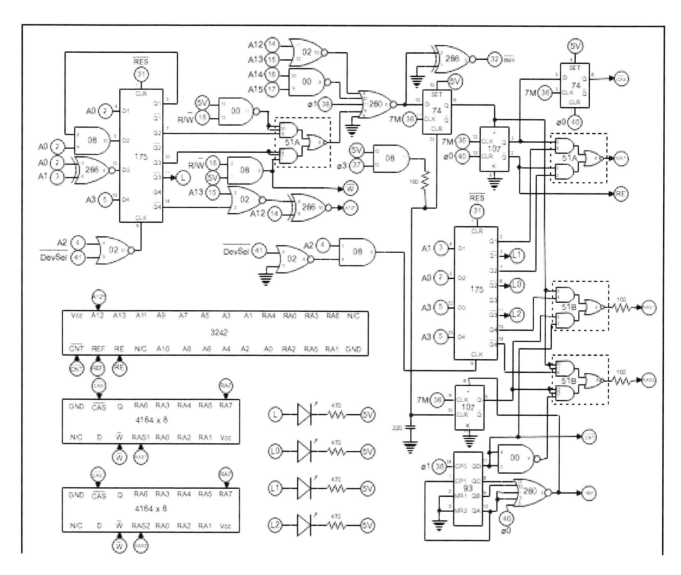

Figure IV.17.1. Original RAM Card Hardware Circuit Diagram

It was around 1992 when I worked out a way to physically modify the RAM Card in order to allow the firmware of the RAM Disk to control it, and to access it as if it was a RAM disk drive having 32 tracks. This modification required me to connect the RAM Card to the RAM Disk using a single wire, however. I found that Slot 3 was the perfect slot for the RAM Card because the RAM Card no longer needed to respond to its own *DEVICE SELECT* signal, but rather responded to the simulated *DEVICE SELECT* signal generated by the RAM Disk firmware. When the RAM Disk connects to DOS 4.1 it puts the address of its disk handlers in the disk address table DISKADRS, one for the RAM Disk and one for the RAM Card. To be sure, the RAM Disk firmware is handling all the RWTS IOCB traffic to and from the RAM Disk as well as the traffic for the RAM Card. Regardless which slot the RAM Card occupies, the RAM Disk saves the track and sector from the RWTS IOCB to the 0xC0s4 (where s is equal to eight plus the slot number of the RAM Disk) peripheral-card I/O memory location on behalf of the RAM Card. Formatting either the RAM Disk drives for 40 tracks or the RAM Card for 32 tracks is easy in DOS 4.1 because the DOS INIT command can set the ENDTRK variable to those specific values using the A keyword.

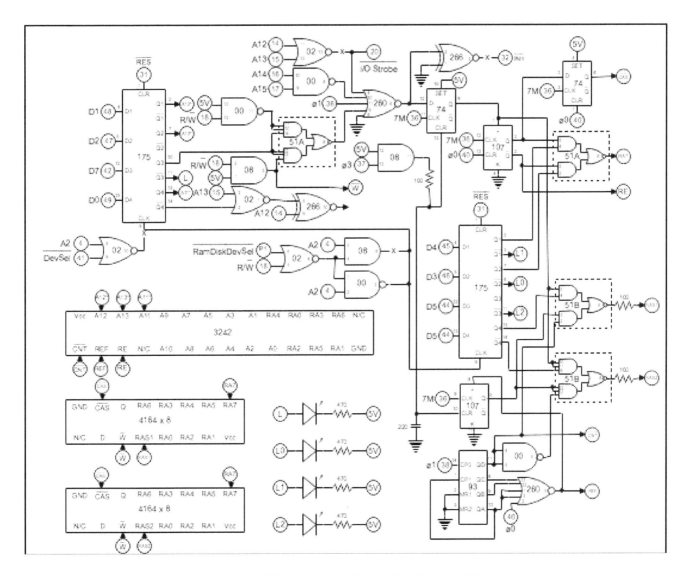

Figure IV.17.2. Modified RAM Card Hardware Circuit Diagram

229

Figure IV.17.2 shows the modified RAM Card hardware circuit diagram. The 74LS175 quad D flip-flops latch the data bus bits except for Data Bit D6. Data Bits D0 to D5 hold the desired sector/track number and Data Bit D7 is used to enable the RAM Card. The desired 6-bit sector/track number is calculated as follows:

```
N = ( track number * 2 ) + ( sector number / 8 )
P = sector number & 7
```

The selected page P within the RAM Card peripheral-card expansion ROM address space is determined from the first three bits of the sector number. The modified RAM Card circuit does not bring the *INH* line low because it is now unnecessary to disable the Apple ROMs. Figure IV.17.3 shows the actual modifications made to Figure IV.17.1 to obtain Figure IV.17.2. One 74LS00 gate was available to use in order to clock the 74LS175 control registers.

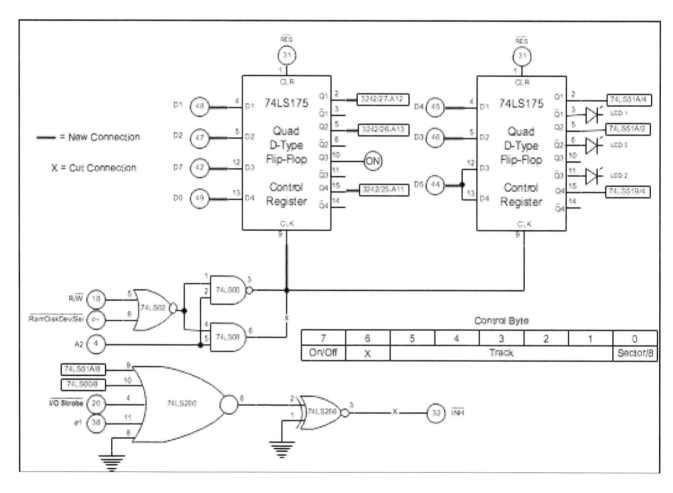

Figure IV.17.3. RAM Card Hardware Modifications

In Figure IV.17.3 the Control Byte is latched into the two control registers on the RAM Card only when Address Bit A02 is high as in "STA 0xC084,X" where register X contains the slot number of the RAM Disk times 16. The RAM Disk hardware does not respond to any value saved to its peripheral-card I/O memory location when Address Bit A02 is high, but it generates a suitable *DEVICE SELECT* signal for the RAM Card. Before the RAM Card is enabled the CLRROM address is read in order to disable the peripheral-card expansion ROM address range 0xC800 to 0xCFFF. The moment the RAM Card is enabled the peripheral-card expansion ROM address range is instantly mapped to eight selected pages of RAM Card memory. Bit 0x0 of the Control Byte contains bit 0x3 of the desired sector number. Therefore, the peripheral-card expansion ROM memory will display sectors 0x0 to 0x7 when Control Byte bit 0x0 is zero and sectors 0x8 to 0xF when Control Byte bit 0x0 is one. Bits 0x1 to 0x5 of the Control Byte contain the desired track number. Bit 0x6 of the Control Byte is not used and bit 0x7 is used to enable or disable the RAM Card. The RAM Card can no longer function as a Language Card after having had these hardware modifications.

Table IV.17.2 shows the firmware entry points for the RAM Disk and for the RAM Card for the firmware that is mapped to the peripheral-card ROM address space of the RAM Disk.

Offset	Name	Description
0x00	RDBOOT	Entry point for PR# DOS command to boot DOS in drive 1
0x10	ROMHOOK	Entry point to connect the RAM Disk and RAM Card to DOS
0x18	ROMUHOOK	Entry point to disconnect the RAM Disk and RAM Card from DOS
0x20	RDENTRY	Entry for DOS 4.1 RAM Disk RWTS processing
0x2B	RDBOOT2	Continuation of RDBOOT
0x30	RDRWTS3	Entry for DOS 3.3 RAM Disk RWTS processing
0x50	RCENTRY	Entry for RAM Card RWTS processing
0x5C	ROMBOOT	Simulate Disk][entry point for Boot Stage 1 code at 0x0801
0x66	TOGGLE	Connect/disconnect continuation code
0x70	MODOS3	Patch DOS 3.3 after Boot Stage 2
0x80	BOOTEXIT	Issue CLRROM, jump to 0x0801
0x87	RCEXIT	Turn RAM Card OFF, fall into RDEXIT
0x90	RDEXIT	Update RWTS error code, issue CLRROM, return to caller
0x97	HOOKEXIT	Exit for ROMHOOK and ROMUHOOK
0xA1	EXIT3	Exit for MODOS3
0xA7	RCRDWRT	Turn on RAM Card, read/write RAM Card, branch to RCEXIT
0xCD	RCFORMT	Issue CLRROM, turn on RAM Card, clear all sectors, branch to RCEXIT

Table IV.17.2. RAM Disk 320 Firmware Entry Points

To assemble the RAM Disk source code place the DOS 4.1 Tools volume DOS4.1.ToolsL in disk drive 1, boot, and start *Lisa*. Enter the SE command-line command to select the SETUP program in order to verify or set the Start of Source Code to 0x2100 and the End of Source Code to 0x6000. Place the RAM Disk Source volume RAMDISK.Source in disk drive 2, load the RD.L file into memory, and start the assembler by entering either the A command-line command or the Z command-line command. If a printed version of the screen output is desired, simply preface the A or Z command with the P1 command-line command. Five object code files will be generated on the RAM Disk Source volume: SEG01 to SEG05. The five object code files can be combined in memory sequentially starting at 0x4000 using the ctrl-P command. The complete binary image can be saved to the RAM Disk Source volume, or to any other volume, as RD.

18. RanaSystems EliteThree

I met a very knowledgeable engineer at Hughes Aircraft Company a year or so after I was hired in 1986. She provided consulting services to small companies for the design of proprietary databases. In order to keep track of her services, she used a database system of her own design hosted on an Apple][using a regular Disk][disk drive and a RanaSystems Elite Three disk drive as her massive database data storage container. She preferred the large storage capacity of the Rana and she thought the access time was a bit faster than the Disk][. When she sold her consulting business she offered to sell me the Rana drive for pennies what it originally cost her. Obviously, the Rana was used, but certainly not dead. Of course, I jumped at the offer. My first investigations into the Rana and its installation software revealed how tightly coupled it was to DOS 3.3. I didn't much care for all the modifications the installation software had to make to DOS 3.3 in order to provide the various configurations the hardware was capable of supporting. These modifications were provided by Rana Enhancement Utilities and were specifically designed to modify DOS and *FID* on a Master DOS diskette. I basically left it at that, and put the Rana away for another time to explore its capabilities: read and write either side of a diskette, create tracks half the size of Disk][tracks, that is, 80 tracks on each side of a diskette, and the slot card was capable of supporting up to four disk drives of any manufacture.

Well, that time is now to have another look at the RanaSystems EliteThree vis-à-vis DOS 4.1. Any configuration utilizing the hardware capabilities of the Rana needs to address the current VTOC structure, and how it can be possibly expanded to provide for more than 50 tracks for a disk volume. The Rana can seek up to 80 tracks on a double-sided, double-density diskette. The Rana can also access both sides of a diskette without having to flip the diskette over to access the backside, thereby providing direct access to 160 tracks. The Rana peripheral slot card can control up to four disk drives of any manufacture, that is, Rana or Disk][or any other manufacture.

I recall fondly the time in 1968 when I sat in the Audio Music Library in Schoenberg Hall at UCLA listening to magnetic tape recordings for my class on Johann Sebastian Bach. The library used an array of four Viking 80 magnetic tape recorders to playback audio assignments for music students. I happened to own a Viking 880. The only difference is that the 880 came installed in a suitcase with two 2x6 inch speakers and a small stereo audio amplifier. This recorder had the ability to physically adjust the erase, record, and playback heads in order to playback magnetic tapes recorded in half-track mode as well as magnetic tapes recorded in quarter-track mode. The signal-to-noise ratio for half-track tapes was obviously far superior to quarter-track tapes because twice as much magnetic material was used to contain the recorded signal. Even though the Viking was using a quarter-track playback head to read a half-track recording, the increased signal-to-noise ratio was still apparent. Why I mention half-track and quarter-track magnetic audio recording is that the concepts are quite similar when applied to magnetic disk recording using a Disk][recorder versus a Rana recorder. The recording head gap, or track size in the Rana is half the width of the recording head gap in the Disk][, so recordings made by the Rana would have a smaller signal-to-noise ratio than those made by the Disk][; that is, half as much magnetic material is used to contain the recorded signal in the Rana. Pure havoc would occur if the Disk][tried to read a Rana disk recorded in 80 track mode.

It is possible to differentiate between diskettes recorded using the standard prologue bytes to the Address Field header and the Data Field header of a sector and those diskettes using other address and data marks for the prologue bytes. This simply makes this diskette readable by one computer and not another. The Rana could certainly use such a protocol but I believe there is simply not enough code space in the peripheral-card expansion ROM memory to make this work for more than one or two configurations regarding number of tracks, number of sectors per track, and VTOC expansion of its bitmap data. Whatever is decided on how to use the full capabilities of the Rana is most likely not going to be compatible with the Disk][. The only place to use the compatibility argument for the Rana and the Disk][must be derived from the DOS 4.1 VTOC structure. Whatever can fit in that VTOC is what should be used to decide how best to utilize the Rana.

Considering the lessons learned from half-track and quarter-track magnetic audio recording, and in view of the rather limited availability of double-sided, double-density magnetic media, I chose to implement full-track stepping for the Rana, thus providing 40 tracks on each side of the diskette knowing full well that the physical width of the recording head gap in the Rana is half that of the Disk][. I also chose to implement recording sectors 0x00 to 0x0F on the notched side of the diskette and recording sectors 0x10 to 0x1F on the un-notched side of the diskette. The VTOC can fully accommodate this configuration. The Rana EPROM can also accommodate this configuration within its available code space and implement all the RWTS commands for both DOS 4.1L and DOS 4.1H. This configuration will provide 40 tracks, each track having 32 sectors, for a total of 1280 sectors. If the VTOC and Catalog use eight of those sectors, a Data disk would have 1272 sectors for storage, a rather massive amount of disk space accessible on a single diskette. This is precisely the configuration I chose to implement. Table IV.18.1 shows the firmware entry points of the firmware that is mapped to the peripheral-card ROM address space of the Rana peripheral slot card.

The signal-to-noise ratio for the Rana drive is still very much a concern because the Rana RWTS FORMAT algorithm rejects many of the double-sided/double-density diskettes I recently purchased as not safely recordable, but they are perfectly useable on the Disk][. Diskettes having previously been recorded by a Disk][will still contain residual and problematic magnetic information even after the Rana overwrites such a diskette using FORMAT due to its smaller head gap size. It was the successful formatting of several virgin diskettes that allowed me to test the Rana firmware I designed when I started to learn more about how DOS was originally designed to use a free sector bitmap for a volume that consisted of tracks having 32 sectors. These bitmap findings are thoroughly discussed in Section I.14 of this book. Needless to say, a CFFA volume having 48 tracks where each track can have 32 sectors is just a minor extension to what I designed and implemented for a Rana volume. Truth be said, the education I received from exploring the Rana and its capabilities proved to be absolutely invaluable in the design of DOS 4.1. Perhaps a future enhancement to DOS 4.1 would be an extension to the VTOC bitmap area.

Offset	Name	Description
0x00	RDBOOT	Entry point for PR# DOS command to boot DOS in drive 1
0x10	ROMHOOK	Entry point to connect the Rana to DOS
0x18	ROMUHOOK	Entry point to disconnect the Rana from DOS
0x20	RANARWTS	Issue CLRROM, enter RWTS processing
0x5C	BOOTFW	Simulate Disk][entry point for Boot Stage 1 code at 0x0801
0x5D	BOOTFW2	Locate address or data header prologue
0x83	FNDADR	Read address field header for volume, track, and sector
0xA6	FNDDATA	Read 342 disk nibbles and post nibblize to memory on a page boundary, jump to 0x0801

Table IV.18.1. Rana Disk Firmware Entry Points

To assemble the Rana source code place the DOS 4.1 Tools volume `DOS4.1.ToolsL` in disk drive 1, boot, and start *Lisa*. Enter the `SE` command-line command to select the `SETUP` program in order to verify or set the `Start of Source Code` to `0x2100` and the `End of Source Code` to `0x6000`. Place the Rana Source volume `RANA.Source` in disk drive 2, load the `RANA.L` file into memory, and start the assembler by entering either the `A` command-line command or the `Z` command-line command. If a printed version of the screen output is desired, simply preface the `A` or `Z` command with the `P1` command-line command. The complete binary image will be saved to the Rana Source volume as `RANA`.

19. The Sider

Around the year 1985 my mother asked me to build her a computer system to store her genealogy records and data. She was becoming overwhelmed with ancestry information, and knew and understood how invaluable a computer would be to store and link all this information. I knew of a product called *Family Roots* by Stephen C. Vorenberg and marketed by Quinsept, Inc., that would give my mother the power and flexibility she needed to contain and organize her ancestry data information. Her *Family Roots* database initially filled four data diskettes besides the three program diskettes when she asked me if there was a better alternative than swapping diskettes in order to generate a family member's report. In its documentation *Family Roots* suggested using the Sider from First Class Peripherals, a fixed disk drive subsystem featuring 10 MB of hard drive disk storage partitioned mostly as DOS 3.3 volumes. And, to tell the truth, I had been very interested in the Sider when I first heard about it but I just didn't have the reason or the bankroll to afford such a luxury. Mom had both. When I inherited my mother's Apple //e computer system she had filled more than 16 DOS 3.3 volumes with genealogy data. The Sider proved to be the perfect data storage system for that era.

The Sider consists of a peripheral slot card connected to an external housing by means of an Integrated Drive Electronics (or IDE) cable. The housing contains a Xebec 1410A controller board and a 10 MB Winchester hard drive. The peripheral slot card contains a 2716 EPROM and uses only two of its sixteen peripheral-card I/O memory locations to communicate with the Xebec controller. Essentially, the firmware transfers an 8-byte Data Context Block, or DCB to the controller. The DCB contains the command, a 24-bit Logical Block Address (or LBA), a block count, a step option, and a buffer address to write 256 bytes of data from computer memory or to read 256 bytes of data into computer memory. Therefore, an LBA address specifies one 256-byte page of data, and a complete DOS 3.3 volume would require 560 of those pages. Even though a Sider may be configured not to use CP/M or ProDOS or Pascal formatted sectors, some sectors are still set aside for those partitions. The Sider is partitioned only once to establish the sizes of the DOS 3.3, CP/M, ProDOS, and Pascal partitions. In the case of my mother's Sider, we partitioned it for the maximum number of DOS 3.3 partitions and the minimum number of CP/M, ProDOS, and Pascal partitions. Her 10 MB Sider contained 69 DOS 3.3 volumes beginning with Volume 0. *Family Roots* utilizes Sider volume number to locate all system programs and all genealogy data. Of course, I was fascinated to learn how the Sider modified DOS 3.3 to "tame" volume number such that programs like *Family Roots* could utilize this valuable parameter.

Table IV.19.1 shows the logical structure of the Sider based on LBA number. The Xebec controller determines how this LBA number, or sector number is mapped to the physical hard drive. It is important to note that a volume is a contiguous group of sectors where each volume follows the previous volume, or group of sectors. Table IV.19.2 show the modifications I made to the Sider Logical Structure to support DOS 4.1. The new Sider peripheral-card ROM firmware I designed boots the DOS 4.1L image starting at sector 264. Alternately, the DOS 4.1H image can be booted by entering 0xCs20, where s is the slot number of the Sider's peripheral slot card, typically slot 7. Either image will insert the Sider's RWTS handler address, 0xCs70, into the DOS 4.1 disk address table. Table IV.19.3 shows all the other firmware entry points of the firmware that is mapped to the peripheral-card ROM address space for the Sider.

There is a mathematical relationship between LBA and volume, track, and sector found in the RWTS IOCB. The first volume is Volume 0 and it begins at LBA address 464, or 0x01D0. There are 35 tracks in a Sider volume and 16 sectors in a track. Each volume is 560 sectors, or 0x0230 sectors.

$$\text{LBA} = (\text{ volume} * 0x230) + (\text{ track} * 0x10) + \text{sector} + 0x01D0$$

LBA Range		Description
Start	End	
0	0	Sider boot block
1	1	Sider parameter block
2	36	DOS 3.3 boot image
37	84	RAM Card image (DOS)
85	135	CP/M boot image point #1
136	255	Reserved for future use
256	258	CP/M boot image point #2
259	463	Free area for any application
464	1023	DOS 3.3 volume 0xFD (BU volume)
1024	????	User data area
????	????	12 alternate tracks

Table IV.19.1. Sider Logical Structure

LBA Range		Description
Start	End	
0	0	Sider boot block
1	1	Sider parameter block
2	36	DOS 3.3 boot image
37	84	RAM Card image (DOS)
85	135	CP/M boot image point #1
136	255	Reserved for future use
256	258	CP/M boot image point #2
259	263	Free sectors
264	295	DOS 4.1L boot image
296	299	Free sectors
300	341	DOS 4.1H boot image
342	463	Remaining Free area for any application
464	1023	Volume 0
1024	39103	Volumes 1 to 68
39136	39136	Park heads address

Table IV.19.2. Modified Sider Logical Structure

In order to calculate the LBA efficiently and with great speed, lookup tables are used that essentially do all the multiplication by using simple addition. There is sufficient room in the 2716 EPROM for these tables. The RWTS IOCB volume, track, and sector values are range-checked before the track and volume are used as indexes into the track and volume tables, and the extracted values are added to the sector value. The offset 0x1D0 is already incorporated within the data of the volume tables. I put the address of the DOS 4.1L image at index 69 and the address of the DOS 4.1H image at index 70 in the volume tables. Either of these DOS images or a selected DOS image using the BOOTVOL entry point from Table IV.19.3 at 0xCs30 can be used to boot the Sider. The track and sector values are set to 0x00 and the regular boot sequence is initiated. If the boot image is a DOS 3.3 image, the SDRWTS3 address is used to replace the RWTS address found at 0xB7B8 and 0xB7B9. Otherwise, if the boot image is a DOS 4.1 image, the SDRWTS address is copied into the DOS disk address table.

Offset	Name	Description
0x00	BOOTLR	Entry point for PR# DOS command to boot DOS 4.1L
0x10	ROMHOOK	Entry point to connect the Sider to DOS
0x18	ROMUHOOK	Entry point to disconnect the Sider from DOS
0x20	BOOTHR	Entry point to boot DOS 4.1H
0x30	BOOTVOL	Entry point to boot DOS from requested volume on Sider
0x40	PARK	Entry point to call ROMUHOOK and park the disk heads
0x5C	ROMBOOT	Simulate Disk][entry point for Boot Stage 1 code at 0x0801
0x70	SDRWTS	RWTS handler in DOS 4.1 disk address table
0x80	SDRWTS3	RWTS handler for DOS 3.3
0xA0	SDRIVER	Read/write a Sider LBA using an 8-byte DCB in regs Y/A
0xC0	GETSTAT	Get Sider status in C-flag
0xD0	READSTAT	Read Sider status into a 4-byte buffer
0xF0	MODOS3	Patch DOS 3.3 after Boot Stage 2

Table IV.19.3. Sider Firmware Entry Points

Family Roots utilizes Diversi-DOS in order to speed up the loading of its humungous Applesoft programs, and it also utilizes Diversi-DOS's DDMOVER to relocate most of DOS 3.3 to the Language Card. Still, *Family Roots* requires four file buffers, and in Diversi-DOS's implementation these buffers remain in lower memory. *Family Roots* CHAIN from program to program keeping all of its global values in memory. This technique certainly makes *Family Roots* appear to seamlessly transfer control from one program to the next particularly with the disk speedup routines in Diversi-DOS. I have to say that I derived my inspiration from Diversi-DOS to incorporate speedup routines native to DOS 4.1, and to move an early version of DOS 4.1, perhaps Build 32 or Build 33, to the Language Card. Diversi-DOS moves pieces and parts of DOS 3.3 to the Language Card and it has to modify the addresses of all JMP and JSR instructions. Diversi-DOS has to create a software interface between the routines it leaves in lower memory and the routines it moves to the Language Card in order to perform all necessary Language Card bank switching. Designing DDMOVER was a momentous effort to be sure, and having most of DOS 3.3 in the Language Card certainly gives *Family Roots* the "breathing room" it needs in view of the size of its Applesoft programs and the size of its variable and ASCII data arrays. And yet the Language Card was less than fully utilized.

I certainly understood how Diversi-DOS by Bill Basham at Diversified Soft Research was able to speed up the File Manager's I/O routines, as well as understanding how SPEEDOS from Applied Engineering worked for its RamWorks products. I also looked at David DOS by David Weston and TurboDOS used for *Lisa*. I'm sure there were others who had forsaken the DOS INIT command and

238

utilized that software space for their particular ingenious speedup algorithm. Even Don Worth and Pieter Lechner went so far as to suggest modifying the sector interleave table to speed up the reading of large Applesoft and Binary program. None of these algorithms seemed to be the very best solution for managing disk I/O in DOS 3.3. At Sierra On-Line a software engineer colleague of mine (a gentleman from the United Kingdom, actually) did provide an additional BLOAD keyword that provided a PAGE parameter. This keyword provided a parameter to an additional and new "read pages" subcode for the File Manager. It certainly was fast and, if I recall correctly, was used on the first version of King's Quest.

I decided that my goal was not to rewrite the File Manager, but to add the idea of reading pages of a file when I could. For example, the first two bytes of an Applesoft file must be read in order to calculate the end of its program address before the rest of the file is read into memory. The remaining 0xFE bytes in its file buffer are copied to memory, one byte at a time. However, the remaining sectors of the file, except for the last sector most likely, can be read into memory one page at a time. If there is a last sector that contains some bytes, that sector can be read into its file buffer and the remaining bytes copied to memory one byte at a time. Binary files are handled in the same way except the first four bytes are copied into the DOS parameter space from its file buffer; that is, the file's target memory address and the file's size in bytes. The remaining 0xFC bytes in its file buffer are copied to memory, one byte at a time.

I am quite sure that if DSR, Inc., had access to Apple's source code for DOS 3.3, it could have generated a native Language Card version of DOS 3.3 that did not require software like DDMOVER. My vision of having DOS 4.1 in the Language Card was that it must boot directly into the Language Card, therefore be wholly resident in the Language Card for the most part. It is one thing to cobble together a system from pieces of a previous system, but quite another thing when a complete system is fully designed from the ground up. I designed DOS 4.1H to occupy the Language Card natively. It has all of the functionality of DOS 4.1L and more. All file buffers, up to five, are fully contained in the Language Card, too. There is even code space to provide a DOS HELP command that provides the syntax for all DOS commands. Regardless of the number of file buffers, HIMEM is set at 0xBE00, the highest possible address perfect for an Applesoft environment for monster programs like those found in *Family Roots*.

Furthermore, DOS 4.1H contains the same CHAIN algorithm found in DOS 4.1L. Preliminary tests have shown that DOS 4.1H and CHAIN function beautifully with *Family Roots*. There are empty volumes on my mother's Sider that I could use to conduct further tests with DOS 4.1H and *Family Roots*. Or, the programs and data for *Family Roots* could be moved to a drive on the CFFA and tested there with DOS 4.1H. Either location would certainly verify the migration of *Family Roots* to DOS 4.1H. I believe my mother would have certainly been very impressed, and she would have certainly provided me with hours of hands-on testing.

20. Sourceror

I first "sourced" *Sourceror* so I could modify its source code in order to create a more pleasing display of its available commands using uppercase and lowercase ASCII before processing object code files. *Sourceror*, like *Big Mac*, was written by Glen Bredon, and it is a Binary program that executes at 0x8900 after MAXFILES is set to one. I found only one error in *Sourceror*, a missing CLC instruction where the software handles 65C02 instructions. Occasionally, not always, the program counter came up one byte too large because a software routine assumed that the C-flag would always be clear on the return from a call to GETNUM at 0xFFA7. Obviously, the C-flag was not always clear.

Sourceror already had a number of built-in equates it would refer to in order to build an equate listing at the end of the source code it generated as per *Big Mac* convention. I added a number of equates to its list that includes CLRROM, RAM2WP, ROM2WE, ROM2WP, RAM2WE, RAM1WP, ROM1WE, ROM1WP, RAM1WE, STROBE, LATCH, DATAIN, and DATAOUT. Figure IV.20.1 shows the initialization screen after LOADSRCRR has launched SOURCEROR. Figure IV.20.2 shows the startup, or HELP screen *Sourceror* displays with its command-line prompt $. Figure IV.20.3 shows the Monitor source listing of code after the first L instruction is issued to *Sourceror*.

I have used *Sourceror* to provide visibility and complete insight into DOS 3.3 first, and recently, insight into the CFFA firmware, and everything that came in between those two projects in the last 35 years. Because of *Sourceror* I understand a fair amount of what there is to know about Apple][hardware architecture and Apple][software that is used to manage that hardware architecture.

```
Press RETURN to accept default Source
Code address 0x2500, or enter 0x3000


If the present location of the code
to be disassembled is at its original
location, press RETURN.  If not,
enter PRESENT location 0x900


In disassembling, use the ORIGINAL
location 0x8900*
```

Figure IV.20.1. Sourceror Initialization

```
 SOURCEROR - 65C02 - DOS4.1
          by Glen Bredon

A HEX byte nn after commands T or H
limits the output to nn bytes.

Commands (alone or after HEX address):

L - Disassemble (current mode)
N - Normal (next mode)
S - Sweet 16 (next mode)
T - Text (TT defeats DCI)
W - Address (W-: Address-1, WW: DDB)
H - HEX data (1 byte default)

R - Read (does not create source)
/ - Retrieve last default address
I - Instructions
Q - Quit

$*
```

Figure IV.20.2. Sourceror Startup/HELP Screen

```
$8900L
                        ORG   $8900
8900-    78             SEI
8901-    20 58 FF       JSR   $FF58
8904-    BA             TSX
8905-    BD 00 01       LDA   $0100,X
8908-    58             CLI
8909-    C9 89          CMP   #$89
890B-    F0 03          BEQ   $8910
890D-    4C D3 03       JMP   $03D3
8910-    4C 06 8D       JMP   $8D06
8913-    8D 8D 3C       STA   $3C8D
8916-    09 0E          ORA   #$0E
8918-    16 05          ASL   $05,X
891A-    12 13          ORA   ($13)
891C-    05 3D          ORA   $3D
891E-    03             ???
891F-    0E 14 12       ASL   $1214
8922-    2E 20 03       ROL   $0320
8925-    08             PHP
8926-    2E 3E 20       ROL   $203E
8929-    7C 46 4C       JMP   ($4C46,X)
$
```

Figure IV.20.3. Sourceror Monitor Source Listing

To assemble the Sourcerror source code place the DOS 4.1 Tools volume `DOS4.1.ToolsL` in disk drive 1, boot, and start *Lisa*. Enter the `SE` command-line command to select the `SETUP` program in order to verify or set the `Start of Source Code` to `0x2100` and the `End of Source Code` to `0x6000`. Place the Sourceror Source volume `SOURCEROR.Source` in disk drive 2, load the `SOURCEROR.L` file into memory, and start the assembler by entering either the `A` command-line command or the `Z` command-line command. If a printed version of the screen output is desired, simply preface the `A` or `Z` command with the `P1` command-line command. The complete binary image will be saved to the Sourceror Source volume as `SOURCEROR`. Also, the *LOADSRCRR* source code is assembled using the same procedure.

21. Parallel Printer Buffer

When I saw the advertisement in one of my 1985 Apple magazines for the JFD Parallel Printer Buffer I just had to have one. As I recall there were two, perhaps more Buffer configurations one could choose: one set of parallel input/outputs or two sets of parallel input/outputs or perhaps a combination of these two configurations. Always budget minded I chose the Buffer with one set of parallel input/outputs. If I had more than one computer or more than one printer I may have chosen differently.

The Buffer came with 256 KB of dynamic RAM, and once an ASCII listing or a page of graphics had printed, the Buffer had a Copy pushbutton to select the number of additional copies (up to 255) to print if desired. I had spent so much time waiting for my computer and printer to print hundreds of pages of source code that I was more than ready to put this Buffer to work: I could work on the computer while the Buffer was supplying the printer with data, especially data from large graphic files. The Buffer connected to the Grappler+ Printer Interface slot card in the computer and to my Epson MX100 printer. A large wall transformer supplying nine volts DC powered the Buffer. Besides the Copy pushbutton there was a Reset pushbutton. The Reset pushbutton caused the Buffer software to initialize and force the input of the next new listing to the beginning of Buffer memory if I needed multiple copies of only that listing, for example. Otherwise, if I used the Copy pushbutton after printing multiple items the Buffer would print everything in its memory again.

The manual that came with the Buffer did not discuss what happened when input data overflowed memory. I had already seen some bizarre behavior like not printing some paragraphs when I used the Buffer to print many listings, and I did not press the Reset pushbutton prior to printing each listing. Momentarily pressing the Copy pushbutton put the Buffer into Pause Mode such that the Buffer could still accept input data; it just did not send that data to the printer. Momentarily pressing the Copy pushbutton again took the Buffer out of Pause Mode and data, once again, was output to the printer. I took advantage of Pause Mode and input a known, and very large amount of data to the Buffer. Then I took the Buffer out of Pause Mode and sent another known, and very large amount of data to the Buffer. When Buffer memory was filled it appeared to me the Buffer was accepting 256 byte chunks of data after it printed approximately 256 bytes of data for a period of time. Then the Buffer started to drop chunks of data, perhaps 256 bytes in size, but I wasn't absolutely sure. I could force this bizarre behavior every time I forced the Buffer memory to overflow. It appeared to me the firmware had some sort of software bug. I saw a challenge waiting to happen.

I opened the Buffer and found a voltage regulator, an 8035 microprocessor, a 2716 EPROM, eight 1257-15 NMOS dynamic RAM chips, and an assortment of eight-bit latches and logic chips. There were PCB locations for an additional input parallel connector and for an additional output parallel connector. The Ready LED was inconveniently located on the rear apron of the Buffer. I moved this LED to the front apron since there was only one input parallel connector and plenty of space next to it. Ideally, I would have liked to have moved that input parallel connector to the rear apron alongside the output parallel connector. At that time I worked at Hughes Aircraft and I had access to virtually any data book available, and I was able to obtain data sheets on the microprocessor and the RAM.

Being able to source and compile the MCS-8048 Instruction Set was certainly going to be a challenge, but I had already had some experience doing that very thing for an external keyboard that used a 6802 microprocessor on its interface board. My technique was to set up a series of equates within *Lisa*, one equate for each MCS-8048 instruction. I had to keep in mind which instructions required additional parameters. Actual coding within *Lisa* simply required the BYT directive followed by the MCS-8048 instruction equate, followed by any required parameter. I put a comment on each line documenting what the BYT directive and instruction equate were actually doing. The next step was to reverse engineer the code contained in the Buffer's EPROM.

Reading the data contained in the 2716 Buffer EPROM was easy using the PROmGRAMER. Sourcing that data was also made easy using an Applesoft program I wrote that translated the MCS-8048 instructions into a Text file using the BYT directive *Lisa* could easily EXEC into its memory. Analyzing that sourced code took the most time and effort because I had to fully understand the architecture of the 8035 microprocessor, the operation of the 1257-15 dynamic RAM for data access and RAM refresh requirements, and the hardware function of the eight-bit latches and supporting logic chips. The Grappler+ and the Epson printer also had handshake and data acknowledgement requirements as well. Slowly I plowed my way through the code finding all the necessary logic to access RAM data, refresh RAM, read Input data, and write Output data as well as perform system initialization, print diagnostic status information, read the Reset and Copy pushbuttons, and control the LED. Unfortunately, I could not locate an error in the software logic that would cause the bizarre behavior I could manufacture. I did locate the general logic where the Buffer would wait for a free page (or 256 bytes) of memory should the write pointer address approach the read pointer address. Dropping or skipping a page of memory was occurring somewhere in this logic when the data pointers were near the end of memory, but I could not find the wrong logic. I'm sure it was some silly addition error, probably involving a carry bit, when transitioning from the 0x3FFxx page to the 0x000xx page of the 256 KB buffer.

I decided to scrape the original code and write my own version of this firmware. Of course, I had to borrow the logic to access and refresh RAM, but I thought I could do a better job at controlling the data pointers and handling the memory overflow situation. I set up hardware to emulate a 2716 EPROM so I could compile and test my software without having to program an EPROM. This hardware setup made it extremely easy to develop MCS-8048 software for the 8035 microprocessor. In May, 1989, I was successful in developing firmware for the Buffer that did not fail any of my previous Buffer overflow tests. This firmware also behaved exactly like the original firmware for Pause Mode and the Copy function. The Reset function also behaved exactly like the original firmware. I programmed a 2716 EPROM, installed it, and used the Buffer with this firmware thereafter.

I performed timing tests and documented the results for the original firmware and for my new Buffer firmware. The initialization routine did not take as long to complete for the original firmware, but that time did not agree with what I had calculated the time should be if all 256 KB was tested with a minimum of a write followed by a read and a compare. My initialization routine actually took precisely the time to complete I had predicted. I also timed how long each firmware took to fill memory with Pause Mode enabled and disabled. With Pause Mode enabled the original firmware took about 2.5 times longer to fill memory: 2.91 KB/sec versus 7.28 KB/sec for my firmware. With Pause Mode disabled the results were 2.91 KB/sec versus 6.90 KB/sec for my firmware. I sent a letter to JFD explaining what I had observed when memory overflow occurred, my timing test predictions and results, and a printed copy of my firmware. I did not receive even an acknowledgement to my letter from JFD. I was terribly disappointed.

Recently I took some time to look over and review the Buffer firmware I wrote back in 1989. I've had a lot of time to add to and mature my programming skills vis-à-vis hardware architecture. I noticed that I used the built-in 8035 microprocessor Interval Timer for timing events such as pushbutton debounce, for example, as in the original Buffer firmware. What a waste of a perfectly good Interval

Timer I thought. What became especially clear to me was how to use the Interval Timer to provide the basic timing for dynamic RAM refresh without having to guess and hope that the RAM refresh routine was called often enough. In my original firmware as well as the JFD firmware the MAIN loop called the REFRESH routine, the CHECKTO routine, and, if the printer was ready to accept another data character, the SENDMEM routine in that order in an infinite loop. The CHECKTO routine checked if the Copy pushbutton was pressed, and if so, would flash the LED ON and OFF at a 0.5 Hz rate in order to set the number of desired copies. CHECKTO could take huge amounts of time away from the REFRESH routine leaving me pondering why memory never became corrupted. I wonder if this was the actual cause of the bizarre behavior I observed so many years ago? Or, did this Buffer RAM have built-in refresh capability? If I followed the 1257-15 dynamic RAM data sheet requirement to perform a RAS-only refresh every 4.0 milliseconds or less I could use the Interval Timer. The Interval Timer could also serve as the base for all other timing requirements like pushbutton debounce and LED flash rate. Central to the 8035 microprocessor are the RESET interrupt, the EXTIRQ interrupt, and the TIMRIRQ interrupt. The Reset pushbutton is connected to the RESET Interrupt pin, the Input connector from the computer is connected to the External Interrupt pin, and the Interval Timer is connected to the Timer Interrupt pin of the 8035 microprocessor. Each of these events is handled by a unique vector to a handler routine at a hard-wired address in page-zero of EPROM memory. There are also 32 bytes of indexed User RAM in internal microprocessor memory that is only slightly clumsy to access, but nevertheless available for use to store program variables and data.

The 8035 microprocessor is clocked using a 6.0 MHz external crystal. This frequency is divided by 15 internal to the microprocessor, so the cycle time (i.e. Tcy for instructions) is 2.5 microseconds. Most instructions require one cycle, and all other instructions require two cycles. The Interval Timer prescaler divides Tcy by 32 making it 80 microseconds in duration. Thus, loading the timer counter with a value of 0xFF will cause a TIMRIRQ interrupt in 80 microseconds when the timer counter overflows to 0x00. Loading the timer with a value of 0xCF will cause a TIMRIRQ interrupt in 3.920 milliseconds. However, the instructions to reset the Interval Timer require 8 cycles, so the total timer interval is 3.940 milliseconds. This time is certainly within specifications to refresh the 1257-15 dynamic RAM. Part of the Interval Timer handler routine is to increment a 2-byte counter. Whatever value is pre-loaded into this counter is incremented every 3.94 milliseconds. Naturally, a number representing the negative of a number would be ideal to use in this application such that when the most significant byte becomes 0x00, the desired time has been reached. For example, if a 63-millisecond debounce time is desired, then -16 must be pre-loaded into the 2-byte counter, or 0xFFF0. Also, an approximate 1.0 second wait time period can be achieved by loading 0xFF00 into the 2-byte counter; that is, 3.940 msec. * 256 = 1.00864 seconds.

Using the Interval Timer as the primary method to refresh the Buffer dynamic RAM changed the code only for the MAIN routine. Now, MAIN simply calls the CHECKTO routine and the SENDMEM routine if the printer is ready to accept another data character, in an infinite loop. The CHECKTO can take all the time it needs in order to count the number of LED flashes representing the desired number of copies. I added another bit-flag to the System Flag Bits byte called the Overflow State Flag. If the write pointer should ever reach 0x00000 and overflow memory, the Overflow State Flag will be turned ON. If that flag is ON the Buffer software will bypass the copy counting logic in the CHECKTO routine and, as protection, not allow whatever there is in memory to be sent to the printer as another copy. Of course, pressing the Reset pushbutton will reset all the State Flag bits including the Overflow State Flag bit, and re-enable the ability to make copies of whatever there is in memory. If copies are selected using the Copy pushbutton immediately after pressing the Reset pushbutton nothing should be printed as expected. I programmed a 2716 EPROM with this version of the firmware, installed it, and will be using the Buffer with this firmware thereafter.

To assemble the Printer Buffer source code place the DOS 4.1 Tools volume DOS4.1.ToolsL in disk drive 1, boot, and start *Lisa*. Enter the SE command-line command to select the SETUP program in order to verify or set the Start of Source Code to 0x2100 and the End of Source Code to 0x6000. Place the Printer Buffer Source volume PRINTBUFFER.Source in disk drive 2, load the PPB.L file into memory, and start the assembler by entering either the A command-line command or the Z command-line command. If a printed version of the screen output is desired, simply preface the A or Z command with the P1 command-line command. The complete binary image will be saved to the Printer Buffer Source volume as PPB. A 2716 EPROM can be programmed with the PPB file.

22. Apple][+ Keyboard Modification

After I started programming on my new Apple][+ my coworker Randy at Rockwell let me borrow a few of his computer magazines. I wanted to read all about the latest enhancements that were available for my computer. The Dan Paymar *Lowercase Adaptor Interface PROM* fascinated me and that adaptor was instrumental in encouraging me to invest in an EPROM programmer so I could design and program into EPROM my own lowercase character set. I was also very interested in adding some digital logic to the piggy-back circuit board of the keyboard in order to provide a CapLock function: I thought that adding a tiny LED to the SHIFT key would be totally awesome to show the shift state. I also wanted to add a pushbutton next to the left SHIFT key. That small pushbutton would set or clear a specific bit in the keyboard data in order to generate all the other ASCII characters the Apple][+ keyboard could not generate.

When I started designing the keyboard modification circuit, I had just accepted employment in the Digital Simulation Laboratory at Hughes Aircraft and I had access to virtually any data book available. I was also not hesitant at all in opening up my Apple][+ and doing some initial testing on the piggy-back circuit board of the keyboard using a few logic chips from my growing toolbox. I had a Heathkit oscilloscope so I could actually view some of the signals on this circuit board. *The Apple][Circuit Description* by Winston D. Gayler helped me to understand the function of S2, a 6-pad connector that contained two electrical bowties that had to be cut in order to modify bits 4 and 5 of the keyboard data byte. If I recall correctly my testing was more trial and error rather than from experience in designing the keyboard modification shown in Figure IV.22.1.

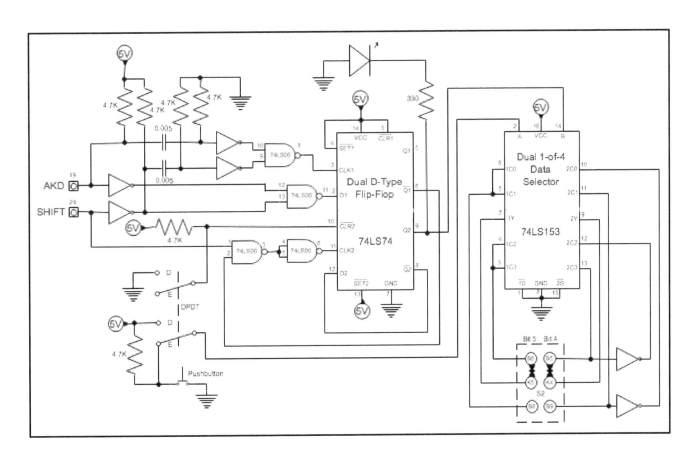

Figure IV.22.1. Apple][+ Keyboard Modification

Select Input		Data Inputs				Strobe	Output
B	**A**	**C0**	**C1**	**C2**	**C3**	**G**	**Y**
X	X	X	X	X	X	H	L
L	L	L	X	X	X	L	L
L	L	H	X	X	X	L	H
L	H	X	L	X	X	L	L
L	H	X	H	X	X	L	H
H	L	X	X	L	X	L	L
H	L	X	X	H	X	L	H
H	H	X	X	X	L	L	L
H	H	X	X	X	H	L	H

Table IV.22.1. 74LS153 Truth Table

Input Character	Input ASCII	SHIFT Key	Push Button	Output Character	Output ASCII
K	0x4B	ON	ON	[	0x5B
L	0x4C	ON	ON	\	0x5C
K	0x4B	OFF	ON	{	0x7B
L	0x4C	OFF	ON	|	0x7C
M	0x4D	OFF	ON	}	0x7D
N	0x4E	OFF	ON	~	0x7E
O	0x4F	OFF	ON	rub	0x7F

Table IV.22.2. Generation of Unavailable Characters

The 74LS153 dual 1-of-4 data selector is the perfect logic chip to generate all of the characters that are unavailable on the Apple][+ keyboard. The truth table for the 74LS153 data selector is shown in Table IV.22.1. Select Input A is controlled by the Pushbutton switch I placed next to the left SHIFT key and Select Input B is controlled by the state of the CapLock flip-flop shown in Figure IV.22.1. Both of these signals are enabled by a Double-Pole Double-Throw (DPDT) switch I added to my keyboard modification circuit. The data selector chip along with S2 and the 6-pad connector on the piggy-back circuit board of the keyboard, passes bit 5 of the generated keyboard data back into keyboard logic in order to derive the lowercase characters. On the other hand, bit 4 must be inverted in order to derive the ASCII characters that are not available on the keyboard from those characters that are available on the keyboard.

Bit 5 is properly handled by means of S2 connectivity in order to create lowercase and uppercase characters. Of course, this assumes the character generator EPROM contains the bit images (or pixels) for the characters normally in the 0x60 to 0x7F ASCII range and not a repeat of the characters from the 0x40 to 0x5F ASCII range. The inversion of bit 4 is accomplished by using the Pushbutton switch next to the left SHIFT key in combination with an available character much like deriving a control character using the CTRL key. Table IV.22.2 shows how to derive the unavailable characters from the available keyboard characters, the SHIFT key, and the Pushbutton. The Pushbutton is a normally open switch so that it does not modify normal keyboard logic when it is not being pressed.

The piggy-back circuit board contains a 555 timer circuit for the REPEAT key that is connected to a signal called Any Key Down (AKD). The REPEAT key in combination with a keyboard key will generate multiple instances of that pressed key. My keyboard modification circuit uses the AKD signal along with an inverted SHIFT key signal to provide automatic toggling of CapLock when the SHIFT key is held a bit longer than normal typing. This is accomplished by generating a digital pulse using a half-monostable circuit made up of a capacitor, a resister, and an inverter for both these signals. When CapLock is ON, an LED mounted in the left SHIFT key glows. The DPDT switch disables CapLock simply by pulling the CLR input of the CapLock flip-flop to ground in order to force its output low. The DPDT switch also disables the Pushbutton by connecting Select Input A to +5 volts.

There is plenty of room to mount the keyboard modification circuit board to the left side of the piggy-back circuit board which is connected to the keyboard using a 40-pin dual incline connector. I used a short length of 10-connector ribbon cable between the keyboard modification circuit board and the piggy-back circuit board. The ten signals are +5 volts, ground, SHIFT, AKD, and the 6-pad connector. The LED and Pushbutton each require two leads to the keyboard modification circuit board. The DPDT slide switch is mounted directly onto the keyboard modification circuit board. I have no idea why anyone would choose to disable the CapLock function or the ability to generate those ASCII characters that are unavailable on the Apple][+ keyboard. Regardless, the keyboard modification can be selectively disabled when desired.

23. Last Concluding Thoughts

There have been many books and articles published telling the story about the history, evolution, and people, some of whom are definitely characters, who have been involved in the Computer Revolution. I must say that I was part of that revolution, though perhaps more realistically on the periphery of that revolution. Ken Williams did attract a host of other entrepreneurs to Oakhurst, California, where Sierra Online was located. Like others, he was involved with developing programs targeted for the soon-to-be-released Apple //c. It was fascinating to be there in that period of time witnessing those events personally and to know that Wozniak and Jobs were among those who occasionally visited Williams. I know there are many others like me who look back on those years with a high degree of nostalgia. It was a glorious time to be writing software for the Apple][family of computers!

Even today I must admit that the Apple][computer holds a unique charm for me that continuously draws me into its technical and software environment. People like Gerard Putter and Richard Dreher certainly must also experience this Apple][charm as well, for they have created invaluable tools, one software and the other hardware, that keep Apple][enthusiasts like me motivated and excited about creating more and more useful software and hardware products for this computer today. I believe that in creating DOS 4.1 is my way of acknowledging and demonstrating the level of understanding I have for the Apple][computer solely in terms of its hardware. It was fortunate that I studied Electrical Engineering at University rather than Computer Science. I certainly absorbed enough Computer Science during my professional career writing software.

Also, DOS 4.1 is the culmination of all the ideas from my DOS "Wish List" and from the DOS "Parameter Needs" of a large number of commercial software programs. Understanding those commercial software programs was vital to focus my attention in providing an interface between DOS 4.1 internals and DOS 4.1 users. I suppose that studying Control Systems in terms of a "black box" having inputs, outputs, and feedback loops all contributed to how I wanted to design DOS 4.1 as the proverbial "black box" not to have its internals recklessly poked and prodded. At least for the most part I believe I have succeeded in designing an Apple][operating system that fulfills all of my needs. I certainly think that it might fulfill the needs of others, particularly the owners of the CFFA card and the users of commercial programs like *Family Roots* who do not use ProDOS. This has been an incredible journey for me and I have enjoyed solving every problem and issue that has come my way while I was developing DOS 4.1

I still believe there is a huge potential use for the 6502 microprocessor IRQ and NMI interrupts in some sort of hardware/software product. What that product is, is yet another mystery to me. But I still keep thinking about it in view of how much fun I had implementing those interrupts on my clock card. And that is part of the charm the Apple][generates because of its open architecture. It allows people to build their own interface slot cards and plug them into a slot in a real computer. I was so fortunate to have the opportunity to experiment and design and tryout my ideas that significantly increased my knowledge and my understanding of digital hardware and software design. There is no better classroom than an engineer's laboratory, which happened to be my garage. Others may have a basement or a spare room for their laboratory. The point is, book knowledge is essential for understanding theory, but the real learning happens when you apply that theory and build something that is your own design, be it something intellectual or something tangible. At least that is the case for me especially when I recall that the original Apple computer was first built in a garage.

I have yet to explore integrating my love for the Apple][hardware and software and my love for model railroading, specifically S-gauge used by the American Flyer model trains. I have boxes and boxes of those trains and many accessories stored in the garage. Perhaps it is time I introduce Mr. American Flyer to Mr. Apple. The relationship could be rather exciting if not downright explosive. Oh, not in the sense of Addams Family explosive, but in the sense of opening up a whole new world of awesome challenges and a whole lot of downright fun.

Today's generation of young engineers have the opportunity to explore computer-assisted or computer-associated projects with the Raspberry Pi computer. The Raspberry Pi is the size of a credit card having four USB ports, an Ethernet port, HDMI, raw video, and stereo sound outputs, and it only requires 5 volts at 2.4 amps for full operation and control. The computer uses a micro SD card that hosts its UNIX operating system and its C language compiler and linker. It provides around 26 Peripheral Input/Output (i.e. PIO) connections to the outside world. The PIOs are software configurable to be an input or an output for 3.3-volt signals.

I designed my Sunrise/Sunset controller around the Raspberry Pi to control all my outside decorative lightening. My software considers my location on planet Earth in terms of longitude, latitude, and azimuth to calculate precisely the time of sunrise and sunset. The software refers to an input configuration file for selectable offsets in order to adjust timing so that my decorative lights turn ON 30 minutes after sunset and they turn OFF 45 minutes before sunrise. One PIO port is used as a 3.3-volt output port to illuminate the LED of a TRIAC controller. When the TRIAC is turned ON, AC voltage is gated to a moderate-duty AC relay. This relay can control a load up to 15 amps at 240 volts AC. The AC transformer that provides the 12 volts AC to the decorative lights draws no more than 8 amps at 120 volts AC through the relay. As the days become longer and the nights shorter my decorative lights turn OFF and ON according to sunrise and sunset, respectively. And, as the days become shorter and the nights longer my decorative lights are appropriately turned OFF and ON.

This Raspberry Pi computer/controller is totally maintenance free because it receives its time of day from the Internet by means of a USB wireless adapter that communicates with my wireless Internet Router. There must be an interesting project or two that could tie Mr. Apple to Mr. Raspberry Pi. I already use a Keyspan serial to USB adapter with my Apple //e and my Apple MacBook Pro. And I already have the programming tools on the Raspberry Pi to write some serious C language programs. The best part is that the Raspberry Pi only costs about $40.00: massive programming power and agility for pennies.

Would I trade those early years learning to program on an Apple][for present day years to program on the Raspberry Pi or another "little" computer? I am very fond of all those past memories, and software in those years did not change very often. It is surprising how many years DOS 3.3 lived and survived. Today, my iPad or my iPhone receives a new iOS update every other month, maybe even more often. Software development occurs at a frenzy pace now, and considerations for size of application and available memory are totally unimportant. Of course I could not last ten minutes in today's aerospace industry because I don't have the experience or the tools young engineers have today nor do I have their intellectual growth processes. So I am quite satisfied with my memories and the fascinating experiences I had, and the interesting characters I met along the way. It is comforting to know that through my travels in time I may have touched someone else's curiosity.

V. Autobiographical Information

Grandfather Vrbančić was born in Trg, Croatia, once a province of Yugoslavia, and he was named Vid. Vid decided to immigrate to the United States around 1907, and he joined his older brother in Rankin, Pennsylvania. There, he and Marko worked in the coal mines. This work did not appeal to him, so he moved to Cleveland, Ohio, to work in the steel mill industry. Vid did not have a profession and he had no desire to learn a trade, so he became one of the many immigrant laborers living in the Cleveland area. There were many other Croatian and Slovenian immigrant laborers living in the same suburbs, and they tended to retain their European style of living and speak their native languages. Vid had lived in America for nearly ten years when he met Veronika Sneperger. Veronika had not been in America as long as Vid, but she became far more fluent in English than he. She was also fluent in six other languages. Vid and Veronika were married on June 25, 1917, in Saint Paul's Church and moved into a lovely, but small apartment on the east side.

Veronika's mother Tvka (Eva) Stefančić had already died in 1910 and the steel mill industry was no longer manufacturing wartime supplies by the 1920's. Vid was finally laid off in 1921 and he could not find any other work in the Cleveland area. He did not want to move his wife, daughter Josephine, and son Andrew to Rankin where his younger brother Franjo was now living and working as a policeman. Veronika's father Jure, a widower for over ten years now, wrote many letters to Vid and Veronika and pleaded with them to return to Croatia. He even promised to give them his home in Maklen and all his farm land if they would agree to care for him in his old age. Vid finally relented and he and his family set sail back to Croatia. Unfortunately, Jure had blatantly lied to both Vid and Veronika as he never intended to give them his home or any of his farm land. He also did not want Vid working his farm land using the methods Vid had learned when he was growing up in Trg. Regardless of their near hopelessness, Mathew was born in February, 1922, in Maklen.

By 1923 the steel mill industry in Cleveland had converted back to manufacturing household and industrial supplies, and they sent pleas to European countries for mill workers. The industry even offered to pay the man's passage and assist him in finding an apartment. Even though Josephine and Andrew were American citizens, Veronika and Mathew were not. When Vid inquired about bringing his family to America, he was told he would need to become an American citizen, have $2000 in a savings account, provide an adequate place for his family to live, and have the required fare for their passage from Maklen to Cleveland. So, if Vid took the job offer, he would have to leave his family behind. After much soul searching and in view of being duped and lied to by Jure, Vid did accept the job offer to return to Cleveland. But, to make financial matters even worse, Vid left Croatia six months before the birth of his fourth child in February, 1924. Grandmother named him Valentin because Father was born on Saint Valentine's Day.

Jure's property would have rightfully gone to his son George (Jure in Croatian) before it would go to Veronika if Jure should die. But George had left for America in 1899 and was never heard from again. Jure never trusted banks or a hiding place at home for his money, so he carried all of his cash with him and made this fact known to all. In 1925 his cousin shot him through the heart and decapitated him while he was taking a shortcut through the woods. To this day there is tree with a four foot cross carved into its bark marking the crime spot. It is believed that teenage boys in the neighborhood keep that cross scrapped clean of bark and retell the killing of Jure. No one was officially charged with the crime, but Jure's cousin admitted to the crime on his deathbed. Even though Veronika inherited her father's home in Maklen and all his farm lands, life was still very hard for Grandmother raising and feeding her four growing children without her husband there.

Josephine and Andrew both attended a one-room school in Brod Moravice; Mathew and Valentin were still too young to attend school. They explored the surrounding villages and farms, but were afraid to venture into the woods where their grandfather had been murdered. They did explore several of the caves in the area only when an older boy accompanied them. Grandmother's farm had many fruit trees they could climb and would feast on the fruit. Vid wrote to his family often and told them he was progressing well with all the requirements needed to bring everyone to Cleveland. He sent Veronika sufficient funds for her to obtain passport photos, visas, clothes, and luggage necessary for the long journey to America. Many government officials had to stamp their passport papers. These included officials in Brod Moravice, officials in the municipality of Delnice, officials in the district of Rijeka, officials in the city of Zagreb (the capital of Croatia), and finally officials in the city of Belgrade (the capital of Yugoslavia). In each case there were fees to be paid to the official for each paper and visa they stamped, and for every outstretched hand (otherwise the papers and visas would be confiscated). In 1930 Veronika and her four children left Maklen, Croatia, forever and boarded the USS Paris in Le Havre, France, for their voyage to the United States of America.

Father says he remembers when the Statue of Liberty first became visible because all the passengers crowded to that side of the ship to get a good look at the Lady who promised so much to newly arriving immigrants. When he gazed upon the statue, he was puzzled why everyone seemed so excited at the sight, but he was only six years old. The ship docked at Ellis Island and everyone had to file through the various designated checkpoints. Father remembers having his hair and body examined, and he was given a mental aptitude test which he thought was some sort of game. Once everyone was examined and tested, Veronika gathered up her children and luggage and boarded a train to Cleveland. When they arrived in Cleveland, Father met his father Vid for the first time. I can only imagine what that stern-faced man had to say, if anything, to his youngest son? Everyone was ushered up to a second floor apartment that had three bedrooms. No one seems to remember when Father's name was changed from Valentin to Walland. Since Father did not speak English, it is believed that a teacher at East Madison Grade School misunderstood the name Valentin when Father pronounced it for her, and she changed it to Walland. Father has been called Wally ever since.

I was named after Father so I was given the Junior suffix. Over the years the name Walland coupled with the last name Vrbančić has given many of my teachers and counselors tremendous pause in how to address me and how to pronounce my name. The diacritic marks over the two "c's" of my last name provided even more confusion except to another Eastern European raised speaking any of the Serbo-Croatian dialects. I have always been called Philip to differentiate me from Father. That part of my journey through life has always been very interesting to me. The fact that I was born with a moderately severe speech impediment, a stutter, has not been so interesting, and only those who also have a stutter know why.

We lived in California and I still have very vivid memories when I was very young, lying on a throw rug in our living room listening to Mother practice her violin. She produced the most wonderful music to my ears and it was then that I became very much attracted to that instrument. Mr. Joe Burger came to my fourth grade classroom looking for potential music students. When he played *The Flight of the Bumblebee* by Nikolai Rimsky-Korsakov, I was forever charmed. I immediately requested a permission slip for my parents to sign so that I could study the violin under Mr. Burger. Mother rented a student-sized violin to see how well I would progress before considering buying a decent instrument. She must have been very happy with my progress because she convinced Father to invest in a "very nice" instrument. Mother took me to meet Mr. Lewis Main in central Long Beach to select my violin. Mr. Main took me alone into his studio at the back of his home where I saw hundreds of instruments, some still wet with varnish, hanging from wires stretched high across the room. He wanted to talk to me privately in order to evaluate what sort of personality I had. He said he could match the violin to the student, much like in the Harry Potter book where Mr. Ollivander matched the wand to the student wizard. I had to wait some months before Mother received a call from Mr. Main. She was so excited and told me Mr. Main had found my violin. Apparently, many appraisers traveled about England to attend estate sales, and the appraiser who worked with Mr. Main only purchased instruments at those particular sort of sales. My violin, a *Gemünder Art* Violin (A266), was handcrafted in 1930 by Oscar A. Gemünder of August Gemünder & Sons, New York, New York. It was purchased new, originally for a young English girl who was beginning her studies on the violin. So, this instrument has traveled across the Atlantic Ocean twice before I became its second owner. Not only did Mr. Main match the instrument to me perfectly, he matched an 1801 French violin to my younger sister a year later. Many years passed when I discovered that the American violinist Camilla Wicks was a close friend to the Main family, and when she and Mr. Main's son were teenagers, they would spar endlessly to see who was the better violinist! When my parents purchased my violin, Mr. Main's son was already a professional violinist and he performed primarily in Las Vegas, Nevada. Camilla Wicks performed as an international soloist. As for my study of the instrument after Mr. Burger, my private violin teachers included Carol Higley (Lakewood, California) in elementary and junior high school, Professor Frank Bellino (Denison University, Granville, Ohio) in high school, Professor Stanley Plummer (University of California, Los Angeles, California) while at University, and Mr. Allan Carter (Long Beach, California) when I wanted to study and perform chamber music in my mid-forties. Plummer and Carter were both students of Vera Barstow (Pasadena, California), though perhaps nearly a generation apart.

I always excelled in mathematics and science classes during high school, so I decided to study Zoology at UCLA as an undergraduate in the mid-sixties after I was graduated from high school. At that time Mother, a registered nurse, was managing the department of surgery at a local hospital and her vision was to send me to medical school after graduation from University. Father, on the other hand, thought my talents were more inclined towards engineering. He was a graduate of the University of Southern California, school of Industrial Engineering, and was a licensed Professional Engineer. My dream or illusion was to become a concert violinist, or at least a professional orchestral musician. Honestly, I was too immature when I attended UCLA, let alone live on campus at Sproul Hall. I was not passionate enough about any of my studies and, unfortunately, I did not have sufficient time nor talent to adequately prepare my lessons for Professor Plummer. It was a dynamic, historical time to attend University during the mid-sixties. The political arena was in an uproar with President Reagan in office. The war in Vietnam was still being waged. Communists like Angela Davis (a student of Herbert Marcuse) were teaching and giving lectures down the hall from my required Political Science (clearly, an oxymoron) class. She and others were permitted to corrupt the minds of children with their lectures of political fantasy, socialism, and the destruction of God-given values and rights. In hindsight, I should have stepped back, attended a community college for a year or two, so I could mature a bit more emotionally.

One particularly horrifying experience I had at UCLA was when I walked into my second quarter German class and saw the instructor's name written on the blackboard: Frau Milovanović. She pronounced my name perfectly and clearly, rolling the "r" in my last name majestically, when she took attendance, and she asked me to stay after class. I knew she was Serbian, or, at least her husband was Serbian, but that did not matter to me. When the other students left the classroom and were out of earshot, she told me I was a "dirty, filthy Croatian" and she wanted to know if I was going to give her any "trouble" (she used other colorful language as well). Literally shaking in my boots, I told her I was born an American and I did not have any resentment towards any ethnic group of people. I worked my tail off in that class and managed to squeak by with a "C" grade. She found fault in most everything I wrote. After the final exam I thanked her for all the "special" attention she gave me! At least I did not have a "melt down" entirely, but finished my studies, and was graduated with a Bachelor's of Science degree in Zoology.

Father suggested I enroll in a two-year program through the USC Medical Center for training as an Orthopedic Physician Assistant. I thoroughly enjoyed every aspect of that program, I completed all the requirements, and I earned my certificate to work as an OPA. I was quickly hired by a local hospital where I worked for over nine years. By the mid-seventies I had already worked as an OPA for about four years when I experienced some sort of intellectual "awakening" and decided Father was right after all: I should have studied engineering, particularly Electrical Engineering. My epiphany to return to another tour of undergraduate studies was perhaps precipitated by the lectures I was attending at that time. The lectures were given by the renowned Astrophysicist Andrew J. Galambos, PhD. Professor Galambos was now an entrepreneur giving lectures on Volitional Science. I had already enrolled in his V-201 course which continued for over a year, one three-hour lecture once a week with a few weekend sessions as well. Previous to the V-201 course, I had enrolled in Professor Galambos's V-50 course which was now being presented by J. S. Snelson. It would not be possible for me to summarize here the knowledge I gained from the V-50 and the V-201 courses, and from several other lectures I attended to celebrate unique and historical events.

Before I enrolled in the OPA program at USC Medical Center, I did work as a phlebotomist in a doctor's office for nearly two years. Both doctors treated obese patients using diet and an array of medications they prescribed and provided onsite. In the early 1970's it was common practice to prescribe either dextroamphetamine sulfate or levoamphetamine sulfate, or any of the combinations of these drugs with other ingredients to help promote weight loss. More importantly, I had a lot of spare time during working hours, and my manager allowed me to read. In fact, she encouraged me to read the works of Ayn Rand. I even attended a few meetings where I was introduced to laissez-faire capitalism. Years later I suppose that when I heard Snelson's presentation of V-50 I was entirely comfortable with the subject of capitalism, and I was amazed at how far the concepts of Galambos had surpassed those of Rand. After attending the V-201 course, it was very difficult for me to manage the "blab forth syndrome", and I was guilty of trying to explain some of the concepts from V-201 to my colleagues for many, many years. Once again, it is something that is difficult to explain in short order.

It was completely normal for me to take apart, dismantle, and study the innards of every toy, train, erector set, chemistry set, or electrical set Santa brought me when I was young, and reconstruct that toy to working order, without inflicting any significant internal damage. Countless times Father would see a radio or tape recorder completely disassembled on the floor of my room and ask me, laughingly, "How long until it works again?" This sense of curiosity even when I was very young should have given me a clue as to what I should have initially studied at University. I have felt some degree of regret that it took me nearly ten years after high school to realize my mistake. Electrical Engineering became my absolute passion: I worked full time on second shift at the hospital and during the morning hours I attended at least three lecture classes and one laboratory class each semester for the next five years. IEEE published my original paper that detailed the theoretical design equations for multiple input operational amplifier summers, and my professors submitted me for the Alton B. Zerby Outstanding Student Award. I won first place in the Region Six IEEE Student Paper contest and placed third nationally that same year during WESCON in 1982. My operational amplifier design equations were also published in a textbook written by one of my professors on that subject. All of these accomplishments coupled with a 4.0 GPA gave me many choices for my next employer. Father worked for Rockwell International, though it was originally known as North American Aviation. I did interview at TRW and I received a very lucrative job offer, but I decided to join the team at Rockwell, in the Space Shuttle Simulation Laboratory. I was hired about five months before the launch of STS-1, thus changing my hospital scrubs for a coat and tie, and a whole lot more money!

About three months after Rockwell hired me, the Simulation Laboratory manager hired a Computer Science Engineer to join the ranks of Initialization Engineers. He and I had the daunting task of learning how to initialize the computers and electronics that comprised the total simulation of a Space Shuttle trajectory from Main Engine Cutoff (MECO) to landing at a few selected sites within the United States. The computers that were initialized with flight and target parameters included a PDP-11 and two Xerox mainframes. The mainframes were initially programmed using front-panel rocker switches: the Sigma 5 had 16 KB of magnetic core memory and the Sigma 9 had 64 KB of magnetic core memory. We used Hollerith cards to insert faults into the General Purpose Computers (GPCs) like those aboard the shuttle. We used a color Eidophor projector to project visual images of our landing site runways into a shuttle cockpit simulator in which the astronauts trained. Finally, we used Nova computers by DEC and DEC word processing software to generate all required customer documentation and, I might add, to play Adventure.

My system initialization colleague was an early Apple][owner when Integer BASIC was first available in ROM. The following year Rockwell offered a home computer purchase program and provided us the choice between an IBM PC or the Apple][+ which had the Autostart ROM. My colleague strongly encouraged me to request the Apple computer, and he assisted me in selecting the monitor, the disk drive, and the printer accessories. The total cost was a lot of money for me, but Rockwell loaned me the money and paid the total cost. I repaid the interest-free loan through weekly payroll deductions making the purchase relatively painless. Thus, my dream of having my own personal computer began. My ever-constant V-50 and V-201 "blab forth syndrome" did interest another colleague of mine who actually enrolled in the V-50T (i.e. "T" for Tape) course. Later, he enrolled in the V-201 and many other "V" courses after completing V-50T. In fact, he became the personal assistant to Professor Galambos during the last and final trip Galambos made to Budapest, Hungary, his native country. Mrs. Galambos stayed behind to manage the curriculum of their Free Enterprise Institute (FEI). Professor Galambos recognized that he was beginning to display the symptoms of Alzheimer's disease and he entrusted my colleague with handling more and more of the private living affairs for both he and his wife. Andrew J. Galambos and Suzanne J. Galambos established their Natural Estates Trust that was to manage all of their Intellectual Property. From my vantage point it appeared to me that my colleague participated in and contributed to what I considered to be dishonorable activities not in the favorable interests of this Natural Estates Trust. My colleague's activities primarily involved the convoluted publishing of *Sic Itur Ad Astra* by Andrew J. Galambos after the death of Galambos on April 10, 1997.

I became fascinated with all aspects of the Apple][+ computer, and I wanted to incorporate it into my studies for my Master's degree. My assigned advisor was analyzing tomographic reconstructions of the human spinal column, and he thought perhaps I could assist him. He wanted to be able to make measurements between any two points within the computer image of a spinal column, even after rotating or enlarging the image. I was tasked to develope the Fortran programs that could be launched on a Microsoft Z80 peripheral slot card in an Apple][+ that would provide him with these capabilities. I found an ingenious way to reduce the size of the three-dimensional rotational matrix in order to accelerate data image processing and the remapping of the resulting HIRES image to the computer screen. My professor was very pleased with my progress. However, I was becoming increasingly interested in high-speed graphics animation, and the only way I thought I could learn that technology was to work for Ken Williams at Sierra On-Line. I terminated my work on my Master's degree, I gave notice to Rockwell, I packed my bags, and I moved to Oakhurst, California.

At Sierra On-Line I was tasked to assist a colleague in migrating *ScreenWriter* to the Apple //e which was recently available for purchase. On another project I wrote all the I/O routines and ICON drawing routines for *HomeWord Speller*. When I started working as a self-employed contractor, I was given the *Goofy's Word Factory* project which was a children's computer game to teach English grammar. Williams had a license to display certain Disney characters on a bit-mapped computer screen per approval by Disney for visual likeness, color, and movement. I would have finished *Goofy's Word Factory* if John (Williams's brother), the assigned designer of the game, could have developed the third game feature (and strategy) in a timely fashion. He apparently could not do so before I secured a position at Hughes Aircraft Company back in Los Angeles. I did utilize Williams's high-speed graphics animation algorithms in *Goofy's Word Factory*, which I had to redesign in order to include collision detection on a dithered background. No other computer game could detect collisions on a dithered background at that time. Williams was impressed, and it was really hard to impress Williams. I stayed all of 18 months at Sierra.

The major observation I made after I was hired by Hughes Aircraft was how different their culture was to the culture I had experienced at Rockwell. At Rockwell I found it exceedingly difficult to have anyone who had written a software tool or program explain to me how that tool or that program worked, and the algorithms the software utilized or exploited. When I was tasked to migrate a software tool from Fortran to C language at Rockwell, I found some incorrect logic that eventually affected the final output data. Given certain input parameters, this tool could calculate a three-dimensional corridor in space and either interpolate points within or extrapolate points outside of that corridor. I presented my findings to its original author showing how I could insert the same incorrect logic into the C code and generate the same wrong output data. He told me to keep the incorrect logic and not disclose my findings to management. I refused. This was totally unthinkable to me, and this would have never happened at Hughes. In fact, CIP awards were given to engineers who found such errors in software and who reported those errors to management. The Hughes culture encouraged the aggressive sharing of knowledge, and it gave rewards to those who made improvements. The Rockwell culture cultivated self-preservation tactics where knowledge was thought to be job security and not to be shared, but to be kept undisclosed. Hughes certainly provided me with a great opportunity in the Digital Simulation Laboratory where I learned about real time executive software that was hosted on Gould SEL mainframe computers (2750, 6750, 8780, and 9780). I also learned about MIL-STD-1553 protocol communication software and real time software interface drivers to a host of various external data processors. Our purpose was to create a digital time frame in order to simulate in real time the environment for a tactical Radar Digital Processor (RDP) flying above the surface of the earth.

Due to the general slowdown in the engineering industry, I returned to Rockwell in 1990. I believed that my knowledge in real time executive software hosted on SEL mainframe computers would be my passport to a nice software engineering career closer to where I wanted to live. How I regret that major blunder in judgment because my employment at Rockwell was terminated just a few years later. I had co-authored a *White Paper* outlining the risks associated with using off-the-shelf RISC processors in certain applications, and the response from my colleagues was very unfavorable. This and my disclosure of software errors I uncovered during a Fortran-to-C language conversion eventually led to my dismissal. Fortunately, my former Hughes management was able to reinstate my position, and I was tasked to gain expertise in real time data collection software for tactical radar systems.

Hughes tactical radar systems are programmed to operate in many different modes depending upon various situations and the immediate needs that are faced by the pilot of a military aircraft. During the development of a radar mode, its processing is heavily instrumented which generates a large amount of output data as the mode progresses through its various processing stages. It is critical to capture all this generated data, primary and incidental in nature, in order to ensure and verify that the mode is behaving as expected and is generating its data according to pre-established boundaries, much like comparing the data to some gold standard. My task was to capture all the In-phase and Quadrature (I/Q) components of radar data in real time, process certain other data components, package the data according to generated source and timestamp, and save the resulting files to some recording device. It is important to understand that there are many independent generating sources of data in a radar system whose timestamps are totally asynchronous. At a later time the data that is packaged in those files would be analyzed to determine if, in fact, the processing modes operated as expected. Physically collecting this I/Q data during real time tactical maneuvers was quite a challenge, and recorders designed to operate in this environment were costly. Preparing for a data collection session involved securing a military aircraft, a flight crew, a ground crew, and people to securely bring the recorded data back to my tempested lab. This certainly added to my responsibilities, and my mantra was to neither add, subtract, nor modify any data word or data bit while that data was in my immediate possession and while my software algorithms extracted and processed that data into prescribed data formats. Those data formats would allow the data analysis tools to function more efficiently for the mode builders.

I was thoroughly vetted and held maximum-security clearances that allowed me to process data from many different and independent classified programs not only in Los Angeles, but also in other locations, and even out of state. The general data collection software engines I began designing in the unclassified world served as my software library for every classified program to which I was assigned. Perhaps I was simply in the right place at the right time that steered my career to become the sole resident expert in Transcription Software Engines. That is, to process, encrypt, and store in real time at least a terabyte of data every second. Or, perhaps I was in the right place at the right time that allowed me to develop a task beyond its envisioned potential. There is a direct ancestral linkage between my unclassified software library of tools, routines, and transcription engines and every single classified program with which I was associated that required my tools, routines, engines, and expertise. I was practicing *code reuse* light-years before it became a topic that some managers thought could reduce software development costs. "How insightful!" I jokingly thought of management, silently and very highly disrespectfully in my private thoughts.

Initially, I was given the opportunity to host my current Transcription Software engine on a newly acquired SGI Origin 300 having four bricks, or 16 CPUs. *Code reuse* made this task fairly straightforward, thus demonstrating the Origin's practicality for this feasibility study. After a fact-finding tour to the SGI facilities at Mountain View, California, I was given the momentous task of designing a Transcription Software engine for an SGI Origin 3000 having eight bricks (i.e. 32 CPUs) running IRIX, and using Big Endian memory management. This turned out to be one of my greatest solo achievements. Even at this time, little did my management understand how effortlessly I could build my Transcription Software engines primarily using *code reuse*. I was extremely fortunate to have had one very intelligent manager who casually asked me to think about the possibility of building a digital playback system. Such a system did not yet exist. Some had tried building an analog playback system a few years earlier with absolutely no success. Instead of analyzing the collected instrumented data, one could observe how the simulated RDP behaved when the recorded high-speed I/Q data and the slow-speed environment data was injected back into its system with a playback system. A few months later I presented my first digital playback recorder and pre-processing system, my last and greatest achievement at Raytheon (former Hughes). I was given the unique privilege to design and build a second digital playback recorder and pre-processing system for another classified program. That program, like the previous program which used my first digital playback recorder and pre-processing system, saved countless hours of analysis time and mission costs before I scheduled my overdue retirement.

A few years after I retired, I was presented with an astonishing diagnosis by my partner that seemed to explain some, if not all of the idiosyncrasies I have displayed my entire life as far back as elementary school: I may have been living with Asperger's. Indeed, how does one know what is truly normal; that which falls under the umbrella of a Gaussian curve? We are all volitional beings and our behavior is internal to each of us. Our brain is composed of carbon-based synapses whose billions of inter-connections and cross-connections compose the very person and personality we have become or have allowed ourselves to become. It is simply miraculous that any of our species reach total fulfillment of their dreams. I would like to believe I have come closer than most in reaching many of my dreams and aspirations.

Now I have the time and the continuing curiosity to delve into the Disk Operating System of the Apple][computer. I now have the opportunity to create my own version of a Disk Operating System that contains the power and the flexibility I always believed an Apple][Disk Operating System ought to and could have.

I call my version of Apple][DOS, DOS 4.1. And DOS 4.1 is now complete with its 46th build. What a ride I have been on! Why? To see what I could do for this wonderful machine and its magnificent architecture!

I completed DOS 4.1 around March, 2019, after I agreed to have the Build 45 Manual published by Call-A.P.P.L.E. I requested no fees, no incentives, nor any royalties. But I continued to innovate DOS 4.1 and Build 46 contains the final modifications I wanted to include in this DOS. I felt that I could not take DOS 4.1 any further due to the memory constraints of DOS 4.1L, and I did not want to increase its size nor add additional sectors to its volume image. However, I could continue to develop Apple][DOS if I concentrated only on the Language Card version. I naïvely thought perhaps I could utilize Auxiliary Memory and move DOS there. To that end, I copied my source code for DOS 4.1H into a new directory and gave it a new name. That moment was the birth of DOS 4.3.

I sincerely hope that the interested user is sufficiently challenged by what I have created in DOS 4.1 as presented in this Second Edition of the DOS 4.1 Disk Operating System. The End (for now?).

After all that I have seen and done during my life and in my travels through time, I am always comforted when I recall the following expressive thought:

The diversity in the human family should be the cause of love and harmony,
as it is in music where many different notes blend together
in the making of a perfect chord.
~~~ Abdu'l-Bahá ~~~